Settlers, Liberty, and Empire

Settlers, Liberty, and Empire traces the emergence of a revolutionary conception of political authority on the far shores of the eighteenth-century Atlantic world, based on the natural right of English subjects to leave the realm, claim indigenous territory, and establish new governments by consent, linked to the center in a loose confederation of equal states. This radical set of ideas culminated in revolution and republicanism. But Craig Yirush eschews the traditional scholarly focus on the late eighteenth century. Instead, he examines how the political ideas of settler elites in British North America emerged out of an imperial world characterized by constitutional uncertainty, geopolitical rivalry, and the ongoing presence of powerful Native American peoples. By taking seriously the often-forgotten years between the Glorious Revolution in America and the American Revolution against Britain, Yirush provides a long-term explanation of the distinctive ideas of the American Revolution.

Craig Yirush is Assistant Professor in the Department of History at the University of California at Los Angeles. He is the author of several articles and book chapters focusing on early American political and legal ideas. He previously served as a Library Associates Fellow at the John Carter Brown Library and a Fellow at Harvard University's Charles Warren Center for American History.

Settlers, Liberty, and Empire

The Roots of Early American Political Theory, 1675–1775

CRAIG YIRUSH

University of California at Los Angeles

CAMBRIDGE
UNIVERSITY PRESS

CAMBRIDGE UNIVERSITY PRESS
Cambridge, New York, Melbourne, Madrid, Cape Town,
Singapore, São Paulo, Delhi, Tokyo, Mexico City

Cambridge University Press
32 Avenue of the Americas, New York, NY 10013-2473, USA

www.cambridge.org
Information on this title: www.cambridge.org/9780521132466

First published 2011

Printed in the United States of America

A catalog record for this publication is available from the British Library.

Library of Congress Cataloging in Publication data
Yirush, Craig, 1968–
    Settlers, Liberty, and Empire : The Roots of Early American Political Theory,
    1675–1775 / Craig Yirush.
        p. cm
    Includes bibliographical references and index.
    ISBN 978-0-521-19330-6 (hardback) – ISBN 978-0-521-13246-6 (paperback)
    1. Political science – United States – History – 17th century. 2. Political science –
    United States – History – 18th century. 3. United States – Politics and government –
    To 1775. I. Title.
    JA84.U5Y57 2011
    320.0973–dc22   2010044678

ISBN 978-0-521-19330-6 Hardback
ISBN 978-0-521-13246-6 Paperback

Contents

Acknowledgments

In writing this book, I have incurred many debts. My dissertation advisor, Jack P. Greene, showed an early interest in my research and provided sage advice at every point along the way. Without his support and scholarly example, this book would never have seen the light of day. I would also like to thank Alan Tully, who was responsible for introducing me to early American history and for encouraging a rather callow undergraduate to enter graduate school and pursue an academic career. Alan also expertly supervised an M.A. thesis, which was the first tentative step toward the argument developed in these pages.

The department of history at Johns Hopkins was a great place to be a graduate student. In his seminar and in many subsequent conversations, John Marshall taught me about the complexities of seventeenth- and eighteenth-century English and European political thought. I was fortunate that Anthony Pagden, whom I first met in Cambridge and who is now a colleague, arrived at Hopkins just after I did. Over many years, I have learned much from him, both in person and in print, about early modern empires. Mathew Lauzon, Paul Tonks, Francois Furstenberg, and Neil Safier all made sure that the years at Hopkins were full of fun as well as substance. Steve Jolivette's insight into the political theory of the American founding is profound. Our conversations about history and philosophy over many years have influenced me immeasurably. Jason Gadd and I have been friends for longer than either of us cares to remember. Over the years, I have benefited from his wide-ranging knowledge of history, as well as his ability to fix old sports cars and appreciate fine ales. He found the time to read an entire draft of this book and to assure me that it did in fact make sense. The Borsos family – Londie, Pete, Delaney,

Spencer, and Connor – always provided timely reminders that there is more to "Uncle Craig's" life than old books. Marc and Nina Lerner made me feel at home in my first years in L.A. and have remained good friends from afar. Pat and Mary Geary provided a home away from home in L.A. when I first arrived and have continued to offer superlative hospitality ever since. Ted and Courtney Balaker were always ready to have a pint at the usual place and to remind me that beyond the academy there is a world of intellectual creativity.

Many years ago, Howard Singleton showed faith in a young historian and generously made possible a year of study in Cambridge. I am also grateful for the support I have received from the University of British Columbia, the Johns Hopkins University, and the Institute of Humane Studies. I was fortunate enough to receive a fellowship from the John Carter Brown Library, which allowed me to complete the research for the dissertation on which this book is partly based. My thanks to Norman Fiering, the Director, and the always helpful staff of the library. David Hall and Jim Kloppenberg were kind enough to invite me to spend a wonderful year at Harvard's Charles Warren Center, where I was able to do some much-needed thinking and writing. Mark Schmeller made the year in Boston a real pleasure.

The history department at UCLA has been a wonderful academic home. For financial support during the research and writing of this book, I would like to thank the Department of History, the Dean of Social Sciences, and the Academic Senate's Council on Research. My colleagues at UCLA provided more than material sustenance. Ruth Bloch and Michael Meranze both gave me much-needed advice and support in a difficult time. I am also indebted to (among many others) Teo Ruiz, Ned Alpers, David Myers, Bill Summerhill, Nile Green, Sanjay Subrahmanyam, Michael Salman, Kevin Terraciano, Naomi Lamoreaux, Gabi Piterberg, Peter Reill, Muriel McClendon, Daniel Walker Howe, and Joan Waugh.

My editor, Eric Crahan, took a chance on a first-time author. For that, and for much valuable advice and encouragement, I am deeply grateful. The comments of the two anonymous readers for Cambridge improved the manuscript greatly. I am also indebted to those who took time out of their busy schedules to read all or part of this book. I would like to thank (in no particular order) Alan Taylor, Eric Hinderaker, Andrew Fitzmaurice, Richard Bushman, Joyce Appleby, Paul Grant-Costa, and Richard Samuelson. Elizabeth Mancke and Trevor Burnard provided crucial support at just the right time. I also benefited from the comments of audiences at the Charles Warren Center Seminar at Harvard, the Legal History Workshop at UCLA, the Omohundro Institute of Early American History and Culture, and the Newberry Library.

I am incredibly fortunate to share with Jessica Stern her passion for ideas, her laughter, and her love. I owe her more than words can say.

My father long ago instilled in me a passion for reading and an interest in history. And he has always been there for me, from standing on the sidelines of countless rainy soccer pitches, to making long-distance phone calls full of good cheer. My mother has been such a source of love, support, and intellectual stimulation over the years that it is hard to put into words. In gratitude, I dedicate this book to them.

Introduction

Jasper Maudit's "Instructions": The Imperial Roots of Early American Political Theory

In June 1762, in the waning months of the Seven Years' War, the Massachusetts General Court sent Jasper Maudit, its new agent in London, a lengthy set of "instructions."[1] Maudit, a London merchant and dissenter, had taken up his appointment at an auspicious time. The colony had been informed by the previous agent, William Bollan, that the Crown was going to require the insertion of a suspending clause in all future laws, ensuring that they would not take effect until approved by the Privy Council.[2] In Bollan's view, this interference with Massachusetts' legislative authority underlined the long-standing need "for a thorough Examination" "of the Original, inherent and just Title of the Colonies in America to the Rights, Liberties and Benefits of the State, whereof they were Members."[3]

---

[1] On Maudit's agency, see *Jasper Maudit, Agent in London for the Province of Massachusetts-Bay, 1762–1765, Massachusetts Historical Society Collections*, Volume 74 (Boston, 1918). (The "Instructions" are reprinted on pages 39–54.) They were a joint effort of the Massachusetts House and the Council.

[2] Bollan, quoted in Maudit's "Instructions," 39. For the provisions of the suspending clause, see James J. Burns, *The Colonial Agents of New England*, (Washington, DC: Catholic University Press of America, 1935) 94, fn. 42. Although they objected to the proposed suspending clause, the Massachusetts House conceded that the Crown could veto their legislation. Like other colonists in the empire, however, they wanted their laws to be in force until vetoed; and they were particularly incensed by any suggestion that their laws would be treated as void *ab initio* after being reviewed in London (see page 51). Bollan had been removed from his job as agent because of the opposition of the Otis faction, which distrusted his Anglicanism (there were fears that he wouldn't support the Congregational Church) and his support for the court party (he was William Shirley's son-in-law and an associate of Thomas Hutchinson). Maudit, his replacement, was thought preferable because he was a dissenter. On the dispute, see Burns, *Colonial Agents*, 4–5; and Bernard Bailyn, *The Ordeal of Thomas Hutchinson* (Cambridge: Belknap Press, 1974), 59–61.

[3] Maudit's "Instructions," 39.

Taking Bollan's warning seriously, the colony's "instructions" to
Maudit laid out a comprehensive account of the rights of the British
American settlers in the empire, one that reveals to the modern reader
the contours of a lost world of early American political theory, stretching
back to before the Glorious Revolution, while anticipating the revolutionary arguments that would convulse the British Atlantic world in the
decade to come.

At the heart of the colony's case was a claim that "The natural Rights
of the Colonists" were "the same with those of all other British subjects,
and indeed of all Mankind." In support of this claim, Maudit's instructions
drew on Locke's *Second Treatise*.[4] According to the colony, "The Principal
of these Rights" was (quoting Locke) to be "free from any superior power
on Earth, and not to be under the Will or Legislative Authority of Man, but
to have only the Law of Nature for his Rule." In society, these natural rights
entailed certain "political or Civil Rights." Once again, the "instructions"
quoted Locke: "The Liberty of all Men in society is to be under no other legislative power but that established by Consent in the Commonwealth." In
other words, to be politically free was to be bound only by rules consented
to by all, and "not to be subject to the inconstant, uncertain, unknown,
arbitrary will of another Man."[5] Moreover, the *instructions* claimed, these
rights were universal: "This Liberty is not only the right of Britons, and
British Subjects, but the Right of all Men in Society, and is so inherent,
that they Can't give it up without becoming Slaves, by which they forfeit
even life itself."[6] And given the universality of these rights, Massachusetts
argued, there could be no basis for denying them to one part of the empire.

The colony's "instructions" to Maudit also defended the settlers' claim
to equal rights by invoking the tie between Crown and subject: Since
the "Allegiance of British Subjects" was "perpetual and inseparable from
their Persons," the colony argued, there could be "no reason" "why a Man
should be abridg'd in his Liberty, by removing from Europe to America,
any more than by his removing from London to Dover, or from one side
of a street to the other." In other words, these rights were not "local, that
is, confined to the Realm," but "extended throughout the Dominions."[7]

In support of this vision of the empire, Maudit's "instructions" cited
the colony's charter, which guaranteed that settlers in Massachusetts

---

[4] The "Instructions" cited Locke without attribution. The quotes are from *The Second
Treatise*, chapter 4, paragraph 22 ("Of Slavery").
[5] This passage is also from chapter four, paragraph 22.
[6] Maudit's "Instructions," 40.
[7] Ibid., 40–41.

enjoyed "all the Liberties and Immunities, of free and natural Subjects ... as if ... every one of them were born within the Realm of England." After all, "the British American Colonies are part of the Common wealth" and thus entitled to "the rights, liberties and benefits thereof." Furthermore, the "instructions" claimed, these charter rights were not mere gifts of the Crown; rather, they were "declaratory of the Common Law, the Law of nature and nations, which all agree in this particular."[8]

Maudit's "instructions" also justified this idea of an empire of equal rights with a claim about the legal status of the territories to which the American settlers had migrated:

By the Laws of Nature and of Nations, which in this Instance at least, are the voice of universal Reason, and of God, when a Nation takes possession of desert, uncultivated and uninhabited Countries, or which to our purpose is the same thing, of a Country inhabited by Salvages [*sic*], who are without Laws and Government, and Settles a Colony there; such Country tho' separated from the principal Establishment or Mother Country, naturally becomes part of the State, equally with its antient possessions.[9]

In other words, the fact that the American colonists had settled among peoples who were in effect stateless meant that the land was legally vacant, and the settlers were free to supplant the natives and establish their own political authority on an equal footing with the mother country.

According to Maudit's "instructions," the settlers' migration to this uncultivated wilderness had also benefited Great Britain: "There are very good judges, who scruple not to affirm, that it is to the Growth of the plantations Great Britain is indebted for her present Strength, and populousness." After all, "as the wild wastes in America have been turned into pleasant Habitations ... so many of the little Villages ... in England, have put on a New Face, suddenly started up and become fair Market Towns, and great Cities." However, these "Mutual Advantages" "derived from the spirit of Trade and Commerce," which was in turn dependent on "that beautifull Form of Civil Government under which we live." As such, it was in the "Interest" of "all those intrusted with the Administration of the Government, to see that every part of the British Empire enjoys to the full the advantages derived from the Laws, and that Freedom which is the Result of their being maintained with Impartiality and Vigour."[10]

---

[8] Ibid., 46.

[9] Ibid., 41.

[10] Ibid., 43–44. The "instructions" refer to the British constitution, but they also claim that colonial prosperity rested on the "reduction" of that constitution to "first principles," which had occurred only in the plantations.

On the basis of these arguments, the Massachusetts General Court told Maudit to resist the King's interference with their legislative authority, for, they insisted, "if these suspensions are Established, it will be in the power of the Crown, in Effect, to take away our Charter without act of Parliament, or the Ordinary process at Common Law." "Surely," the colony pleaded, "the laws of England, will never make such Construction of the King's Charter, as to put it in the power of the donor or his Successors to take it away when he pleases."[11]

Not long after Maudit's instructions crossed the Atlantic, the long, costly, and punishing war against the French ended, and the British empire emerged triumphant, masters of the continent. Yet within a decade, the North American colonies were on the brink of a revolt caused by the kind of infringement on settler rights that the General Court of Massachusetts had complained about in 1762. The fact that the colony was able to offer a coherent account of its inhabitants' rights in the early 1760s indicates that the settlers' response to parliamentary taxation and legislation was informed by a long history of thinking about their autonomy in the empire. Most histories of early American political thought, however, begin where Maudit's instructions leave off, with the looming imperial crisis in the aftermath of the Seven Years' War, as if the ideas that drove opposition to imperial reforms from the mid-1760s on had no antecedents.

This book moves in the opposite direction and explores the imperial roots of the distinctive set of ideas expressed in Maudit's "instructions" – the forceful grounding of settler rights in both common law and natural law; the denial of the sovereignty and property of the indigenous peoples of the New World; and the related claim that the settlers had undertaken a risky migration across the Atlantic to what was in effect a wilderness, and then by their labor had established flourishing polities which had benefited Britons on both sides of the ocean. In order to understand this settler vision of the empire, we need to eschew the current scholarly focus on the origins of the nation and take seriously the imperial world out of which it came. Only then will we have a long-term perspective on the political theory of the founding and be able to see the important continuities between colony and nation, empire and republic.[12]

[11] Ibid., 53.
[12] I have chosen to refer to the subjects of my study as "settlers" rather than employ the more traditional "colonist." The term "settler" better captures their ambiguous status in the empire, for while they were subjected to metropolitan control, they were also agents of empire in their own right, appropriating native land and establishing local

Scholarship on the early modern world is increasingly taking the history of empire as seriously as it used to take that of states.[13] In the guise of Atlantic history, the impact on early American historiography has been profound, with the American colonies now seen as integral parts of a broader British world of commerce, religion, culture, law, and politics.[14] This Atlantic turn in the study of early America is itself part of a broader trend toward transnational and comparative histories of the United States.[15]

Yet scholarship on early American political thought has not taken this imperial turn. Dominated in the last generation by the "classical republican" challenge to an older "liberal" interpretation of the founding, it has reached an impasse, with the republican contention that a classical politics of virtue dominated early American political theory proving unsustainable in the face of the strong counter-evidence that liberal ideas of rights, property, and consent, often associated with John Locke, were an important part of the ideology of the Revolution.[16] While

authority in a quasi-autonomous manner. By using this term, I also hope to encourage early Americanists to engage with the burgeoning literature on settler colonialism. On which, see Anna Johnston and Alan Lawson, "Settler Colonies," in Henry Schwartz and Sangeeta Ray, eds., *A Companion to Postcolonial Studies* (Malden: Blackwell, 2000), 360–376.

[13] For a recent discussion of the centrality of empire in an era we usually see as heralding the rise of the nation-state, see Jeremy Adelman, "The Age of Imperial Revolutions," *American Historical Review* 113 (2008), 319–340; and Trevor Burnard, "Empire Matters? The Historiography of Imperialism in Early America, 1492–1830," *History of European Ideas* 33, 1 (2007), 87–107.

[14] On the British Atlantic, see the essays collected in David Armitage and Michael Braddick, eds., *The British Atlantic World, 1500–1800* (New York: Palgrave Macmillan, 2002). On early American history in an Atlantic context, see Bernard Bailyn, *Atlantic History: Concept and Contours* (Cambridge: Harvard University Press, 2005). According to Jack Rakove, the revival of interest in empire in Anglo-American historiography is a corollary of the rise of Atlantic history, both of which allow for the examination of colonial American politics in a more expansive framework. Rakove, "An Agenda for Early American History," in Donald A. Yerxa, ed., *Recent Themes in Early American History: Historians in Conversation* (Columbia: University of South Carolina Press, 2008), 38.

[15] Thomas Bender, *A Nation among Nations: America's Place in World History* (New York: Hill and Wang, 2006).

[16] The literature on this debate is extensive. For an up-to-date and judicious account, see Alan Gibson's *Understanding the Founding: The Crucial Questions* (Lawrence: University Press of Kansas, 2007). For the state of the debate as it was waxing, see Daniel Rodgers, "Republicanism: The Career of a Concept," *Journal of American History* 79 (1992), 11–38. For an example of the Lockean liberal consensus that prevailed before the rise of classical republicanism, see Carl Becker's *The Declaration of Independence: A Study in the History of Political Ideas* (New York: Alfred. A. Knopf, 1942). Three books are usually cited as inaugurating the classical republican challenge to a liberal

this debate has enriched our understanding of the intellectual context of the American Revolution, scholars on both sides failed to explore the ways that the political ideas of the English settlers who eventually created a republican revolution were shaped by the experience of living in an Atlantic world of jurisdictional plurality and contested sovereignty. Instead, despite their differences, all of the major contributors to the debate sought to explain the ideas of the founding by tracing the impact of one strand of European or English political thought – be it Renaissance civic humanism, or English radical whiggism, or the Scottish Enlightenment, or Lockean natural law theory – on the political thinking of British Americans in the two decades before the Revolution. In doing so, however, they ignored the intellectual world of the settlers in British America in the crucial century between the Glorious Revolution and the American Revolution entirely.[17] As a consequence, we have an

account of the founding: Bernard Bailyn's *The Ideological Origins of the American Revolution* (Cambridge, MA: Belknap Press, 1967); Gordon Wood's *The Creation of the American Republic, 1776–1787* (Chapel Hill: University of North Carolina Press, 1969); and J.G.A. Pocock's *The Machiavellian Moment: Florentine Political Thought and the Atlantic Republican Tradition* (Princeton: Princeton University Press, 1975). But while Bailyn did downplay Locke's influence, preferring, like Wood and Pocock, to stress the influence of English radical Whig thought on the revolutionaries, unlike them he never understood this strand of thought as centrally concerned with civic virtue. Rather, Bailyn stressed the individualism of the radical Whigs, arguing that their central concern was with protecting the individual from the depredations of power. For the liberal response to the republican thesis, see Joyce Appleby, *Liberalism and Republicanism in the Historical Imagination* (Cambridge: Harvard University Press, 1992); Thomas Pangle, *The Spirit of Modern Republicanism: The Moral Vision of the American Founders and the Philosophy of Locke* (Chicago: University of Chicago Press, 1988); Paul Rahe, *Republics Ancient and Modern: Classical Republicanism and the American Revolution* (Chapel Hill: University of North Carolina Press, 1992); and Steven Dworetz, *The Unvarnished Doctrine: Locke, Liberalism and the American Revolution* (Durham, NC: Duke University Press, 1990). The downplaying of Locke's influence in revolutionary America was also due to John Dunn's influential article "The Politics of John Locke in England and America in the Eighteenth Century," in John Yolton, ed., *John Locke: Problems and Perspectives* (Cambridge: Cambridge University Press, 1969), 77. For a convincing riposte, see Yuhtaro Ohmori, *"The Artillery of Mr. Locke": The Use of Locke's "Second Treatise" in Pre-Revolutionary America, 1764–1776* (Ph.D. Dissertation, Johns Hopkins University, 1988).

For an insightful attempt to combine the two perspectives, see Michael Zuckert's "amalgam" thesis in which the republican concern with virtue is seen as the means to the liberal end of rights. Zuckert, *Natural Rights and the New Republicanism* (Princeton: Princeton University Press, 1994), 164–166.

[17] This focus on the late eighteenth century is ubiquitous in the secondary literature on early American political theory, although some older studies – for example, Lawrence Leder's *Liberty and Authority* (Chicago: Quadrangle Books, 1968) and Clinton Rossiter's *Seedtime of the Republic* (New York: Harcourt, Brace, 1953) – dealt with

account of early American political ideas focused largely on the late eighteenth century, the traditional founding, and disconnected from the larger Atlantic and imperial world out of which the Revolution came.

Two bodies of scholarship, both largely ignored by historians of early American political theory, allow us to explore the ways in which the early modern Atlantic world – and in particular the contested constitutional structure of the empire – shaped colonial political thought. The first is the efflorescence of writing on the constitutional history of the empire which began with Barbara Black's pioneering bicentennial argument that the settlers had a compelling constitutional case against metropolitan authority in the revolutionary crisis.[18] In a series of dense and learned volumes, the legal historian John Philip Reid has also argued that in the 1760s and 1770s the colonists articulated a sophisticated vision of their rights in the empire, one which was as legally sound as that propounded by

political ideas in British America, as did Bernard Bailyn's seminal *Origins of American Politics* (New York: Vintage Books, 1967), though Bailyn's focus on the prerogative powers of the royal governors made it difficult to fit the private colonies into his explanation for the salience of radical Whig thought in eighteenth-century America. For a recent example, see Lee Ward's *Politics of Liberty in England and Revolutionary America* (New York: Cambridge University Press, 2004). Ward offers a superb account of the complexity of seventeenth-century English political thought, placing the radical Whig ideas that influenced the American revolutionaries alongside a range of other discourses. Yet by failing to deal with the transmission of these ideas across the Atlantic in the crucial decades following the Glorious Revolution, he is unable to explain why the settlers were so receptive to this strand of Whig ideology when English people at home were not. An exception to this narrow focus on the founding appears in a series of superb studies of political culture in individual colonies – for example, Richard Bushman, *King and People in Provincial Massachusetts* (Chapel Hill: University of North Carolina Press, 1985); and Alan Tully, *Forming American Politics: Ideas, Interests and Institutions in Colonial New York and Pennsylvania* (Baltimore: Johns Hopkins University Press, 1994). Richard Beeman's *Varieties of Political Experience in Eighteenth-Century America* (Philadelphia: University of Pennsylvania Press, 2004) is the most recent account of politics in the mainland colonies.

[18] Barbara Black, "The Constitution of Empire: The Case for the Colonists," *University of Pennsylvania Law Review* 124 (1976), 1177. Black took the side of Charles McIlwain in his debate with Robert Schuyler about the authority of the English Parliament in the American colonies. See McIlwain *The American Revolution: A Constitutional Interpretation* (New York: Macmillan, 1923); and Schuyler, *Parliament and the British Empire: Some Constitutional Controversies Concerning Imperial Legislative Jurisdiction* (New York: Columbia University Press, 1929). For contemporaries of McIlwain's whose arguments about the empire as a federation or commonwealth of separate states are also back in vogue, see R.G. Adams, *The Political Ideas of the American Revolution: Brittanic-American Contributions to the Problem of Imperial Organization, 1765–1775* (1922; New York: Barnes and Noble, 1958); and Andrew C. McLaughlin, *The Foundations of American Constitutionalism* (New York: New York University Press, 1932).

ministers in Parliament.[19] Black and Reid have been joined in this recon-struction of colonial constitutional arguments by, among others, Jack P. Greene.[20] According to these historians, the colonists based their case against Parliament on the arguments of seventeenth-century common lawyers like Edward Coke, who held that English subjects lived under an "ancient" and unwritten customary constitution that guaranteed them certain liberties, including the right to be secure in their person and prop-erty, to consent to taxation, to be represented in parliaments, and to par-ticipate in lawmaking through juries. The fact that these rights of English subjects were seen as "immemorial," that is, in the parlance of common lawyers, they had existed "time out of mind," was also the basis for their legitimacy, for they had been tested by long experience and consented to by the community as a whole. This idea of an ancient constitution also served to limit the scope of the royal prerogative as the king was bound to obey these fundamental liberties as well.[21]

[19] John Phillip Reid, *Constitutional History of the American Revolution*, 4 volumes (Madison; University of Wisconsin Press, 1986–1993).

[20] For an overview of this literature, see Jack P. Greene, "From the Perspective of Law: Context and Legitimacy in the Origins of the American Revolution," in Greene, ed., *Interpreting Early America: Historiographical Essays* (Charlottesville: University Press of Virginia, 1996), 467–492; as well as Greene, "John Phillip Reid and Reinterpretation of the American Revolution," in Hendrick Hartog and William E. Nelson, eds., *Law as Culture and Culture as Law: Essays in Honor of John Phillip Reid* (Madison: Madison House, 2000), 48–57. For Greene's own contribution, see *Peripheries and Center: Constitutional Development in the Extended Polities of the British Empire and the United States, 1607–1788* (Athens: University of Georgia Press, 1986). In addition to the work of Black, Reid, and Greene, see the important article by Thomas C. Grey, "Origins of the Unwritten Constitution: Fundamental Law in American Revolutionary Thought," *Stanford Law Review* 30 (1978), 843–893.

[21] The classic account of common law thought is J.G.A. Pocock, *The Ancient Constitution and the Feudal Law: A Study of English Historical Thought in the Seventeenth Century* (1957; expanded edition, Cambridge: Cambridge University Press, 1987). According to Glenn Burgess, English jurists didn't think that the common law was literally unchang-ing but rather that customary practices were subject to constant change over time as they evolved to suit the needs of the polity. See Burgess, *The Politics of the Ancient Constitution: An Introduction to English Legal and Political Thought, 1603–1642* (University Park: Pennsylvania State University Press, 1992), 37, 57–58. For an argu-ment that the origin of this idea of English legal rights as inherent in the individual (and hence akin to the modern idea of subjective rights) lay in the parliamentary struggle against James I, see James H. Hutson, "The Emergence of the Modern Concept of a Right in America: The Contribution of Michael Villey," *American Journal of Jurisprudence* 39 (1994), 185–224. According to Hutson, the modern idea of subjective individual rights was more influential in the American colonies in the eighteenth century than in the sev-enteenth when the older medieval idea of liberties as (unequally distributed) grants from the king was still dominant.

These legal historians contrast this seventeenth-century constitution of customary rights with the gradual emergence following the Glorious Revolution of the idea that Parliament was supreme not only over the Crown but over the law and the constitution as well.[22] By pointing out the newness of the doctrine of parliamentary sovereignty within the realm, they are able to legitimate the colonial arguments against parliamentary taxes and legislation in the 1760s and 1770s. For, they argue, if parliamentary sovereignty was a recent phenomenon in England, then students of the Revolution should not assume that it applied across the Atlantic in the American colonies.[23] Rather, these historians redirect scholarly attention to the existence of a customary imperial constitution based on the settlers' long experience of governing themselves through local assemblies, subject only to the oversight of the king-in-council, but not – apart from a small number of ineffectual mercantile regulations – to the authority of the king-in-Parliament.[24] The rights the settlers enjoyed under this imperial constitution were bolstered by what Reid calls "the colonial original contract," according to which the king had promised them that in return for undertaking the risks of migrating to America they would be as secure in their rights as if they had never left home.[25] For these legal historians, then, the empire was a federation, a union of quasi-autonomous states, much like the composite monarchies of early modern Europe, in which authority was consensual, the settlers offering allegiance to a monarch who in turn was bound to respect their constitutional rights.[26]

[22] According to Jack P. Greene, this "great constitutional change" meant that "increasingly during the eighteenth century, the constitution came to be seen – in Britain – as virtually identical with Parliament itself: the constitution became precisely what Parliament said it was." Greene, *Peripheries and Center*, 57–58.

[23] According to John Phillip Reid, "the eighteenth century can be called the epoch of two constitutions in both Great Britain and the American colonies." Reid, "The Jurisprudence of Liberty: The Ancient Constitution in the Legal Historiography of the Seventeenth and Eighteenth Centuries," in Ellis Sandoz, ed., *The Roots of Liberty: Magna Carta, the Ancient Constitution, and the Anglo-American Tradition of the Rule of Law* (Columbia: University of Missouri Press, 1993), 194.

[24] Greene is most responsible for the idea that there was an imperial constitution as distinct from the English (later British) constitution and the constitutions of the individual colonies. See *Peripheries and Center*, xi, and passim.

[25] John Phillip Reid, *The Constitutional History of the American Revolution: The Authority of Rights* (Madison: University of Wisconsin Press, 1986), 114–145. Once granted, these rights were held by the settlers to be irrevocable.

[26] See John Elliott, "A Europe of Composite Monarchies," *Past and Present* 137 (1992), 48–71; and H.G. Koenigsberger, "Composite States, Representative Institutions and the American Revolution," *Historical Research* 62 (1989), 135–154. On the first British empire as characterized by consensual authority, see Greene, *Negotiated Authorities: Essays in*

The work of these scholars is indispensable to any full account of the Revolution. Nevertheless, their focus on the conservative, prescriptive nature of the colonial case, and in particular their denial that the idea of natural rights had any influence on settler thought, ignores the fact that even in its seventeenth-century heyday, the common law was not a solely customary legal system.[27] Rather, common lawyers often proclaimed that custom needed to be based on reason. And, as the historian J.P. Sommerville argues, "in emphasizing the rational nature of English liberties, the lawyers came close to asserting that these liberties did, in fact, belong to everyone by nature."[28] Moreover, despite the insistence of revisionist historians[29] on the hegemony of the ancient constitution in seventeenth-century England, the descent into Civil War in the 1640s led to a proliferation of new legal and political ideas, from parliamentary sovereignty, to natural rights, to republicanism, to the resurgence of absolutism following the Restoration, all of which shaped political debate in the British Atlantic world.[30] As well, recent work on legal pluralism in early modern England has shown that common lawyers were

---

Colonial Political and Constitutional History (Charlottesville: University of Virginia Press, 1994). On consensual authority as a feature of early modern empires in general, see Christine Daniels and Michael V. Kennedy, eds., *Negotiated Empires: Centers and Peripheries in the Americas, 1500–1820* (New York and London: Routledge, 2002). On the culture of constitutionalism in the empire, see Mary Sarah Bilder, *The Transatlantic Constitution: Colonial Legal Culture and the Empire* (Cambridge: Harvard University Press, 2004); and Daniel J. Hulsebosch, *Constituting Empire: New York and the Transformation of Constitutionalism in the Atlantic World, 1664–1830* (Chapel Hill: University of North Carolina Press, 2005).

[27] For John Phillip Reid's intransigent rejection of natural rights, see his *Constitutional History of the American Revolution: The Authority of Rights*, 90–95; and "The Irrelevance of the Declaration," in Hendrik Hartog, ed., *Law in the American Revolution and the American Revolution in the Law: A Collection of Essays on American Legal History* (New York: New York University Press, 1981), 46–89. For a milder version of this argument, see Jack P. Greene, "Law and the Origins of the American Revolution," in Michael Grossberg and Christopher Tomlins, eds., *The Cambridge History of Law in America: Volume 1, Early America (1580–1815)* (New York: Cambridge University Press, 2008), 481.

[28] J.P. Sommerville, *Royalists and Patriots: Politics and Ideology in England, 1603–1640* (New York: Longman, 1999), 102. According to Sommerville, by reason the common lawyers usually meant an "artificial reason" which "could be acquired only by those who had spent long years studying the law." See *Royalists and Patriots*, 84, and the discussion at 89.

[29] On revisionism, see J.P. Kenyon, "Revisionism and Post Revisionism in Early Stuart History," *Journal of Modern History* 64 (1992), 686–699. Despite the revisionist support for their contention that a customary ancient constitution dominated Anglo-American legal thought, Reid and the other legal historians discussed above do not cite this literature.

[30] According to Glenn Burgess, there was "a new structure of political discourse in the 1640s" as "thinkers began to explore modes of political thinking not related to common

not so insular that they were ignorant of other systems of law. In particular, this new work argues, they drew on Roman law when addressing legal questions arising outside the realm, such as the acquisition of new territories by the Crown. In such a situation, English jurists held that the prerogative was not subject to the legal limits placed upon it by the common law and the ancient constitution.[31] This recognition that the common law had territorial limits is an important one for early Americanists, for it meant that even staunch Whigs like Edward Coke, whom the colonists venerated, was equivocal about whether the rights of Englishmen had traversed the Atlantic.[32] Moreover, even when the king did extend English law outside the realm, the prerogative still played a far greater role in governing subjects in the royal dominions than it did within the realm, especially if the dominion in question had been conquered.[33] And, as we will see in Chapter 1, these English jurists also claimed that once English law extended, so did the jurisdiction of the English Parliament, which could then bind subjects in the colonies without their consent if it named them in its legislation. The fact that eminent common lawyers could make a legally sound argument that the colonies were subordinate parts of the empire made it unlikely that precedent or custom alone would be determinative in debates about the rights of Englishmen outside the realm.[34]

law." Burgess, *Politics of the Ancient Constitution*, 229, 221. The classic account of political thought in early Stuart England is Margaret Judson, *The Crisis of the Constitution: An Essay in Constitutional and Political Thought in England, 1603–1645* (1949; New Brunswick: Rutgers University Press, 1988).

[31] On legal pluralism, see Burgess, *Politics of the Ancient Constitution* and Ken MacMillan, *Sovereignty and Possession in the English New World: The Legal Foundations of Empire, 1576–1640* (New York: Cambridge University Press, 2006). On the role that civil lawyers played in developing an absolutist conception of the prerogative, see Brian P. Levack, "Law and Ideology: The Civil Law and Theories of Absolutism in Elizabethan and Jacobean England," in Dubrow and Strier, eds., *The Historical Renaissance: New Essays on Tudor and Stuart Literature and Culture* (Chicago: University of Chicago Press, 1988), 220–241; and, more generally, his *The Civil Lawyers in England, 1603–1641* (Oxford: Clarendon Press, 1973).

[32] This is the central contention of an important article by Daniel J. Hulsebosch, "Edward Coke and the Expanding Empire: Sir Edward Coke's British Jurisprudence," *Law and History Review* 21 (2003), 439–482.

[33] For the use of a Roman law doctrine of conquest in Ireland, see Hans Pawlisch, "Sir John Davies, the Ancient Constitution, and Civil Law," *Historical Journal* 23 (1980), 689–702. On the force of the prerogative in eighteenth-century British North America, see Bailyn, *Origins of American Politics*, 59–105.

[34] A point made in Michael Zuckert's "Natural Rights and Imperial Constitutionalism: The American Revolution and the Development of the American Amalgam," *Social Philosophy and Policy* 22 (2005), 27–55.

The embrace of Roman law by English jurists was part of a larger turn toward transnational legal doctrines in the early modern Atlantic world. As an important body of recent work by historians of political thought has shown, European expansion into the Americas was closely connected to the revival of natural law theory in early modern political and legal thought. Beginning in the sixteenth century, jurists developed a new law of nations (*ius gentium*) in order to govern relations between the European empires and the indigenous peoples they encountered, as well as between the empires themselves as they competed for territory. Because the tenets of this early modern law of nations were seen as a codification of natural law, Europeans deemed them binding on all peoples everywhere.[35] The turn to nature and reason as the foundation of this new law of nations also led to a downplaying of scriptural claims in legal debates in the Atlantic world.[36] As developed in the seventeenth and eighteenth centuries by such thinkers as Grotius, Locke, and Vattel, natural law theory held that Europeans had a superior right to territory in the Americas because the indigenous peoples who lived there were not cultivating the land in a manner that Europeans deemed necessary to establish ownership or sovereignty.[37] Moreover, as Edward Keene has recently argued, the early modern law of nations authorized private individuals and corporations to settle on native land and establish

---

[35] See Robert A. Williams, Jr., *The American Indian in Western Legal Thought: The Discourses of Conquest* (New York: Oxford University Press, 1990); Richard Tuck, *The Rights of War and Peace: Political Thought and the International Order from Grotius to Kant* (New York: Oxford University Press, 1999); Anthony Anghie, "Francisco De Vitoria and the Colonial Origins of International Law," *Social and Legal Studies* 5 (1996), 321–336; and Anthony Pagden "Dispossessing the Barbarian: The Language of Spanish Thomism and the Debate over the Property Rights of the American Indians," in Anthony Pagden, ed., *The Languages of Political Theory in Early Modern Europe* (Cambridge: Cambridge University Press, 1987), 99–119. For a comparative account of European justifications of empire, see Anthony Pagden, *Lords of All the World: Ideologies of Empire in Spain, Britain and France c.1500–c.1800* (New Haven: Yale University Press, 1995); as well as Patricia Seed, *Ceremonies of Possession in Europe's Conquest of the New World, 1492–1640* (New York: Cambridge University Press, 1995).

[36] According to Lauren Benton and Benjamin Straumann, the desire of northern European Protestants to refute papal claims led to the development of "a fresh doctrine of sources of law" based on "nature," the content of which was provided in part by Roman law texts. See Benton and Straumann, "Acquiring Empire by Law: From Roman Doctrine to Early Modern European Practice," *Law and History Review* 28 (2010), 20.

[37] On Locke as theorist of empire, see James Tully's seminal articles: "Rediscovering America: The *Two Treatises* and Aboriginal Rights," in Tully, ed., *An Approach to Political Philosophy: Locke in Contexts* (Cambridge: Cambridge University Press, 1993), 137–176; "Aboriginal Property and Western Theory: Recovering a Middle

governments with the "marks of sovereignty," including the ability to levy taxes, pass laws, and wage war.[38] By allowing private individuals to wield delegated political authority in the extra-European world, these theorists accentuated the individualism of early modern natural law theory, bringing to the fore the argument that individuals had natural rights to liberty and property which they could exercise outside the confines of the state from which they had emigrated.[39] According to Barbara Arneil, one of the pioneers in placing early modern thinkers in an imperial context, "the originality of Locke's arguments on property lies in the way

Ground," *Social Philosophy and Policy* 11 (1994), 153–180; and "Placing the 'Two Treatises'," in Nicholas Phillipson and Quentin Skinner, eds., *Political Discourse in Early Modern Britain* (Cambridge: Cambridge University Press, 1993), 253–280; as well as Barbara Arneil, *John Locke and America: The Defence of English Colonialism* (Oxford: Clarendon Press, 1996); Duncan Ivison, "Locke, Liberalism and Empire," in Peter Anstey, ed., *The Philosophy of John Locke: New Perspectives* (London: Routledge, 2003), 86–105; and David Armitage, "John Locke, Carolina, and the *Two Treatises of Government*," *Political Theory* 32 (2004), 618. On the connection between indigenous systems of property and their incapacity to govern themselves, see Bruce Buchan, "The Empire of Political Thought: Civilization, Savagery, and the Perceptions of Indigenous Government," *History of the Human Sciences* 18 (2002), 1–22. As Andrew Fitzmaurice has recently argued, however, the natural law idea that property rights derived from use was invoked to *defend* indigenous rights in the Iberian world on the grounds that they were in fact occupying and using the land. Nevertheless, he maintains that the English, beginning in the early seventeenth century and culminating in the work of John Locke, inverted this argument, contending that the indigenous peoples of North America were *not* in fact using the land in ways that would confer legitimate rights of ownership and sovereignty. On these points, see Fitzmaurice, The Genealogy of *Terra Nullius*," *Australian Historical Studies* 129 (2007), 7–8; and "Moral Uncertainty in the Dispossession of the Native Americans," in Peter Mancall, ed., *Virginia in the Atlantic World, 1550–1624* (Chapel Hill: University of North Carolina Press, 2007), 383–409.

[38] Edward Keene, *Beyond the Anarchical Society: Grotius, Colonialism and Order in World Politics* (New York: Cambridge University Press, 2002), 67–68. According to Benjamin Straumann, Grotius's "secular doctrine of natural rights" – which was formulated "independently from Christian sources" – "acknowledged both private entities – individuals and trading corporations – and states as subjects." Straumann contends that this had a "double-edged implication for sovereignty: not only were states endowed with certain rights, but so were individuals and private entities." Straumann, "Is Modern Liberty Ancient? Roman Remedies and Natural Rights in Hugo Grotius' Early Works on Natural Law," *Law and History Review* 27 (2009), 84–85. Alison LaCroix argues that the founders' conception of federalism was influenced by such a "Continental notion of divisible sovereignty" which she contrasts with "the common law vision of unitary sovereignty." LaCroix, *The Ideological Origins of American Federalism* (Cambridge: Harvard University Press, 2010), 18–20.

[39] On the individualism of early modern natural law theory, see Richard Tuck "The 'Modern' Theory of Natural Law," in Pagden, ed., *Languages of Political Theory*, 99–119. According to Benjamin Straumann, Grotius's "influential doctrine of individual natural rights" was derived from Roman law and ethics; and therefore, contra the claims

English colonization is justified, not just because God or natural law has commanded it, as Winthrop and others had argued, but because each colonist has a natural right within himself, through his labour, to appropriate land."[40]

Given that the English settlers had to think about both the rights of the indigenous peoples of eastern North America and the nature of their own delegated authority in the empire, it should not surprise us if this early modern natural law theory resonated with them. By taking the insights of this scholarship seriously, early Americanists can begin to develop an account of political and legal ideas in British North America more attuned to the legally contested world that the settlers inhabited. In particular, they can begin to understand why those who made a republican revolution did so in the name of natural rights, an idea which, as this new scholarship has shown, was not a peripheral creed (as the partisans of classical republicanism claimed), but rather was central to political debate within the early modern Atlantic world.[41]

of the classical republican historians discussed above, there was an idea of individual or subjective rights in the ancient world that was transmitted to the seventeenth and eighteenth century Atlantic world by Grotius and others. See Straumann, "Is Modern Liberty Ancient?" 55.

[40] Barbara Arneil, "The Wild Indian's Venison: Locke's Theory of Property and English Colonialism in America," *Political Studies* 44 (1996), 74. The fissiparous implications of an individual natural right to appropriate indigenous land and establish (via delegated authority) quasi-sovereign colonial governments are discussed in Keene, *Beyond the Anarchical Society*, 67–68 ("the rights in property through occupation and the marks of sovereignty granted under the Charter were both used to justify resistance, much as they were later used in the more decisive revolution of the eighteenth century" – referring to the settler opposition to the Dominion of New England in the late seventeenth century); and Anthony Pagden, "The Struggle for Legitimacy and the Image of Empire in the Atlantic to c. 1700," in Nicholas Canny, ed., *The Oxford History of the British Empire. Volume One, The Origins of Empire* (New York: Oxford University Press, 1998), 53 ("the reliance on the 'agriculturalist argument' implied a large measure of self-determination on the part of the colonists themselves"; and "Locke's ... legitimation for the English colonization of America ... depended not upon concessions made from, or on behalf of, the metropolitan power, but on the actions of the settlers themselves").

[41] The idea that Locke was a peripheral figure was of course the original battle cry of the republican revisionists; however, J.G.A. Pocock, one of the original debunkers, has recently conceded the centrality of natural law (as well as the *ius gentium*) to political debate in the early modern British Atlantic. See Pocock, "Political Thought in the English-Speaking Atlantic, 1760–1790. Part I: The Imperial Crisis," in J.G.A. Pocock, Gordon J. Schochet, and Lois G. Schwoerer, eds., *The Varieties of British Political Thought, 1500–1800* (Cambridge: Cambridge University Press, 2003), 246–282.

Building on these two bodies of scholarship, *Settlers, Liberty, and Empire* explores the political world that British Americans encountered as they faced east from the periphery of the Atlantic in the crucial century before the Revolution, when the empire took shape, and settler elites confronted the question of their relationship to the center for the first time. Drawing on a body of hitherto unexamined political pamphlets, tracts, newspaper essays, and legal cases, it argues that there was a transatlantic debate about the rights of settlers in the first British empire, a debate that decisively shaped the nature of colonial – and thus early American – thinking about rights, law, and political authority. As subjects of the Crown, the settlers lived in polities removed from the realm and its institutions, inhabiting lands that were also occupied by powerful Native American nations. This novel situation raised a series of difficult questions. Did, for example, English law and rights extend to the settlers, allowing them to be governed by consent *via* local assemblies? Or were they to be directly subject to the Crown's prerogative? And, if English rights did extend to these new colonies, what was the relationship between local institutions and royal authority and parliamentary authority? And finally, what was the legal status of the Native American peoples on whose lands the colonies were established? The response of British people on both sides of the Atlantic to these difficult questions forms the heart of this study.[42]

Settlers, Liberty, and Empire begins with the crucial years of the late seventeenth century when the English Crown began the first serious attempt to undermine the de facto autonomy that had characterized the pre-Restoration empire. In order to do so, the Crown reversed the policy of previous decades in which it had delegated its political authority to chartered corporations and proprietors in a vain attempt to have an empire without paying for it. *Settlers, Liberty, and Empire* then traces the response of settler elites to a series of metropolitan attempts to take back this delegated authority – from the ill-fated Dominion of New England in the 1680s, to the failed attempt to revoke the charters of the private colonies in the early 1700s, to the final imperial crisis in the 1760s and 1770s. Given the episodic nature of constitutional strife in the empire, *Settlers, Liberty, and Empire* doesn't attempt a narrative covering the whole of British America; instead, it offers detailed accounts of imperial conflict

---

[42] On the jurisdictional complexity of early modern empires, see James Muldoon, *Empire and Order: The Concept of Empire, 800–1800* (New York: St. Martin's Press, 1999), 145.

in colonies ranging geographically from Massachusetts to Virginia, and chronologically from the Glorious Revolution in America to the American Revolution against Britain.

Two different visions of the empire emerged from these successive waves of imperial reform. The English Crown argued that the American colonies were subordinate polities in which the royal prerogative could trump settler rights. In this view, the settlers had no inherent claim to English law or representative institutions; rather, they enjoyed them only at the pleasure of the Crown. And even when these rights had been extended, their exercise was limited by periodic royal attempts to override colonial legislation, to erect juryless courts, to make governors' instructions legally binding, and, in extremis, to revoke colonial charters altogether. Following the Glorious Revolution, Parliament became an increasingly important part of imperial governance, adding its claims to sovereignty over the colonies to those of the Crown. In the early 1700s, the Board of Trade enlisted parliamentary aid in its attempt to revoke the charters of the private colonies. And, beginning in the mid-eighteenth century, metropolitan officials began to argue that the new idea of the unitary sovereignty of the king-in-Parliament should apply throughout the empire, giving parliamentary legislation the authority to trump colonial rights.[43]

This authoritarian royal policy was driven by economic and geopolitical considerations – most centrally the desire to reap commercial benefits from the colonies and to secure the imperial frontiers from the French and the Spanish. Influential officials at the Board of Trade and the Privy Council believed that both of these goals were jeopardized by the political autonomy the colonies had enjoyed in the early to mid-seventeenth century and which these officials strove (albeit intermittently) to undermine beginning in the 1670s. The Crown's desire to reform the empire also derived from a concern that an excessively decentralized empire was detrimental to its vital alliances with those Native Americans who faced dispossession by a growing settler population.

In response to these centralizing imperatives, settler elites crafted an alternate account of their place within the empire. Drawing on the seventeenth-century idea of the common law, they claimed that their migration from the realm had not weakened their claim to the enjoyment

---

[43] On the rise of Parliament in the eighteenth century, see H.T. Dickinson, "The Eighteenth-Century Debate on the Sovereignty of Parliament," *Royal Historical Society Transactions* 26 (1976), 189–210.

of English rights, rights they contended were the birthright of all English subjects, and which had their basis in both reason and a customary ancient constitution. The adoption by the settlers of these English legal norms was in part the product of Anglicization and the increase in transatlantic economic and cultural ties that characterized the eighteenth-century British world; however, the transmission of these norms to the settlers was in tension with this cultural and economic convergence, as the growing influence of common law constitutionalism made it hard for the center to assert its authority in ways that contravened the settlers' expectation of consensual government in the empire.[44]

In order to bolster their claim to English rights, the settlers also argued that they had undertaken the risks of colonization, had labored to subdue a "wilderness," and had thereby benefited the metropole. In this view, colonization was contractual: In return for their efforts on its behalf, the Crown guaranteed them equal rights with subjects who had stayed at home. And beginning in the first decades of the eighteenth century, the settlers drew on the early modern natural law tradition – in particular, John Locke's variant of it – to argue that they had a natural right to migrate and then establish both property rights and political authority in the New World. The settler adoption of natural rights was part of a transformation in their political thought in which the particularism of the English common law was gradually incorporated into a universalistic account of rights, one more suitable to a transatlantic and jurisdictionally contested imperial polity.

Instead of seeing England as the ultimate locus of authority, the settlers envisioned a decentralized empire, one in which authority was divided between London and the several colonial governments, and in which the greater good of all Britons depended on colonial autonomy. The empire was thus not a unitary state, but a collection of equal dominions tied together by allegiance to a common monarch, an allegiance which in turn was conditional on the Crown's respect for colonial rights. Although the Crown held the executive authority of the empire in its hands, all local authority remained in the several American polities, which were each governed by an assembly of their own choosing. This nascent federal conception of the empire partook of older ideas about the bonds of allegiance between king and subject; but it also looked ahead to the federal division of authority that would be the

---

[44] On Anglicization, the classic study is John Murrin, *Anglicizing an American Colony: The Transformation of Provincial Massachusetts* (Ph.D. Dissertation, Yale University, 1966).

hallmark of the new republican empire of the United States. Although this settler vision of the transatlantic connection contained a strong defense of local autonomy, it was not latently republican; rather, it was a wholehearted embrace of empire, but one in which the settlers were its agents and not subalterns whose liberty and property was subject to metropolitan control.

Settlers, Liberty, and Empire also takes seriously the rights of the Native Americans, a subject that has been absent from most of the scholarship on early American political theory.[45] The land the English settled was occupied by ancient cultures used to governing themselves on their traditional territories. As such, the settlers had to think about the juridical status of Native Americans as part of the larger project of justifying their presence in America. The settlers made several distinct but interrelated arguments about Native American rights. In some cases, they acknowledged indigenous rights to property, arguing that the Crown was violating the natives' natural law rights by claiming to hold ultimate title to the soil in the New World. The settlers then claimed that they had purchased the land from the natives fairly, thereby legitimating their own settlement while undermining the authority of the Crown in America. The settlers also invoked the right of conquest, arguing that they had defeated the natives in war and thus had a superior title to their land. At other times, they argued that the natives were not cultivating the land in a way that would establish property rights or jurisdiction according to the dictates of natural law and thus could be dispossessed without consent. Although distinct, these arguments were (creatively) combined by settler spokesmen, for they all had the same end: to base the legal foundation of the colonies on the right of the settlers – via purchase, labor, or conquest – to replace indigenous authority with their own. Seen in this light, the old question of the constitutional status of the American colonies in the empire was intimately related to the question of the rights of the indigenous peoples of the Americas.

The political theory of the American Revolution was the outcome of this century-long debate about settler rights in the empire. After a period of lax oversight in the early to mid-eighteenth century, the settlers confronted a renewed metropolitan challenge from king and Parliament in the 1760s and 1770s. Building on previous settler arguments, they

---

[45] This neglect is at odds with the efflorescence of scholarship on all aspects of Native American society in the last generation. For an incisive synthesis of this new history, see Daniel Richter, *Facing East from Indian Country: A Native History of Early America* (Cambridge: Harvard University Press, 2001).

responded with a compelling pan-colonial account of their natural right to equality, to consent, and, ultimately, to revolution.

This book does not make any claims to comprehensiveness, still less to be constructing an all-encompassing explanatory paradigm for early American political thought (which was the great fault of both sides in the republicanism-liberalism debate). Rather, it focuses on one important but neglected aspect of the political experience of settler elites – their attempt to define their legal rights in the first British empire, a vast, extended polity riven by constitutional uncertainty. In order to uncover the contours of this settler vision of the empire, it focuses on close readings of a series of important but little-studied settler texts, each representative of a particular type of constitutional conflict in the empire – from the attempt to revoke colonial charters, to the debate over the extension of English law, to the nature of indigenous rights, to the power of the Crown over colonial legislation – and each the product of a particular (and often long forgotten) political and institutional context, which the book reconstructs. And because this story of constitutional conflict is told chronologically and covers a representative sample of the mainland colonies, the book serves as a history (albeit incomplete) of colonial politics in the empire.

As well, although *Settlers, Liberty, and Empire* shows that the settlers were influenced by Locke's political theory much earlier than usually thought, it pays more attention to the content of their thought, to the way that they creatively combined European and English legal and political ideas, than it does to tracing the impact of particular thinkers or texts in British North America.[46] And despite the fact that the book focuses on imperial conflict, I have tried to avoid the teleological assumption that the natural course of empire was revolution and republicanism. Rather, I argue that the settlers were willing participants in the British imperial project, albeit on their terms; and that it was the desire of Crown and Parliament to centralize the empire that ultimately forced them to contemplate resistance.

---

[46] I also do not trace the circulation and reception of these texts. Rather, I demonstrate the ways in which settlers in these disparate colonies developed a shared account of their place in the empire. For which European texts were available to colonial readers, see David Lundberg and Henry F. May, "The Enlightened Reader in America," *American Quarterly* 28 (1976), 262–293; and Donald S. Lutz, "The Relative Influence of European Writers on Late Eighteenth-Century American Thought," *American Political Science Review* 78 (1984), 189–197. On the reception of Locke's *Second Treatise* in the colonies on the eve of revolution, see Eric Slauter, "Reading and Radicalization: Print, Politics and the American Revolution," *Early American Studies* 8 (2010), 5–40.

A fuller study of the impact of empire on settler legal and political norms would also have to take into account the experience of the West Indian islands. Apart from constraints of time and space, I have chosen to focus on the mainland colonies because they had a different relationship to the imperial center in the eighteenth century. As Richard Dunn has recently argued, following the Glorious Revolution there were "two varieties of colonial relationship, a West Indian kind and a North American kind." Although in the seventeenth century the islanders were in the forefront of resistance to imperial authority, after the overthrow of the Stuarts they asked for and got beneficial trade regulations, as well as military protection from the British army and navy, in return for which, Dunn argues, they were willing to accept a "dependent colonial status" in the eighteenth-century empire.[47] The mainland colonies, by contrast, faced more political pressure from the center while at the same time were less able to influence policy makers in London. As a consequence, they had to think more deeply and creatively about their rights as subjects outside the realm.[48] My focus on the mainland colonies, then, is not an exercise in anachronism but rather an attempt to relate a part of what I hope one day will be a broader, comparative history of settler ideas of liberty in the early modern British world, taking into account the experience of such far-flung places as Ireland, Nova Scotia, British India, and South Africa.[49]

[47] Richard Dunn, "The Glorious Revolution and America," in Canny, ed., *The Origins of Empire*, 465. Dunn's student Andrew O'Shaughnessy carries this argument forward into the revolutionary era in his superb *An Empire Divided: The American Revolution and the British Caribbean* (Philadelphia: University of Pennsylvania Press, 2000). For the opposition of Barbados to Parliament in the mid-seventeenth century, see Liam S. O'Melinn, "The American Revolution and Constitutionalism in the Seventeenth-Century West Indies," *Columbia Law Review* 95 (1995), 104–159.
[48] This study is thus an exercise in what David Armitage has called "Cis-Atlantic history," which he defines as "the history of any particular place – a nation, a state, a region, even a specific institution – in relation to the wider Atlantic world." Although Armitage does not specify a principle by which to select one part of the Atlantic world to investigate, for the reasons outlined above, I believe that the mainland colonies constitute a discrete component of the larger eighteenth-century British Atlantic world. Armitage, "Three Concepts of Atlantic History," in Armitage and Braddick, eds., *The British Atlantic World*, 22.
[49] On which, see Jack P. Greene, ed., *Exclusionary Empire: English Liberty Overseas, 1600–1900* (New York: Cambridge University Press, 2010). On Ireland, see Neil York, *Neither Colony nor Kingdom: The Irish Quest for Constitutional Rights, 1698–1800* (Washington, DC: Catholic University of America Press, 1994). For a comparative account stressing the divergence between one of the oldest mainland colonies and Nova Scotia, see Elizabeth Mancke, *The Faultlines of Empire: Political Differentiation in Massachusetts and Nova Scotia, ca. 1760–1830* (New York: Routledge, 2005). Like

Settlers, Liberty, and Empire is divided into three parts. The first – "Restoration and Rebellion" – begins with the new imperial policies of Charles II and his brother James in the crucial decades following the Restoration. Their attempt to centralize the empire raised the question of what rights Englishmen had in the king's dominions in America. This was a potentially explosive issue, coming at the end of a century in which England had been plunged into civil war and revolution in part over the Stuarts' exalted conception of the royal prerogative. And it was a question to which leading English jurists had at best equivocal answers, with Crown lawyers (and later parliamentary ministers) able to furnish good legal arguments for metropolitan authority in the colonies, while the settlers were able to draw on some of the same cases and treatises to bolster their claim to autonomy in the empire. The fact that leading common lawyers were never able to come to a consensus on the legal status of the colonies was central to constitutional conflict in the empire.

The book's second chapter narrates the consequences of the Stuarts' imperial vision, principally the establishment of the Dominion of New England and its downfall in a series of settler rebellions that echoed the larger upheaval with the realm. In the three colonies – Massachusetts, New York, and Maryland – that took up arms against the Dominion in the spring and summer of 1689, we see the contours of an emerging discourse about empire based on the legal equality of all of the king's subjects, the contractual guarantee of settlers' rights in the colonial charters, the purchase of the land from the natives independent of any Crown grant, and the transformation of this uncultivated land into flourishing civil societies. For the settlers, then, the resistance to the Stuarts validated their vision of an empire of equal rights. However, in the center the legacy of the Glorious Revolution was more equivocal, with many royal officials holding that the limits placed on prerogative within the realm did not extend to the peripheries. As well, the victory of Parliament over the king raised the questions of whether its newfound authority extended across the Atlantic.

The second part of the book – "Empire" – deals with the uncertain aftermath of the Glorious Revolution. Beginning in the 1690s, the settlers were increasingly drawn into the orbit of an expanding empire. Under the new king, William III, renewed warfare with the French; rising levels of trade, commerce, and migration; the growth of transatlantic political

O'Shaugnessy, Mancke argues that the continental colonies were exceptional in their resistance to metropolitan centralization.

ties; and a shared embrace of the ideology of English constitutionalism all knit the British world more closely together.[50] At the same time, however, this integration was imperfect, and the empire continued to experience tensions between local and central authority, exacerbated by the intermittent revival of the Stuarts' dream of centralized rule.

The first of the four chapters in this part of the book analyzes the impact of imperial centralization in the 1690s and early 1700s. In the middle of two cycles of war against the French and eager to reap the commercial benefits of empire, William III created the Board of Trade in 1696, which then embarked on a series of reforms, most notably an attempt to revoke the charters of the private colonies. By turning them into royal colonies, the Board hoped to weaken their autonomy, bringing much needed order to the empire following the settler revolts of 1689. When its initial attempts to rein in the private colonies failed, the Board turned to Parliament, setting the stage for later assertions of its sovereignty across the Atlantic. In addition to undermining chartered governments, the Board also attempted to augment its authority in the existing royal colonies by insisting on the Crown's right to review colonial legislation; to suspend its operation until it had received royal approval; to create juryless prerogative courts; to have its instructions to its governors treated as law; and finally, to force the colonial assemblies to pay the governor's salary.

To examine the impact on the private colonies of this second wave of imperial centralization, this chapter focuses on the 1721 pamphlet of the agent for all of the New England colonies, Jeremiah Dummer. In this sophisticated polemic, Dummer defended the American charters on the

---

[50] For a provocative reinterpretation of British America that argues for its imperial and monarchical character, see Brendan McConville, *The King's Three Faces: The Rise and Fall of Royal America, 1688–1776* (Chapel Hill: University of North Carolina Press, 2006). McConville dissents from what he sees as anachronistic interpretations of early American political culture that stress its latently republican and democratic character. While I am sympathetic to McConville's critique, I think he ignores the extent to which the settlers conceived of monarchical authority as connected to the protection of their rights, and thus as contractual and conditional. On liberty as a central component of an emerging imperial identity, see Jack P. Greene, "Empire and Identity from the Glorious Revolution to the American Revolution," in P.J. Marshall, ed., *The Eighteenth-Century: Volume Two, The Oxford History of the British Empire* (New York: Oxford University Press, 1998), 208–230. On transatlantic politics, see Alison G. Olson, *Making the Empire Work: London and American Interest Groups, 1690–1790* (Cambridge: Harvard University Press, 1992). And on war and imperial integration, see Bruce Lenman, "Colonial War and Imperial Instability, 1688–1793," in Marshall, ed., *The Eighteenth-Century*, 151–168.

grounds that they represented a contract between the king and the settlers in which the settlers expanded the Crown's empire in return for the
recognition of colonial rights. Dummer also grounded the settlers' rights
to the land in the colonies in a preexisting native title that the settlers had
fairly purchased. However, he then contended that before the English
arrived, America was, due to the "savage" nature of the indigenous population, akin to an uninhabited wilderness. By laboring on this land and
improving it, the settlers created a right to the soil that the Crown could
not abrogate. This argument about the legal status of America as both
native soil and *terra nullius* ran throughout settlers' discourse about their
rights in the empire. Dummer also dealt with the new issue of Parliament's
authority in the empire by arguing that it was morally bound to respect
the rights of the settlers.

The book's fourth chapter deals more fully with the tension between
Native American rights and those of the settlers in this age of imperial
integration. In the early eighteenth century, the Mohegan Indians appealed
to the Crown against Connecticut's encroachment on their tribal lands.
Imperial officials were eager to listen as they wanted to use Connecticut's
ill treatment of the tribe in their ongoing attempt to revoke the charters
of the private or corporate colonies. The colony responded by arguing
that they had obtained the disputed land by both conquest and purchase and had then improved it with their labor. By this account, their
own efforts had given them title; the subsequent grant of a royal charter
merely confirmed their preexisting claim. Above all, Connecticut insisted
that the Mohegans were not a nation as the Crown had claimed and
therefore had no right of appeal against the colony's authority. As such,
the Mohegan case exemplifies the way in which the settlers based their
rights in the New World on the denial of those of the natives. The fullest articulation of this settler viewpoint was the 1725 pamphlet of John
Bulkley, a prominent Connecticut clergyman. Bulkley contended that
the Mohegans were still in a state of nature, thereby denying the tribe
the sovereign status that the Crown had accorded them and justifying the
colony's appropriation of their land. In making this argument, Bulkley
drew extensively on Locke's *Second Treatise*, illustrating the extent to
which early modern natural law theory was becoming central to the settlers' justification of their rights in America.

Chapter 5 deals with an important but neglected instance of constitutional conflict in Maryland, one of the colonies that had revolted in
1689. Although it had been made a royal colony following the Glorious
Revolution, Maryland had been returned to its original proprietors, the

Baltimore family, in 1715. In the early 1720s, a decade-long dispute broke out between the proprietor and the assembly over whether the settlers were entitled to the enjoyment of English laws by right, or whether their extension depended on the proprietor's discretion. The result was a political crisis that made the province ungovernable for nearly a decade. This chapter focuses on the colonial assembly's response to the proprietor, and in particular that of its leader Daniel Dulany, who in 1728 wrote a powerful polemic defending the rights of the settlers in Maryland to English laws. Drawing on Coke's idea of the ancient constitution, Dulany contended that English laws were the subjects' "birthright," something they could claim everywhere in the king's dominions. He also argued that Maryland was, before the English came, a "wilderness," inhabited by native peoples who lacked even the semblance of law and government. As a consequence, the settlers in Maryland had the right to take English laws with them to the New World. As with Bulkley's argument against Mohegan rights, Dulany's pamphlet shows the extent to which the assertion of settler rights depended on the denial of those of the natives. Dulany concluded his pamphlet with a long invocation of Locke on the natural right to migrate, which was, along with Bulkley's, one of the earliest uses of the *Second Treatise* in British America.

Chapter 6 turns to Virginia, the oldest of the royal colonies, which had largely avoided clashes with imperial authority in the early eighteenth century. However, in the 1750s two disputes, one over the pistole fee – a tax on land levied by the royal governor – and the other over payments to the Anglican clergy (the Parson's Cause) engendered a debate within the colony about the Crown's prerogative right to set taxes and to veto colonial legislation. This chapter deals with these neglected episodes via a close examination of the arguments of prominent Virginians – principally Landon Carter and Richard Bland – against both of these exercises of the prerogative. Their defense of the colony's legislative authority was similar to previous arguments for settler rights in the empire, strongly suggesting the existence of a common legal and political theory in eighteenth-century British North America. In his opposition to the royal veto, Bland also developed a nascent federal theory of the empire, with a delineation of zones of internal and external authority intended to safeguard Virginia's autonomy while allowing for the delimited exercise of metropolitan oversight. In doing so, he made explicit what had only been implicit in previous iterations of settler discourse and laid the foundation for the emergence of a federal theory of the empire in the late 1760s and early 1770s.

The third and final part of the book – "Revolution" – narrates the collapse of this period of uncertain imperial integration and its descent into revolution. In the aftermath of the failed attempt to revoke the colonial charters in the early 1700s, a small group of officials at the Board of Trade, unhappy with the lax oversight that characterized imperial governance after the Treaty of Utrecht, began to agitate for a more centralized empire able to defend itself against imperial rivals and extract economic rents from its colonies. Like earlier reformers, these policy makers were driven by geopolitical concerns, in particular the looming threat from the French to the north, as well as the growing importance of the colonies to the wealth and power of the British fiscal-military state. In order to restructure the empire, all of these reformers called for Parliament to have a greater role in imperial governance, believing that its authority was necessary to enforce royal instructions, levy taxes, and, in extremis, annul the colonial constitutions entirely. As well, they pointed out that the Native Americans of the interior would have to be protected from encroachment by the settlers if the empire was to be able to defend itself against the French. The visions of these reformers inspired the reinvigoration of the Board of Trade in 1748, and provided the blueprint for the more ambitious attempts to restructure the empire in the 1760s and 1770s.

The book's final chapter relates the consequences of this reforming impulse in the crucial years following the Seven Years' War. Anxious to recoup the large sums spent to defeat the French, Parliament proposed a series of taxes to raise revenue in the colonies. But what began as a dispute over taxation soon escalated into a deeper conflict over where the ultimate locus of authority in the empire lay. Although many of the settlers remained cautious, not wanting to provoke Parliament and desirous of staying in the empire, the intransigent metropolitan insistence on the unitary sovereignty of the king-in-Parliament – exemplified in the Declaratory Act's claim to legislate for the colonies "in all cases whatsoever" – led others to think more deeply about the basis of their rights in the empire.

Reading closely both official statements of settler thought (e.g., in the Stamp Act Congress and the two Continental Congresses) as well as a representative sample of the extensive revolutionary pamphlet and newspaper literature, this final chapter examines the ways in which the settlers confronted this imperial challenge. In doing so, it charts the emergence of a radical theory of empire in the late 1760s and early 1770s in which the settlers' authority in America was grounded entirely on a natural law right to migrate, to acquire property, and to establish legitimate polities with full rights of sovereignty. As a consequence, any jurisdiction Parliament had over the colonies resulted from the settlers' consent; and even the tie to the monarch was revocable if the settlers did not receive protection for their rights in return for allegiance.

This radical theory of the empire contained a robust defense of federalism in which imperial authority was delegated to the center from the periphery and encompassed only those matters that were of common concern. It also drew on the earlier settler discourse about native rights in the empire to argue that the settlers could displace indigenous authority with their own.

The culmination of this long settler reflection on empire was revolution and republicanism. But in order to explain this momentous development we must go back to the seventeenth century and a world of constitutional upheaval within the realm and the quest for empire beyond it.

PART I

RESTORATION AND REBELLION

I

English Rights in an Atlantic World

In Philadelphia in 1687, William Penn printed a small pamphlet entitled *The Excellent Priviledge of Liberty and Property Being the Birth-Right of the Free-born Subjects of England.*[1] The *Excellent Priviledge* was an abridgement of a longer tract called *English Liberties: Or, the Free-Born Subject's Inheritance* published by the radical Whig Henry Care in 1682.[2] Care wanted to provide religious dissenters, then facing the full force of the Test and Corporation Acts, with an accessible guide to English law should they be hauled into court. But Care's primer outlived its dissenting roots to become a publishing phenomenon, with successive editions circulating around the Atlantic world in the eighteenth century, its small size – it could literally fit into a pocket – enabling knowledge of English rights to reach the peripheries of the empire.[3]

[1] (Philadelphia: Printed by William Bradford, 1687).
[2] On the publishing history of this neglected tract, see Winthrop S. Hudson, "William Penn's *English Liberties*: Tract for Several Times," *William and Mary Quarterly* 26 (1969), 578–585. As the title indicates, Hudson argues that Penn and not Care was the author. On Care, see Lois Schwoerer, *The Ingenious Mr. Care, Restoration Publicist* (Baltimore: Johns Hopkins University Press, 2001). Although Schwoerer agrees with Hudson about the important role *English Liberties* played in spreading the ideas of common law constitutionalism to British America, she disagrees with his claim that Penn was the author.
[3] In addition to the 1682 edition, it was also published in England in 1688, 1691, 1692, 1700, 1703, 1719, 1721, 1766. There was a Boston edition in 1719 and another published in Providence, Rhode Island, in 1774. In 1766, two London publishers who regularly exported to America put out a book entitled *British Liberties* that was based on Care's compilation and was intended to reach an American audience concerned about the rights of Englishmen in the wake of the Stamp Act Crisis. On the publishing history, see Schwoerer, *The Ingenious Mr. Care*, 232–235; and Hudson, "William Penn's *English Liberties*," 584–585.

Penn had a similar aim for his abridgment of *English Liberties*, hoping
it would aid the settlers in his new colony to understand the laws that
were "their native Right and Inheritance." Penn thought his version
would be particularly valuable for those "who may not have leisure from
their Plantations to read large Volumes." The centerpiece of Penn's com-
pendium was "*Magna Charta*," "the Store-house of all our Liberties,"
to which Penn appended a lengthy comment, drawn largely from the
writings of the great seventeenth-century jurist Edward Coke.[4] Penn also
reprinted the royal patent that he had received from Charles II, as well as
"The Charter of Liberties" which Penn had granted to "the Free-men and
Inhabitants" of his new colony. He hoped that, read together, these documents "may raise up Noble Resolutions in all the Free-Holders in these
new Colonies, not to give away any thing of Liberty and Property." After
all, he warned, "it is easier to part with or give away great Priviledges."
"Once lost," however, they were "hard to be gained."[5]

Penn prefaced these documents with a short essay laying out what he
saw as the essential features of the English constitution. According to
Penn, "the Fundamental Laws of England" guaranteed that "every Free-
Born Subject" was "Heir" by "Birthright" to the "unparalell'd Priviledge
of Liberty and Property." For Penn, these constitutional principles ensured
that all Englishmen were "to be freed in Person & Estate from Arbitrary
Violence and Oppression." Two institutions that were at the heart of the
early modern English polity safeguarded these rights: "Parliaments and
Juries." "By the first," Penn argued, "the subject has a share by his chosen
Representatives in the Legislative (or Law making) Power." It ensured that
"no new Laws bind the People of England, but such as are by common
consent agreed on in that great Council." The second right of Englishmen
was equally important. By serving on juries, Penn argued, every freeman
"has a share in the *Executive* part of the Law, no Causes being tried, nor
any man adjudged to loose [*sic*] Life, member or Estate, but upon the
Verdict of his Peers or Equals." According to Penn, "These two grand
Pillars of English Liberty" were "the *Fundamental vital Priviledges*" of
Englishmen.[6]

This system of law meant that English monarchy was fundamentally different from its Catholic competitors. Drawing on a distinction
first elaborated by the jurist Fortescue in the fifteenth century, Penn

---

[4] *Excellent Priviledge*, 19–34. Coke's commentary was taken from the "second part of his
    Institutes."
[5] From Penn's note "To the Reader."
[6] *Excellent Priviledge*, 3.

argued that royal power in England was limited because the Crown was unable to tax its subjects or change the laws of the realm without their consent.[7] As Penn put it, "*In England*" the "Law is both the measure and the bound of every Subject's Duty and Allegiance, each man having a fixed Fundamental-Right born with him, as to Freedom of his Person and Property in his Estate." Furthermore, an English subject "cannot be deprived of" these rights save "by his Consent, or some Crime, for which the Law has impos'd such a penalty or forfeiture." By contrast, "*In France, and other Nations, the meer Will of the Prince is Law, his Word takes off any mans Head, imposeth Taxes, or seizes a mans Estate, when, how and as often as he lists.*" And, Penn warned, if an unfortunate Frenchman were "*accused, or but so much as suspected of any Crime,*" the king "*may either presently Execute him, or banish, or Imprison him at pleasure.*"[8]

Unlike in France, then, the English king was bound to rule according to known laws and by respecting the inherent rights of his subjects. It was this obedience to the law and respect for liberty that created the bond of allegiance between the English king and his subjects. Furthermore, as Penn pointed out, "all our Kings take a solmn [*sic*] Oath ... At their Coronation, Too Serve & cause the Laws to be kept." Equally important, royally appointed justices took a similar oath, whereby "they swear to do equal Law and Right to all the King's Subjects, Rich and Poor, and not to delay any person of common Right for the Letters of the King, or of any other Person, or any other cause."[9] According to Penn, this English system of law – protecting as it did the "unparalell'd Priviledge of Liberty and Property" – had made the English "more free and happy than any other People in the World."[10]

The common law constitutionalism defended by Care and Penn was the product of a tumultuous century of political conflict, war, and revolution. Beginning in the early 1600s, jurists and parliamentarians like Edward Coke transformed English common law from a bundle of specific privileges granted by the monarch into a body of rights and liberties that subjects could claim against royal power.[11] And, in the crucial decades

---

[7] Sir John Fortescue, *On the Laws and Governance of England*, ed. Shelley Lockwood (Cambridge: Cambridge University Press, 1997).

[8] *Excellent Priviledge*, 1.

[9] Ibid., 11.

[10] Ibid., 3.

[11] J.H. Baker, "Personal Liberty under the Common Law of England," in R.W. Davis, ed., *The Origins of Modern Freedom in the West* (Stanford: Stanford University Press, 1995), 178–202. On Coke's role in Parliament, see Stephen D. White, *Sir Edward Coke and*

leading up to the civil war, they invoked these common law rights against
the prerogatives of successive Stuart monarchs, arguing that they were
part of an ancient constitution whose central tenets were not "meer
Emanations of Royal Favor."[12] Rather, they were a "birthright"; that is,
something that English subjects inherently possessed, the product of long
usage, of legal principles sanctified by time.[13] As a result, their legal force
did not derive from positive law. Instead, their statutory instantiation –
for example, in charters like *Magna Carta* – was merely "Declaratory" of
the "Fundamental Laws and Liberties of England."[14]

Most Englishmen in the early seventeenth century adhered to this idea
of the ancient constitution, with its balancing of the subject's rights and
the monarch's authority.[15] If, on this view of the English polity, the king
had legal prerogatives that allowed him to govern, he was also bound to
respect the liberties of his subjects. However, James I and in particular his
son Charles I held a much more robust view of royal authority in which
the rights of the subject were the gift of the monarch who held absolute sovereignty and was free to rule without Parliament if he so chose.[16]
These claims for absolute monarchy periodically threatened to shatter

the *"Grievances of the Commonwealth," 1621–1628* (Chapel Hill: University of North
    Carolina Press, 1979).
[12] *Excellent Priviledge*, 20.
[13] The classic study is J.G.A. Pocock, *The Ancient Constitution and the Feudal Law: A
    Study of English Historical Thought in the Seventeenth Century* (1957; revised edition,
    Cambridge: Cambridge University Press, 1987). See also, J.P. Sommerville, *Royalists and
    Patriots: Politics and Ideology in England, 1603–1640* (New York: Longman, 1999),
    81–104; and Alan Cromartie, *The Constitutionalist Revolution: An Essay on the History
    of England, 1450–1642* (Cambridge: Cambridge University Press, 2006).
[14] *Excellent Priviledge*, 20. On Magna Carta in America, see A.E. Dick Howard,
    The Road from Runnymede: Magna Carta and Constitutionalism in America
    (Charlottesville: University Press of Virginia, 1968).
[15] This has been the argument of the revisionist historians who want to deny the existence
    of both absolutism and radicalism in seventeenth-century English political culture. See
    Conrad Russell, *Unrevolutionary England* (London: Hambledon Press, 1990). For good
    accounts of the historiography of the revisionist turn, see Thomas Cogswell, "Coping
    with Revisionism in Early Stuart History," *Journal of Modern History* 62 (1990), 538–
    551; Glenn Burgess, "On Revisionism: An Analysis of Early Stuart Historiography in the
    1970s and 1980s," *Historical Journal* 33 (1990), 609–627; and J.P. Kenyon, "Revisionism
    and Post Revisionism in Early Stuart History," *Journal of Modern History* 64 (1992),
    686–699. I have been particularly influenced by Burgess's account of the origins and
    nature of revisionism.
[16] For a rebuttal to the revisionist view that there were no advocates of absolutism in
    early modern England, see Johann P. Sommerville, "English and European Political
    Ideas in the Seventeenth-Century: Revisionism and the Case of Absolutism," *Journal of
    British Studies* 35 (1996), 168–194. On Charles's personal rule, see Mark Kishlansky, *A
    Monarchy Transformed: Britain 1603–1714* (New York: Penguin, 1996), 113–133.

the precarious balance between the subject's liberties and the prerogatives of the monarch. In 1629, following a battle with Parliament over forced taxation, Charles I dismissed the body and ruled without it for eleven years. When he was forced to recall Parliament in 1640, the constitutional tensions that had plagued the first years of his reign returned with a vengeance and ultimately cost him his throne.[17]

The shattering effect of the English Civil War weakened the hegemony that the common law had previously exercised over the English legal imagination and led to an outpouring of political writing, all of it trying to come to terms with the fall of the monarchy, the subsequent collapse of the ancient constitution, the rise of Parliament, and the declaration of a republic.[18] The de facto seizure of power by the House of Commons in the 1640s forced the Crown to respond by arguing for mixed monarchy, with sovereignty being shared between the Parliament and the king. Other theorists contended for outright legislative or parliamentary sovereignty.[19] Also in the 1640s, more radical writers, such as the Levellers, made a case for political authority based on natural rights and popular sovereignty, ideas that would be revived in the 1670s and 1680s. And in the 1650s, following the execution of the king, a body of explicitly republican political theory emerged in the English world.[20]

---

[17] John Kenyon, *The Civil Wars of England* (London: Weidenfeld and Nicolson, 1988), 5–47.

[18] John Marshall, "Some Intellectual Consequences of the English Revolution," *European Legacy* 5 (2000), 515–530. To get a sense of the sheer range of political ideologies in England post-1640, see David Wootton, ed., *From Divine Right to Democracy: An Anthology of Political Writing in Stuart England* (New York: Penguin, 1986). On the breakdown of the old consensus, see Margaret Judson, *The Crisis of the Constitution: An Essay in Constitutional and Political Thought in England, 1603–1645* (New Brunswick: Rutgers University Press, 1949).

[19] See Michael Mendle, "Parliamentary Sovereignty: A Very English Absolutism," in Nicholas Phillipson and Quentin Skinner, eds., *Political Discourse in Early Modern Britain* (Cambridge: Cambridge University Press, 1993), 97–119. The best account of the ideas of mixed monarchy and coordinate sovereignty is Corinne C. Weston and Janelle R. Greenberg, *Subjects and Sovereigns: The Grand Controversy over Legal Sovereignty in Stuart England* (Cambridge: Cambridge University Press, 1981). On the radical implications of this idea of coordinate or shared sovereignty, see Corrine C. Weston, "Co-ordination – a Radicalising Principle in Stuart Politics," in Margaret Jacob and James Jacob, eds., *The Origins of Anglo-American Radicalism* (Boston: George Allen & Unwin, 1984), 85–104.

[20] For a survey of the political thought of this period, see J.G.A. Pocock and Gordon Schochet, "Interregnum and Restoration," in J.G.A. Pocock, Gordon J. Schochet, and Lois G. Schwoerer, eds., *The Varieties of British Political Thought* (Cambridge: Cambridge University Press, 1993), 146–179. On the influence of Leveller radicalism in the late seventeenth century, see Tim Harris, "The Leveller Legacy: From the Restoration to the Exclusion Crisis," in Michael Mendle, ed., *The Putney Debates of 1647: The Army,*

As these constitutional tensions mounted in the realm, the Stuart kings granted charters to some of their subjects to settle colonies in America. The creation of this new empire meant the devolution of royal authority to corporations and proprietors at a time when the king's prerogatives were being contested in England. As a result, the conflict between subjects and sovereigns that plagued the realm in the seventeenth century was replicated on the other side of the Atlantic. Moreover, these tensions were magnified by the presence of indigenous peoples inhabiting the lands the English coveted and living under their own forms of law and government. The subsequent debates over whether the rights that Penn and Care thought so valuable extended to English subjects on the far shores of the Atlantic world forms the heart of this book.[21]

The starting point for English thinking about the rights of subjects in the empire in the seventeenth and eighteenth centuries was Edward Coke's decision in *Calvin's Case*, which concerned the legal status of Scotsmen born after the union of the Crowns in 1603 (the *post-nati*). Were they, as the king and his legal advisors argued, naturalized subjects of the king with the full rights of Englishmen – in particular, the right to inherit land in England? Or was the English parliament correct when it held that they were aliens at English law? In order to answer this complex question, Coke constructed a legal theory of the relationship between Crown and subject, realm and dominion. The result was a ruling that influenced debates about the rights of English subjects in the empire down to the era of the American Revolution.[22]

Coke held that Robert Calvin (and thus all of the *post-nati*) were not legal aliens in England and therefore had the right to inherit land under English law. In deciding for Calvin, Coke did not base his decision on the common law as he felt it was ill-suited to deal with the complex legal problems posed by the relationship of England and Scotland. As he put

---

the Levellers and the English State (Cambridge: Cambridge University Press, 2001), 219–240.

[21] On the extension of English law to the colonies, see Joseph Smith, *Appeals to the Privy Council from the American Plantations* (New York: Columbia University Press, 1950), 464–522.

[22] For a good overview of the case, see Sir William Holdsworth, *A History of English Law*, Volume IX (London: Methuen, 1926), 74–86; and Polly J. Price, "Natural Law and Birthright Citizenship in *Calvin's Case*," Yale Journal of Law and Humanities 73 (1997), 73–145. Coke's great contemporary, Sir John Davies, articulated some of the same ideas as Coke and the later jurists in his defense of the English conquest of Ireland. On Davies, see Hans S. Pawlisch, *Sir John Davies and the Conquest of Ireland: A Study in Legal Imperialism* (Cambridge: Cambridge University Press, 1985).

it: "this little plea is a great stranger to the laws of England." In its place, Coke drew on the law of nations, arguing that the bond of allegiance between subject and sovereign transcended national or municipal legal systems like the common law.[23]

Coke reasoned as follows: "ligeance or obedience of the subject to the Sovereign" is "due by the law of nature." He then argued that "the law of nature is immutable, and cannot be changed." Indeed, he insisted, it was "before any judicial or municipal law in the world." However, the "law of nature" was also "part of the laws of England."[24] From this it followed that the common law of England was bound to recognize the bond of allegiance between Calvin and James I. As long as Calvin was born a subject of James after the union of Scotland and England, he could not be deemed an alien at English law simply because he resided outside the realm. For Coke, then, "it followeth that Calvin ... cannot be an alien born" as he was "naturalized by procreation and birth-right, since the descent of the Crown of England."[25] Conversely, the *ante-nati* were aliens at English law because when they were born James was only King of Scotland. As Coke put it: "the time of his birth is of the essence of a subject born; for he cannot be a subject to the King of England, unless at the time of his birth he was under the ligeance and obedience of the King." Coke's conception of allegiance also contained an important limitation on royal authority. Although all subjects owed fealty to their sovereigns by natural law, Coke held that rulers had a corresponding obligation to their subjects: "for as the subject oweth to the King his true and faithful ligeance and obedience, so the Sovereign is to govern and protect his subjects."[26]

The fact that Englishmen and Scotsmen were both subjects of the same king did not, however, mean that there would be a political union between

---

[23] *Calvin v. Smith* (1608) *English Reports*, Vol. 77, 398. Patrick Kelly claims that the legal categories Coke employed in *Calvin's Case* – conquest and inheritance – were part of "a common law theory of acquisition." See his "Conquest *versus* Consent as the Basis of the English Title to Ireland in William Molyneux's *Case of Ireland ... Stated* (1698)," in Ciaran Brady and Jane Ohlmeyer, eds., *British Interventions in Early Modern Ireland* (Cambridge: Cambridge University Press, 2005), 334–356. Gavin Loughton notes that, unlike the Roman tradition of just war, "one of the most salient features of 'conquest' at common law is the irrelevance of motivation or justification." Loughton, "Calvin's Case and the Origins of the Rule Governing 'Conquest' in English Law," *Australian Journal of Legal History* 8 (2004), 143–180 (quote at 145).

[24] *Calvin v. Smith* (1608) *English Reports*, Vol. 77, 382 (also see the discussion at 391–392).

[25] Ibid. at 394.

[26] Ibid. at 392.

Scotland and England. Rather, Coke held, "England and Scotland" continued to be "several and distinct kingdoms." They were both governed by separate "municipal laws" and "have several distinct and separate Parliaments."[27] Having explained the legal relationship between Scotland and England, Coke turned to the legal status of the inhabitants of those territories that had not been acquired by descent or inheritance (like Scotland) but had been acquired by conquest (like Ireland and many of the English Crown's other dominions).[28] In answering this question, Coke laid out an alternate account of the relationship between realm and dominion, one that was less favorable to the rights of English subjects outside the realm.

According to Coke, there were only two classes of persons recognized by English law: subjects (by birth or by descent) and aliens. Coke further held that there were several categories of aliens recognized by English law. There were those whom the law viewed as friendly aliens. They could own goods and trade freely under English law. There were also aliens who were enemies (such as the subjects of monarchs who were at war with the English Crown). According to Coke, the latter could not maintain a suit or hold any property at common law. However, Coke also argued that there was a third category of alien: those who were "Infidels" and thus irremediably hostile to the interests of the Crown. As he put it: "All Infidels are in Law *perpetui inimici*, perpetual enemies (for the Law presumes not that they will be converted, that being *remota potentia*, a remote possibility)." "Between them," Coke argued, "and the Christian, there is perpetual hostility, and can be no peace."[29]

Coke then related this distinction about the types of aliens to the legal status of the inhabitants of territories conquered by the Crown. For Coke, these territories fell into two categories: those inhabited by Christians and those inhabited by infidels. According to Coke, "if a King come to a Christian kingdom by conquest ... he may at his pleasure alter and change the Laws of that kingdom." However, "until he doth make an alteration of those Laws, the ancient Laws of that kingdom remain." But in the case of the conquest of the "kingdom of an Infidel" by a Christian king, Coke held that "the Laws of the Infidel are abrogated, for that they be not only against Christianity, but against the Law of God and Nature,

---

[27] Ibid. at 394.
[28] On the history of this doctrine, see Sutherland, "Conquest and Law," *Studia Gratiana* 15 (1972), 35–38.
[29] *Calvin v. Smith* (1608) *English Reports*, Vol. 77, 397.

contained in the Decalogue." Given that the indigenous laws were nullified by the conquest, Coke instructed the king to "judge them and their causes according to natural equity" until "certain Laws be established among them."[30]

For Coke, then, conquest was a powerful legal claim, for all conquerors could claim an unlimited legal power over their conquests. In the case of a conquest by the English Crown over a Christian people, the king could grant them English law but was not legally obliged to do so. Nevertheless, until he changed the legal system of the conquered territory, the old laws stayed in place. This was an important proviso for seventeenth-century Englishmen who wanted to make sure that the Norman Conquest could not be used as a legal precedent to undermine the ancient constitution or the common law. However, in a claim of some significance for the English settlement of North America, Coke also argued that conquered countries inhabited by "Infidels" immediately lost the right to their own laws following the conquest, and, as a result, should be governed according to the dictates of natural equity.

Coke then applied these distinctions to the legal status of the several dominions of the Crown.[31] He held that Scotland was "a kingdom by title of descent," which meant that the king "cannot change" their laws "himself, without consent of Parliament." By contrast, Ireland was a Christian kingdom that English kings had acquired by conquest. As such, it was subject to the strictures Coke laid out above – its existing laws had remained in force until the conqueror decided to alter them. However, once the English king had extended English laws to Ireland, then "no succeeding King could alter the same without Parliament."[32] For Coke, then, the extension of English law meant that the king's authority to act in conquered dominions was now circumscribed; however, it also rendered these territories subject to the authority of the English parliament. As Coke put it: "the title thereof being by conquest," Ireland "might by express words be bound by Act of the Parliament of England." As well, he held that the rulings of Irish courts were subject to review by English judges.[33] Despite its subordinate status, however, Ireland remained "a distinct dominion."

[30] Ibid. at 398.
[31] On the dominions that comprised the medieval empire, see A.F. Madden, "1066, 1776 and All That: The Relevance of English Medieval Experience of Empire to Later Imperial Constitutional Issues," in John E. Flint and Glyndwr Williams, eds., *Perspectives of Empire: Essays Presented to Gerald S. Graham* (London: Longman, 1973), 9–26.
[32] *Calvin v. Smith* (1608) *English Reports*, Vol. 77, 398.
[33] Ibid.

In particular, Coke held, because "the laws of England" were now "the proper laws of Ireland," the Irish were able to "have Parliaments holden there" where they "made divers particular laws concerning that dominion." In addition to this local lawmaking authority, the Irish were also allowed to "retain unto this day divers of their ancient customs." As a result, they are "governed by laws and customs, separate and diverse from the laws of England."[34]

So according to Coke, the conquered Irish, despite being able to retain some of their own laws, were subject to the overarching authority of the English parliament. But what about those who had conquered in the name of the English king and then settled in Ireland? Was their status different from that of the indigenous inhabitants? According to Coke: "in the case of a conquest of a Christian kingdom, as well those that served in wars at the conquest as those that remained at home for the safety and peace of their country ... are capable of lands in the kingdom or country conquered." Furthermore, they could "maintain any real action, and have the like privileges and benefits there, as they may have in England."[35]

Coke's sketch of the legal status of the king's dominions can be summed up as follows. His conception of allegiance, based on natural law, allowed inhabitants of inherited dominions to claim that they were subjects of the king and entitled to royal protection in return for their allegiance. This part of Coke's decision could be cited in support of an empire of equal rights in which no one born under allegiance to the English king was an alien and all could inherit land in England. Indeed, Coke compared his account of Calvin's legal status to that of St. Paul, who, though a Jew from Tarsus, "was born under the obedience of the Roman emperor," and was therefore "by birth a citizen of Rome in Italy," and "capable of and inheritable to all privileges and immunities of that city."[36] According to Coke, subjects in these inherited dominions also had the right to separate laws, courts, and parliaments, rendering them immune from the jurisdiction of the English parliament.[37] By contrast, in conquered Christian territories, the Crown could either leave the existing laws in place, or it could extend English laws to the inhabitants (as had been done throughout the British Isles). If it chose the

---

[34] Ibid. at 404.
[35] Ibid. at 398.
[36] Ibid. at 406.
[37] The settlers in Barbados used this argument against Cromwell in the 1650s. See Liam S. O'Melinn, "The American Revolution and Constitutionalism in the Seventeenth-Century West Indies," *Columbia Law Review* 95 (1995), 104–159.

latter, its legal authority was circumscribed by the English parliament, which could then legislate for the conquered inhabitants.[38] Even after extension, however, these conquered dominions remained legally separate from the realm of England, with their own institutions, though they would be subordinate to the overarching authority of the English parliament. Coke also held that those who made the conquest in the name of the Crown (or who later migrated to the conquered dominion) had the same rights as the original inhabitants; but they were also subject to the same oversight from king and Parliament.

In the case of the conquest and acquisition of a non-Christian territory, however, the existing laws were abrogated, and the king was to govern the indigenous inhabitants by natural equity. Although this was the category that most closely approximated the new English empire in America, Coke had relatively little to say about the legal status of this kind of territory. Unlike in his discussion of conquered Christian countries, he did not specify whether those Englishmen who had made the conquest in the name of the king would be allowed to take English laws with them; or if they, like the conquered inhabitants, would be governed by the will of the king alone. Nor did he indicate whether, if the king granted them English law, they would be subject to the authority of the English parliament, or what the relationship should be between their laws and those of the indigenous inhabitants (assuming the latter would retain any).[39]

Given the extent to which English Whigs like Penn and Care venerated Coke's vision of the English constitution, these lacunae in the great jurist's account of the rights of Englishmen outside the realm is somewhat paradoxical. For all his efforts to limit royal authority within the realm, Coke was ultimately less concerned about the rights of Englishmen beyond it. While those who resided in inherited dominions would have equal status with subjects within the realm, those in conquered dominions would be at the mercy of the prerogative (for it was up to the conqueror to extend rights), or, if they did receive English

[38] For a contrary reading of Coke, see Barbara Black, "The Constitution of Empire: The Case for the Colonists," *University of Pennsylvania Law Review* 124 (1976), 1157–1211. Despite an ingenious effort to make the case that Coke was an advocate of consensual rule in the empire, Black concedes that "the implications of Calvin's Case were multiple and inconsistent" (1198).

[39] On the relationship between English and indigenous law, see Mark D. Walters, "*Mohegan Indians v. Connecticut* (1705–1773) and the Legal Status of Aboriginal Customary Laws and Government in British North America," *Osgoode Hall Law Journal* 33 (1995), 789–793.

law, would find themselves living in subordinate polities subject without their consent to the English parliament.[40]

Coke's near contemporary Mathew Hale also dealt with the legal relationship between realm and dominion. Hale was one of the most important jurists in the seventeenth century, responsible in part for reestablishing the authority of the common law and the ancient constitution following the Interregnum.[41] As with Coke, Ireland was central to Hale's imperial jurisprudence. According to Hale, Ireland had been acquired "by conquest" for the Crown of England, after which English laws were introduced. For Hale, this extension meant that the "native Irish descended from the first conquered inhabitants" were "no longer under the unlimited power of a conqueror, but under the legal and regular government of a king." According to Hale, the influx of English settlers further reduced the power of the conquering monarch, for "these English planters ... were free English men and carried with them their rights and liberties of Englishmen," even though they entered "a country acquired ... by the conquering king."[42] The extension of English laws also ensured that Ireland had its own "courts, parliaments," and "peers." However, just because subjects in Ireland enjoyed English rights did not, according to Hale, change the fact that it was still a "subordinate and dependent" dominion,[43] where "Judgments in the king's bench of Ireland are reversible for error in the king's bench" in England,[44] and where "the subordination of the Parliament of Ireland" to "the parliament of England is considerable." Hale did add that acts of the "English Parliament doth not regularly extend to Ireland, unless specifically named," because they have "a parliament of their own."[45] That is, Ireland and the other conquered dominions were not automatically bound by all statutes of the English parliament. But he also maintained that if it applied legislation to them specifically then they were (even without representation) bound by its authority.

---

[40] On this paradox, see the important article by Daniel J. Hulsebosch, "Edward Coke and the Expanding Empire: Sir Edward Coke's British Jurisprudence," *Law and History Review* 21 (2003), 439–482.

[41] On Hale, see Alan Cromartie, *Sir Mathew Hale, 1609–1676: Law, Religion, and Natural Philosophy* (Cambridge: Cambridge University Press, 1995).

[42] Mathew Hale, *The Prerogatives of the King*, ed., D.E.C. Yale (London: Selden Society, 1976), 34–35. Hale added that "all those acts of Parliament preceding" Poyning's law were "as much the birthright of the native Irish as they are of the subjects of England, if they do not forfeit them."

[43] Hale, *Prerogatives of the King*, 35.

[44] Ibid., 37.

[45] Ibid., 38

What, according to Hale, was the basis for the subordination of Ireland to England "even after English laws had been extended and they had their own local Parliament"? After all, he noted, "the jurisdiction both here and there is derived from the same fountain, *viz.* the king." As well, "the courts in both places are royal courts," and "the acts of parliament here and there are effectual by the king's royal assent." Hale's answer was that when Ireland had been acquired by the English king, his courts "immediately" had "jurisdiction" there, and his "parliament" "a legislative authority." As a result, even after the Irish were allowed to have their own courts and parliament, this original jurisdiction remained, giving the English king a "super-intendency" over Ireland. Hale added that this subordination was "consonant to natural justice," for all "new acquired territory should be subject to the jurisdiction of that country whereunto it is now annexed."[46]

Unlike Coke, Hale was writing in the mid-seventeenth century, and so he did address, albeit briefly, the legal status of the American colonies. According to Hale, they were "acquired in right of the crown of England" by settlers who planted the king's "standard" as a "token of his possession." As a result, they were "parcel of the dominions though not of the realm of England,"[47] and therefore "English laws" were "not settled there, or at least are only temporary till a settlement made." Instead, the king, who was "lord and proprietor of them," could decide at his "pleasure" what the laws would be until he "shall dispose of them by patent." As a result, Hale argued, "we see that there is in all these plantations administration of justice and laws much differing from the English laws." Nevertheless, Hale insisted that "the English planters carry along with them those English liberties that are incident to their persons." For Hale, then, the legal settlement of the king's American plantations was similar to the way Ireland had been acquired, where "English laws were gradually introduced by the king without the concurrence of an act of Parliament."[48] But for both Coke and Hale, the rights of the settlers in both Ireland and America were ultimately dependent on royal grant; and,

[46] Ibid., 39–40. Hale also discussed the other dominions of the King in the British Isles. Berwick, which was conquered, became "parcel of the dominion and crown of England," but was not part of the realm ("*infra regnum Angliae*"). As a result, it had its own "customs and usages," but "by charter granted they send burgesses to parliament." The Isle of Man and the Channel Islands, "though originally parcel of the duke of Normandy," were now "annexed unto the crown of England, and though not *infra regnum*, yet they are *infra dominium regni sui Angliae*" (pp. 40–42).

[47] Hale, *Prerogatives of the King*, 43.

[48] Ibid., 43–44.

even after they had received the blessings of English law and rights, they might be made subject to the English parliament without their consent.

In the late seventeenth century, a new doctrine regarding the extension of English law to the king's dominions emerged alongside the Cokean categories of inheritance and conquest. In 1670, Chief Justice Vaughan made a distinction between countries acquired by conquest and those settled as plantations, arguing that in the latter type the colonists were entitled to all of the rights of Englishmen.[49] In *Dutton v. Howell* (1693), counsel for one of the parties utilized Vaughan's new category, contending that when "certain subjects of England, by consent of their Prince, go and possess an uninhabited desert Country; the Common Law must be supposed their Rule, as 'twas their Birthright." After all, he reasoned, "When they went thither, they no more abandoned English laws, than they did their Natural Allegiance."[50] This settlement doctrine was also employed in a 1693 case by Chief Justice Holt who held that "in case of uninhabited country newly found out by English subjects, all laws in force in England are in force there."[51] Unlike the older doctrines of inheritance or conquest, then, this new theory applied to the acquisition of land that was unoccupied, or, which amounted to the same thing, was inhabited by peoples who lacked what the English considered to be settled law, governments, and property rights.[52] And in contrast to conquest, the new settlement doctrine held that the extension of English law was automatic; that is, it did not depend on the explicit grant of the Crown. Richard West, who was legal counsel to the Privy Council, laid out the substance of this settlement doctrine in 1720. According to West:

The Common Law of England is the Common Law of the Plantations, and all statutes in affirmance of the Common Law passed in England, antecedent to the settlement of a colony, are in force in that, unless there is some private Act to the contrary; though no statutes made since those settlements, are there in force, unless

---

49 *Craw v. Ramsey* (1670) *English Reports*, Vol. 124, 905–909. See Smith, *Appeals to the Privy Council from the American Plantations*, 469–470.
50 *Dutton v. Howell* (1693) *English Reports*, Vol. 1, 22.
51 *Blankard v. Galdy* (1693) *English Reports*, Vol. 90, 1089. The case involved Jamaica, which Holt deemed to be conquered, and thus English laws "did not take place there, 'till declared so by the conqueror or his successor." Before extension, Holt said, the old laws remained in place and the people there were "not bound by our laws, unless particularly mentioned."
52 On this, see Holdsworth, *A History of English Law*, Volume XI (London: Methuen, 1938), 241. Most scholars ignore the problematic consequences of the settlement doctrine for indigenous rights. But see Hulsebosch, "The Ancient Constitution and the Expanding Empire," 471–472.

the colonies are particularly mentioned. Let an Englishman go where he will, he carries as much of law and liberty with him, as the nature of things will bear.[53]

In 1722, the Privy Council asked its legal counsel for a ruling on the extension of English law to Barbados. The resulting "Memorandum" held that

If there be a new and uninhabited country found out by English subjects as the law is the birthright of every subject, so, wherever they go, they carry their laws with them and therefore such new found country is to be governed by the laws of England.

Like West, this author argued that "after such a Country is inhabited by the English, Acts of Parliament made in England, without naming the foreign plantations, will not bind them."[54]

This settlement doctrine was also central to a 1724 decision regarding Jamaica; and it was also employed in a 1729 case involving Maryland.[55] However, despite the support that this new doctrine gave to the settlers' claim to English law and rights, it was ultimately unable to resolve the problem of what rights Englishmen enjoyed outside the realm. For even though it held that the extension of English law no longer depended on the discretion of the monarch, it allowed Parliament to legislate for settled dominions if it chose to. In this sense, the reduction of the power of the prerogative was offset by the fact that Parliament was able to legislate for settled dominions without the consent of the inhabitants. Moreover, under the settlement doctrine it was not clear just how much of English law extended to new territories. Advising the Privy Council, Richard West had said that only "as much of law and liberty" as "the nature of things will bear" should apply in the dominions. There was a further gray area about which statutes applied in the dominions. Were they to receive all English

---

[53] Cited in George Chalmers, *Opinions of Eminent Lawyers on Various Points of English Jurisprudence* (Burlington: C. Goodrich, 1858), 207.

[54] "Privy Council Memorandum on English Law in Settled and Conquered Countries," in Frederick Madden and David Fieldhouse, eds., *Select Documents on the Constitutional History of the British Empire and Commonwealth: Volume II, The Classic Period of the First British Empire, 1689–1783: The Foundations of a Colonial System of Government* (Westport, CT: Greenwood Press, 1985), 192–193.

[55] For both decisions, see the excerpts in Madden and Fieldhouse, eds., *The Classical Period of the First British Empire*, 193–194. For a full text of the 1724 decision rendered by Sir Philip Yorke and Sir Clement Wearg, respectively Attorney General and Solicitor General, see George Chalmers, *Opinions of Eminent Lawyers*, 215–232. Holdsworth, *A History of English Law*, Volume XI, 243, fn., 4, says that long usage could also be grounds for inhabitants of a dominion to get the benefit of parliamentary statutes.

statutes? Or just those passed prior to the settlement of the colony? And what about those statutes that confirmed important common law rights (such as the Habeas Corpus Act of 1679), or the various guarantees of English liberties passed by Parliament following the Glorious Revolution (such as the Bill of Rights and the Act of Settlement)?[56]

Despite the advent of this new settlement doctrine, claims that the king's dominions were conquered continued to be made by English jurists. In a 1688 case involving Barbados, the defendant's lawyers (seeking to support the authority of the governor) argued that "the King is not restrained by the laws of England to govern that island ... by the common law," for "those islands were gotten by conquest or by some of his subjects going in search of some prize, and planting themselves there."[57] And in 1702, Chief Justice Holt held that "the laws of England do not extend to Virginia, being a conquered country their law is what the King pleases."[58] Although the conquest doctrine remained alive well into the eighteenth century, English jurists modified its stance on the rights of non-Christians. Where Coke had claimed that their laws were abrogated following the conquest of their territories, later jurists held that only those that were "against the law of God" would be abrogated.[59] This had the effect of making their legal status the same as that of conquered Christians. It did not, however, clarify the question of the rights of the settlers who had undertaken the conquest and who desired to enjoy the benefits of English law in the newly acquired territory. As one late seventeenth-century lawyer complained, it was "unreasonable that Englishmen should lose their laws by the conquest of a nation." After all, these "laws are their birthright," something "they carry with them wherever they go." And, he cautioned, the consequence of not extending English laws was that "by the conquest of an infidel country," the English "must be subject to those of the Al-coran."[60]

Writing on the eve of revolution, William Blackstone, the most influential common law jurist of the latter half of the eighteenth century, offered

---

[56] For a range of different sources on this question, see Madden and Fieldhouse, eds., *The Classical Period of the First British Empire*, 190–270.

[57] *Wytham v. Dutton* (1688) *English Reports*, Vol. 87, 104.

[58] *Smith v. Brown and Cooper* (K.B. 1705 [1702]) *English Reports*, Vol. 91, 567.

[59] Chief Justice Holt in *Blankard v. Galdy* (1693). Cited in Madden and Fieldhouse, eds., *The Classical Period of the First British Empire*, 205. On the judicial recognition of indigenous laws and institutions in the late seventeenth-century, see Walters, "*Mohegan Indians v. Connecticut*," 790–792.

[60] The case was *Blankard v. Galdy* (1693). Quoted in Madden and Fieldhouse, eds., *The Classical Period of the First British Empire*, 204.

the fullest account of the constitutional status of the king's dominions. In his *Commentaries on the Laws of England*, first published in 1765 as tensions in the empire were building, Blackstone followed Coke's lead and discussed the American colonies alongside the king's other dominions closer to home.[61] In a section of the *Commentaries* entitled "Of the Countries Subject to the Laws of England," Blackstone argued that "The kingdom of England, over which our municipal laws have jurisdiction, includes not, by the common law, either Wales, Scotland, or Ireland, or any other part of the king's dominions, except the territory of England only."[62]

Blackstone began by discussing Wales, which had once been "independent of England, unconquered and uncultivated." However, in the reign of "Edward the first" it had been "entirely annexed to the dominion of the crown of England," although the Welsh continued to live to some extent by their own laws. However, by "subsequent statutes their provincial immunities were still farther abridged," but the "finishing stroke to their independency" came in the reign of Henry VIII when "the dominion of Wales" was united to the "kingdom of England." As a result, "all Welchmen [*sic*] born shall have the same liberties as other the king's subjects." By this incorporation, Blackstone argued, "this brave people" were "gradually conquered into the enjoyment of true liberty" and "made fellow-citizens with their conquerors."[63]

By contrast, Scotland, not withstanding "the union of the Crowns" following the accession of James I, remained "an entirely separate and distinct kingdom for above a century." However, following the parliamentary union of 1707, both were "united into one kingdom, by the name of Great Britain." Despite this political union, many of the laws of Scotland remained in force, though, apart from those relating to "private rights," they were "alterable by the parliament of Great Britain."[64]

Blackstone also dealt with the legal status of several smaller dependencies of the English Crown. He argued that Berwick upon Tweed was

---

[61] William Blackstone, *Commentaries on the Laws of England*, Volume I. Stanley N. Katz, ed. (1765; Chicago: University of Chicago Press, 1979), 93. On Blackstone's jurisprudence, see David Lieberman, *The Province of Legislation Determined: Legal Theory in Eighteenth-Century Britain* (Cambridge: Cambridge University Press, 1989).
[62] Blackstone, *Commentaries on the Laws of England*, I, 93.
[63] Ibid., 93–94. He added that this incorporation "gave the utmost advancement to their civil prosperity, by admitting them to a thorough communication of laws with the subjects of England." According to Blackstone, this was "a generous method of triumph, which the republic of Rome practiced with great success."
[64] Ibid., 95–96.

"subject to the crown of England ever since the conquest of it," but it was "not part of the kingdom of England, nor subject to the common law; though it is subject to all acts of parliament, being represented by burgesses therein."[65] As for the Isle of Man, it was also claimed by "right of conquest." As such, Blackstone held that it is a "distinct territory and is not governed by our laws," although it could be subject to acts of the British parliament if specifically named in them. In addition, "Jersey, Guernsey, Sark, Alderney" were all governed by their own laws derived principally from the ducal customs of Normandy. Although they were united to the Crown by the first princes of the Norman line, Blackstone contended that they were not bound by the English parliament unless named in one of its Acts.[66]

Blackstone discussed the legal status of Ireland at length, arguing that it was a "distinct ... though a dependent, subordinate kingdom." For Blackstone, Ireland's dependence on Great Britain rested on conquest. As he put it: "King John in the twelfth year of his reign went into Ireland ... and there by his letters patent, in right of the dominion of conquest, is said to have ordained and established that Ireland should be governed by the laws of England."[67] As a result, in the reign of Henry II, the settlers "carried over the English laws along with them." But, even after the extension of English laws, Ireland "continues in a state of dependence," and "must necessarily conform to, and be obliged by such laws as the superior state thinks it proper to prescribe."[68]

For Blackstone, then, Ireland was in this dependent state despite the fact that the common law had been extended to it after the conquest, and despite the fact that it remained "a distinct dominion" with "parliaments of its own." Blackstone underscored the extent of Ireland's dependence on both Crown and Parliament by noting that the ultimate court of appeal for Ireland was the court of King's Bench in England. He thought that such judicial oversight was necessary or else the laws of an "inferior dominion" could be changed without the assent of "the superior."[69]

---

[65] Ibid., 98. Indeed, Blackstone noted, "the general law there used is the Scots law."

[66] Ibid., 102–104.

[67] Ibid., 99.

[68] Ibid., 98–99. According to Blackstone, "The original and true ground of this superiority is the right of conquest: a right allowed by the law of nations, if not that of nature; and founded upon a compact either expressly or tacitly made between the conqueror and the conquered, that if they will acknowledge the victor for their master, he will treat them for the future as subjects and not as enemies." Ibid., 101.

[69] Ibid., 102. On Parliamentary authority in Ireland, see Martin Flaherty, "The Empire Strikes Back: *Annesley v. Sherlock* and the Triumph of Imperial Parliamentary Supremacy," *Columbia Law Review* 87 (1987), 593–622.

Not surprisingly, given the fraught moment at which he was writing, Blackstone provided a more extensive discussion of the legal status of the American colonies than the other jurists we have discussed. According to Blackstone, there were two types of "Plantations, or colonies in distant countries." First, were those "where the lands are claimed by right of occupancy only, by finding them desert and uncultivated, and peopling them from the mother country." The second type consisted of lands which were "already cultivated," and had "either been gained by conquest, or ceded to us by treaties."[70] Although "both these rights are founded upon the law of nature or at least that of nations," Blackstone held that "there is a difference between these two species of colonies, with respect to the laws by which they are bound." As he put it: "if an uninhabited country be discovered and planted by English subjects, all the English laws are immediately there in force. For the law is the birthright of every subject, so wherever they go they carry their laws with them." However, "in conquered or ceded countries, that have already laws of their own, the King may indeed alter and change those laws; but, till he does actually change them, the antient laws of the country remain, unless such as are against the law of God, as in the case of an infidel country."[71]

In Blackstone's view, the American colonies were "principally of this latter sort, being obtained in the last century by right of conquest and driving out the natives (with what natural justice I shall not at present enquire) or by treaties." As a result, "the common law of England, as such, has no allowance or authority there; they being no part of the mother country, but distinct (though dependent) dominions." However, they were "subject" "to the control of the parliament; though (like Ireland, Man, and the rest) not bound by any acts of parliament, unless particularly named."[72] Although they were subordinate dominions, the American colonies, like Ireland, had their own institutions. They had governors named by the king. They also had "courts of justice of their own, from whose decisions an appeal lies to the king in council here in England." And they had their own assemblies, which, according to Blackstone, "are their house of commons." However, Blackstone insisted, these local institutions were subject to parliamentary legislation. For Blackstone, then, Parliament, or the king-in-Parliament as opposed to the king-in-Council, was the ultimate authority in the empire.

[70] Ibid., 104–105.

[71] Ibid. Blackstone cites *Calvin's Case*, although, following Holt's opinion in *Blankard v. Galdy*, he holds that only those laws contrary to God's are abrogated; the rest remain in force.

[72] Ibid., 105.

Although this imperial jurisprudence provided a framework for the constitutional relationship between the settlers and metropolitan authority, it
ultimately posed more questions than it answered about the rights of subjects in England's expanding empire. For if the settlers could invoke Coke's
idea of allegiance to claim English law anywhere in the king's dominions,
including the right to have their own courts and assemblies, Crown officials could claim that the American colonies, like Ireland, had been conquered, and that as a result the grant of English rights was subject to the
royal prerogative. Furthermore, even if the king granted English law and
rights to the settlers (as he was to do in the colonial charters), thus limiting
his legal powers as conqueror, Parliament could still bind the colonies if it
chose to name them in its acts. Moreover, the settlement doctrine, while it
gave the colonists an automatic claim to English law, also brought with it
the heavy hand of parliamentary authority. The gradual reduction of royal
authority over the dominions brought about by these largely Whig jurists
was thus counterbalanced by their insistence that the English (and later
British) parliament could override settler rights.[73] Blackstone exemplified
this transformation with his concern that the "dependence" of the dominions be to "the crown of England" and not "of the person of the king."[74]

   This imperial jurisprudence also had no clear category for the Native
Americans. They could, following Coke, be seen as conquered infidels
whose laws were abrogated upon contact. However, this meant that the
territories they inhabited would be classified as conquered and the rights
of the settlers who migrated there rendered uncertain. Jurists who came
after Coke held that the laws of Native Americans (like those of conquered Christians) survived the conquest.[75] But this judicial recognition
of indigenous rights failed to grapple with the problem of how their law
would coexist with that of the settlers, which in turn set up a conflict
between imperial officials who wanted to treat native peoples as a separate part of the empire's composite polity, and the settlers who thought
that this policy undermined their ability to control American territory.[76]
Further complicating matters, the settlement doctrine, with its assumption

[73] On the shift from royal to parliamentary authority over the dominions, see Black, "The
    Constitution of the Empire," 1205.
[74] Ibid., 102.
[75] Later formulated as the common law principle of "continuity," which influenced the pro-
    tection of the rights of the conquered in the Royal Proclamation of 1763 and the Quebec
    Act in 1774.
[76] According to Daniel Hulsebosch, "Coke believed there should be a distinction between
    the conquered aborigines and English settlers who migrated to that conquered colony."
    However, as Hulsebosch notes, "Coke never applied this dichotomy to Virginia even

that the colonies were legally vacant, provided some protection for the rights of Englishmen outside the realm, but it did so by denying the very existence of indigenous jurisdiction, making the claims of the settlers and the natives mutually exclusive.

The fact that eminent common lawyers offered such equivocal guidance about the legal status of the colonies fueled constitutional tensions in the empire, for if royal officials (and later parliamentary ministers) could draw on this jurisprudence to make an argument for colonial subordination, the settlers could also utilize aspects of it (in particular, Coke's arguments about the reciprocal nature of allegiance) to claim the rights of Englishmen outside the realm. The result was that from the earliest settlements in Virginia to the eve of the revolution there was never any agreement about the constitutional principles that governed the empire. Responding to this ambiguity, the settlers developed a set of arguments about their rights that drew from their common law inheritance, reshaping it to fit their New World circumstances by arguing that they had made a contract with the king in which he guaranteed their rights in return for the risks they had undertaken to expand his dominions. They also appropriated the doctrine of conquest, turning the tables on royal officials by arguing that it was they who had conquered in the name of the king and thus were entitled to equal rights in the empire. In addition to their creative use of English legal doctrines, the settlers also drew from natural law theory, which, as we discussed in the introduction, was transformed in the early modern period in order to defend European rights in the extra-European world. The legal problems the settlers faced – the need to construct authority outside the realm in the face of the claims of prerogative as well as the existence of the indigenous peoples of the New World – made this body of ideas particularly attractive. As well, the advent of the settlement doctrine encouraged the settlers to see the New World as an uninhabited place, which fit with the natural law idea of the New World as a state of nature where property was open for the taking by industrious colonists.[77] The settler adoption of natural rights in order

though he surely would have seen it as a conquered and not an inherited territory." Hulsebosch, "The Ancient Constitution and the Expanding Empire," 470.

[77] Daniel Hulsebosch argues that the doctrine of settlement "drew on the civilian principle of *res* nullius," and also speculates that it "may have derived from John Locke's contemporary writings on the labor theory of property." This is a fruitful suggestion that, given the recent interest in Locke's role as theorist of empire, deserves further investigation. See Hulsebosch, "The Ancient Constitution and the Expanding Empire," 471.

to make sense of their place in a broader Atlantic world had far-reaching consequences for early American political theory.

For most of the seventeenth century, English officials – both royal and republican – paid little attention to the king's American possessions. This neglect allowed for a decentralized and de facto self-governing English empire to arise in America. But this period of lax oversight ended with the Restoration, when, for the first time, the Crown began to tighten the reins of empire, challenging the settlers' claim to enjoy the rights of Englishmen in the New World. The result was a series of rebellions in the late 1680s that would shape the empire down to the Revolution.[78]

On Locke and empire, see James Tully, "Rediscovering America: The *Two Treatises and Aboriginal Rights*," in his *An Approach to Political Philosophy: Locke in Contexts* (Cambridge: Cambridge University Press, 1993), 137–176.

[78] For a recent challenge to this argument about the centrality of the Restoration, see Carla Pestana, *The English Atlantic in an Age of Revolution* (Cambridge: Harvard University Press, 2004).

2

The Glorious Revolution in America

The first British Empire was acquired in a decidedly ad hoc fashion. Beginning in the early sixteenth century, the Crown added to the remnants of its medieval territories several previously independent kingdoms. It acquired Wales and Ireland by conquest, incorporating the former into the realm in 1536, while leaving the latter in a rather ambiguous status somewhere between dependent colony and independent kingdom until the late eighteenth century.[1] The accession of James VI of Scotland to the English throne (as James I) brought Scotland into this loose association of political entities in 1603, although a full political union would not be completed until 1707.

From the early 1600s, the Crown allowed various private interests to establish English colonies on the eastern seaboard of North America, sanctioning these ventures with either a corporate or a proprietorial charter.[2] In the former, a group of individuals who formed a company (as in Massachusetts) received a royal charter (or letters patent). In the latter, the Crown granted the right to settle to a courtier or royal favorite (such as Lord Baltimore in Maryland or William Penn in Pennsylvania). And, beginning with Virginia in the 1620s, the Crown created royal colonies

---

[1] On Ireland's uncertain constitutional status, see Neil L. York, *Neither Kingdom nor Nation: The Irish Quest for Constitutional Rights, 1698–1800* (Washington, DC: Catholic University Press of America, 1994).

[2] On the private and decentralized nature of the English empire, see Jack P. Greene, "Metropolis and Colonies: Changing Patterns of Constitutional Conflict in the Early Modern British Empire, 1607–1763," in Greene, ed., *Negotiated Authorities: Essays in Colonial Political and Constitutional History* (Charlottesville: University Press of Virginia, 1994), 43–77.

ruled directly by a governor it appointed. Although rare in the seventeenth century – they often resulted from the Crown's revocation of a corporate or proprietary charter – royal colonies became increasingly common in the eighteenth-century empire.[3]

The Crown authorized these private entities to conquer and settle; in return, the patentees were responsible for underwriting the expense of these enterprises. In doing so, the Crown retained *imperium* or sovereignty, but it delegated many of the prerogatives that comprised its authority – the power to tax, to pass laws, to create courts, to assemble militias – to these chartered entities, creating what were de facto self-governing polities.[4] For their part, the patentees held their land by a royal tenure[5] and had to ensure that the laws they passed were not repugnant to those of England.[6] The patentees were also subject to the legal oversight of the Privy Council, which could revoke the royal charter if the patentees abused its terms.

[3] On the constitutional structure of the empire, see Charles M. Andrews, "The Government of the Empire, 1660–1763," in J. Holland Rose, A.P. Newton, and E.A. Benians, eds., *The Old Empire*, Volume One of *The Cambridge History of the British Empire* (Cambridge: Cambridge University Press, 1929), 405–435; and A.B. Keith, *The Constitutional History of the First British Empire* (Oxford: Oxford University Press, 1930). For a range of colonial charters, see Jack P. Greene, ed., *Great Britain and the American Colonies, 1606–1763* (New York: Harper and Row, 1970), 11–26.

[4] On the authority of the royal prerogative in the empire, see Ken MacMillan, *Sovereignty and Possession in the English New World: The Legal Foundations of Empire, 1576–1640* (New York: Cambridge University Press, 2006), 79–120. For the gradual emergence of the common law in Virginia, a development that favored the power of colonial elites as against the private jurisdiction of the company, see David Konig, "Colonization and the Common Law in Ireland and Virginia, 1569–1643," in James A. Henretta, Michael Kammen, and Stanley N. Katz, eds., *The Transformation of Early American History: Society, Authority, Ideology* (New York: Alfred A. Knopf, 1991), 70–92.

[5] The trading companies were usually granted land "by free and common socage" as of "our manor of East Greenwich." This form of tenure required no feudal service; and it was also often granted in fee simple, which was more easily sold or alienated. Proprietorial colonies, by contrast, often received land *in capite* (and thus not of a manor), which allowed the holders to grant land to subordinates and live as manor lords collecting rent from their tenants. Edward P. Cheyney, "The Manor of East Greenwich in the County of Kent," *American Historical Review* 11 (1905), 29–35. On the much-neglected subject of landholding in the American colonies, see Beverly Bond, *The Quit Rent System in the American Colonies* (New Haven: Yale University Press, 1919).

[6] In the words of the third Virginia charter (1612), the company had "full Power and Authority, to ordain and make such Laws and Ordinances, for the Good and Welfare of the said Plantation" provided they "be not contrary to the Laws and Statutes of this our Realm of England." Francis Thorpe, ed., *The Federal and State Constitutions, Colonial Charters and Other Organic Laws* (Washington, DC: U.S. Government Printing Office, 1909), VI, 3802–3810.

To induce English people to expand the king's dominion, these charters also contained clauses that accorded the patentees the same legal rights and privileges as subjects in England. And in 1619, after a period of disastrous quasi-military rule, the Virginia Company of London granted the settlers a representative assembly through which they could consent to the laws that governed them. Directed by company leaders "to imitate and follow the policy of the form of government, laws, customs, and manner of trial; and other administration of justice, used in the realm of England," the assembly claimed the right to consent to all taxes levied on the inhabitants of Virginia.[7] In similar fashion, the Maryland charter (1632) stipulated that the settlers should enjoy "all Privileges, Franchises and Liberties of this our Kingdom of England, freely, quietly, and peaceably to have and possess ... in the same manner as our Liege-Men born, or to be born within our said Kingdom of England." As well, the charter decreed that Lord Baltimore's "absolute Power" to "Ordain, Make, and Enact Laws, of what Kind soever" was subject to the "Advice, Assent, and Approbation of the Free-men" who "shall be called together for the framing of Laws."[8]

The Maryland assembly took advantage of this grant, and in 1637–1638 passed an act "for the liberties of the people," which stated that subjects in Maryland should "have and enjoy all such rights, liberties, immunities, priviledges, and free customs as any naturall born subject of England hath or ought to have or enjoy in the Realm of England by force or vertue of the common law or Statute Law of England." The act also decreed that no one should "be imprisoned nor disseissed or dispossessed of their freehold goods or Chattels or be out Lawed, Exiled or otherwise destroyed fore judged or punished then according to the Laws of this Province."[9]

By contracting colonization out to these chartered enterprises, the Crown allowed the settlers on the ground to establish authority and property with limited oversight. Over time, the settlers came to see the charters as their constitutions, written documents that guaranteed their rights and liberties outside the realm.[10] And in the mid-seventeenth century, when

---

[7] Ordinance of July 24, 1621, in Jack P. Greene, ed., *Great Britain and the American Colonies, 1606–1783* (Columbia: University of South Carolina Press, 1970), 28, 30.

[8] Maryland Charter, June 30, 1632, in Greene, ed., *Great Britain and the American Colonies*, 23–24.

[9] Quoted in George Dargo, *Roots of the Republic: A New Perspective on Early American Constitutionalism* (New York: Praeger, 1974), 58.

[10] Herbert L. Osgood, "The Corporation as a Form of Colonial Government, Part I," *Political Science Quarterly* 11 (1896), 259–277; and Part II, 11 (1897), 502–533.

England was plunged into civil war, the chartered colonies used their delegated authority to act in effect as states, trading freely, waging war, making peace, and concluding treaties, both with other European powers, and with the indigenous people of the Americas.[11]

Although they provided a legal framework for settlement, and thus filled in the outlines of the inchoate Cokean jurisprudence on royal power in the dominions, the charters ultimately posed as many questions as they answered about the legal status of English subjects outside the realm. Could, for example, the Crown revoke the charters at its pleasure, on the grounds that the settlers owed "absolute obedience to the King's authority"?[12] Or did the settlers enjoy the legal protections of the charters as a matter of right? The exact meaning of the nonrepugnancy clause was also a source of disagreement. Beginning in the late seventeenth century, the Privy Council used it as the legal basis for its authority to review colonial laws. Many settlers, by contrast, claimed that the intent of the clause was to guarantee them English law outside the realm, including in some cases the right to pass local laws without royal oversight. Also in dispute was the Crown's authority to create juryless prerogative courts within the chartered boundaries of the colonies.

As well, the charters offered little guidance on the crucial question of the rights of the indigenous peoples that the English encountered in the New World. The third Virginia charter (1612) enjoined the settlers to "the Propogation of Christian Religion and Reclaiming of People barbarous to Civility and Humanity"; and the Maryland charter (1632) spoke of establishing a colony "in a Country hitherto uncultivated" and "partly occupied by Savages"; but neither charter was clear about the property rights or jurisdictional status of the peoples who were inhabiting the lands the settlers intended to settle on. Were they conquered peoples, or independent nations? Allies or subjects? Did they own the land, or did industrious colonists have a superior claim to it?[13]

---

[11] On the political independence of the Massachusetts Bay colony in the seventeenth century, see Michael Winship, "Godly Republicanism and the Origins of the Massachusetts Polity," *William and Mary Quarterly* 63 (2006), 427–462. On chartered colonies acting as states, see Max Savelle, *Seeds of Liberty: The Genesis of the American Mind* (New York: Alfred A. Knopf, 1948), 343–344.

[12] Report of the Commissioners sent to New England (April 30, 1661), in W. Noel Sainsbury et al., eds., *Calendar of State Papers, Colonial, 1661–68* (London, 1860 –), 25 (hereafter, *CSPC*).

[13] The secondary literature on this question is equally diffuse. Paul McHugh claims that "the early Stuart grants contained no assertion of jurisdiction over the Indian tribes, the powers of corporate governance they constituted being expressed" in "personal terms"; as a result, he contends that "the charters' constant references to 'Barbarous Nations' indicated a class outside the ordinary scope of their constituted governance." McHugh,

These questions mattered little in the early seventeenth century when the Crown took scant interest in the governance of the colonies. But in the aftermath of the Civil War, the new monarch, Charles II, sought to reverse the "sweeping devolution of power" that had characterized the early decades of English empire in America.[14] Faced with Charles's attempt to extend royal authority across the Atlantic, settler elites defended their autonomy by drawing on the common law and its conception of the subjects' rights. As well, they began to draw on the idea of natural rights to think about their place in an increasingly complex transatlantic empire. Both of these traditions of thought would shape legal and political discourse in the empire down to the era of the American Revolution.

Charles's imperial policy in the early years of the Restoration was conservative. The Earl of Clarendon, the king's chief minister, sought to rebuild royal authority in the empire by granting the settlers in Connecticut a charter in 1662, renewing Rhode Island's parliamentary grant from the 1640s, while, at the same time, converting the disordered settlements in the Caribbean (principally Barbados and Jamaica) into royal colonies. In doing so, Clarendon appealed to colonial elites, sanctioning their authority in return for allegiance to the restored monarchy.[15]

Under Charles, royal officials also continued the Cromwellian policy of trade regulations, passing Navigation Acts in 1660, 1663, and 1673, the last of which created customs officers who would be independent of local authority, a move that "marked a potentially revolutionary change in colonial government."[16] The animating principle of the Navigation Acts

Aboriginal Societies and the Common Law: A History of Sovereignty, Status, and Self-determination (New York: Oxford University Press, 2004), 94. By contrast, Christopher Tomlins claims that the charters called for evangelization and asserted the superior rights of those who possessed and then transformed the land. Tomlins, "The Legal Cartography of Colonization, the Legal Polyphony of Settlement: English Intrusions on the American Mainland in the Seventeenth Century," *Law and Social Inquiry* 26 (2001), 335–336.

[14] John Murrin, "Political Development," in Jack P. Greene and J.R. Pole, eds., *Colonial British America: Essays in the New History of the Early Modern Era* (Baltimore: Johns Hopkins University Press, 1984), 419.

[15] On the attempt to restore royal authority in English America after the Restoration, see Robert M. Bliss, *Revolution and Empire: English Politics and the American Colonies in the Seventeenth Century* (Manchester: Manchester University Press, 1990), 132–160. Bliss refers to Clarendon's imperial policy in the 1660s as a "conservative contractual approach" (160).

[16] Bliss, *Revolution and Empire*, 174. For the text of these acts, see Jack P. Greene, ed., *Settlements to Society, 1607–1763: A Documentary History of Colonial America* (New York: W.W. Norton, 1975), 134–139. On Restoration commercial policy, see J.M. Sosin, *English America and the Restoration Monarchy of Charles II: Transatlantic Politics, Commerce, and Kinship* (Lincoln: University of Nebraska Press, 1980), 49–73. For

was that trade should serve the state, and in particular that the wealth it generated was crucial to the king's ability to project power against his enemies. On this view, the colonies, as repositories of vital raw materials, must be subject to metropolitan control. As well, by limiting imperial trade to English shipping, the Navigation Acts would provide a cadre of trained seamen who could bolster the naval power of the realm in time of war, further enhancing the Crown's ability to defend its interests in a dangerous Atlantic world.[17]

In the mid-1670s, the Lord Treasurer, the Earl of Danby, sought to further centralize the empire by creating a new body, the Lords of Trade, which replaced the old system whereby several ad hoc committees of the Privy Council had jurisdiction over the colonies.[18] The new Lords of Trade began to enforce the provisions of the Navigation Acts more aggressively, requiring that royal governors take an oath to uphold them, as well as report to London regularly on their operation.[19] Danby also made an ambitious young man by the name of William Blathwayt the clerk of the new Lords of Trade. And he appointed Edmund Randolph, another aspiring office-seeker, as the customs collector in Massachusetts. Both men

an argument that the English Civil War was in fact the transformative moment in the empire, see Carla Pestana, *The English Atlantic in an Age of Revolution, 1640–1661* (Cambridge, MA: Harvard University Press, 2004).

[17] Bliss, *Revolution and Empire*, 169–171. In this sense, the policy was neither commercial nor military; rather, it saw both aspects of imperial power as interrelated. On the genesis of Restoration colonial policy, see W.A. Speck, "The International and Imperial Context," in Greene and Pole, eds., *Colonial British America*, 388–389; and Charles Andrews, *The Colonial Period of American History: Volume IV, England's Commercial and Colonial Policy* (New Haven: Yale University Press, 1938), 370–372. Andrews sees the need to enforce the Navigation Acts and a fear of the French threat as driving the Privy Council toward centralization. This "commercial reason of state" (to quote Bliss) also entailed the constitutional subordination of the royal dominions to the English Parliament. On this point, see David Armitage, *The Ideological Origins of the British Empire* (Cambridge: Cambridge University Press, 2000), 146–169. For the ideas on trade and empire of a prominent royal advisor, see E.E. Rich, "The First Earl of Shaftesbury's Colonial Policy," *Transactions of the Royal Historical Society* 7 (1957), 47–70. John Murrin points out that we still lack a good account of the acceptance by settler elites of these new restrictions. See Murrin, "Political Development," 427.

[18] On this new body, see Ralph Bieber, *The Lords of Trade and Plantations, 1675–1696* (Allentown, PA: H. R. Haas, 1919); and Winifred T. Root, "The Lords of Trade and Plantations, 1675–1696," *American Historical Review* 23 (1917), 20–41. On the earlier system of ad hoc committees, see Charles Andrews, *British Committees, Commissions, and Councils of Trade and Plantations, 1622–1675* (Baltimore: Johns Hopkins University Press, 1908). For an overview of the Privy Council and the empire, see H.E. Egerton, "The Seventeenth and Eighteenth Century Privy Council in Its Relations with the Colonies," *Journal of Comparative Legislation and International Law* 7 (1925), 1–16.

[19] Bliss, *Revolution and Empire*, 179.

were aggressive centralizers, who felt the empire was being undermined by the political autonomy enjoyed by the American colonies.[20]

Several factors contributed to Danby's decision to tighten the bonds of empire in the mid-1670s. Massachusetts had rebuffed the royal commission sent out in 1665 by Clarendon in order to get them to agree to a new charter, insisting on its right to remain a virtually self-governing polity, and declining to accede to royal demands to expand the suffrage to non-Puritans, tolerate the Anglican Church, and allow for the king to hear appeals from the colony's courts and the neighboring Native American peoples.[21] The Bay Colony's intransigence hardened metropolitan attitudes toward chartered autonomy throughout the empire.[22]

As well, a devastating war against an Indian confederacy led by the Wampanoag Sachem Metacom (King Philip) in the mid-1670s alerted the Crown to the destructive consequences of New England's autonomy.[23] And in the spring of 1676 Virginia's western borders exploded when Berkeley, the long-serving royal governor, angered aggressive frontier settlers with what they saw as a conciliatory Indian policy. Further south, the royal colonies in the Caribbean were havens for pirates, playing havoc with Charles's diplomatic overtures to Spain.

Jamaica was the first colony to have its internal autonomy threatened by the new Lords of Trade. Reacting to a series of laws passed by the Jamaican assembly that it felt violated the royal prerogative, the Lords proposed that the colony be subjected to a version of Poynings's Law. First applied to the Irish Parliament in the sixteenth century, it meant that the assembly would be forced to simply ratify laws written by the Privy

---

[20] Michael Hall, *Edward Randolph and the American Colonies, 1676–1703* (Chapel Hill: University of North Carolina Press, 1960). On Blathwayt, see Stephen Saunders Webb, "William Blathwayt, Imperial Fixer: From Popish Plot to Glorious Revolution," *William and Mary Quarterly* 25 (1968), 3–21; and Barbara C. Murison, "The Talented Mr. Blathwayt: His Empire Revisited," in Nancy L. Rhoden, ed., *English Atlantics Revisited: Essays Honouring Professor Ian K. Steele* (Montreal: McGill-Queens University Press, 2007), 33–58.

[21] On this episode, see Paul Lucas, "Colony or Commonwealth: Massachusetts Bay, 1661–1666," *William and Mary Quarterly* 24 (1967), 88–107. For the Crown's complaints, see the royal letter of 1662, reprinted in Nathaniel B. Shurtleff, ed., *Records of the Governor and Company of Massachusetts Bay in New England*, Volume IV, Part 2 (New York: A.M.S. Press, 1968), 165–166.

[22] Bliss, *Revolution and Empire*, 160, argues that it led to a rethinking of Clarendon's contractual approach to the empire.

[23] On the role that Indian warfare (and Indian appeals to the Crown) played in imperial politics, see Jennifer Pulsipher, *Subjects unto the Same King: Indians, English, and the Contest for Authority in Colonial New England* (Philadelphia: University of Pennsylvania Press, 2005), passim.

Council. In support of this policy, the attorney general, William Jones, contended that the king was the "absolute sovereign" in Jamaica and "may impose what form of constitution both of government and laws, he pleaseth." According to Jones, "the inhabitants are in no sort entitled to the laws of England," save "by the mere grace and grant of the king."[24] After hearing from the attorney general, in April 1677 the Privy Council took the decision to draft all of Jamaica's laws in London and then present them to the assembly for ratification.[25]

The Jamaican assembly, despite internal strife between planters and buccaneers, presented a united front and refused to ratify the laws that the new governor, the Earl of Carlisle, brought over, including the crucial one providing the governor with a permanent salary. After several years of conflict, a compromise was reached in 1683.[26] The assembly agreed to pass a long-term revenue law for the support of royal government. As well, it conceded to the Crown the right to review (and possibly veto) its legislation. In return, the Crown granted the assembly the right to initiate legislation.[27]

[24] Quoted in Bliss, *Revolution and Empire*, 182.

[25] For the royal commission authorizing this, see Leonard Labaree, ed., *Royal Instructions to British Colonial Governors, 1670–1776* (New York: D. Appleton-Century, 1935), I, 125–126. On this episode, see Richard S. Dunn, "Imperial Pressures on Massachusetts and Jamaica, 1675–1700," in Alison G. Olson and Richard M. Brown, eds., *Anglo-American Political Relations, 1675–1775* (New Brunswick: Rutgers University Press, 1970), 52–75.

[26] For the Privy Council's response to the assembly's rejection of Poynings's Law, see W.L. Grant, James Munro, and Sir Almeric Fitzroy, eds., *Acts of the Privy Council of England, Colonial Series*, Volume I (London: His Majesty's Stationery Office, 1910), 827–833 (hereafter, *APCC*). According to the council, the colony "never had any other right to Assemblies than from the Permission of the Governors, and that only Temporary and for Probation."

[27] On Jamaica's resistance, see Bliss, *Revolution and Empire*, 182–186; and Agnes M. Whitson, *The Constitutional Development of Jamaica, 1660–1729* (Manchester: Manchester University Press, 1929), 70–109. Leonard Labaree, *Royal Government in America: A Study of the British Colonial System before 1783* (1930; New York: Frederick Ungar, 1958), 220–221, contends that without Jamaica's stand against Poynings's Law all of the royal colonies might have been reduced to the status of the Irish Parliament. Even after Danby had been impeached by the Whigs and Shaftesbury had briefly returned to office, the whole Privy Council agreed that Jamaica's resistance to the Crown was illegitimate. That is, both Whigs and Tories "supported royal supremacy in the empire." Bliss, *Revolution and Empire*, 188–189. As Blathwayt later recollected, at the meeting Shaftesbury opined that "all plantations were of the King's making, and that he might at any time alter or dispose of them at his pleasure." *CSPC*, 1681–1685, #1087. Though see David S. Lovejoy, *The Glorious Revolution in America* (1972; Hanover, NH: Wesleyan University Press, 1987), 56, for a different account in which Shaftesbury opposed Poynings's Law as it would treat the settlers like Irishmen and drive away the planters.

Virginia, the oldest royal colony on the mainland, met a similar fate in the late 1670s. Hit hard by the 1673 Plantation Act that cut into its tobacco profits, and threatened by the king's plan to grant the entire Northern Neck of the colony to Lords Culpepper and Arlington, Virginia sent agents to court in 1675 to obtain a new royal charter. By doing so, it sought to ensure its territorial integrity and corporate autonomy.[28]

In lobbying for the new charter, Virginia's agents wrote a defence of its main provisions that reveals the way settler elites understood their place in the empire in the late seventeenth century. To convince the king not to carve up the colony for his courtiers, the agents argued that all land in the colony should be "assured to the present possessors and owners of it" on the grounds that they had relied on a royal grant "to lay out their estates, and employ their industry" thereon "for the improvement and advancement" of the "country." The agents also insisted on the settlers' right to be taxed by an assembly of their own choosing, for "both the acquisition and defense of this country hath been, for the most part, at the country's charge." As well, the agents argued, "legislative power" in Virginia has "ever resided" in such an assembly, and "by fifty years' experience, had been found a government more easy to the people, and more advantageous to the crown." Above all, the agents contended, the colony's claim to property, legislative autonomy, and consensual taxation were the rights of "natural born subjects of England," rights the colony had enjoyed in its original charter, and which "in truth, without any declaration or grant, they ought by law" to enjoy. For if the king allowed his subjects to settle in "an uncultivated part of the world," the "planters and their heirs ought to enjoy ... the same liberties and privileges as Englishmen in England." "Such plantation," the agents reasoned, was "but in nature an extension or dilation of the realm of England."[29]

Before the Crown could approve the charter, the colony was convulsed by Bacon's rebellion.[30] In response, the Crown sent out a royal commission, which determined that Governor Berkeley and the assembly had

[28] CSPC, 1675–1676, #602–3/696/697. On the quest for the charter, see David Lovejoy, "Virginia's Charter and Bacon's Rebellion, 1675–1676," in Olson and Brown, eds., *Anglo-American Political Relations*, 31–51.

[29] For the agents' defence of their proposed charter, see John Burk, *History of Virginia from the First Settlement to the Present Day* (Petersburg, VA: Dickson and Pescud, 1805), II, xlv–l.

[30] The 1676 charter is reprinted in *Virginia Magazine of History and Biography* 56 (1948), 264–266. On Bacon's rebellion, see Richard L. Morton, *Colonial Virginia: The Tidewater Period, 1607–1710* (Chapel Hill: University of North Carolina Press, 1960), 227–277.

badly mismanaged the colony, alienating the majority of the settlers and
reducing the Crown's valuable tobacco revenues. Although Berkeley was
ordered home in 1677, the Virginia assembly refused to cooperate with
the commission's investigation. Robert Beverly, its clerk, even refused to
hand over the assembly's records to the royal commissioners.[31]

Although Bacon's Rebellion provided a pretext for the denial of the
charter, it is likely that the plan of the new Lords of Trade to centralize the empire, which involved sending Lord Culpepper to Virginia as
governor, was the real reason it was never granted.[32] And indeed, when
Culpepper finally arrived in 1680, he came armed with three bills, which,
in the manner of Poynings's Law, the Lords of Trade wanted the assembly
to ratify. In contrast to the intransigence of the Jamaicans, the Virginia
assembly agreed to pass all three into law, one of which granted the royal
governor a permanent salary.[33] And when Culpepper's replacement, Lord
Howard of Effingham, arrived in 1683, he insisted on the Crown's right
to review the assembly's laws in London and to have the Privy Council,
rather than the assembly, be the final court of appeal for the colony.[34]

Concerned by these aggressive assertions of prerogative, in 1684 the
burgesses petitioned the king, arguing that the Virginia settlers had left
their "Natiue Soyle," and "Aduentered" their "Liues, fortunes and all that
are deare to us" by "Inhabiting a Barbarous and Malancholy part of the
world," where they were "subject to the Incursions ... and depredations
of a skulking, Cruell, inhumane ... Enemie." Despite undertaking this
perilous venture for "the enlargement of your Majesties Dominions," they
were being denied their "Antient" right to pass laws for their own welfare
as many lesser corporations within the realm could do. To remedy this
situation, they asked the king to ensure that all of their laws would remain

[31] For an argument that the Crown was motivated by a desire to protect the interests
of the common planters, see John C. Rainbolt, "A New Look at Stuart 'Tyranny': The
Crown's Attack on the Virginia Assembly, 1676–1689," *Virginia Magazine of History
and Biography* 75 (1967), 387–406. Rainbolt argues that the common planters wanted
lower taxes and fewer meetings of the assembly but did not desire the abolition of representative government in the colony. The same could be said of many Baconians. Giles
Bland, the royal collector of customs, also thought that Berkley and the assembly had
engrossed too much power. Stephen Webb notes the irony of those like Bland who, by
complaining to the Crown about Berkeley, undermined the passage of the charter and
thereby thwarted their desire for a royal declaration of English liberties. See Webb, *The
Governors General: The English Army and the Definition of Empire, 1569–1681* (Chapel
Hill: University of North Carolina Press, 1979), 340–343.

[32] See Lovejoy, "Virginia's Charter and Bacon's Rebellion," 40–42.

[33] For the preparation of Culpepper's instructions, see *CSPC, 1677–1680*, #917.

[34] On Effingham's term as governor, see Morton, *Colonial Virginia*, I, 310–329.

in force until "declared voyd" by the governor or the Privy Council in London.[35] However, their petition never reached the king; instead, the Privy Council returned it to Effingham, who castigated the assembly for having sent it in the first place. As a final indignity, he fired the burgesses' clerk, replacing him with a royal appointee.

As the controversies in Jamaica and Virginia were dying down, settlers in New York made a bid for English rights. Conquered from the Dutch in 1664, New York was a proprietorial colony, owned by the king's brother, James, Duke of York, whose letters patent gave him "full and absolute power to Correct punish Pardon Governe and Rule all."[36] In addition, the first English governor, Richard Nicolls, drafted a legal code for the province after consulting the laws of other colonies. Proclaimed before deputies from the towns, both English and Dutch, the Duke's Laws (March 1665) did not allow for an elected assembly; instead, all authority was held by the governor and council, though there was a Court of Assize that also functioned as a consultative body.[37]

Following a brief reconquest by the Dutch (1672–1674), Edmund Andros, soldier and courtier, became governor.[38] Soon after arriving, Andros suggested to the Duke of York that he grant New Yorkers an assembly, but he demurred, opining that an assembly was "of dangerous consequence."[39] The duke had cause to regret his decision, when, in 1680, the law authorizing the governor to collect the customs duties expired, leaving the collector, William Dyer, without legal sanction for his activities. When Dyer attempted to collect the customs duties anyway, the merchants balked, and a tax revolt ensued. A grand jury charged Dyer

[35] Petition of the Burgesses to the King, May 16, 1684, in H.R. McIlwaine, ed., *Journals of the House of Burgesses of Virginia, 1659/60–1693* (Richmond, VA: Colonial Press, E. Waddey Co., 1914), 228–230.

[36] See the discussion in Daniel Hulsebosch, *Constituting Empire: New York and the Transformation of Constitutionalism in the Atlantic World, 1664–1830* (Chapel Hill: University of North Carolina Press, 2005), 44–45.

[37] The most comprehensive account of politics in Restoration New York remains Robert C. Ritchie, *The Duke's Province: A Study of New York Politics and Society, 1664–1691* (Chapel Hill: University of North Carolina Press, 1977). On the structure of government in the newly conquered province, see Ritchie, *The Duke's Province*, 25–46; and on the Duke's Laws, see Wesley Craven, *The Colonies in Transition, 1660–1713* (New York: Harper and Row, 1968), 74–78.

[38] On Andros, see Mary Lou Lustig, *The Imperial Executive in America: Sir Edmund Andros, 1637–1714* (Madison, NJ: Farleigh Dickinson University Press, 2002).

[39] The Duke of York to Andros, April 6, 1675, and January 28, 1676, in Edmund O'Callaghan, ed., *Documents Relative to the Colonial History of the State of New York* (Albany: Weed, Parsons, 1858), III, 230, 235.

with imposing "unlawful Customs," thereby subverting the "Ancient and Fundamentall Lawes of the Realme of England." Moreover, it held that he had abused his "Regall Power" over the king's subjects in a manner contrary to "the great charter of Libertyes," and the "Petition of Right."[40]

The grand jury also convinced the Court of Assize to petition James, telling him that an assembly was the "undoubted birthright" of all the king's subjects.[41] The political upheaval along with the loss of customs' revenue to the government changed James's mind about the propriety of representative government in the colony.[42] As a result, when the new governor, the Catholic Thomas Dongan, arrived in August 1683, he carried royal instructions authorizing him to call an assembly.

The new assembly, the first in the colony's history, convened in October and quickly passed a "Charter of Liberties," intended to provide New Yorkers with a constitutional framework more hospitable to English legal norms.[43] Under it, the unelected governor and council exercised the "Chiefe Magistracy and Administration"; however, according to the "usage Custome and practice of the Realme of England," the assembly had the right to initiate as well as consent to all legislation. The charter also contained a provision requiring that the governor call an assembly at least once every three years.

At the heart of the charter were a series of guarantees for the legal rights of the settlers. No one was to be imprisoned but by "the Lawfull Judgment of his peers and by the Law of this province." And no taxes were to be imposed but by consent of the governor, the council, and "the

---

[40] O'Callaghan, ed., *Documents*, III, 289.

[41] Quoted in Lovejoy, "Equality and Empire: The New York Charter of Libertyes, 1683," *William and Mary Quarterly* 21 (1964), 500.

[42] John Murrin suggests that York had one eye on the generous grant of political and religious rights being extended settlers in New Jersey and Pennsylvania at this time. Murrin, "English Rights as Ethnic Aggression: The English Conquest, the Charter of Liberties, and Leisler's Rebellion in New York," in William Pencak and Conrad Wright, eds., *Authority and Resistance in Early New York* (New York: New York Historical Society, 1988), 72.

[43] Lovejoy, "Equality and Empire," 493–515; and Ritchie, *The Duke's Province*, 155–179. In characteristically revisionist fashion, John Murrin has argued that the motive behind the charter was not primarily local autonomy but English ethnic chauvinism against the Dutch population who up to that point had shown no interest in English law or liberties (and legislation accompanying the charter imposed English land laws and local government on the Dutch population). He also claims that the Englishmen behind the charter comprised the anti-Leislerian (and hence anti-Dutch) faction following the Glorious Revolution. See Murrin, "English Rights as Ethnic Aggression," 56–94.

Representatives of the people in Generall Assembly." As well, all subjects would be protected against unlawful seizure of property. Martial law was forbidden; and there was to be no quartering of troops, save in time of war. The charter also proclaimed that all "Tryalls shall be by the verdict of twelve men" who are "peers or Equalls" of the accused and "of the neighbourhood." As well, in "all Cases Capitall or Criminal," no charges were to be laid but by "a grand Inquest."[44]

Although Governor Dongan and the council approved the charter, it still required the Duke of York's sanction. To provide James with an incentive to grant it, the assembly passed a generous new revenue act. Despite this, the charter was derailed by the mounting troubles at home, as Charles, in the wake of the Exclusion Crisis and the Rye House plot, sought revenge against the Whigs, one consequence of which was that many English corporations, including London, lost their charters, as their juries had repeatedly thwarted the King's will.[45]

As a consequence, when the Lords of Trade considered the charter in early 1685, it claimed that the right of New Yorkers to "be governed" by "the Laws of England" was a "Priviledge," which was "not granted to any of His Majesties Plantations where the Act of Habeas Corpus and all such other Bills do not take Place." The same reasoning was applied to the provision for triennial assemblies. The Lords also objected to the phrase "*The People* met in General Assembly," which, they claimed, was "not used in any other Constitution in America." As well, they worried that the powers the charter granted the governor, council, and assembly would "abridge the Acts of Parliament that may be made concerning New York." The Lords of Trade were also concerned that the governor and council would lose the "power of framing Laws as in the other Plantations," for the charter said that bills approved by the representatives of the people would be presented to the executive for approval. The lords also deemed "inconvenient" the control the charter gave the assembly over the sitting of its own members. As well, they objected to the fact that bills passed by the assembly remained in force for two years, unless the proprietor dissented, a provision they thought would "abridge the King's power."[46]

[44] The charter is reprinted in Greene, ed., *Settlements to Society*, 159–164.
[45] Paul Halliday, *Dismembering the Body Politic: Partisan Politics in England's Towns, 1650–1730* (New York: Cambridge University Press, 1998), 149–263.
[46] "Observations upon the Charter of New York," March 3, 1685, in O'Callaghan, ed., *Documents*, 357–359.

The main target of the Stuarts' centralizing policies, however, was Massachusetts, which had long been suspect for its religious heterodoxy, its violation of the Navigation Acts, its refusal to send its laws home for review, and its less than accommodating attitude toward the Anglican Church. In the mid-1670s, as the royal colonies of Virginia and Jamaica were facing Poynings's Law, Edmund Randolph arrived in Massachusetts to investigate its conduct on behalf of the Lords of Trade.[47] This heightened scrutiny culminated in the surrender of the Massachusetts charter in 1684 (via a writ of quo warranto). Later that year, Charles II, emboldened by his rout of the Whigs at home and the Puritans in America, began to discuss the possibility of revoking all of the remaining American charters.[48] In early December, the Privy Council agreed that the empire should be governed without assemblies, as New York had been before 1683. William Blathwayt, now auditor of the plantation revenues and a rising star in the colonial bureaucracy, hoped that the revocation of the charters would "bring about that Necessary union of all the English colonies in America which will make the King great & Extend his real Empire in those parts."[49]

In early 1685, Charles II died, and his brother, the Duke of York, became James II. Under James, the revocation of the Massachusetts charter was soon followed by similar assaults on other colonial charters; and, finally, by the consolidation of Massachusetts, Connecticut, Rhode Island, Plymouth, and New Hampshire into a new entity, the Dominion of New England.[50] The Crown appointed Edmund Andros, rehabilitated after he had been dismissed as governor of New York, to rule the dominion in conjunction with an appointed council. Significantly, no provision for an elected body was included in the new plan of government.[51] In 1688, James expanded the dominion to include New York and East and West Jersey.[52] With this addition, representative government in America was extinguished from the banks of the Delaware to the border of Maine.

---

[47] Michael Hall, *Edward Randolph and the American Colonies, 1676–1703* (Chapel Hill: University of North Carolina Press, 1960).

[48] Haffenden, "The Crown and the Colonial Charters, 1675–1688: Part I," *William and Mary Quarterly* 15 (1958), 307.

[49] Quoted in Lovejoy, *Glorious Revolution in America*, 68.

[50] Viola F. Barnes, *The Dominion of New England: A Study in British Colonial Policy* (New York: Frederick Ungar, 1960). On James's absolutism, see Steve Pincus, *1688: The First Modern Revolution* (New Haven: Yale University Press, 2009).

[51] For Andros's commission, see Kammen et al., *The Glorious Revolution*, 25–26.

[52] Lovejoy, *The Glorious Revolution in America*, 172, 211–212.

As well as governing the dominion without an assembly, Andros wanted all land grants to recognize "the King as ultimate owner of the soil."[53] To implement this policy, Andros announced that he would honor only land titles that had the official seal of the colony on them. This decree caused all landholders whose titles were now in doubt to petition the dominion government for a legal patent to their land.[54] Needless to say, New Englanders were not eager to accept a tenurial relationship to the Crown, nor did they want to pay quit rents to support royal government.[55]

When Andros instructed each town to select the land assessors who would then levy the requisite taxes, Ipswich refused. Led by John Wise, a then unknown Congregationalist minister, the town meeting defied Andros, contending that "the said act doth infringe their liberty as free-borne English subjects." They further charged that "the Statute Laws of the Land" "enacted that *no taxes shall be levied on the subjects* without the consent of an assembly chosen by the freeholders for assessing the same." For their troubles, Wise and the other men involved were arrested. At their trial, one of Andros's judges informed them that their rights as Englishmen did not follow them across the Atlantic. Rather, the judge claimed, "You have no more Privileges left you, but this, that you are not bought and sold for Slaves."[56]

In addition, Andros denied the legitimacy of Indian title and thus of any land that the colonists claimed to have purchased from local tribes.[57] In the words of Increase Mather, one of the dominion's most severe critics, "The property of his Majesty's loyal subjects ... has been invaded by their present Rulers. The Governor has taken away the Lands belonging to some particular persons, & given them to his owne creatures."[58]

Andros also allowed Anglicans a much wider freedom of worship than they had previously enjoyed in New England. In a particularly contentious move, he allowed Anglican worshippers to use Congregationalist meeting houses, thereby simultaneously transgressing both a religious freedom and a civil one, for the churches were also considered private property. In addition, Andros introduced the practice of swearing oaths on the Bible, something that the Puritans considered idolatrous.

---

[53] Barnes, *The Dominion of New England*, 188.

[54] T.H. Breen, *The Character of the Good Ruler: A Study of Puritan Political Ideas, 1630–1730* (New Haven: Yale University Press, 1970), 146–147.

[55] On the response to Andros's policies, see Breen, *The Character of the Good Ruler*, 141–150.

[56] Quoted in ibid., 145.

[57] Barnes, *The Dominion of New England*, 193–194.

[58] Quoted in Breen, *The Character of a Good Ruler*, 147.

In the wake of the Ipswich revolt, Andros restricted town meetings to one a year, limited solely to the purpose of electing local officials.[59] This interference in local affairs was exacerbated by the widespread provincial perception that Andros was doing little or nothing to protect them from the threat of both the French and the Indians. Indeed, the failure of Andros's military expedition to Maine gave rise to wild charges that he was supplying the Indians with arms and had made a secret covenant with the French.[60]

Finally, Andros attempted to control the trade of the northern colonies via a more rigorous enforcement of the Navigation Acts. For years, New Englanders had imported staple goods from the West Indian colonies and then exchanged them with European merchants, all without paying the duty required by imperial legislation. When Andros started assiduously collecting all of the relevant duties, local trade suffered as Boston merchants could no longer undercut their British competitors. The resultant desertion of the non-Puritan merchants from the Andros camp further weakened him politically.[61]

Discontent with Andros's rule forced Increase Mather, scion of an old Puritan family, to leave for London in the spring of 1688 to lobby for the return of the charter. While he sought an audience with James II and courted anyone influential enough to help him, Mather published *A Narrative of the Miseries of New England*. In recounting the misfortunes that had befallen Massachusetts under the dominion, Mather contrasted English liberty with a polity governed by "a Despotick and Absolute Power." Mather dated the change from one type of government to another in New England to "the *Quo Warranto* issued out against their *Charters*, by means whereof they have been deprived of their *ancient Rights and Privileges*."[62] For Mather, the loss of the New England charters had resulted in the erection of "a French Government in that part of the Kings Dominions,"[63] with Andros having the power "to make Laws and

---

[59] On this issue, see ibid., 149.

[60] Ibid., 149.

[61] On the New England merchants' attitude to the dominion, see Bernard Bailyn, *The New England Merchants in the Seventeenth Century* (1955; New York: Harper Torchbooks, 1964).

[62] Increase Mather, *A Narrative of the Miseries of New England, by Reason of an Arbitrary Government Erected there under Sir Edmund Andros* (Boston, 1688), 1. Ian Steele says that it was printed in London and dated 1688 in Boston when it was reprinted there in early 1689. See Steele, "Communicating an English Revolution to the Colonies, 1688–1689," *Journal of British Studies* 24 (1985), 348, fn. 64.

[63] Ibid., 2.

raise moneys on the Kings Subjects, without any Parliament, Assembly, or Consent of the People."[64]

Mather also complained of Andros's violation of colonial land titles. As Mather put it, colonists were told by "their new Masters" that "their Charter being gone, their Title to their Lands and Estates is gone therewith, and that all is the Kings."[65] Mather maintained that such an attack on their property rights was unjust. After all, the settlers in New England should have a clear right to "enjoy the Houses which their own Hands have built, and the Lands, which at vast Charges in subduing a Wilderness, they have for many Years had a rightful possession of, as ever any People in the world had or can have."[66]

Although Mather's pleas fell on deaf ears, the invasion of England by the Dutch prince, William of Orange, in November 1688, and the subsequent fall of the Stuarts, proved the undoing of Andros and the dominion. In the spring of 1689, news of Williams's triumph reached Massachusetts. In a matter of hours on April 18, 1689, leading townsmen in Boston rose up and seized Andros along with all of the major dominion leaders, and jailed them.[67] They then issued a declaration, insisting that their uprising was modeled on "the Patterns which the Nobility, Gentry and Commonality" of England "have set before us" when they overthrew James II the previous year.

The declaration offered a forceful critique of Andros's rule, which had brought "multiplied Contradictions to Magna Charta," among them the passing of laws and the levying of taxes without consent, the presence of troops to enforce the dominion's rule, as well as arbitrary arrests and fines, "Packt" juries, and the denial of habeas corpus. Indeed, the declaration noted, it was "plainly affirmed" by Andros's council that "the People in New-England were all Slaves," who "must not think the Privileges of English men would follow us to the End of the World." As if that were not egregious enough, Andros had also denied the legitimacy of the settlers' land titles, notwithstanding "our purchase of them from the Natives," and "our actual peaceable Possession of them for near threescore Years." And finally, Andros's bungled war against the Native Americans in Maine

---

[64] Ibid., 2.
[65] Ibid., 3.
[66] Ibid., 3.
[67] Lovejoy, *The Glorious Revolution in America*, 240–241. For an argument that Bostonians knew of James's fall at least a month before the uprising, see Ian K. Steele, "Origins of Boston's Revolutionary Declaration of 18 April 1689," *New England Quarterly*, 62 (1989), 75–81.

had been so ineffectual and had led to so many casualties that the rebels could not but suspect that the whole enterprise was part of "a Branch of the Plot to bring us low."[68]

The constitutional case made in the declaration was, in the words of Ian Steele, "overwhelmingly secular," concentrating on "political liberties," in order to appeal to those rebels – like the merchant John Nelson – who were not Puritans, as well as to a broader English world that didn't find New England's particular reading of scripture compelling.[69] However, the resistance to the dominion in New England – and indeed in the rest of English America – also contained a powerful critique of Andros and the Stuarts as agents of the papacy. This powerful strain of anti-popery was nondenominational and thus could be embraced by all English Protestants. As well, it was perfectly compatible with the constitutional claims made in the declaration, as it tapped into a widespread fear in the English world that the pope, in league with Catholic powers like the France of Louis XIV, sought to replace parliaments with arbitrary government, thereby undermining an Englishman's religion as well as his liberties.[70]

Benjamin Harris, a radical Whig émigré who had printed the declaration, combined anti-popery and English constitutionalism in a broadside he published in Boston in 1689.[71] In it, he connected New England's travails under the dominion with the struggle in England against the arbitrary and crypto-Catholic monarch James II.

> Those Laws, which Parliaments had made to live,
> Were laid in Dust by Grand Prerogative ...
> Nor could the Vastness of his damn'd design
> The Limits of his Popish Rage confine,
> But or'e the Ocean to *this* world it flew;
> Reformed America must suffer too.

[68] "The Boston Declaration of Grievances" (April 18, 1689), in Michael G. Hall, Lawrence H. Leder and Michael Kammen, eds., *The Glorious Revolution in America: Documents on the Crisis of 1689* (New York: W.W. Norton, 1964), 42–46.

[69] Steele, "Origins of Boston's Revolutionary Declaration," 80. On the secularization of New England's legal and political culture, see Breen, *The Character of a Good Ruler*.

[70] On anti-popery, see Peter Lake, "Anti-Popery: The Structure of a Prejudice," in Richard Cust and Ann Hughes, eds., *Conflict in Early Stuart England: Studies in Religion and Politics, 1603–1642* (London: Longman 1989), 72–106. For its role in the Glorious Revolution in America, see Owen Stanwood, "The Protestant Moment: Antipopery, the Revolution of 1688–1689, and the Making of an Anglo-American Empire," *Journal of British Studies* 46 (2007), 481–508.

[71] On Harris, who was Mather's printer, see Ian K. Steele, *The English Atlantic, 1675–1740: An Exploration of Communications and Community* (New York: Oxford University Press, 1986), 106, 136.

And when Andros, "the Jersy Knight," arrived:

> We were not treated by the insulting Knaves
> As free-born English, but as poor French Slaves
> Taxes were rais'd, without Mercy, or Measure,
> To keep us low, and fill our Tyrant's treasure
> To MAGNA CHARTA we could claim no Right ...

But then the New Englanders heard of the coming of William of Orange, and

> ... by Your great Example sway'd,
> A *just* Attempt *opprest* New-England Made,
> Not to revenge our wrongs but set us free
> From arbitrary Power and Slavery.[72]

Having overturned constituted authority, it was imperative that the rebels in Massachusetts justify their actions to authorities in London, especially since they hoped that the new sovereigns, William and Mary, would sanction their resistance and restore their old charter. Increase Mather, still in London, continued to lobby for its return. As well, many New Englanders wrote impassioned critiques of Andros's rule.[73] But the dominion did not lack defenders, the most sophisticated of whom was John Palmer, a judge and councilor under Andros, who had been jailed by the Boston rebels.[74] His exchange with Edward Rawson, the secretary of the Bay Colony before the revocation of the charter, was the most thorough exploration to date of the rights of settlers in English America.

For Palmer, the dominion was justified because the prerogative powers of the Crown in America were legally unlimited. As he put it, "Tis a fundamental point, consented unto by all Christian Nations, that the first Discovery of a Countrey inhabited by Infidels, gives a Right and Dominion of that Countrey to the Prince, in whose Service and

[72] *The Plain Case Stated of Old – but especially of New-England, in an Address to His Highness the Prince of Orange* (Boston, Printed for and Sold by Benjamin Harris at the London Coffee-House).

[73] For example, A.B., *An Account of the Late Revolution in New England* (Published in Boston by Benjamin Harris, and sold at the London-Coffee House there 1689).

[74] It appeared in two versions. The first, entitled *The Present State of New England* was published in Boston in 1689. The second, slightly emended version was called *An Impartial Account of the State of New England: Or, the late Government there, Vindicated In Answer to the Declaration* ... (London, 1690). I have drawn on the later version. For details on both versions of Palmer's pamphlet, along with a reprint of *An Impartial Account*, see W.H. Whitmore, ed., *The Andros Tracts*, Volume One (Boston: The Prince Society, 1868), 21–61.

Imployment the Discoverers was sent."[75] New England, having been inhabited by "Infidels," and then discovered and conquered under the aegis of the Crown, was thus subject to royal authority in a way that Englishmen at home were not.

Palmer held that Ireland and the other dominions of the Crown in the British Isles were also conquered dependencies. As a result, the Englishmen who first settled among the conquered Irish "were neither governed by their own Laws, nor the Laws of *England*, but according to the good pleasure of the Conqueror."[76] Palmer adduced the best of authorities for this claim: "if you will take the Opinion of Sir *Edward Coke*, in his Annotations on the *Great Charter*, he tells you plainly, That *at the making thereof, it did not extend to* Ireland, *or any of the King's Foreign Dominions*."[77] And the same was true of Wales. According to Palmer, it was "once a Kingdom, or Territory, govern'd by its own Laws; but when it became of the Dominion of the *Crown of England*, either by Submission or Conquest, it became subject also to such Laws as King *Edward* the First (to whom they submitted) thought fit to impose."[78] For Palmer, then, "*Englishmen permitted to be transported into the Plantations* (for thither without the King's License we cannot come) *can pretend to no other Liberties, Privileges, or Immunities there, than anciently the Subjects of* England, *who removed themselves into* Ireland *could have done*." In both cases, he argued, "it is from the Grace and Favour of the *Crown* alone that all these Flow, and are dispensed at the pleasure of him that sits upon the Throne."[79]

Palmer did concede that "*New England* had a *Charter*," but he held that "no one will be so stupid to imagine that the King was bound to grant it them." Rather, the charter was a revocable gift, one which the New Englanders had forfeited by their disobedience.[80] Palmer applied the same reasoning to the settlers' claim to representative government

---

[75] Palmer, *An Impartial Account*, 17–18.

[76] Palmer added: "it is evident, That after the Conquest, and before the recited Charters, the Inhabitants there, although composed of many *Free-born English Subjects, who settled themselves amongst them*, were neither governed by their own Laws, nor the Laws of *England*, but according to the good pleasure of the Conqueror" (16–17).

[77] Ibid., 16–17. "That it is a Conquer'd Kingdom is not doubted, [*Cooke Rep. Fol. 18*] but admitted in *Calvin's* case, and by an Act of the 11th. 12th. And 13th. Of King *James*, acknowledging in express Words, *viz. Whereas in former times the Conquest of this Realm, by His Majesty's most Royal Progenitors, Kings of* England, &c. That by virtue of this *Conquest*, it became of the Dominion of the *Crown* of *England*, and subject to such Laws as the Conqueror thought fit to impose " (15).

[78] Ibid., 14.

[79] Ibid., 18. Palmer cited *Craw v. Ramsey*, a late seventeenth-century naturalization case involving Ireland that drew heavily on Coke's decision in Calvin's Case.

[80] Ibid., 19.

throughout the king's dominions. For Palmer, "*Barbados, Jamaica, the Leeward Islands,* and *Virginia* have their Assemblies: but it is not *sui juris.*" Moreover, the laws made by these bodies were only "in force" until "the King is pleased to signifie his Disapprobation of them, which power he hath always reserved to himself." As such, the king "can, whenever he thinks fit, Repeal and Annul all" of their laws that "have not been before confirmed by him, or some of his Predecessors."[81]

In Palmer's view, such extensive royal power also characterized the "usage of Foreign Nations in their Plantations and Settlements abroad." According to Palmer: "The Governments of the *United Provinces,* and *Denmark,* are well known in *Europe*; and yet in all their Plantations, their Governments are despotical and absolute, all the power is in the hands of a Governour and Council, and everything is ordered and appointed by them, as is sufficiently manifest to those that are acquainted with *Batavia, Surinam, Curasao, New York* (when formerly in their hands) *and the Island of St. Thomas.*"[82]

In addition to their dependence on the Crown, Palmer argued that the settlers in America were subordinate to the English Parliament. As he pointed out, "the *Parliament of England* have never by any Act of theirs favoured the Plantations, or declared or inlarged their Privileges." On the contrary, Parliament had always "demonstrated, that they were much differenced from *England,*" lacking "those Privileges and Liberties which *England* enjoyed, being in all Acts relating to the Plantations, restrained and burthened beyond any in *England.*" For Palmer, the proof of this assertion "appears by the several Acts made for the increasing of Navigation, and for regulating and securing the Plantation Trade."[83] Furthermore, Palmer held that parliamentary statutes like the Habeas Corpus Act did not extend to the colonies. As he put it: "let any man peruse the Act, and I believe he will be easily convinced, that it is particularly limited to the Kingdom of *England.*"[84] Palmer also denied colonial claims to the privileges of the common law on the basis of long usage. After all, if "Prescription is intended," then "the Colony hath not been long enough settled, to claim any advantage by that Right."[85]

Not surprisingly, then, Palmer explicitly disavowed any parallel between the English and colonial constitutions, arguing that "the Plantations"

[81] Ibid., 17–18.
[82] Ibid., 17.
[83] Ibid., 19.
[84] Ibid., 25.
[85] Ibid., 26–27.

may, "without any regard to *Magna Charta*," be "Ruled and Governed, by such wayes and methods, as the Person who wears that Crowne, for the good and advancement of those Settlements, shall think most proper and convenient." Indeed, he insisted "that we can not justly call that Arbitrary, which by the Law we are obliged to submit to: So that betwixt their Condition and ours, there can be no Parity." Palmer also held that there was no parallel between the colonial rebellions and the actions of the English nation in overthrowing the Stuarts. According to Palmer: the "People of England" did not take "up Arms to right themselves; but instead thereof, they became humble Supplicants to his *Highness* for his Favour and Protection." Moreover, even the peers of the realm had "never left their Duty and Allegiance to his late MAJESTY, until he first left the Kingdom." Indeed, "all Things were transacted in his Name, and by his Authority, until the very minute *the Prince* was proclaimed."[86]

In his response to Palmer, Edward Rawson crafted a complex defense of the rights of the settlers in English America.[87] According to Rawson, Palmer's arguments from conquest and discovery were "clearly against *Jus Gentium & Jus Naturale*, which instructs every man ... that shall violently, and without any just cause take from infidels their lands, where they plant, and by which they subsist, does them manifest injury."[88] As a consequence, the "first Planters in *New-England*" were not "willing to *wrong the Indians in their properties*." Instead, they "purchased from the natives their right to the soil in that part of the world, not withstanding what right they had by virtue of their charters from the kings of *England*."[89] Because of this purchase, Rawson argued that the New Englanders were not, like the Welsh and Irish had been, a conquered people. On the contrary, the settlers in New England had "at vast charges of their own conquered a wilderness, and been in possession of their estates forty, nay sixty years."[90] As a result, Palmer's "alledging the case of *Wales* and *Ireland* before English liberties were granted to them, is an impertinent story."[91]

In addition to denying that New England had been conquered, Rawson argued "that there was *an original contract* between the king and the first

---

[86] Ibid., 37.
[87] On Rawson's resistance to Andros, see Lovejoy, *The Glorious Revolution in America*, 182.
[88] Edward Rawson, *The Revolution in New England Justified, and the People there Vindicated from the Aspersions cast upon them By Mr. John Palmer* (Boston, 1691), 44.
[89] Ibid., 44.
[90] Ibid., 17–18.
[91] Ibid., 46.

Planters in *New-England*, the king promising them, if they at their own cost and charge would subdue a wilderness, and enlarge his dominions, they and their posterity after them should enjoy such privileges as are in their charters expressed, of which that of not having taxes imposed on them without their consent was one." In Rawson's view, the reason for such a contract was obvious. After all, "what Englishmen in their right Wits will venture their Lives over the seas to enlarge the King's dominions, and to enrich and greaten the English nation, if all the reward they shall have for their cost and adventures shall be their being deprived of *English liberties*, and in the same condition with the *slaves in France or Turkey*."[92]

As well as this contractual argument for settler rights, Rawson also denied Palmer's claim that whatever rights New Englanders had were lost when the charter was annulled. According to Rawson, the mere removal of a legal guarantee in no way affected the settlers' rights, for "the judgment against their charter" did not make "them cease to be *Englishmen*."[93]

Finally, Rawson drew a clear parallel between the Glorious Revolutions in England and America. As he put it: "No man does really approve of the *revolution* in *England*, but must justify that in *New-England* also; for the latter was effected in compliance with the former."[94] According to Rawson, "the men usurping government in *New-England* were king *James's* creatures, who had invaded both the *liberty and property of English protestants* after such a manner as perhaps the like was never known in any part of the world where the English nation has any government." But despite the perfidy of Andros and his councillors, the settlers "designed not to revenge themselves on their enemies." Instead, they decided to "*leave it to the king and parliament of England, to inflict what punishment they should think meet for such criminals*."[95] Although Rawson defended the rebellions on both sides of the Atlantic, he denied that there was ever any "design among the *people in New-England* to reassume their ancient *charter-government*, until his present majesty's intended descent into *England*, to rescue the nation from *slavery* as well as *popery*, was known to them."[96]

In the spring and summer of 1689, rebellions also broke out in New York and Maryland. In New York, Francis Nicholson, the young lieutenant

[92] Ibid., 46.
[93] Ibid., 46.
[94] Ibid., 7.
[95] Ibid., 8.
[96] Ibid., 7.

governor, despite being faced with a restive population, refused to pro-
claim William and Mary. Instead, he informed a militiaman that New
Yorkers were a conquered people and therefore "could not so much claim
rights and privileges as Englishmen in England, but that the prince might
lawfully govern us by his own will and appoint what laws he pleases
among us."[97] Unable to govern, Nicholson fled to England in mid-June.
In the resultant power vacuum, Jacob Leisler, a militantly anti-Catholic
Calvinist, seized power at the head of the local militia.[98] To justify its
actions, the militia composed an address to the new sovereigns, William
and Mary, in June 1689, informing them that "in so remote a part of the
world" they had of late been governed "by papists" "who had in a most
arbitrary way subverted our ancient priviledges making us in effect slaves
to their will contrary to the laws of England." In response, the militia had
taken control of the colony "for the preservation of our Religion, liberty
and property," and were now awaiting "your Majestyes will and pleasure
in the disposing of our Government."[99]

With this coup, Leisler began a two-year reign characterized by increasingly arbitrary and erratic behavior. After arresting and jailing most of
those who challenged his authority, attempting to collect revenues in
contravention of the 1683 charter, coercing the residents of Albany, and
embarking on a failed attack on New France, he then refused to hand over
power when Henry Sloughter, the new royal governor, finally arrived in
the spring of 1691. Upon Sloughter's arrival, Leisler was tried, convicted,
and executed, leaving a legacy of political factionalism that haunted New
York politics for the next two decades.[100]

[97] Deposition of Charles Lodwick, July 25, 1689, in *Collections of the New-York Historical Society for the Year 1868* (New York, 1868), 295. On Nicholson, who was to have a long career in colonial administration, see Stephen Saunders Webb, "The Strange Career of Francis Nicholson," *William and Mary Quarterly* 23 (1966), 513–548; and Randy Dunn, "Patronage and Governance in Francis Nicholson's Empire," in Rhoden, ed., *English Atlantics Revisited*, 59–80.
[98] David Vorhees, "The 'fervent Zeale' of Jacob Leisler," *William and Mary Quarterly* 51 (1994), 470–471.
[99] "Address of the Militia of New York to William and Mary," in E.B. O'Callaghan, ed., *Documents Relative to the Colonial History of the State of New York*, Volume III (Albany: Weed, Parsons, 1853), 583–584. The address was signed by "Lieut. Hendrick Cuyler, of Captain De Peyster's company." If, as seems likely, Cuyler was Dutch, it would shed some light on the old question of whether the Dutch embraced English law and liberties. In any case, the official proclamations of both the Leislerians and the anti-Leislerians contained similar invocations of English rights, the Protestant religion, and the new monarchs.
[100] On Leisler's tumultuous year and a half in office, see Ritchie, *The Duke's Province*, 198–231.

As Leisler was consolidating power in New York, Protestant settlers in Maryland, long hostile to the proprietor, Lord Baltimore, and worried about the Catholic sympathies of Governor Joseph, seized power in the name of the new monarchs in June 1689.[101] The Maryland rebels then issued a declaration, which was printed in both the colony and London, and then presented before the Lords of Trade on December 5, 1690. In order to justify taking up arms, the rebels argued that they had been "threatened every day with the Loss of our Lives, Liberties, and Estates." The governor had suspended their laws, declaring them "null and void by Proclamation." He had also collected taxes without consent, even going so far as to dissolve the assembly. As well, he had failed to support the Anglican Church. On account of these depredations, the rebels in Maryland considered the settlers "Free from all manner of Duty, Obligation, or Fidelity" to the proprietary, whose officers had "Departed from their Allegiance" on which "alone our said Duty ... depends." And, worried that Baltimore would soon regain the colony, they pleaded with the new monarchs to deliver them from "the Yoke of Arbitrary Government, Tyranny and Popery."[102]

The settler resistance to the Stuarts in the 1670s and 1680s was crucial to the formation of early American legal and political ideas. Faced with the first concerted attempt to centralize the empire, settler elites from Virginia to New England responded with a remarkably uniform defense of their rights as Englishmen outside the realm. Rejecting the conquered status that royal officials accorded them, they argued that their rights did not depend on the prerogative or on a royal grant; rather, they were a "birthright," something that inhered in all English subjects, and which could thus be claimed anywhere in the empire. Moreover, the fact that they had migrated from the realm and risked their lives to settle a wilderness, expanding the King's territories in the process, only strengthened their claim to equal rights with their fellow subjects at home. Indeed, they would not have undertaken the arduous task of settlement had their rights not been confirmed to them by the monarch in the colonial charters.

---

[101] The definitive account is Lois Green Carr and David W. Jordan, *Maryland's Revolution of Government, 1689–92* (Ithaca, NY: Cornell University Press, 1974).

[102] "The Declaration of the Reasons and Motives for the Present Appearing in Arms of their Majesties Protestant Subjects in the Province of Maryland" (Printed by William Nuthead at the City of St. Maries. Reprinted in London, and Sold by Randal Taylor near Stationers Hall, 1689), in Charles M. Andrews, ed., *Narratives of the Insurrections, 1675–1690* (New York: Charles Scribner's Sons, 1915), 305–314.

This settler variant of English constitutionalism became central to political debate in the eighteenth-century empire. And it was reinforced by a widely shared belief that Protestantism and English liberty went hand in hand, forming necessary bulwarks to the twin perils of popery and arbitrary government.[103]

In defending their autonomy in the empire, the settlers also engaged in a complex consideration of the rights of the Native Americans. In order to deny the Cokean claim that they were residing in conquered territories, they defended native rights, claiming, as Rawson did in his debate with Palmer, that the natives were the original owners of the soil and that the settlers had purchased the land from them. But this position was largely instrumental, invoked to undermine the Crown's claim to property in the Americas.[104] At the same time, the settlers argued that they had migrated to what was in effect a wilderness and had then applied their labor to the uncultivated land, in the process generating property rights independent of royal grant or purchase.

The fact that the colonists had left the jurisdiction of the common law by crossing the Atlantic also disposed them to think of their rights in more universal terms. In this, they were influenced by contemporary theorists like Grotius and Locke who developed a new, individualistic idea of natural rights to justify trade, conquest, and settlement by private corporations in the non-European world. Not surprisingly, this emerging idea of natural rights provided Englishmen on the far side of the Atlantic with a set of norms to justify their own imperial ambitions. Rawson's use of natural law to undermine Palmer's claims that the Native Americans had been conquered was one early example of this phenomenon in English America. The settler adoption of natural rights also helped to transform the disparate liberties and privileges of the English common law into

[103] On the connection between Protestantism and English constitutionalism in the eighteenth-century empire, see Jack P. Greene, "Empire and Identity from the Glorious Revolution to the American Revolution," in P.J. Marshall, ed., *The Oxford History of the British Empire*: *The Eighteenth Century* (New York: Oxford University Press, 1998), 208–230.

[104] William Blathwayt saw the danger in such a claim. In his June 25, 1691, comments on a draft of the new Massachusetts charter, he contended that "the Crown asserting the right of soil will much Strengthen and Confirme the power of government." If the Crown did not make such a claim, the colony will argue that "the Soil is the peoples by purchase from the Natives, and that having settled and subdued the same by their own Industry and Charge they have an absolute and Independent right and power of government in themselves," in Robert Earle Moody and Richard Clive Simmons, eds., *The Glorious Revolution in Massachusetts: Selected Documents* (Boston: Colonial Society of Massachusetts, 1988), 556.

a set of fundamental rights that subjects could claim anywhere in the empire.[105]

In the wake of the Glorious Revolution, then, a view of the empire crystallized in English America which was based on the equal rights of all of the king's subjects; the grounding of those rights outside the realm in the efforts and risk taking of the settlers themselves; the confirmation of these rights in charters and other royal grants; the subsequent acquisition of territory from the natives by purchase or conquest; and the transformation of what the settlers saw as a "wilderness" into flourishing civil societies.

If settler elites celebrated the Glorious Revolution as the triumph of English liberty under their new Protestant monarchs, the view from London was very different, as William along with many royal officials maintained that the limits placed on prerogative as a result of the revolution settlement did not extend to the colonies.[106] Despite Increase Mather's best efforts, Massachusetts had to accept a new charter in 1691, with a governor appointed by the Crown, who could veto legislation passed by the General Court, as well as prorogue or dissolve it at will.[107] Massachusetts was also now required to submit its laws for review by the Crown in London. And its courts, though still locally controlled, were subject to the appellate jurisdiction of the Privy Council in London. As well, it was no longer able to limit the franchise to members of the Congregational churches.[108]

[105] On this development, see Hulsebosch, *Constituting Empire*, 28–29, who argues that in "the unsystematic mass of common-law property writs were flowering into rules that could be understood apart from the executive directives in which they originated. Writs were becoming rights."

[106] On this disjuncture, see Bernard Bailyn, *The Origins of American Politics* (New York: Vintage Books, 1967). For the limitation on prerogative in seventeenth-century England, see Howard Nenner, *By Colour of Law: Legal Culture and Constitutional Politics in England, 1660–1689* (Chicago: University of Chicago Press, 1977), 53–57, 61–75.

[107] See Richard Johnson, *Adjustment to Empire: The New England Colonies, 1675–1715* (New Brunswick, NJ: Rutgers University Press, 1981), 183–241

[108] According to R.C. Simmons, the 1691 charter was gradually accepted by both the moderates and the defenders of the old Puritan polity, which led to "the old stress on the preservation of a godly society" giving way to "a more secular and Whiggish emphasis on political and constitutional freedoms." Simmons, "The Massachusetts Charter of 1691," in H.C. Allen and Roger Thompson, eds., *Contrast and Connection: Bicentennial Essays in Anglo-American History* (London: G. Bell & Sons, 1976), 66–87 (quote at 82). On the use of the 1691 charter to defend rights in the eighteenth-century empire, see Theodore B. Lewis, "A Revolutionary Tradition, 1689–1774: 'There Was a Revolution Here as Well as in England'," *New England Quarterly* 46 (1973), 424–438.

Connecticut and Rhode Island, by contrast, were allowed to retain their old charters, but they were subject to far more intrusive scrutiny of their legislation, their courts, and their trade.[109] The rebels in Maryland succeeded in overthrowing the hated proprietor, but he was replaced by a royal governor who had extensive prerogative powers.[110] And in New York, the Crown finally granted settler elites a representative assembly, but their attempt to pass a declaration of rights in 1691 (akin to the 1683 Charter of Liberties) was vetoed by the king on the grounds that it contained too many "great and unreasonable privileges."[111]

To add insult to injury, William reappointed many of the men who had run the empire under the Stuarts. Edmund Andros, exonerated by the Lords of Trade after spending months in a Boston jail, was made royal governor of Virginia in 1692.[112] Francis Nicholson, who had fled New York in ignominy, became governor of Maryland in the early 1690s, and then, after much scheming, replaced the aged Andros in Virginia. He ended his time in royal service as governor of South Carolina, which had become a royal colony following a settler rebellion in 1719 against the proprietors. Moreover, two of the architects of Stuart policy, William Blathwayt and Edward Randolph, remained in the service of the new king, their zeal to undermine colonial autonomy undiminished in the years following the Glorious Revolution.[113]

It would be a mistake, however, to portray the post–Glorious Revolution empire as simply a replay of the ill-fated reign of the Stuarts, for in practice William and his successors tolerated representative government throughout English America, as well as significant local control of the

---

[109] Andrews, *Colonial Period*, IV, 373.

[110] Which was accompanied by Chief Justice Holt ruling in 1690 that the Crown could appoint a governor in Maryland without any judicial proceeding required against the charter. On this, see Charles H. McIlwain, *The American Revolution: A Constitutional Interpretation* (1923; Ithaca, NY: Cornell University Press, 1958), 179. McIlwain claims that Holt's ruling stripped the settlers in Maryland of English rights that their charter – in effect "a provincial constitution" – had granted them.

[111] The 1691 charter is reprinted in Hall et al. eds., *The Glorious Revolution in America*, 121–123. On the repeal of the 1691 Charter, see *CSPC*, 1696–7, #846, 952, 1010, 1012. On royal government, see Charles Worthen Spencer, *Phases of Royal Government in New York, 1691–1719* (Columbus, OH: Fred J. Heer, 1905).

[112] Lustig, *Imperial Executive*, 227–265; Webb, "The Strange Career of Francis Nicholson."

[113] Webb, "William Blathwayt, Imperial Fixer: Muddling through to Empire, 1689–1717," *William and Mary Quarterly* 26 (1969), 374–377.

administration of justice.[114] This concession to the settlers was due in part to the libertarian legacy of the revolution as well as to the unwillingness of the Crown to pay the salaries of royal officials out of its own pocket.[115] In the eighteenth century, these assemblies became the vehicles for more open and responsive elites in English America, who replaced the narrow oligarchies that held sway in the previous century.[116] As well, the bonds of empire were strengthened by an increasingly integrated and prosperous Atlantic world in which goods, ideas and people moved freely, providing both the Crown and the colonists with an incentive to make the empire work.[117]

Nevertheless, it remained the case that there was no agreement on either side of the Atlantic about what rights the settlers could claim in America. As an anonymous Virginian complained in 1701, "No one can tell what is law and what is not in the Plantations."[118] And despite the settler resistance to the Stuarts, in the aftermath of the Glorious Revolution, the Crown continued to claim the right to veto the acts of the assemblies in the royal colonies, to prorogue or dissolve them at will, and to suspend their legislation if it was contrary to the provisions of the royal governor's commissions or instructions (which served as the equivalent of a charter, and could, the law officers of the Crown claimed, be altered by

---

[114] Craven, *Colonies in Transition*, 284–285.

[115] According to J.M. Sosin, this was the empire's Achilles' heel. See the final volume of his three-part history: *English America and Imperial Inconstancy: The Rise of Provincial Autonomy, 1696–1715* (Lincoln: University Press of Nebraska, 1985).

[116] On the expansion of the "governing class" in the colonies, see Richard Dunn, "The Glorious Revolution and America," in Nicholas Canny, ed., *The Oxford History of the British Empire: Volume One, The Origins of Empire* (New York: Oxford University Press, 1998), 462. On the rise of such an elite in Virginia in the aftermath of Bacon's Rebellion, see Bernard Bailyn, "Politics and Social Structure." The classic account of the rise of the assemblies is Jack P. Greene, *The Quest for Power: The Lower Houses of Assembly in the Southern Royal Colonies, 1689–1776* (Chapel Hill: University of North Carolina Press, 1963). For an argument that the eighteenth-century empire, with authority divided between the Crown and the colonial charters, worked well, see Mary Bilder, *The Transatlantic Constitution: Colonial Legal Culture and the Empire* (Cambridge: Harvard University Press, 2004).

[117] To borrow a phrase from Alison Olson, who argues that the existence of transatlantic lobbies in the eighteenth century served to further cement the bonds of empire. See Olson, *Making the Empire Work: London and American Interest Groups, 1690–1790* (Cambridge: Harvard University Press, 1992). On the growth of these transatlantic ties, see Ian K. Steele, *The English Atlantic, 1675–1740: An Exploration of Communication and Community* (New York: Oxford University Press, 1986).

[118] Anonymous, *An Essay upon the Government of the English Plantations in America* (London, 1701), 23.

prerogative). As for the corporate and proprietary colonies, the Crown insisted that they submit their laws to the Privy Council in London for review, allow the decisions of their courts to be overturned on appeal by the Privy Council, and face prosecution in juryless Admiralty courts for violations of the Navigation Acts.

In isolation, the Crown's demands would probably not have amounted to much. However, as a result of William's accession to the throne, English America became embroiled in the first of two long wars against the France of Louis XIV. Viewed from London, colonial conduct in the early phase of this two-decade long struggle left much to be desired. As a result, beginning in the early 1700s, a revamped royal bureaucracy attempted something much more ambitious: A parliamentary bill that would revoke all of the American charters, putting the whole empire under the direct control of the Crown.[119]

---

[119] After the Glorious Revolution, many Whigs were eager to assert parliamentary authority in the empire. William Attwood, who had defended the antiquity of parliaments against the Stuarts in the Exclusion Crisis, saw nothing incongruous in asserting Parliament's authority over both Scotland and Ireland, notwithstanding the fact that neither was represented in it: William Atwood, *The Superiority and Direct Dominion of the Imperial Crown of England over the Crown and Kingdom of Scotland* (London, 1705); *The History and Reasons of the Dependency of Ireland upon the Imperial Crown of the Kingdom of England. Rectifying Mr. Molineux's State of the Case of Ireland's Being Bound by Acts of the Parliament in England* (London, 1698); *An Answer to Mr. Molyneux his Case of Ireland's Being Bound by Acts of Parliament in England, stated; and His Dangerous Notion of Ireland's Being Under no Subordination to the Parliamentary Authority of England Refuted; by Reasoning from His own Arguments and Authorities* (London, 1698).

PART II

EMPIRE

3

Jeremiah Dummer and the Defense of Chartered Government

The collapse of the Dominion of New England left the American colonies in the same fragmented state they had been in prior to the accession of James II. However, the old Stuart dream of a centralized empire persisted among imperial administrators in London in the decades immediately following the Glorious Revolution.[1] In 1696, nearing the end of the first of two long wars with the French, William III replaced the old and by now ineffectual Lords of Trade with a new body, the Board of Trade. Along with the Privy Council, the secretary of state, the Admiralty, and other agencies with responsibility for colonial governance, the Board of Trade then embarked on a series of measures to extend royal authority more effectively across the Atlantic, culminating in a wholesale assault on the charters of the private colonies. The result of these policies was an eighteenth-century empire more integrated than the Stuarts' scattered and highly autonomous plantations, but one whose inhabitants were subject to royal authority in a way that, following the revolution settlement, was no longer the constitutional norm within the realm.[2] The ongoing

[1] According to Charles Andrews, the Board continued the policies of its predecessor, the Lords of Trade. As such, the "Plantation Office had an unbroken and an unchanging policy from 1675–1782." Charles M. Andrews, *The Colonial Period of American History*, Volume IV (New Haven: Yale University Press, 1938), 291. There was continuity in personnel too, as key figures in the new Board of Trade, like William Blathwayt, had been involved with the old Lords of Trade. According to Stephen Webb, at the new Board of Trade Blathwayt continued the "pre-revolutionary program of imperializing colonial government." Webb, "William Blathwayt, Imperial Fixer: Muddling Through to Empire, 1689–1717," *William and Mary Quarterly* 26 (1969), 377.
[2] According to John Murrin: "Within a few years either side of 1700 virtually every institutional feature we associate with the eighteenth-century empire had taken shape."

assertion of prerogative outside the realm ensured that the Restoration-
era debate about colonial rights continued into the eighteenth century,
as settlers periodically clashed with imperial officials over the distribution of political power and legal rights in the empire. Furthermore,
as a consequence of the Board's centralizing policies, a newly empowered Parliament began to exert its sovereignty across the Atlantic with
ultimately revolutionary consequences.

Although these policies affected the entire empire, the private colonies
(both corporate and proprietary) were hit hardest. Indeed, the Board's
nearly two-decade long legal assault on their charters was the most concerted attempt to centralize the empire until the mid-century reforms inau-
gurated by the Earl of Halifax. The most sophisticated settler response
to this policy was the 1721 pamphlet of Jeremiah Dummer – the agent
for all of the New England colonies and a quintessentially Atlantic figure,
involved in imperial politics in both Old and New England.

The establishment of a new Board of Trade in 1696 was one part of a
larger policy of imperial centralization designed to secure the commercial
and military interests of the empire in the midst of two cycles of warfare against the French.[3] The idea behind this policy was that increasing
the Crown's executive and judicial authority in the American colonies
would foster better military coordination as well as greater obedience
to the acts of trade, which in turn would enrich the empire and help it
to defeat the French in North America.[4] Several factors contributed to
the Crown's renewed desire to centralize the empire in the latter half of
the 1690s. The first was a concern that following the dissolution of the
Dominion of New England, the empire had – with the exception of the
new Massachusetts charter in 1691 and the conversion of Maryland into
a royal colony – returned to the status quo ante, divided up into multiple

Murrin, "Political Development," in Jack P. Greene and J.R. Pole, eds., *Colonial British America: Essays in the New History of the Early Modern Era* (Baltimore: Johns Hopkins University Press, 1984), 432. On the continuing force of the prerogative in British America after the Glorious Revolution, see Bernard Bailyn, *The Origins of American Politics* (New York: Vintage Books, 1967), 50–105.

[3] On William's imperial policies, see G.H. Guttridge, *The Colonial Policy of William III in America and the West Indies* (London: Cambridge University Press, 1922).

[4] On the conflict between the French and English in North America between 1689 and 1713, see Howard Peckham, *The Colonial Wars, 1689–1762* (Chicago: University of Chicago Press, 1964), 25–76. Peckham paints a picture of relatively effective intracolonial military cooperation combined with a lack of serious English assistance. In Peckham's view, English officials preferred that the settlers foot the bill for their own defense.

jurisdictions, each with a large degree of autonomy.[5] More immediately, in the mid-1690s there was a crisis in England's trade and finances brought on by the cost of war against Louis XIV.[6] Imperial officials believed that the colonies were exacerbating this situation by failing to unite militarily against the French on the northern border, by violating the acts of trade and navigation, and by harboring pirates.[7] According to Charles Andrews, "all of these circumstances were demanding the inauguration of a more drastic and efficient colonial program," which would "centralize, as had never been done successfully before, authority in the hands of the crown."[8]

The crucial year was 1696. As the first period of warfare against the French was coming to a close, Parliament passed a new Navigation Act.[9] The creation of the colonies' old nemesis, Edward Randolph, that tireless proselytizer for imperial integration, the new act did not alter the details of previous trade legislation, but it did contain several provisions designed to exert greater control over the American colonies.[10] It required all the colonial governors to take an oath to uphold the act, with removal from office as the penalty for malfeasance. It also required the governors in the private colonies to be approved by the king; and it empowered customs officials to enter and search houses and warehouses. In addition, the act declared that any colonial law "repugnant to this present act" shall be "illegal, null and void," setting a precedent for parliamentary interference with colonial legislation. Finally, it allowed for transgressions of the act to be tried in juryless vice-admiralty courts.[11] According to Michael Hall,

---

[5] According to Ian Steele, "there was a pressing need to restore authority in the colonies after the disturbances of 1688–9." Ian K. Steele, *Politics of Colonial Policy: The Board of Trade in Colonial Administration* (Oxford: Clarendon Press, 1968), 9–10.

[6] Steele, *Politics of Colonial Policy*, 10 and Andrews, *Colonial Period*, IV, 275–285, discuss the concerns of English merchants, including the loss of shipping and inadequate protection from the Admiralty.

[7] J.M. Sosin, *English America and the Revolution of 1688: Royal Administration and the Structure of Provincial Government* (Lincoln: University of Nebraska Press, 1982), 231.

[8] Andrews, *Colonial Period*, IV, 375.

[9] Reprinted in Jack P. Greene, ed., *Settlements to Society: A Documentary History of Colonial America* (New York: W.W. Norton, 1975), 210–215.

[10] Randolph was the surveyor general of the customs in America. See Michael Hall, *Edward Randolph and the American Colonies, 1676–1703* (Chapel Hill: University of North Carolina Press, 1960). On the origins of the act, see Hall, "The House of Lords, Edward Randolph, and the Navigation Act of 1696," *William and Mary Quarterly* 14 (1957), 494–515; and Sosin, *English America and the Revolution of 1688*, 232–233.

[11] Helen Crump, *Colonial Admiralty Jurisdiction in the Seventeenth Century* (London: Longmans, 1931).

this provision of the act "struck so closely at the government of the colonies as to alter fundamentally their relationship to the Crown."[12]

In the spring of 1696, following the passage of the Navigation Act, the Crown authorized the creation of the Board of Trade.[13] From its inception until 1768 when a secretary of state for the colonies was created, the Board of Trade was the only agency solely responsible for the administration of the empire.[14] In his commission, William III authorized the Board to promote "the Trade of our Kingdome," including that of the "Plantations in America and elsewhere." In order to do so, the Board's members were to inform themselves "of the present condition of Our respective Plantations," paying particular attention to "the Administration of Government and Justice in those places," as well as "the Commerce thereof," and then to report to the king or the Privy Council. As part of this task, the Board's members were also empowered to examine (and propose changes to) the instructions for the royal governors, suggest "proper persons to be Governors or Deputy Governors," and "examin into and weigh" the "Acts of the Assemblies of the Plantations," setting down their "Usefulness or Mischief thereof to Our Crown." As well, the Board had authority "To heare complaints of Oppressions and maladministrations, in our Plantations."[15]

[12] On the constitutional significance of the Navigation Act, see Hall, "The House of Lords," 502. According to Hall, the private colonies had previously had no royal courts. As a result, the vice-admiralty courts constituted an intrusive new legal system. Randolph had also wanted royally appointed attorney generals in the private colonies, but the proprietors resisted and the Board of Trade (in December 1696) accepted a compromise: there would be colonial attorney generals, but the king would have the right to appoint Crown advocates to try cases before the admiralty courts. On this, see Hall, "Edward Randolph," 506–508.

[13] William III created the new Board of Trade in part to ward off an attempt by disaffected parliamentarians to establish their own trade council. On the constitutional question raised by Parliament's attempt to assume executive authority, see R.M. Lees, "Parliament and the Proposal for a Council of Trade, 1695–6," *English Historical Review* 54 (1939), 38–66.

[14] The fullest study is still Ian Steele, *The Politics of Colonial Policy*. But see also Olive Dickerson, *American Colonial Government, 1696–1765: A Study of the British Board of Trade in Its Relation to the American Colonies, Political, Industrial and Administrative* (Cleveland: Arthur H. Clarke, 1912); Andrews, *The Colonial Period*, IV, 272–317; and Mary P. Clark, "The Board of Trade at Work," *American Historical Review* 17 (1911), 17–43. For the later years of the Board, see Arthur H. Basye, *The Lords Commissioners of Trade and Plantations, 1748–1782* (New Haven: Yale University Press, 1925).

[15] The Board's commission is reprinted in Greene, ed., *Settlements to Society*, 218–220. Steele, *Politics of Colonial Policy*, 29–30, describes the Board's rather limited powers of colonial patronage, though it did acquire (and defended against the secretary of state) the right to nominate colonial councillors (87–88).

The new Board's centralizing mandate was part of a shift in English thinking about empire in the late seventeenth and early eighteenth centuries in which trade was increasingly seen as crucial to the building of a strong metropolitan state and the projection of imperial power.[16] This policy of "commercial reason of state" entailed the constitutional subordination of colonies and plantations to the imperial goals of the metropole.[17] In order to promote the trade of the plantations, then, the Board consistently supported measures to reduce the political-constitutional autonomy of the American colonies.[18] Over the next two decades, the Board pursued these policies without being much influenced by the vagaries of party politics in the England of William and Anne.[19] According to W.A. Speck, the Board's core members "were not party zealots" and were in fact split between Tories and Whigs.[20] Although the new Board

[16] On the rise of the "fiscal-military" state, see John Brewer, *The Sinews of Power: War, Money and the English State, 1688–1788* (New York: Alfred A. Knopf, 1989); and Laurence Stone, ed., *An Imperial State at War: Britain from 1689 to 1815* (London: Routledge, 1994).

[17] See David Armitage, *The Ideological Origins of the British Empire* (Cambridge: Cambridge University Press, 2000), 146–169 (quote at 168). According to Armitage, such figures as John Cary, John Locke, and Charles Davenant agreed that "a flourishing empire" required "firm regulation of the colonies" (167). In addition, Armitage argues that the period after 1688 was marked by an "English Parliamentary mercantilism" (158). See also the important essays by Istvan Hont, *Jealousy of Trade: International Competition and the Nation-State in Historical Perspective* (Cambridge: Belknap Press, 2005).

[18] According to Charles Andrews, "no part of the English executive was more consistently mercantilist ... or more conservative in defense of the king's prerogative in America than this advisory body." Andrews, *Colonial Period*, IV, 291. Dickerson contends that the Board consistently sought to "preserve the dependence of the colonies on the home government by retaining control of the executive and the judiciary and by making the colonies conform to one administrative type of government. Closely connected with these schemes were its plans for protecting the colonies by the creation of a central military government in America, which could be used to maintain order and protect the frontiers." Dickerson, *American Colonial Government*, 180.

[19] At least until 1707 when several members, including Blathwayt, were dismissed. Steele, *Politics of Colonial Policy*, 132, sees 1707 as marking the end of the Board as a relatively apolitical body whose members could serve Whig and Tory ministries alike.

[20] Speck, "The International and Imperial Context," in Greene and Pole, eds., *Colonial British America*, 402. For example, John Locke and William Blathwayt had, despite their domestic political differences, broadly similar attitudes to colonial governance and commercial regulations. According to Steele, "Even a Whig philosopher and a Tory civil servant had relatively few disputes about the status and function of the colonies." *Politics of Colonial Policy*, 25. Indeed, on the question of colonial rights, Locke was unsympathetic to William Molyneux's critique of Parliament's attempt to impose trade legislation on Ireland, despite the fact that Molyneux drew extensively on the *Second Treatise*. On this, see Laslett, "John Locke, the Great Recoinage, and the Origins of the Board of Trade, 1695–1698," *William and Mary Quarterly* 14 (1957), 396. As well, the Board's secretary during its initial attempts to resume the charters (down to 1707) was the radical

contained many able and experienced men, it was a weaker body than its predecessor. Crucially, unlike the old Lords of Trade, who were Privy Councilors, the new Board's members lacked any executive authority.[21] Instead, its main function was administrative – to gather data on the state of trade and to advise the Privy Council and Parliament about the governance of the empire. The Board was also subordinate to the secretary of state for the Southern Department.[22] As such, it usually reported to the king in council through the secretary of state.[23] In addition, the king and Privy Council heard all colonial appeals and appointed the governors.

However, the Board's formal weaknesses were less important in practice.[24] Since the Board was the sole body with responsibility for the colonies during most of the eighteenth century, it alone coordinated the often scattered efforts of other departments and agencies, functioning as a clearing house for information on the empire, and acquiring an expertise that commanded respect. The Board also influenced imperial policy via its relationship with the Crown's lawyers "whose rulings on colonial

---

Whig William Popple. On Popple, see Caroline Robbins, "Absolute Liberty: The Life and Thought of William Popple," in Robbins, ed., *Absolute Liberty: A Selection from the Articles and Papers of Caroline Robbins* (Hamden, CT: Shoe String Press, 1982), 3–30. In contrast, Stephen Webb contends that Blathwayt was only able to proceed with resumption after Locke retired, the latter having a whiggish reluctance to limit colonial rights. See Webb, "Imperial Fixer," 398. However Webb erroneously assumes that metropolitan Whigs like Locke were in favor of colonial equality. By contrast, Alison Olson argues that it was the Tories who opposed resumption because they perceived it as an attack on vested rights. See Olson, "William Penn, Parliament and Proprietary Government," *William and Mary Quarterly* 18 (1961), 176–195.

[21] According to Charles Andrews, "they had no right to order, punish, or execute, except that in the pursuit of information they could summon men before them and take evidence under oath." Andrews, IV, *Colonial Period*, 291. Steele argues that a more effective way to govern the colonies would have been to establish another committee of the Privy Council having both executive and advisory functions; however, the Privy Council would not relinquish its "executive power in colonial affairs to a body which was not composed exclusively of Privy Councillors." Steele, *Politics of Colonial Policy*, 17–18.

[22] On the working relationship between the Board and the secretary of state, see Andrews, *Colonial Period*, IV, 309–314.

[23] Steele, *Politics of Colonial Policy*, 29. See also Louise P. Kellogg, *The American Colonial Charter: A Study of English Administration in Relation Thereto, Chiefly after 1688* (Washington, DC: Government Printing Office, 1904), 225. But Andrews, *Colonial Period*, IV, 312–313, says that the Board could report to the secretary of state directly if the secretary had requested information, though the norm was to report to the Privy Council, copying the secretary of state.

[24] While it did not have "executive, financial, or penalizing powers, it was able to exercise both directly and indirectly, through its reports and recommendations to the crown and in its correspondence with the colonial governors, a far-reaching and often determinative influence." Andrews, *Colonial Period*, IV, 290–291.

legislation determined in most cases the final decision of the king in council on the confirmation or disallowance of colonial laws."[25]

In its first four years of operation, the Board orchestrated a series of policies designed to increase the Crown's authority in the colonies. In the fall of 1697, taking advantage of the king's appointment of Lord Bellomont as governor of Massachusetts, New York, and New Hampshire, the Board successfully urged that he also be given control over the militias of Connecticut, Rhode Island, and East and West Jersey, thus creating (until Bellomont's death in 1701) a captain general for the northern colonies.[26] The Board was also behind other measures to increase royal authority in the colonies. It supported the commissioner of customs in implementing the vice-admiralty courts[27]; and, with the aid of Parliament, began to tackle the problem of piracy in the empire.[28] As well, in 1697 the Board wrote to the private colonies requiring them to send copies of their laws to England for review, thus giving the Crown the ability to disallow colonial laws via the Privy Council.[29] The Board also supported the Crown's right to hear appeals from colonial courts.[30] And it began a policy that lasted into the era of the American Revolution of trying to make the governors' instructions in the royal colonies binding on the assemblies.[31] Although it wanted to increase the Crown's executive and

---

[25] Andrews, *Colonial Period*, IV, 296. Andrews claims that the Board of Trade or the Privy Council "rarely, if ever" reversed "the opinion of the standing counsel" (300). See also Dickerson, *American Colonial Government*, 24.

[26] See Steele, *Politics of Colonial Policy*, 36–37; and Sosin, *English America and the Revolution of 1688*, 229–230, 238–239. Andrews, *Colonial Period*, IV, 377–378, notes that the Board's report calling for "one Military Head or Captain General" drew on a legal opinion that in emergencies the Crown could appoint a governor general with civil and military powers. According to Andrews, the Board wanted Governor Phips's successor to "become civil head of all New England and New York and general of all the forces from New Hampshire to the Jerseys," but Connecticut resisted on the grounds that its charter gave it a right to elect its governor.

[27] Steele, *Politics of Colonial Policy*, 46–47, describes the Board support for Randolph's vice-admiralty courts; and Sosin, *English America and the Revolution of 1688*, 241–242, describes the efforts of Randolph and the commissioners of customs to erect courts of admiralty over the opposition of the proprietors.

[28] For the attack on piracy, see Steele, *Politics of Colonial Policy*, 56 (Captain Kidd was the catalyst). For the Board's inclusion of a provision that the private colonies could lose their charters if they violated the act, see Leo F. Stock, ed., *Proceedings and Debates of the British Parliament Respecting North America*, Volume II (Washington, DC: Carnegie Institute, 1927), 369.

[29] Kellogg, *The American Colonial Charter*, 274.

[30] See Joseph H. Smith, *Appeals to the Privy Council from the American Plantations* (New York: Columbia University Press, 1950), 140–141.

[31] Dickerson, *American Colonial Government*, 115–116, 200–201, 204.

judicial authority in the empire, the Board did not attempt to govern the American colonies without assemblies as James II had done in the 1680s. Instead, following the Glorious Revolution, political debate in the empire centered on how far royal (and later parliamentary) authority could be extended before it violated what the settlers considered to be their rights as Englishmen outside the realm.

From the outset, the private colonies challenged this post-1696 extension of royal authority. Connecticut and Rhode Island opposed the Board's attempt to have one captain general for all of the northern colonies on the grounds that it violated their charter right to control their own militias.[32] The vice-admiralty courts engendered opposition too.[33] In 1699, Massachusetts passed a judiciary act designed to circumvent the vice-admiralty courts by claiming that all prosecutions in the colony required jury trials at common law.[34] The Crown's claim to review and disallow colonial laws was also the subject of much dispute. Although Connecticut consented to have its laws reviewed by the Board, it insisted that the sole power of repealing them lay with the colony's assembly. As the colony informed the Board, "it is the privilege of Englishmen and the natural right of all men who have not forfeited it to be governed by laws made by their own consent."[35]

The private colonies also resisted the Crown's claim to be the highest court of appeal for their laws and judicial decisions. For example, Governor Treat of Connecticut held that the charter of 1662 gave no right to appeal from colonial courts to the king in council.[36] As well, despite the requirement that all of the private colonies send their laws

[32] Ibid., 209–211. The policy of putting the militias of the chartered colonies under the command of neighboring royal governors was begun under Phips and Fletcher in the early to mid-1690s during the war, continued under Bellomont who became "military governor of all colonies north and east of Pennsylvania," and lasted through the terms of Dudley, Cornbury, and Hunter. See ibid., 212, on the Board's (late 1690s) conclusion that there could be no effective military command without the powers of government in the private colonies being returned to the Crown.

[33] J.W. Fortescue, ed., *Calendar of State Papers, Colonial Series: America and West Indies, 1697–1698*, Volume 25 (London: Her Majesty's Stationery Office, 1905), # 240, 241, 252, 256 (hereafter, CSPC). See also Sosin, *English America and the Revolution of 1688*, 241; and Kellogg, *American Colonial Charter*, 264–265.

[34] Provincial officials had allowed these cases to be tried by common law and when the jury decisions went against the customs officers they denied their right to appeal to England. See Dickerson, *American Colonial Government*, 236, for the Board's objections.

[35] Quoted in Kellogg, *American Colonial Charter*, 274–275.

[36] Kellogg, *American Colonial Charter*, 275; and Sosin, *English America and the Revolution of 1688*, 248.

to the Privy Council for review, many continued to be governed by laws long since repealed by the Crown. In order to get around the need for royal review of their legislation, they also passed laws for a brief period, ensuring they expired before the Privy Council could vet them. In addition, the private colonies resisted having their governors take an oath to uphold the acts of trade, or post a bond to guarantee that they would enforce the provisions of the act.[37]

By 1700 the private colonies' resistance to these individual reforms led the Board to contemplate a more radical step: revoking their charters and making the whole empire subject to the direct government of the Crown.[38] To do this, the Board could obtain either a writ of *quo warranto* or of *scire facias*,[39] as the Stuarts had done in the 1680s; however, these writs required legal proof that the chartered governments had violated the terms of their royal grant.[40] Alternately, the Board could purchase the rights of the proprietors. Or, it could take the unprecedented step of asking Parliament to pass a bill annulling the charters.

The Crown had used the courts to revoke colonial charters before – in Virginia in the 1620s, in New England in the 1680s, and in Maryland and Pennsylvania in the early 1690s. And, as late as 1699, the Board had contemplated a *quo warranto* against Rhode Island for its opposition to the Navigation Acts.[41] However, legal proceedings would allow the private colonies to argue that their defiance of imperial regulations was justified on the basis of the authority granted to them in their charters. And, given

---

[37] This was a complaint made frequently by Edward Randolph upon returning from his transatlantic journeys. On Rhode Island's attempts to avoid sending its laws to England, see Mary Bilder, *The Transatlantic Constitution: Colonial Legal Culture and the Empire* (Cambridge: Harvard University Press, 2004), 51–69.

[38] Steele, *Politics of Colonial Policy*, 62–65. Steele claims that the reports of Nicholson, Bellomont, Randolph, and Quary about illegal practices in the private colonies influenced the Board's decision.

[39] According to Blackstone: "When the Crown hath unadvisedly granted any thing by letters patent, which ought not to be granted, or where the patentee hath done an act that amounts to a forfeiture of the grant, the remedy to repeal the patent is by writ of *scire facias* in chancery." William Blackstone, *Commentaries on the Laws of England*, Volume III, ed. Stanley N. Katz (1765; Chicago: University of Chicago Press, 1979), 260.

[40] According to Elizabeth Mancke, the legal basis for royal oversight of charters was the idea that "civil governance of British subjects, regardless of their location in the world, originated with and remained tied to the Crown" (though over time the locus of sovereignty became the Crown-in-Parliament). See Elizabeth Mancke, "Chartered Enterprises and the Evolution of the British Atlantic World," in Elizabeth Mancke and Carole Shammas, eds., *The Creation of the British Atlantic World* (Baltimore: Johns Hopkins University Press, 2005), 253.

[41] Steele, *Politics of Colonial Policy*, 66.

the contested nature of the empire's constitutional structure, there was a chance that they could win their case at law.[42]

This was a chance the Board of Trade was unwilling to take. As a result of the time and uncertainty of a legal suit, it turned to Parliament and tried to get both the Lords Commons to pass a bill revoking the charters of all of the private colonies.[43] Two years earlier, in a 1698 report on combating piracy in the empire, the Board had warned, "If the Proprieties and Charter Governments do not speedily comply with what is required of them ... we see no means to prevent a continuance of this mischief without calling in the further assistance of Parliament."[44] In March 1700, the Board of Trade used the occasion of a report to Parliament on its work since 1696 to urge it to pass a resumption bill.[45] Parliament was prorogued two weeks after the Board delivered its report, but when it met the next year the Board was ready.[46] On March 29, 1701, William Blathwayt, the leading advocate of resumption, presented the essence of the Board's complaints about the private colonies to the Commons as part of a broader report on the nation's trade.[47] In it, the Board charged that the private colonies "have no-ways answered the chief design, for which such large tracts of land, and such privileges and immunities were granted by the Crown." In particular, they had failed to conform to the "several acts of Parliament for regulating trade and navigation." According to Blathwayt, they had also "assumed to themselves a power to make laws, contrary and repugnant to the Laws of England," thereby

[42] For example, in 1714 the attorney general reporting to the House of Lords on the legality of the colonies issuing paper money bills, claimed that the powers granted in charters could not be limited by the Crown, though they could by Parliament. On this opinion, see Kellogg, *American Colonial Charter*, 275. For a collection of important legal cases on the rights granted to the settlers under charters, see George Chalmers, *The Opinions of Eminent Lawyers on Various Points of English Jurisprudence, Chiefly Concerning Colonies, Fisheries, and Commerce*, 2 volumes (1814; New York: Burt Franklin, 1971).
[43] Steele, *Politics of Colonial Policy*, 68, argues that the Board turned to Parliament as it wished to avoid the use of the prerogative in post-Jacobean England. As well, the Board's successful collaboration with Parliament on the piracy act provided a model for the Resumption Bills. Andrews, *Colonial Period*, IV, 379, notes that after 1688 "a legislative act was becoming recognized as likely to be obeyed more willingly than an order in council."
[44] *CSPC*, Volume 16 (1697–1698), #265, 121.
[45] Steele, *Politics of Colonial Policy*, 68. For the report, see Stock, ed., *Proceedings and Debates*, II, 364–369.
[46] Steele, *Politics of Colonial Policy*, 68–69.
[47] Stock, ed., *Proceedings and Debates*, II, 382–389 (the charges against the private colonies are on 385–386). Blathwayt's report repeated charges also made in the Board's March 26 report to the King. See Colonial Office Papers (hereafter, C.O.) 5/1289, pp. 12–17 (National Archives, United Kingdom).

further prejudicing "our trade." Indeed, some of them had even "refused to send hither such laws as they have there enacted; and others having sent them, but very imperfectly." Furthermore, the private colonies had "denied appeals to his Majesty in Council," thereby depriving "the inhabitant of those colonies" of the "benefits enjoyed in the Plantations under your Majesties immediate Government." Blathwayt also informed the Commons that the private colonies continued to harbor pirates and to trade illegally with foreigners. As well, they manufactured goods "proper to England" (such as woolens), while exempting their inhabitants from "duties and customs" to which "the other colonies are subject." Finally, they had not made provisions for their own defense, failing to "provide themselves with arms and ammunition" or "a regular militia." According to Blathwayt, the solution to these pressing problems was that the charters "intitling them to a right of government, should be reassumed to the crown, and these colonies put into the same state and dependency as those of his Majesty's other plantations, without further prejudice to every man's particular property and freehold." The report concluded by saying that this would be best "effected" by "the Legislative power of this Kingdome."[48]

After hearing this report, the Commons asked the Board to provide it with a more detailed account of trade and governance in all of the colonies.[49] On April 24, the Board delivered its findings but focused its ire on the private colonies, urging once again that Parliament revoke the charters.[50] On the same day the Board was making its representations before the Commons, the Lords had a bill before it to reunite the private colonies with the Crown, claiming that "no power in the plantation should be independent of England."[51] This bill would not have annulled the charters entirely, but it would have removed clauses "which stated or implied rights to govern the people of the colonies."[52] The Board

---

[48] Stock, ed., *Proceedings and Debates*, II, 386. The report to the King on March 26 noted the urgency of this matter: "They do not in generall take any due care for their own defense and security against an enemy ... in case they should be attacked, which is every day more and more to be apprehended, considering how French power encreases in those parts." C.O. 5/1289, pp. 12–17.

[49] Stock, ed., *Proceedings and Debates*, II, 389–90.

[50] Ibid., 392–401.

[51] Quoted in Steele, *Politics of Colonial Policy*, 70 (in the words of one of the Board's solicitors). Sosin, *English America and the Revolution of 1688*, 252, says that Jeremiah Basse and Joseph Dudley spoke to the Lords in favor of resumption; and Lord Baltimore and some of the Carolina proprietors who sat in the Lords made the case against.

[52] Steele, *Politics of Colonial Policy*, 70.

supported this measure, but the Lords' Resumption Bill failed to get to the committee of the whole, even though a vote on June 11, 1701, of thirty-three to twenty-seven was in favor.[53]

The failure of the 1701 Resumption bill caused the Board to "redouble its efforts in preparation for the next session."[54] On January 24, 1702, in the shadow of renewed war with the French, the Board reported to the secretary of state (the Earl of Manchester) on the poor state of imperial defenses in North America. According to the Board, the proprietary colonies were to blame, having failed to comply "with what has been demanded of them, or may be thought necessary for the common safety of your Majesty's subjects during a war." As it had the previous year, the Board advocated revoking the charters: "the mutual defence of the Plantations," it argued, requires that they be "put into the same state of dependency as those of your majesty's other Plantations"[55] In February, William Blathwayt once again used the occasion of a report on the nation's trade to make the case for annulling the charters.[56] At the same time, the Lords asked for and received a report from the Board which urged further action against the proprietary colonies in particular.[57] As evidence of the Board's determination to push ahead with resumption, they rejected a compromise proposal from the secretary of state, granting the Crown extensive authority in the private colonies, but allowing "the Civil authority and Administration" to "rest where they are, as they do in those Corporations in England where the King has his Governours."[58]

The death of William III in March 1702 prevented the Board from reintroducing the same bill that had narrowly failed in the Lords the

---

[53] Ibid., 70–71. On the role of Ashurst, Connecticut's agent, in defeating the Lords' Bill, see Stock, ed., *Proceedings and Debates*, II, 418; and Kellogg, *American Colonial Charter*, 288.

[54] Steele, *Politics of Colonial Policy*, 76.

[55] C.O. 324/8, pp. 37–63.

[56] Steele, *Politics of Colonial Policy*, 76–77; Stock, ed., *Proceedings and Debates*, II, 427–442.

[57] Presented by Lord Stamford on February 16, 1702. See Steele, *Politics of Colonial Policy*, 77.

[58] C.O. 5 1289, pp. 381–382 (February 17, 1702). Steele, *Politics of Colonial Policy*, 77, contends that the Board rejected the proposal as they suspected it came from William Penn and was designed to ward off a total loss of the charter (in his letter to the Board, Manchester explicitly referred to Pennsylvania as one of the colonies it would affect). It was also likely that the Board feared that this proposal was too much like the situation in Massachusetts post-1691, where a royal governor with executive authority had hardly proved a panacea. Kellogg, *American Colonial Charter*, 291, thinks that if the Board had accepted this more moderate proposal it might have passed.

year before.[59] However, Queen Anne's accession did not change the Board's desire to reduce the autonomy of the private colonies. For the next few years, Lord Cornbury and Joseph Dudley, the newly appointed governors of, respectively, New York and Massachusetts, kept up a constant stream of complaints against them over their opposition to the admiralty courts and their refusal to cede control of their militias or contribute to the defense of the northern frontier against the French.[60] And, as we will see in the next chapter, in order to undermine Connecticut's charter, Dudley supported the Mohegan Indians' legal challenge to that colony's land policy.[61] As well, the Board successfully purchased the rights of the proprietors of the Jerseys in August 1701, uniting them into one royal colony.[62] And in 1702, Robert Quary, the inveterate enemy of William Penn, replaced Randolph as surveyor general, and continued to press the Board about the malfeasance of the private colonies, causing Penn to consider selling his proprietary rights to the Crown.[63] Finally, as a result of the lobbying of Cornbury and Dudley, the Board made another attempt on the charters in 1706. It sent a long report to the queen on January 10, 1706, laying out the now familiar list of complaints against the private colonies.[64] This led to the introduction of a resumption bill in the Commons on February 23; however, like the Board's efforts in 1701 and 1702, it failed, unable to pass on second reading.[65]

---

[59] For a copy of an Act (dated April 8, 1702) to make the charters "utterly void of none effect," see C.O. 5/1289, pp. 426–430.

[60] Kellogg, *American Colonial Charter*, 298–299. For Dudley's moves against Rhode Island, see Edward M. Cook, "Enjoying and Defending Charter Privileges: Corporate Status and Political Culture in Eighteenth-Century Rhode Island," in Robert Olwell and Alan Tully, eds., *Cultures and Identities in Colonial British America* (Baltimore: Johns Hopkins University Press, 2006), 255; and Smith, *Appeals to the Privy Council*, 150–151.

[61] Kellogg, *American Colonial Charter*, 302–303.

[62] Ibid., 240.

[63] Ibid., 242, 293. However, Steele claims that in June 1702, once the new ministry was established, which included new peers on the Board, Penn found that he had more influence with the ministry and was able to counter Quary's testimony before the Board, get him replaced as judge of the vice-admiralty courts, and have his own choice as deputy-governor approved. On Penn's lobbying, see also Gary Nash, *Quakers and Politics, 1681–1726* (1968; Boston: Northeastern University Press, 1993), 217–224.

[64] *CSPC*, Volume 23 (1706–08), #18. [C.O. 5/1291, pp. 238–253].

[65] It lost by fifty votes to thirty-four. Stock, ed., *Proceedings and Debates*, III, 114, 118. On the Bill's fate in Parliament, see J.M. Sosin, *English America and Imperial Inconstancy: The Rise of Provincial Autonomy, 1696–1715* (Lincoln: University of Nebraska Press, 1985), 28. Andrews, *Colonial Period*, IV, 385, attributes its failure to concerns about executive authority due to the place bill debates.

Two years after the failure of the 1706 Resumption Bill, a young New Englander by the name of Jeremiah Dummer (1681–1739) came to London. A graduate of Harvard, Dummer had also studied at the universities of Leyden and Utrecht, becoming, in 1703, the first Harvard graduate to receive a doctorate in philosophy.[66] Due to accusations of religious unorthodoxy, Dummer was unable to get a job at his alma mater or at the pulpit in Boston. Stymied at home, he sought his fortune in the imperial capital, first in commerce and then in politics. Dummer invested in the South Sea company and associated with a wide range of people, including the Whig Bishop Burnet and the Tory Bolingbroke.[67] His contacts in imperial circles led to Massachusetts appointing him as their agent in London in 1710. Connecticut followed suit in 1712.[68] In addition to his involvement in imperial politics, Dummer was also central to the efforts to found a new college in Connecticut, procuring money and a large number of books from the school's eventual namesake, Elihu Yale.[69]

In his capacity as agent for the New England colonies, Dummer urged imperial officials in London to make a major assault on New France. He even wrote a legal memorandum supporting the English Crown's claim to the lands surrounding the Saint Lawrence.[70] And when the assault on Quebec in 1711 turned out to be a disaster, Dummer wrote a pamphlet defending the New England colonies' role in the enterprise. According to Dummer, "the Reduction of Canada" was "a Truly Great and Noble Design,"[71] justified by the access it would allow the English to the lucrative fur trade; and more important, by the safety it would provide the English colonies. As Dummer put it, the queen's object in authorizing the invasion was "to make Her good Subjects in that Part of the World easy and happy, which they can never be whilst the French are Masters

---

[66] There is no biography of this important transatlantic figure. But see Sheldon S. Cohen, "The Diary of Jeremiah Dummer," *William and Mary Quarterly* 24 (1967), 397–422; the essay on Dummer in Clifford K. Shipton, ed., *Sibley's Harvard Graduates: Biographical Sketches of Those Who Attended Harvard College in the Classes 1690–1700* (Boston: Massachusetts Historical Society, 1933–64), IV, 454–468; and Charles L. Sanford, *The Days of Jeremiah Dummer, Colonial Agent* (Ph.D. diss., Harvard University, 1952).

[67] Cohen, "The Diary," 405, 419.

[68] Ibid., 415; Shipton, ed., *Sibley's Harvard Graduates*, 457.

[69] Shipton, ed., *Sibley's Harvard Graduates*, 462–463.

[70] Reprinted in *Collections of the Massachusetts Historical Society*, Volume I, third series (Boston: Phelps and Farnham, 1825) 231–234.

[71] *A Letter to a Noble Lord, concerning the Late Expedition to Canada* (London, 1712), 11. On this failed attempt to take Quebec and the earlier successful attack on Port Royal, see W.T. Morgan, "Some Attempts at Imperial Co-Operation during the Reign of Queen Anne," *Transactions of the Royal Historical Society* 10 (1927), 171–194. Morgan claims that Dummer was consulted by the secretary of state as to whether Port Royal or Quebec should be attacked (190); and describes the "zeal" of Dummer in urging more attacks (194).

of Canada."[72] After all, the location of New France, stretching as it does down the "Back-Side" of the English colonies from New Hampshire to Virginia, gave it "an Opportunity to invade all the British Colonies when-ever they please."[73] By contrast, a victory over the French would allow the English to annex "a large Country extending above a thousand Leagues towards the Mississippi," territory that was both rich in furs and a potential place to export "our Woollen Manufactures and other European Commodities" to both the new settlers and "the adjacent Indians."[74] Dummer also warned that Newfoundland and the Hudson Bay forts were still at risk, which was especially problematic as the former is a "great Nursery for Sailors," as well as being home to a lucrative "Fishery."[75] Furthermore, Dummer argued, defeating the French was necessary in order to weaken their native allies who butcher "the People" of the colonies "in cold Blood." In Dummer's view, the threat posed by the French was the result of the "Assistance of the Indian Nations, who are blindly bigoted to their Superstitions, and therefore entirely devoted to their Interest."[76] As Dummer reminded his readers, the Indians have an "insuperable Advantage" over the English colonists as they "live in a Vast Wilderness, and are therefore themselves inaccessible, but can fall upon the English Towns whenever they please." The only way, then, to disarm the Indians and remove the threat to the English empire was "by extirpating the French."[77]

The end of the war with the French in 1713 led to a renewed desire among imperial officials in London to resume the charters.[78] Dummer was alive to this threat, sending word to Connecticut in August 1713 that "a design was on foot for a new modeling of the plantations."[79] In August 1715, the new Whig ministry introduced a Resumption Bill in Parliament, occasioned by a plea from some South Carolinians about the failure of the proprietors to defend them in the wake of an attack by the Yamasee Indians.[80] The bill was defeated after concerted lobbying from

---

[72] *A Letter*, 5.
[73] Ibid., 5.
[74] Ibid., 10.
[75] Ibid., 10–11.
[76] Ibid., 8.
[77] Ibid., 9.
[78] Andrews, *Colonial Period*, IV, 386.
[79] Quoted in ibid., IV, 386.
[80] For the petition of the agent and merchants trading to South Carolina, see Stock, ed., *Proceedings and Debates*, III, 359–360. For background, see Sosin, *Imperial Inconstancy*, 105–106.

the colonial agents, including Dummer, as well as Lord Carteret, one of the principal Carolina proprietors and secretary of state for the Southern Department.[81] In order to aid in the lobbying efforts, Dummer wrote a lengthy pamphlet entitled *A Defence of the New-England Charters*.[82] Although the final version was likely written sometime in 1715, it was not published until 1721, in the middle of an ongoing dispute between the Massachusetts assembly and Governor Shute over his salary, a dispute that had required Dummer's intervention on the colony's behalf and which, he feared, might spark another attempt on the charters.[83] In the *Defence*, Dummer built on the arguments that the New England colonists had made against the incursions of royal authority from the Restoration on, constructing a wide-ranging case for a free, equal, commercial empire, able to defeat the French and allow all Englishmen to benefit from the conquest. Not only was the *Defence* representative of the official position of the New England colonies (whose employee Dummer was) but it was also the most comprehensive case for settler rights in the empire to date.

Dummer began the *Defence* by claiming that he was representing all of the New England colonies, that is, Massachusetts, Connecticut, Rhode Island, as well as "the Province of New Hampshire," which "never had

---

[81] Andrews, *Colonial Period*, 387; Sosin, *Imperial Inconstancy*, 28–29; and Kellogg, *American Colonial Charter*, 310. On Dummer's role in defeating the bill, see James J. Burns, *The Colonial Agents of New England* (Washington, DC: Catholic University of America, 1935), 92; and Stock, ed., *Proceedings and Debates*, III, 362–363. For Dummer's arguments.

James Henretta criticizes the Board during this period, noting that it turned down the chance to purchase Penn's charter in 1713, put up little opposition to the return of Maryland in 1715 to the Calverts following their conversion to Anglicanism, and didn't respond when the settlers in Carolina petitioned for royal government following the Yamasee War in 1715. Henretta also blames the influence of Dummer's dedicatee, Lord Carteret, who was secretary of state for the Southern Department as well as a proprietor of Carolina. Henretta, *"Salutary Neglect": Colonial Administration under the Duke of Newcastle* (Princeton: Princeton University Press, 1972), 57–58.

[82] (London: W. Wilkins, 1721). There was also a Boston edition in 1721. It was republished in the 1740s, and, significantly, also in the 1760s.

[83] Andrews, *Colonial Period*, IV, 386–387, claims that Dummer wrote it in 1712–1713, and added to it afterward. On the reason for its printing in 1721, see Kellogg, *American Colonial Charter*, 311. Ironically, Dummer was dismissed by the Massachusetts House the day before the pamphlet appeared over his opposition to the charges that Elisha Cooke had sent to London against Governor Shute. On this, see Shipton, ed., *Sibley's Harvard Graduates*, 461; and Perry Miller, *The New England Mind: From Colony to Province* (1953; Boston: Beacon Press, 1961), 388. See also, Burns, *Colonial Agents*, 3–4. According to Burns, Dummer's crime was to inform the assembly that London was supporting Shute in the battle over the governor's salary.

any peculiar Privileges, but is under the immediate and absolute Direction of the Crown."[84] He noted that their charters conferred on "the Patentees" a "Title to the Soil," as well as "ample Privileges for the well ordering and governing the respective Plantations." The latter category was extensive, including the right "to call General Assemblies; to make Laws, so as they were not repugnant to the Laws of England; to assess the Freemen; to constitute all Civil Officers; to array the Inhabitants in a warlike Posture, and use the Martial Law, when Occasion requir'd."[85] For Dummer, then, property rights as well extensive powers of self-government were at stake in the debates about resumption.

Dummer offered several arguments in defense of chartered government. Central to his case was the claim that the charters had been granted in exchange for the settlers' service to the Crown. Indeed, like Rawson, he argued that the American charters constituted a contract between Crown and settlers. In return for chartered rights, the colonists increased "the Nation's Commerce" and enlarged "her Dominions," doing so at great expense and risk in "a waste Wilderness," following a dangerous voyage "over the Atlantick." Upon arrival in America, the settlers had encountered "the Extremity of the Seasons" and "a War with the Savages," and many of "the first Planters soon found their Graves."[86] As such, "to strip the Country of their Charters" would "deprive the Patentees of the only Recompence they were to have for all their Toils and Fatigues." After all, Dummer asked, "Could they have imagin'd, could they have foreseen that their Privileges were such transitory things, as to last no longer than their Work should be done, and their settlements completed, they had never engag'd in so hazardous and difficult an Enterprize."[87] Indeed, according to Dummer, because of the circumstances under which they were granted, "the American Charters are of a higher Nature and stand on a better Foot than the Corporations in England." Since, Dummer held, they "were given as Pramiums for Services to be perform'd," they should "be consider'd as Grants upon a valuable Consideration; which adds Weight and Strength to the Title." By contrast, domestic charters "were granted upon Improvements already made, and therefore were Acts of meer Grace and Favour in the Crown."[88]

---

[84] *A Defence*, 1–2.
[85] Ibid., 2.
[86] Ibid., 8.
[87] Ibid., 15.
[88] Ibid., 7. Although he drew on Coke for his discussion of charters, Dummer's claim about the greater legal force of the American charters is (as far as I know) original to him.

Dummer's defense of the American charters, then, turned on the fact that the king's patent was worthless until the settlers expended the requisite blood and treasure. It was this that gave them a greater immunity from the prerogative than the domestic charters. Underlining the differences between domestic and colonial charters, Dummer contended that without the American charters "those Countries which have since added so much to the Wealth and Greatness of the Crown, might have been a barren Wilderness to this Day; or what is worse, and more probable, might have been fill'd with French Colonies, whereby France would have reign'd sole Mistress of North America."[89]

As with the debates over the Dominion of New England, the question of who owned the land in America was central to the debate about charter rights. Imperial officials who argued for resumption – for example, Blathwayt in the 1701 report to Parliament – claimed that they intended to strip the authority to govern from the proprietors or corporations, but would leave the settlers' property rights intact. According to Dummer, however, "The Crown, strictly speaking, neither did nor could grant the Soil, having no Right in it self" [sic]. Although "Queen Elisabeth gave out the first patent to Sir Walter Rawleigh in 1584," she had neither a claim based on "a Right of Inheritance, because those Countries did not descend to her from her Ancestors," nor one based on "Conquest, because she neither conquer'd, nor attempted to conquer them." After all, Dummer reasoned, "it would be pretty hard to conceive how a Conquest, where there was no preceeding Injury or Provocation, could create a Right." Furthermore, any claim based on "the prior Discovery or Pre-occupancy, as the Civilians speak" was invalid "because that gives a Right only to derelict Lands, which these were not, being full of Inhabitants, who undoubtedly had as good a Title to their own Country, as the Europeans have to theirs." Dummer also denied any Crown claim to the New World based "upon the Foot that we were Christians, and they Heathen," adding that "Rome it self, as imperious as she is, never carry'd her Pretences to this Height: For though some of her Doctors have taught absurdly enough, that Dominion is founded in Grace, none of 'em ever said that Property was."[90]

If not Crown grant, then what legitimated the English presence in America? For Dummer, such a right could only be "deriv'd from the native Lords of the Soil, and that is what the honest New-England Planters rely

[89] Ibid., 15–16.
[90] Ibid., 13–14.

on having purchas'd it with their Money." As a result, "Indian Title" was "the only fair and just" basis for property rights in America. By contrast, Dummer argued, a royal grant could convey nothing more "than a bare Right of Preemption."[91] By basing his case for the charters on purchase from the Indians, Dummer gave them a foundation independent of the Crown. But purchase was not the end of the story for Dummer. As he pointed out, even "admitting that the Crown granted the Soil," "how little must the Value of such Grants amount, all Circumstances consider'd?" After all, "The Patentees were not only oblig'd to travel Thousand Leagues beyond the Sea, but to purchase their Grants over again of the Natives, before they could be put into Possession." More important, "The Land it self was of a tough savage Nature, incumbr'd with unprofitable Woods, and of no Use till by vast Labour and Expence subdu'd and cultivated." Indeed, Dummer argued, the land the New Englanders settled on was "but bare Creation to the first Planters, and their Labour like the Beginning of the World."[92]

Like Rawson, Dummer combined this argument about the uncultivated nature of the New World with his claim that the settlers had purchased the land from the Native Americans. As a result, he was able to concede that they were the original owners, while also contending that the land "was of little Use to the Natives" as "They liv'd chiefly on Fish and Fowl, and Hunting, because they would be at the Pains to clear and break up the Ground."[93] In other words, it was the settlers' labor and not just purchase (let alone a royal grant) that grounded their claim to the soil of America. The implication of Dummer's argument was that even though the Indians had possessed an original title, all the value in the land had been added by the cultivation of the English purchasers. Indeed, their labor had been solely responsible for creating civilized polities out of what was in effect a state of nature. Consequently, the New Englanders possessed a superior title to that of either the Crown or the natives. In addition, the settlers' initial title to the land by purchase and

---

[91] Ibid., 13–14. Dummer added in an aside that "Indian title" was "decry'd and undervalu'd here" (i.e., in England).

[92] Ibid., 15. Dummer also noted that "the Colony made a Law to forbid any Person's purchasing Land of the Indians without the Approbation of the General Court, to prevent their being over-reached or ill us'd in their private Bargains: and some Land, lying very convenient for them, was by another Law made inalienable, and never to be purchased out of their Hands, than which nothing could more demonstrate the Colony's Care and Concern for the Natives." Ibid., 21.

[93] *A Defence*, 20.

improvement was further strengthened by prescription or long usage. As Dummer reminded his readers, the New England charters had already been in existence for what "the Civilians call Immemorial, one of them being above Fourscore Years standing."[94]

One of the arguments made by imperial officials against the American charters was that the patentees had failed to defend their inhabitants against the French and Indians. Dummer adamantly denied this accusation, insisting that the New England colonies had borne the brunt of the fighting against the French, even defending another province (New York), which had failed to defend itself. Indeed, not only had they kept their "Militia well train'd and disciplin'd,"[95] Dummer insisted, but they had also tried "to enlarge the British empire by undertaking several chargeable expeditions against the strongest French settlements in America."[96] In these expeditions, they had lost "robust young Men, such as no Country can spare, and least of all New Settlements, where Labour is the dearest thing in the World, because nothing so much wanted as Hands."[97] Such was their commitment to the empire that they had even sent men to aid Jamaica and the Carolinas.[98] Reflecting on their efforts, Dummer thought it "astonishing" that "these little Governments" were able to "perform such great Things."[99]

Dummer's vigorous defense of the military achievements of the chartered governments led him back to a discussion of the Native Americans. In Dummer's view, not only had the New England settlers fairly purchased the land from the Indians but they had also treated them well, eschewing "the barbarous Methods practis'd by the Spaniards on the Southern Continent," and instead seeking "to gain the Natives by strict Justice in their Dealings with them."[100] Furthermore, they had tried "to bring them from their wild manner of Life to the civil and polite Customs of Europe," building "Indian Towns," prescribing to them "Forms of Government," and making them "acquainted with the Gospel."[101] Despite the solicitousness

[94] Ibid., 76.
[95] Ibid., 27.
[96] Ibid., 29.
[97] Ibid., 30.
[98] Ibid., 33–34.
[99] Ibid., 29.
[100] Ibid., 19–20. Dummer felt obliged to defend the New Englanders' treatment of the Indians in order to "wipe off an unworthy Aspersion" that that they had "encroach'd on their Land by Degrees, till they fraudulently and forcibly turn'd them out of all."
[101] Ibid., 21.

of the New England colonies for native rights, however, "nothing could oblige the Indians to Peace and Friendship." Rather, they were "alarm'd with strong Jealousies of the growing Power of the English, and therefore began a War to extirpate them, before they had too well establish'd themselves." In the face of this threat, Dummer noted, the New England colonies, though young and facing famine, "made no Application to the Crown for Assistance," but instead created a confederacy for mutual defense. The New Englanders pursued the Indians and made them sue for peace, though such "was the perfidious Nature of the American Savages" that they "renew'd the Hostilities" and after several years and "many terrible Slaughters" were finally "subdu'd and utterly extirpated."[102]

In addition to neglecting the defense of their inhabitants, the private colonies had also been accused of exercising arbitrary power, principally by denying appeals to the Crown, and by not dispensing equal justice in their courts.[103] Dummer, however, argued that chartered government was far more conducive to liberty than royal rule. "For in the Governments, where there are Charters ... all Officers Civil and Military are elected by the People, and that annually; than which Constitution nothing under Heaven can be a stronger Barrier against arbitrary Rule." Charter governments, then, "far from retrenching the Liberty of the Subject, have improv'd it in some important Articles."[104]

To underline this point, Dummer recalled for his readers the experience of the New England colonies under the Dominion of New England, when they "lost their Charters" and were subjected to royal government without even the benefit of local assemblies. With the charters gone, the governor and his council – "Men of desparate Fortunes" – made "what Laws, and levy'd what Taxes they pleas'd on the people."[105] Subjects who protested were jailed and denied the writ of habeas corpus.[106] The officers of the dominion had also undermined the subject's property rights. In Dummer's recounting, "Their Title to their Lands was absolutely deny'd by the Governour and his Creatures." As a result, those "who had fairly purchas'd their Lands, and held them in quiet Possession for above Fifty

---

[102] Ibid., 23.

[103] Dummer wasn't specific about what the charge of arbitrary government consisted of. On this point and the previous one (on defense) he is referring to allegations contained in the Parliamentary Bill of 1715. There is no extant copy of this bill.

[104] Ibid., 36.

[105] Ibid., 39–40.

[106] Dummer is referring here to the protests of John Wise and the other residents of Ipswich described in Chapter 2.

Years, were now obliged to accept new Deeds from the Governour …
otherwise they would be seized for the Crown."[107]

For Dummer, however, the worst aspect of the dominion was its denial
that Englishmen outside the realm were entitled to the same rights and
liberties as those at home. As he put it in an emotive passage which
recalled the travails of the New England colonies under the Dominion
of New England:

And to compleat the Oppression, when they upon their Tryal claim'd the
Privileges of Englishmen, they were scoffingly told, Those things would not follow them to the Ends of the Earth. Unnatural Insult; must the brave Adventurer,
who with the Hazard of his Life and Fortune, seeks out new Climates to inrich
his Mother Country, be deny'd those common Rights, which his Countrymen
enjoy at Home in Ease and Indolence? Is he to be made miserable, and a Slave by
his own Acquisitions? Is the Labourer alone worthy of his Hire, and shall they
only reap, who have neither sow'd nor planted? Monstrous Absurdity! Horrid
inverted order![108]

In Dummer's view, the lesson of this dark episode in New England's past
was that "Charters are not the Causes of Arbitrary Government, but
indeed strong Works rais'd against it." And, crucially, once charters were
revoked, "Oppression rushes in like a Tide, and bears down every thing
before it."[109]

Having dealt with several of the charges made against the private colonies before Parliament, Dummer turned to consider "such Arguments
as I have met with in Conversation from Persons in the Ministry." The
first of these concerned the acts of trade and navigation, whose purpose, Dummer's interlocutors maintained, was to make the "Plantations
beneficial to Great-Britain." According to Dummer, the ministry complained that these acts "are disregarded in the Charter Governments;
and that this Evil cannot be effectually cur'd, but by a Resumption of the
Charters."[110] In response, Dummer first denied any widespread wrong-
doing on the part of the New England colonies, adding that in both
the royal colonies and England obedience to the acts of trade was not
perfect either. Indeed, he believed that the New England colonies were
more sinned against than sinning, given that under the 1696 navigation
act, they were now subject to the jurisdiction of juryless vice-admiralty

---

[107] *A Defence*, 41.
[108] Ibid., 40–41.
[109] Ibid., 42.
[110] Ibid., 42–43.

courts. Although he didn't challenge the legitimacy of London's restrictions on colonial trade, Dummer did make a case for limiting their impact on the chartered colonies by asserting the right of the colonial courts to "issue Prohibitions to the Court of Vice-Admiralty" on the grounds that they violated English rights. Dummer's reasoning was as follows: "It has bin ever boasted as the peculiar Privilege of an Englishman, & the grand Security of his Property to be try'd by his Country and the Laws of the Land." By contrast, the "Admiralty Method of Tryal deprives him of both, as it puts his Estate in the Disposal of a single Person, and makes the Civil Law the Rule of Judgment." For Dummer, the vice-admiralty courts had also not been "consented to" by any subject "or his Representative for him." For Dummer, such "A Jurisdiction," which did not observe English legal norms, should be limited to "what is really transacted on the High Seas."[111]

Dummer next addressed a long-standing grievance against "the American Charters" which he claimed was also circulating in the ministry: "That their Governments have made Laws repugnant to the Laws of Great-Britain contrary to the Powers given them, and thereby have incurr'd a Forfeiture." As we have already seen, the relationship between English and colonial law was one of the unresolved issues in the imperial constitution.[112] Dummer offered several arguments against the metropolitan understanding of the nonrepugnancy provisions in the colonial charters. He first argued that English laws bound the American colonies only if they were specifically named in them. For example, "if a Law was pass'd here has it's Force restrain'd to England, Wales, and the town of Berwick on the Tweed, no Law in the Plantations can properly be said to repugn it"[113] Second, Dummer defended the colonies' right to make local laws at variance with English ones. If they could not do this, he argued, "these Governments must make no Laws at all, which no Body will say, who knows that a Right of Legislature is the most essential Part of their Charters." Dummer also defended colonial legislative autonomy on the grounds that "Every Country has Circumstances peculiar to it self in Respect of its Soil, Situation, Inhabitants, and Commerce." In Dummer's view, "the Laws of England are calculated for their own Meridian, and

---

[111] Ibid., 50–51. However, Dummer conceded that admiralty jurisdiction was not entirely foreign as it was based on the civil law which in turn was derived from the law of nations.

[112] On this issue, see Mary Bilder, *The Transatlantic Constitution*, 31–51.

[113] *A Defence*, 57.

are many of them no ways suitable to the Plantations, and others not possible to be executed there."[114]

To this defense of legal pluralism in the empire, Dummer added a final
argument about the relationship of colonial to English law. In his view,
conformity to English law meant adhering to the principles of English
constitutionalism and not to the edicts of Crown or Parliament. As
such, by insisting on nonrepugnancy, the Crown was ensuring "that the
Patentees should not under color of their particular Charters presume
to make any Laws inconsistent with the Great Charter and other Laws
of England, by which the Lives, Liberties and Properties of Englishmen
are secur'd."[115] In so doing, Dummer argued, the Crown's intent was "to
provide for all it's Subjects, that they might not be oppressed by arbitrary
Power, but in whatever distant Part of the World they were settled, being
still Subjects, they should have the Usage of Englishmen, be protected
by the same mild Laws, & enjoy the same happy Government, as if they
continued within the Realm." By this standard, Dummer contended, the
chartered colonies which he was defending had acted properly, "having in
no respect impair'd, but many Ways improv'd the Liberty of the Subject."
In his view, then, the royal mandate that colonial laws be not repugnant
to those in England was not intended to subject the colonies to specific
English statutes, nor to allow colonial laws to be repealed for not con-
forming to English law; rather, its purpose was to secure the colonies
against arbitrary government by extending royal protection for their
rights across the Atlantic.

Having dealt with the main charges against the charters, Dummer
laid out a vision of the benefits that had accrued to England when it
protected settler rights. On this score, he noted, other empires had les-
sons to teach the British. For example, Holland "did not entertain these
Jealousies of their Subjects in India," and as a result have "drawn such
immense Riches from that Part of the World."[116] So certain was Dummer
of this point that he was even prepared to claim that "London has risen
out of the Plantations, and not out of England." It was to the colonies,
Dummer contended, that England owed its "vast Fleets of Merchant
Ships, and consequently the Increase of our Seamen and Improvement of
our Navigation." Furthermore, it was the colonies' commodities that had
allowed England to increase its balance of trade "and to make the Figure

[114] Ibid., 55–56.
[115] Ibid., 59.
[116] Ibid., 62.

we do at present, and have done for near a Century past, in all Parts of the commercial World."[117] For Dummer, these commercial ties underpinned the mutual dependence of the constituent parts of the empire. Indeed, he went so far as to claim that "the Body Politick" of the empire was analogous to a "Natural Body," arguing that "a Finger can't ake, but the Whole feels it, so in the other the remotest Plantation can't decay, but the Nation must suffer with it."[118] Given this mutual dependence, Dummer contended that even if the charter colonies had "forfeited their Charters back to the Crown," it "was not the true Interest of the Crown to resume them."[119]

Finally, Dummer insisted that the prosperity generated by this empire of liberty was vital if the English were to match the French in North America. This was a pressing issue for Dummer as he foresaw that "in a few Years" the "British Empire in America" will need to be protected "against the formidable Settlement of Loisiana." If not checked, Dummer warned, the French will "have a Chain of Towns on the Back of all our Colonies from the Borders of Cape-Breton to the westernmost Part of Carolina."[120]

Dummer also contrasted the benefits of chartered government with what he saw as the ill effects of rule by royally appointed governors. Dummer contended that royal government would harm the empire's prosperity, as governors have an interest in "private Gain, which being too often acquir'd by discouraging and oppressing Trade, is not only an Interest distinct from that of the Crown, but extreamly prejudicial to it." As Dummer reminded his readers, "The Trade of a young Plantation is like a tender Plant, & should be cherish'd with the fondest Care." By contrast, royal rule would bring with it "the rough Hand of Oppression," ensuring that colonial trade "will soon die." If the governors' rapacity endangered colonial commerce, what political principles were conducive to flourishing colonies? According to Dummer, "The proper Nursery for this Plant is a free Government, where the Laws are sacred, Property secure, & Justice not only impartially, but expeditiously distributed."[121]

In addition to its impact on trade, Dummer feared that royal government would result in arbitrary rule in the colonies. After all, even the ancient Romans, the most virtuous people in the world, had suffered abuses from

[117] Ibid., 64.
[118] Ibid., 64.
[119] Ibid., 67.
[120] Ibid., 65–66.
[121] Ibid., 68.

their proconsuls. And, Dummer noted, this was also the case in the contemporary French and Spanish empires. For Dummer, then, the lesson was clear: To "vacate the Charters" would give the governors "greater Power to oppress," as they would then have "the intire Legislative and Executive Powers" in their hands, along with command of the militia, and the right to appoint "Judges, Justices, Sherifs and other Civil Officers." As well, Dummer warned, "in those Plantations which never had any Charters, but are immediately dependent on the Crown," there were equity courts in which "the Governour is always Chancellor, and for the most part Chief Justice." The governors' control of these courts, Dummer was certain, "puts the Estates, Lives, and Liberties of the Inhabitants, saving the Liberty of Appeal at Home, intirely in his Disposal."[122]

The Crown and its agencies were not the only threat to the private colonies. As we have seen, between 1701 and 1715 the Board of Trade made four attempts to enlist Parliament's help in resuming their charters. Although both the Lords and Commons ultimately failed to support resumption, the Board's attempts to involve Parliament in colonial governance created a constitutional conundrum that was to ultimately tear the empire apart. Dummer's attempt to grapple with the complicated question of the relationship between parliamentary authority and settler rights gives us a sense of just how intractable this issue would become later in the eighteenth century.

Dummer first questioned the legality of removing the charters by "an Act of Parliament." It would, he argued, be akin to a bill of attainder, "an extrajudicial Proceeding," rarely used in England and only then for "flagrant Crimes." Dummer pointed out that proceeding in such a manner would "deprive the Colonies of their Charters, without giving them a fair Tryal or any previous Notice."[123] For Dummer, therefore, vacating the charters by Parliamentary Bill would be "a Severity without a Precedent." Considering that the people of New England were already suffering "the Misfortune of being a Thousand Leagues distant from their Sovereign," Dummer felt it would be unjust that they should also "UNSUMMON'D, UNHEARD, IN ONE DAY be depriv'd of all their valuable Privileges, which they and their Fathers have enjoy'd for near a Hundred Years."[124]

---

[122] Ibid., 73.
[123] Ibid., 74.
[124] Ibid., 76.

Although Dummer acknowledged the sovereignty of Parliament post-1688, noting that "the Legislative Power is absolute and unaccountable, and King, Lords, and Commons may do what they please," he insisted that "the question is not about Power, but Right: And shall not the Supream Judicature of all the Nation do right?" Indeed, he argued, what "Parliament can't do justly, they can't do at all"[125] For Dummer, this normative limit on Parliament's legislative authority also applied to its judicial capacity. Although as a "High Court" it was "not strictly confin'd to the Forms of the Courts below, yet it is not doubted but the great Fountain of Law & Justice will have some regard, if not to all the Rules made for inferior Judicatures, yet to such as are essential to Justice." For example, Dummer noted, any parliamentary bill that concerned property rights in Ireland must "lie 30 Days" so that those affected had time to respond. Why not, Dummer asked, allow an equivalent time for "Subjects in America"? After all, "they are no less the Subjects of the Crown ... and Liberty is at least as valuable as Property."[126]

Dummer also argued that unlike subjects in England the settlers were not represented in Parliament. Although he agreed that "it is indeed very reasonable that all publick Affairs be subject to the Determination of the publick wisdom," he held this maxim only obtained in situations where "every Body is suppos'd to be present in the Representative Body of the Whole." Yet, as Dummer pointed out, "the Provinces to be censur'd and depriv'd have no Representative in Parliament, and consequently must be consider'd as absent Persons suffering unheard."[127] Despite these admonitions, however, Dummer was careful to exhibit the deference due to Parliament in a British world that saw it as the guarantor of liberty following the Glorious Revolution. As a result, he conceded that "if such an Act should pass" the charter colonies "would receive the News with the lowest Submission: So great is their Loyalty to the King, and so profound their Regard for the Resolutions of a British Parliament, the wisest and most august Assembly in the World."[128]

For Dummer, then, the New England colonies had flourished despite Indian wars, the pervasive threat from the French, and the need to create civilized polities in a harsh wilderness. All of these accomplishments, he held, would not have been possible without the charters. As a result,

[125] Ibid.
[126] Ibid., 78.
[127] Ibid., 77–78.
[128] Ibid., 75.

"These Governments" "reckon the Loss of their Privileges a greater Calamity, than if their Houses were all in Flames at once." After all, houses can be rebuilt, but "Liberty once lost, is lost for ever."[129] Furthermore, Britain had benefited from chartered government every bit as much as the American colonies. Indeed, for Dummer, so great were the benefits of charters that it would be better for "the Crown and Nation to incorporate those Governments which have no Charter rather than Disfranchize those that have."[130]

Dummer's comprehensive defense of the New England charters allows us to reconstruct the settlers' vision of their place in the empire at the end of a long period of warfare and following two attempts at imperial centralization. Central to this vision was the common law, and in particular the idea that English rights applied equally to the inhabitants of the colonies across the Atlantic. Enshrined in charters, these rights entailed extensive powers of self-government under the Crown. But the principles of English constitutionalism did not exhaust the intellectual content of Dummer's *Defence*, for in it we see again the distinctively settler amalgam of legal-political ideas displayed in the late seventeenth-century arguments against the legitimacy of the Dominion of New England. This strand of thought saw colonization as inherently contractual, grounding charter rights in the efforts, the labor, and the risk taking of the settlers themselves, and not on a royal grant. Complementing the idea of English law as a birthright that traversed the Atlantic, this labor-based justification of colonial rights made the settlers themselves the primary source of legal and political authority in the empire.

This settler theory also entailed an understanding of the empire as a loose confederation of autonomous polities under the Crown. In Dummer's vision of the empire, the corporate colonies possessed considerable legislative, judicial, and executive authority. And the Crown, far from exerting its prerogative to undermine colonial rights, stood as the ultimate guarantor of them. Such an empire, Dummer argued, was not only conducive to liberty; it was also better suited to matching the territorial ambitions of the French. Dummer's defense of colonial autonomy, however, was not an incipient call for independence, let alone republicanism. Rather, he openly embraced an imperial future, but one in

---

[129] Ibid., 79.
[130] Ibid., 73. Earlier Dummer had used the first person plural to refer to England or Britain, but on the last page of the pamphlet he claims that he is a native of one of the New England colonies.

which the settlers were the agents of empire and not its subalterns; and in which the fruits of conquest would be shared by all Britons.

As in the late seventeenth-century debates about the legitimacy of resistance to the Stuarts, the rights of Native Americans were inextricably linked to those of the settlers. By positing an indigenous right to the soil, Dummer gave the settlers a claim to territory in America independent of the Crown. However, as we saw with Rawson's similar argument, this defense of native rights was primarily instrumental. It was further weakened by Dummer's argument that the natives were not cultivating the soil properly; lacked towns, religion, and government; and despite the generous treatment they had received from the colonists, were unremittingly hostile and warlike, especially when allied to the French. For Dummer, then, the natives might have been the original owners of the soil, but their lack of civility vitiated their rights. As a result, it was the settlers – via purchase and labor – who had the superior claim to the New World.

The publication of Dummer's pamphlet in 1721 marked the end of the Board's efforts to annul the charters of the private colonies. It had been unable to interest the other imperial agencies or Parliament in resumption. Furthermore, its plans had been checked by powerful colonial interests, including the lobbying of agents like Dummer. Despite intense pressure, Pennsylvania's charter had survived, though only at the cost of major concessions by the proprietor to the assembly.[131] And Lord Baltimore, upon converting to Anglicanism, was given Maryland back in 1715, which, as we will see in a subsequent chapter, led to a constitutional crisis in the 1720s. Moreover, the colonial assemblies survived the vicissitudes of war and revolution, and were able to begin the long process of accruing power and authority from royal governors, largely by denying them a permanent salary and the funding necessary for a civil list. The growing power of the assemblies in the eighteenth century would make it increasingly difficult to assert royal authority in the empire.[132]

Despite the failure of resumption, the Board's attempts at centralization had not been entirely in vain.[133] By the early eighteenth century,

---

[131] See Nash, *Quakers and Politics*, 231–232.

[132] According to Sosin, this lack of funding for the executive was the weak link in the empire's chain of authority. See Sosin, *English America and the Revolution of 1688*, 261–262. The classic account of the rise of the assemblies is Jack P. Greene, *The Quest for Power: The Lower Houses of Assembly in the Southern Royal Colonies, 1689–1776* (Chapel Hill: University of North Carolina Press, 1963).

[133] For a list of the Board's achievements, see Dickerson, *American Colonial Government*, 31.

admiralty courts had been set up in most of the British American colonies. In addition, "the right to take appeals from all colonies, whether protected by charters or not, was asserted as a prerogative of the Crown, and was successfully maintained against all resistance."[134] As well, the Navigation Acts were accepted by the colonists in principle, if not always obeyed in practice. And the Board succeeded – albeit by purchase and not resumption – in reducing the number of proprietary colonies to two on the mainland.[135] As a result, the empire in 1715 was a far more cohesive entity than it had been in 1675 when the Lords of Trade had first attempted to undermine colonial autonomy. But if the empire had become more integrated by the early eighteenth century, there was still a range of unsettled constitutional questions concerning the Crown's prerogative powers outside the realm that periodically disturbed its calm. In addition, the attempt to resume the charters highlighted an ultimately fatal flaw in the empire's political structure: the uncertain relationship between parliamentary sovereignty and colonial rights. Indeed, what is striking about the resumption debates is how early this issue came up and how widespread the consensus was among imperial officials in London – Whig and Tory alike – that Parliament had the authority to revoke the charters and restructure the internal constitutions of the colonies, a view that was not universally shared on the other side of the Atlantic.[136]

The delicate and uncertain balance between local and central authority that emerged in the crucial years following the Glorious Revolution shaped the politics of the empire down to the era of the American Revolution. In the next chapter, we turn to one example of that uncertain balance – the long dispute between the Crown, the colony of Connecticut, and the Mohegan Indians over property and autonomy in the empire.

[134] Kellogg, *American Colonial Charter*, 272.

[135] Andrews, *Colonial Period*, IV, 402.

[136] On Parliament's role in the eighteenth-century empire, see the suggestive essay by Ian K. Steele, "The British Parliament and the Atlantic Colonies to 1760: New Approaches to Enduring Questions," in Philip Lawson, ed., *Parliament and the Atlantic Empire* (Edinburgh: Edinburgh University Press, 1995), 29–46.

4

John Bulkley and the Mohegans

In the early 1700s, as Connecticut and the other private colonies were combating the Board of Trade's attempts to revoke their charters, a long-running dispute between the colony and the Mohegans, a once-powerful Native American tribe, came to the attention of royal officials. The dispute centered on a large tract of land (approximately 20,000 acres) in southeastern Connecticut, which, the Mohegans claimed, the colony had reserved for them in the late seventeenth century. Concerned that the colony had violated its agreements, the Mohegans, aided by powerful colonists with a pecuniary interest in this tract of land, appealed to the Privy Council. As a result of this appeal, what had been a narrow dispute over land became part of a larger conflict between the Crown, the colony, and the tribe over property and autonomy in the empire.[1]

[1] There is no book-length history of the Mohegan case. I have relied on the following: J.W. De Forest, *History of the Indians of Connecticut from the Earliest Known Period to 1850* (Hartford: W.J. Hammersley, 1852); J.H. Smith, *Appeals to the Privy Council from the American Plantations* (New York: Columbia University Press, 1950), 422–442; Michael Leroy Oberg, *Uncas: First of the Mohegans* (Ithaca: Cornell University Press, 2003); Richard Bushman, *From Puritan to Yankee: Character and the Social Order in Connecticut, 1690–1765* (Cambridge: Harvard University Press, 1967); David Conroy, "The Defense of Indian Land Rights: William Bollan and the Mohegan Case in 1743," *Proceedings of the American Antiquarian Society* 103 (1993), 395–424; and Amy E. Den Ouden, *Beyond Conquest: Native Peoples and the Struggle for History in New England* (Lincoln: University of Nebraska Press, 2005), 91–141. See also my "Claiming the New World: Empire, Law, and Indigenous Rights in the Mohegan Case, 1704–1743," *Law and History Review* (forthcoming, 2011). Paul Grant-Costa's 2008 Yale dissertation, *The Last Indian War in New England: The Mohegan Indians v. The Governour and Company of the Colony of Connecticut, 1703—1774*, was not available to scholars while I was researching and writing this chapter. Most of the recent interest in the case has come from lawyers and legal historians who are primarily concerned with native rights in the modern

The origins of the conflict between the Mohegans and Connecticut lie in the complicated aftermath of the Pequot War in the late 1630s.[2] Uncas, sachem of the Mohegans, used the warfare between the English and the Pequots to undermine the powerful Pequot sachem, Sassacus.[3] According to Michael Oberg, "With the Pequots under attack by the Narragansetts and the Dutch, and ensnared in an increasingly tangled web of controversy with the English, Uncas saw alliance with the newcomers as a means to increase his power and that of the Mohegans."[4] In his bid to usurp Sassacus, Uncas allied with Major John Mason, an English soldier of fortune who prosecuted the war against the Pequots with particular brutality, torching their fort at Mystic and killing hundreds of men, women, and children.[5] Through Uncas's strategic alliance with the English, the Mohegans were able to replace the defeated Pequots and create a new Mohegan confederation that included Pequots and former Pequot tributaries.

The relationship between Uncas and Mason was central to the ensuing conflict over the Mohegans' land. As a result of his help in defeating the Pequots in the 1630s, Uncas came to control a large amount of territory east of the Connecticut River. Facing encroachment from the Dutch, the French, and their Native American allies, as well as the other English colonies, it was in the best interest of Connecticut "to help Uncas consolidate lands and Indian peoples under his rule. Uncas obliged by claiming a

commonwealth countries and the United States. See, for example, the superb article by Mark D. Walters, "*Mohegan Indians v. Connecticut* (1705–1773) and the Legal Status of Aboriginal Customary Laws and Government in British North America," *Osgoode Hall Law Journal* 33 (1995), 785–829. The major documents for the case can be found in an eighteenth-century collection: *The Governor and Company of Connecticut and Mohegan Indians, by their Guardians. Certified Copy of the Book of Proceedings before the Commissioners of Review,* 1743 (London: W. and J. Richardson, 1769).

2 According to Richard Johnson, the Mohegans were "born of intra-tribal factionalism ... they elected from the first to consolidate their separate identity through alliance with the whites, as when they promptly joined in the coalition already forming against their own Pequot kinsmen and shared the spoils of victory." Johnson, "The Search for a Usable Indian: An Aspect of the Defense of Colonial New England," *Journal of American History* 64 (1977), 646.

3 For an account of his life, see Oberg, *Uncas.* For the conflict between Uncas and Sassacus as an example of precontact native factionalism, see P. Richard Metcalf, "Who Should Rule at Home? Native American Politics and Indian-White Relations," *Journal of American History* 61 (1974), 651–665.

4 Oberg, *Uncas,* 50.

5 For the relationship between Uncas and Mason, see Wendy B. St. Jean, "Inventing Guardianship: The Mohegan Indians and their Protectors," *New England Quarterly* 72 (1999), 362–387.

huge tract of land that constituted most of southeastern Connecticut and a small part of what is today Rhode Island."[6]

In the decades following the defeat of the Pequots, Uncas's control over this territory was tenuous at best. Massachusetts, as well as the Narragansetts under their Sachem, Miantonomo, made claims to the former Pequot lands, as did factions within Connecticut opposed to Mason's alliance with Uncas.[7] In 1659, beset by the Narragansetts and by expanding English settlements, Uncas deeded the Mohegans' territories to Mason, who now would have to consent to any alienation of the tribe's land.[8] By doing so, Uncas intended to protect the tribe from being cheated by unscrupulous colonists and to use Mason's connections in the councils of Connecticut to shield them militarily from their tribal enemies.[9] For his part, Mason hoped to profit from his privileged access to the lands the tribe controlled east of the Connecticut River.[10] In 1660, hoping to aid the colony in securing a royal charter, Mason transferred control over this land to the colonial government on the condition that when they opened it for settlement, sufficient land would be set aside for the Mohegans.[11] In 1662, helped in part by the land deeded to the colony by Mason, Connecticut received a royal charter, the boundaries of which included the Mohegans' territory.

In 1671, the year before he died, Mason entailed a tract of land eight miles by four miles – or approximately 20,000 acres – lying between the towns of New London and Norwich for the exclusive use of the tribe.[12]

---

[6] Ibid., 368. For a detailed description of these lands, see Bushman, *From Puritan to Yankee*, 85.

[7] On Connecticut's territorial ambitions, see Richard Dunn, "John Winthrop, Jr., and the Narragansett Country," *William and Mary Quarterly* 13 (1956), 68–86.

[8] Oberg, *Uncas*, 155.

[9] Ibid., 154. Wendy St. Jean compares the relationship between Mason and Uncas to that of the "squirrel king," a practice common among "southeastern Indian clans" who cultivated a relationship with a powerful individual in a rival tribe so that he would promote their interests with his people. St. Jean sees the close ties between Roger Williams and the Narragansetts as akin to that between Mason and Uncas (although the ties that John Winthrop, Jr., and the Reverend James Fitch cultivated with other New England Indians differed in that they sought to subordinate these Indians to English law). See St. Jean, "Inventing Guardianship," 366–367.

[10] David Conroy, "The Defense of Indian Land Rights," 401. In 1661 and again in 1665 Mason had Uncas sign documents entitling him to half the profits from the sale of Mohegan lands. On this, see St. Jean, "Inventing Guardianship," 377; and *The Governor and Company*, 41–42.

[11] De Forest, *History*, 292.

[12] Jean, "Inventing Guardianship," 378. It is not clear from the surviving records just what percentage of the lands the Mohegans held prior to Uncas's alliance with Mason

This tract – referred to subsequently as the "sequestered lands" – was to be the principal (though not the only) one in question in the ensuing legal dispute. Despite the entailment, and despite the Mohegans' aid to the colony during King Philip's War, in the decade following Mason's death, the towns of New London and Norwich began to encroach on the Mohegans' reserved lands.[13] As a result, in 1681, Uncas concluded a treaty with the colony in which it undertook to provide "a sufficiency of land" for the tribe to plant on and to ensure that "a just price be paid" for "Whatever plantations we grant to any people in their countries and territories." As well, the colony pledged that the Mohegans "shall have *equal justice* from us as our own people, in all manners which they shall bring before us," adding that this would be the case if *"they shall have before-hand declared their subjection to our laws."* The colony also undertook to help defend the Mohegans should they be attacked by their enemies. In return, Uncas granted the colony "all my lands and territories," pledging that he would not dispose of them to anyone else without the colony's consent.[14] In return for these concessions, he demanded a "reasonable satisfaction for my propriety in them as we shall agree." In addition to this transfer of territory, Uncas promised that he and his successors will be "friends and allies to the said colony" and not make "peace and war" without taking "advice" from "the general court of Connecticut." Uncas also pledged "to assist" the colony against any "enemy" with *"a competent number of fighting men."*[15]

Upon Uncas's death in 1684, his son, Oweneco, became sachem. In the same year, John Mason's son, Samuel, assumed his father's role as the colony's legal guardian. Samuel Mason used his long tenure as an assistant in the General Court to defend the tribe, arguing that the colony still needed the Mohegans for defense, and trying to preserve their land from settler encroachment.[16] However, despite Mason's best efforts, by the late

---

were left at the time of Mason's entailment. On this entailment, see also De Forest, *History*, 293–294.

[13] See De Forest, *History*, 294–295.

[14] Oberg argues that Uncas most likely understood this grant to be a right of preemption or first purchase, much like his earlier dealings with the Masons. See Oberg, *Uncas*, 200–201.

[15] For the text of the treaty, see *The Governor and Company*, 39–41. The terms of the treaty are discussed in De Forest, *History*, 295. The colony also attempted to ascertain the boundaries between it and the Mohegan lands in 1683 and 1684 (via the Treat and Talcott commission).

[16] St. Jean, "Inventing Guardianship," 382–385.

1680s much of the territory the Mohegans had occupied at the end of the Pequot war was gone. All that remained was the land that Mason had entailed in 1671, as well as another tract on the northern boundary of Lyme, and a "third, usually styled the Mohegan Hunting Grounds," which "lay between the townships of Norwich, Lebanon, Lyme, Haddam and Middleton."[17] And in the late 1690s, despite the terms of the 1681 treaty, Connecticut began to grant away even the entailed or "seques-tered" land to new townships, often without the Mohegans' consent or that of the Mason family.[18] In 1698, the colony's assembly granted the governor, Fitz-John Winthrop, a farm out of these lands.[19] In 1699, part of the Mohegan hunting grounds was included within a grant made to the new town of Colchester.[20] And, in 1703, the remainder of the seques-tered lands was annexed to New London "without the Mohegans or their English protectors being consulted."[21]

Nicholas Hallam, a political ally of the Masons, observed the effect of the colony's usurpations on the Mohegans. In 1703, he was attempting to ascertain the boundaries between the Mohegans and the town of New London for Samuel Mason when he came across about thirty to forty "Mohegan Indians, men, women, and children, in a very poor and naked condition, many of them crying lamentably." When he asked them the reason for their plight, they told him "that the governor had been up with them that day, and had drove them from their planting land, which they had enjoyed ever since the English came into the country, and that they were not willing to leave the English, unless they were forced to it."[22]

In addition to the colony's appropriation of their lands, the Mohegans – Uncas as well as his sons – had also deeded large tracts of land to various colonists, often without the consent of the Mohegan community.[23] In

[17] Oberg, *Uncas*, 204–205. De Forest, *History*, 297, refers to other, smaller tracts, as well as "considerable quantities of land in Windham county."

[18] *The Governor and Company*, 27–28. For the continual incursions on the Mohegans' planting and hunting grounds, see Smith, *Appeals to the Privy Council*, 424; and St. Jean, "Inventing Guardianship," 385.

[19] On this, see *The Governor and Company*, 51–52.

[20] The hunting grounds lay between "Norwich, and Haddam, Lyme, Lebanon, and Metabesset." See *The Governor and Company*, 28.

[21] Oberg, *Uncas*, 206. According to Den Ouden, by 1704 the planting grounds – the "thirty-two-square-mile tract of land (20,480 acres) between New London and Norwich" – were "encompassed by the newly enlarged town of New London." See Den Ouden, *Beyond Conquest*, 98.

[22] *The Governor and Company*, 54–55.

[23] Den Ouden claims that "such transactions may have regularly taken place without the consent or consideration of the larger community of Mohegans." Den Ouden, *Beyond Conquest*, 102. Den Ouden also cites the work of an anthropologist who estimates that

1659, there was a large sale to the town of Norwich, made with the consent of Mason.[24] A similar alienation occurred in 1668, this time to New London.[25] And in 1680 Oweneco deeded all the lands his father had given him in Quinnebag to the powerful Fitch family.[26] However, as was the case with many of these deeds, the land Fitch received from Oweneco overlapped with land claimed by Governor Winthrop, leading to decades of conflict between these two powerful families. The result of these cessions, both consensual and nonconsensual, was the loss of the bulk of the tribe's property, as well as mounting intra-settler conflict as the competing deed holders clashed.[27]

In 1703, worried that the General Court was going to annex all of the remaining lands, Mason's son, Samuel, and Uncas's son, Oweneco, sought redress from the General Court.[28] Failing to obtain it, they appealed to Queen Anne, claiming that the colony was violating the terms of the various agreements that had set aside land for the tribe.[29] Pursuant to the appeal, Oweneco published a "Letter to a Gentleman now in London" requesting that "Our Hereditary Right to the Soyl and Royalties of our Dominions and Territories, before the English came into our Country" be made known "to the Great Queen Ann, and her Noble Council." The letter went on to say that "Owaneko, and his Ancestors, were formerly Chief Princes, and Owners of All, or great Part of the Country now called Connecticut-Colony in New-England." Furthermore, it claimed that "when the English first came, these Indians received them very kindly, and for a very small and inconsiderable Value, parted with all or most of their Lands to the English, reserving to themselves only a small Quantity of Land to Plant upon, and Hunt in." In addition, Oweneco noted that the Mohegans had also "assisted" the colony "in their wars against the other Indians; and have, until of late, quietly enjoyed their reserved Lands."

Oweneco made at least twenty-five deeds of sale to colonists between 1659 and 1710. However, according to William Bollan, the Mohegans' lawyer before the 1743 royal commission, Uncas deeded the sequestered lands to the tribe in 1683. See *The Governor and Company*, 89.

[24] De Forest, *History*, 290–291. According to De Forest, "The Norwich and New London records abound with deeds, conveying tracts, of usually from one to five or six hundred acres, to various persons of these towns."

[25] For the deed, see *The Governor and Company*, 43.

[26] De Forest, *History*, 290.

[27] For example, Governor John Winthrop got a tract of land along the Quinebaug river from another tribe, yet in 1680 Oweneco sold the same tract of land to Captain James Fitch. See Bushman, *From Puritan to Yankee*, 86–87.

[28] *The Governor and Company*, iii.

[29] Ibid., 58.

However, "about a Year or two ago" the colony annexed "these lands to the Townships of Colchester and New London." As a result, "these poor Indians have been unjustly turn'd out of Possession, and are thereby destitute of all means of Subsistence."[30]

In making this appeal, Oweneco and the Masons received assistance from powerful elites in Connecticut, including Nicholas Hallam, who had observed the plight of the dispossessed Mohegans in 1703. Hallam was angry with Connecticut's government for claiming that the colony's charter barred his right to appeal to the Crown against a court decision that had gone against him. As such, Hallam had an interest in the Mohegans' case as he hoped it would weaken Connecticut's legal autonomy.[31] In December 1703, and again in February 1704, Hallam appeared before the Board of Trade to convince them that Connecticut's charter should not be a barrier to the Mohegans' attempts to seek redress. As he put it: "this being a controversy between the Indians and that Government, H.M. may, notwithstanding the privileges then granted to the said Government, grant a Commission to indifferent persons in this or adjacent Colonies to enquire into and determine the matter." Hallam also told the Board that such a commission should be authorized "to put the Indians into possession of their lands in case it shall duly appear they have been wrongfully disseised."[32]

The Board of Trade referred the question to the Crown's legal advisors. On February 29, 1704, the attorney general gave his opinion on the merits of the Mohegans' appeal:

It doth not appear to me that the lands now claimed by the Indians were intended to pass or could pass to the Corporation of the English Colony of Connecticut

---

[30] Owaneko, *Chief Sachem or Prince of the Moheagan-Indians in New England, HIS Letter to a Gentleman Now in London* (London: Printed for Daniel Brown at the Black Sawn without Temple-Bar, 1704). The gentleman in question was Nicholas Hallam.

[31] Hallam and his brother John were challenging the disposition of their stepfather's estate by a Connecticut court. They were joined in their appeal to the Crown by Edward Palmes, the brother-in-law of Fitz-John Winthrop, who was also contesting the legality of a will. The Privy Council ruled against them, though it upheld their right to appeal to the Crown notwithstanding the charter. See Robert Taylor, *Colonial Connecticut: A History* (New York: KTO Press, 1979), 195–197. On the Crown's inherent right to hear appeals from all of its subjects, see J.M. Sosin, *English America and Imperial Inconstancy: The Rise of Provincial Autonomy, 1696–1715* (Lincoln: University of Nebraska Press, 1985), 179. As we have seen, the private colonies' denial of such a right was a central grievance in the Board of Trade's case against the chartered colonies. On this, see Louise P. Kellogg, *The American Colonial Charter* (Washington, DC: Government Printing Office, 1904), 267–272.

[32] For Hallam's memorial to the Board of Trade, see Cecil Headlam, ed., *Calendar of State Papers, Colonial Series: America and West Indies, 1704–1705*, Volume 22 (London: Her Majesty's Stationary Office, 1916), #56 (page 25); (hereafter, *CSPC*).

or that it was intended to dispossess the Indians who before and after the Grant were the owners and possessors of the same, and therefore what ye Corporation hath done by ye Act mentioned is an apparent injury to them, and H.M., notwithstanding the power granted to that Corporation, there not being any words in the Grant to exclude H.M., may lawfully erect a Court within that Colony to doe justice in this matter, and in ye erecting such Court may reserve an Appeale to H.M. in Council, and may command ye Governors of that Corporation not to oppress those Indians or deprive them of their right, but to doe them right notwithstanding the Act made by them to dispossess them, which I am of opinion was illegall and void.[33]

According to the attorney general, the Mohegans were the original owners of the land in question. Furthermore, the royal charter had not dispossessed them, nor did it stop them from appealing to the Crown for redress. Following this opinion, the queen authorized a royal commission to hear the dispute, informing the colony that "complaints have been made to us in behalf of the Mohegan Indians, that you have by an Act or Order of your General Court or Assembly taken from the said Indians that small tract of land which they have reserved to themselves." In addition to its concern that the colony's law was "unjust," the Crown also warned the colony that, in the middle of war with the French, its treatment of the Mohegans "may be of fatall consequence by causing a defection of the Indians to our enemies." As such, the Crown instructed the colony "to pay all due obedience" to its commission, and, if "upon enquiry it be found that the said Indians have been deprived of their lands," to "immediately cause them to be put into possession thereof."[34]

The language the Crown used in establishing the commission indicates that it did not view the Mohegans as subjects, but rather as allies, who, in addition to being the "chief proprietors of all the land in those parts," had "entertained and cultivated a firm friendship by league, with our said subjects of Connecticut, and have, at times, assisted them when they have been attacked by their enemies."[35] However, if the Mohegans were a separate people governed by their own rulers and capable of entering into treaties with the Crown's subjects, they were also, in the words of the Board of Trade, "under your Majesty's Dominion," a status which gave them a right to appeal to the Crown for redress.[36]

33 *CSPC, 1704–05*, #146, pp. 60–61.
34 *CSPC, 1704–05*, #181, pp. 76–77.
35 *The Governor and Company*, 24.
36 *CSPC, 1704–05*, #171, pp. 72–73.

The Crown's desire to protect the Mohegans did not arise solely from a desire for justice. In securing a royal commission to hear their grievances, the Mohegans and their colonial allies benefited from the Board of Trade's attempt to revoke the charters of the New England colonies and convert them to direct royal rule.[37] Finding that Connecticut had mistreated the Mohegans suited imperial reformers as it gave them a pretext to weaken or undermine the colony's chartered autonomy. Not surprisingly, the Crown chose Joseph Dudley, the governor of Massachusetts, to head the royal commission. For years, Dudley had been hostile to what he saw as the excessive autonomy afforded Connecticut by its charter, which had survived the Dominion of New England, and which still featured an elected governor.[38] Indeed, due to the lobbying of both Dudley and Lord Cornbury, the royal governor of New York, Connecticut's dispossession of the Mohegans was one of the charges in the 1706 Parliamentary Bill designed to annul the charters of all of the private colonies.[39]

Given the threat to its charter rights, Connecticut refused to appear before the Dudley commission, claiming that the Crown had no legal right "to enquire and judicially determine concerning the matter in controversy."[40] Such royal oversight, its lawyers argued, was "contrary to law and to the letters patent under the great seal." In addition, the colony maintained that the establishment of a juryless royal commission with authority over the private property would violate "the known rights of her majesty's subjects throughout all her dominions."[41]

On August 24, 1705, the Dudley commission unanimously decided in favor of the Mohegans and the Masons. The commissioners held "That the said Moheagans are a considerable tribe or people ... and cannot subsist without their lands, of which they have been deprived

---

[37] On the Crown's attempts to revoke the charters of the private colonies, see Steele, *The Politics of Colonial Policy: The Board of Trade in Colonial Administration, 1696–1720* (Oxford: Clarendon Press, 1968), 60–81.

[38] On Dudley's enmity toward the private colonies (which he shared with Hallam and Palmes and the others who supported the Mohegans), see Kellogg, *American Colonial Charter*, 301–302 (as well as Chapter 3).

[39] Kellogg, *American Colonial Charter*, 303. For an example of Dudley's complaints against Connecticut for – among other things – its treatment of the Mohegans, see CSPC, 1706–08 (Volume 23), #69, pp. 29–32.

[40] The colony also forbade individual colonists from giving testimony before the commission.

[41] *The Governor and Company*, 32–33. The colony also accused Dudley and the other commissioners of having an interest in the land in question. On this point, see Richard S. Dunn, *Puritans and Yankees: The Winthrop Dynasty of New England, 1630–1717* (Princeton: Princeton University Press, 1962), 340.

and dispossessed." Furthermore, Oweneco and his people "have at all
times served the interests of the crown of England and the colony of
Connecticut" and "have *faithfully kept their leagues and treaties* with the
said colony."[42] However, the colony, "contrary" to these "reservations,
treaties, and settlements," had "*granted away considerable tracts of the
planting grounds of the said Moheagans.*"[43] As a result of the colony's
encroachments on their lands, the tribe has "been reduced *to great want
and necessity*, and, in this time of war, are in great danger of deserting
their ancient friendship."[44] Accordingly, the commissioners ruled that the
Mohegans "had a very good and undoubted right to a very large tract
of land within the colony of Connecticut"[45]; and it ordered the colony
to return to them the tract that Mason had entailed in 1671 between
New London and Norwich, as well as several smaller tracts of land.[46]
Upon hearing the verdict, Oweneco pledged that he and his sons would
be "ever under the allegiance and government of the queen and crown of
England." Captain Ben Uncas, his brother, also thanked the court, claiming that its favorable decision prevented him from "staining his hands
with the blood of the English, notwithstanding the many and frequent
provocations from them." In reply, the commissioners thanked "the said
Indians for their zeal and affection to her majesty, the crown, and the
government of England, and the interests of the English nation," assuring
them that "her majesty would always be ready to take care of them and
their people, both in protecting them and preserving of their rights and
properties."[47]

Following the Dudley commission's adverse verdict, the colony
instructed Henry Ashurst, its agent in London, to appeal the decision.[48]
In his petition to Queen Anne, Ashurst informed the monarch that the
colony had obtained the disputed territory from the Pequots by conquest.
As he put it: "your petitioners and their ancestors did formerly, with great
difficulty, and by their only endeavours, expenses and charge, acquire,
by conquest, the plantation of Connecticut, within the territories called
New England, whereby a large addition was made to the dominions of
the crown of England." In conquering the Pequots, Ashurst argued, "your

---

[42] *The Governor and Company*, 26–27.
[43] Ibid., 28.
[44] Ibid., 29.
[45] Ibid., 27.
[46] Ibid., 29.
[47] Ibid., 66–67.
[48] Ibid., 153–157.

petitioners ... became absolute owners of the lands and plantations of Connecticut."[49] Furthermore, Ashurst noted, the Pequots had themselves recently "subdued and conquered Unca Sachem, a subordinate tributary chief under him, who had then lately revolted and rebelled." As a result, Uncas, having been "expelled" from "his government and country," joined with the English in the wars against the Pequot. According to Ashurst, however, he "served them in no greater station than a pilot to steer their vessels upon waters in those parts."[50] In return for his assistance, the colony had allowed Uncas and the Mohegans "to possess some part of the said conquered lands, under such terms as your petitioners thought fit." Ashurst added that the amount of land the colony granted him was small, as Uncas barely had "enough to make a hunt." More important, this "reservation" did not mean that Uncas had "any right" to the land, but "only the *permission* of your petitioners, *the conquerors*, to *suffer* him to possess the same."[51]

Ashurst also grounded the colony's title to the land in question on the settlers' labor. According to him, they had built "upon, planted and greatly improved the said country and plantation." In addition, he invoked prescription or long usage, arguing that the colonists "have had the general possession" of the land in question "ever since the said conquest, being now near seventy years since."[52] As well, many of "the freeholders and planters" have held their individual plots of land "for thirty, others forty, and others fifty years last past."[53] In addition to conquest, labor, and prescription, Ashurst also held that Connecticut had obtained a deed from the Mohegans granting it the disputed land, though he clearly thought that this had been done to clarify the colony's title and not because the Mohegans had a legitimate claim to the territory. As he put it: "your *petitioners, to obviate all further pretences, took an instrument in writing, whereby said Unca Sachem did freely give and grant to your petitioners and their successors all the lands that ever had belonged to him ... reserving only for his own use that ground which*

[49] Ibid., 154. On the use of arguments from conquest to justify English colonization, see Robert A. Williams, *The American Indian in Western Legal Thought: The Discourses of Conquest* (New York: Oxford University Press, 1990).

[50] *The Governor and Company*, 154.

[51] Ibid., 154.

[52] On prescription as one of the most important European justifications for dispossession, see Anthony Pagden, *Lords of All the World: Ideologies of Empire in Spain, Britain and France, c. 1500–1800* (New Haven: Yale University Press, 1995), 89–91.

[53] *The Governor and Company*, 155–156.

at that present time was planted and improved by him."[54] According to Ashurst, it was only after the settlers had acquired the land for themselves that the Crown had "erected your petitioners into a corporation, and granted and confirmed to them and their successors all the said country or province called Connecticut." For Ashurst, then, the charter merely confirmed preexisting rights; it did not create them. Moreover, he added, with the Dudley commission very much in mind, the royal charter gave the colony the final say in "all manner of judicatories for the trial of all causes therein."[55]

Following Ashurst's appeal, the Crown overturned the Dudley commission's award of costs to the Mohegans and granted a commission of review, this time under the direction of Connecticut's other nemesis, Lord Cornbury. However, due to Ashcraft's opposition to Cornbury's appointment, this commission never met.[56] Despite its willingness to reconsider Dudley's verdict, the Privy Council upheld the legality of the Crown's jurisdiction over the colony, arguing that because "the Mohegan Indians are a Nation with whom frequent Treatys have been made, the Proper way of Determining the aforesaid Differences, is by her Matys Royall Commission."[57] The Privy Council's determination that the Mohegans were a "Nation" with treaty rights was an emphatic rejection of the colony's claim that the tribe was subordinate to it. In his year-end letter to the Board of Trade, Governor Dudley seconded the Privy Council's conclusion: "if H.M. cannot grant commissions to hear so apparent a breach between that Government and a Tribe of independent [Indians] ... that Corporation must be beyond all challenge."[58]

The legal position taken by the Mohegans and the Masons, and accepted by the royal commissioners, depended on the Mohegans' original

---

54 Ibid., 155.
55 Ibid.
56 For the Queen's order-in-council overturning "the sentence of costs," see *CSPC, 1706–08*, #368, pp. 150–151. The stages of Connecticut's appeal can be followed in W.L. Grant, James Munro, and Sir Almeric Fitzroy, eds., *Acts of the Privy Council of England, Colonial Series, 1680–1720*, Volume II (London: His Majesty's Stationery Office, 1910), 460–461 (hereafter *APCC*). On Ashurst's role in getting the ruling on costs reversed, see George Washburne, *Imperial Control of the Administration of Justice in the Thirteen American Colonies, 1684–1776* (New York: Longmans, Green, 1923), 103; and Sosin, *English America*, 181.
57 This is from the report of the appellate committee of the Privy Council (quoted in Walters, "*Mohegan Indians v. Connecticut*," 814). On the 1706 appeal, see also Smith, *Appeals to the Privy Council*, 427.
58 *CSPC, 1704–05*, #1422, 659–660.

"Hereditary Right," which had survived contact with the English and the granting of a royal charter.[59] In addition, the Mohegans, the Masons, and the royal commissioners all held that the colony had made several treaties and agreements with the tribe, all of which they had broken. For its part, the Crown agreed that the Mohegans were politically independent from the colony, though under the dominion of the Crown.[60] As a result, the colony's ability to take Indian land was legally limited and subject to the higher authority of the Privy Council in London. In its appeal, the colony based its claims to the disputed territory on conquest, labor, and improvement; long usage; and Indian grant, all of which were confirmed by the royal charter and underpinned by the rights of Englishmen throughout the empire to freehold property.[61]

Due in part to Ashurst's appeal and the subsequent decision of the Privy Council to set up a new commission, the judgment of the royal commission in favor of the tribe was never executed.[62] Instead, the towns that had been founded on the Mohegans' lands continued to expand, and none of the landholders were ejected. Samuel Mason, on the winning side in the case, found himself politically isolated. The nadir of the Mason family's political fortunes came in 1711, when John Mason, Samuel's nephew, surrendered the family's rights to the territory that Captain Mason had entailed for the tribe in 1671.[63] And in 1718 the colony removed John Mason as the tribe's legal guardian, appointing in his stead others who would Christianize the Mohegans, funding this proselytization from the sale of their lands.[64]

[59] From Oweneco's letter cited earlier in the text.
[60] On the Crown's defense of the Native Americans' jurisdictional independence, see P.G. McHugh, *Aboriginal Societies and the Common Law: A History of Sovereignty, Status, and Self-Determination* (Oxford: Oxford University Press, 2004), 61–116. James Tully has made a similar argument. According to Tully, the Crown recognized "the Aboriginal First Nations as a mirror image of itself: as equal in status and to be dealt with on a nation-to-nation basis." See his "Aboriginal Property and Western Theory: Recovering a Middle Ground," *Social Philosophy and Policy* 11 (1994), 170. The Mohegan case tends to support McHugh's and Tully's characterization of Crown policy.
[61] Though forbidden by the colony from appearing before the Dudley commission, the tenants on the disputed territory echoed Ashurst's arguments, claiming they did "improve the lands belonging to the Mohegan Indians, formerly reserved to the said Indians in the tract of their hunting ground." *The Governor and Company*, 64.
[62] Conroy, "The Defense of Indian Land Rights," 404.
[63] A copy of Mason's grant is in Mary Kingsbury Talcott, ed., *Collections of the Connecticut Historical Society*, Volume V (Hartford, 1896), 123–125.
[64] St. Jean, "Inventing Guardianship," 385.

The Mohegans' power also declined in the first two decades of the 1700s. Before his death in 1715, Oweneco continued to sell tribal lands to the settlers, further reducing the amount of land under the Mohegans' control.[65] In 1718, hoping to reverse the loss of their territory, the Mohegans petitioned the General Court, complaining of "entries, made upon the said land, and damage sustained by them in their fields."[66] Desiring to forestall another appeal to the Crown, the colony appointed a commission of its own to settle definitively the Mohegans' land claims. In 1721, this commission granted the colony the bulk of the "sequestered lands," apart from four to five thousand acres which it set aside for the Mohegans.[67] However, even this small set-aside came with an important qualification, the colony promising that it "shall for ever belong to the Moheagan Indians," but only "so long as there shall be any of the Moheagans found or known of alive." However, "when the whole nation, or stock of said Indians are extinct, and none of them to be found," the colony decreed, "the said eastern part, which is now settled upon the Indians, shall for ever belong to the town of New London, as their full, free, and indefeasible estate in fee."[68]

In addition to dispossessing the Mohegans, the colony left the Masons with no chance of recompense for the large legal costs incurred before the Dudley commission in 1705. As a result, in 1722, John Mason appealed to the General Court for redress but was unsuccessful. In 1725, he presented a second petition asking that the decision of the Dudley court be enforced, and that he be compensated. The colony once again refused to oblige, noting that Mason had been compensated in 1711 for renouncing his interest in the disputed land. The colony did, however, allow Mason to settle on the Mohegans' remaining lands and once again take charge of their affairs. But the colony's concession did not temper Mason's sense

---

[65] De Forest, *History*, 313, provides details of these sales and argues that they angered members of the tribe.

[66] *The Governor and Company*, 187.

[67] Several documents pertaining to the commission are collected in *The Governor and Company*, 189–195. According to De Forest, this assembly committee "assigned the Hunting Grounds to Colchester; the tract stretching from the Niantic to the Connecticut to Lyme, and three-quarters of the Sequestered Lands to the various persons who had obtained deeds of them. Between four and five thousand acres remaining were granted to the Mohegans, and were entailed in their possession as long as a single one of them should remain in existence. This decision was ratified by the government of Connecticut, and thus ended the proceedings resulting from the complaint that Hallam had presented seventeen years before to the Crown." See De Forest, *History*, 315.

[68] *The Governor and Company*, 194.

of grievance. Instead, the growing discontent of the Masons and the Mohegans led to several more decades of legal and political conflict.[69]

In 1725, John Bulkley, a Connecticut clergymen, published a powerful polemic against the Mohegans' rights to property and political autonomy. John Bulkley was the son of Gershom Bulkeley, a staunch defender of the Dominion of New England and the prerogative rights of the Stuarts in the 1680s. Born in 1679, John Bulkley attended Harvard and in 1703 was ordained a minister in the small frontier town of Colchester. Although he felt isolated in what he called his "long confinement here in the wilderness," he had access to a considerable library (partly inherited from his father) and was involved in many of the colony's theological and political disputes.[70] No less a person than Charles Chauncy counted Bulkley (along with Jeremiah Dummer and Thomas Walter) among "the three first for extent and strength of genius and powers New England has yet produced"[71]

Bulkley's critique of Native American rights appeared as the preface to Roger Wolcott's *Poetical Meditations*. Wolcott was a young poet (and future governor of Connecticut) whose literary endeavors Bulkley had patronized.[72] In the *Meditations*, Wolcott rendered in verse the efforts of John Winthrop, Jr., in obtaining the Connecticut charter. Wolcott's subject matter led Bulkley to use his preface to discuss the colony's rights to the Mohegans' land. As he put it, "my Tho'ts are here led to it by some Passages in the Ensuing Muse. Tis the matter of Native Right as it is commonly called, or the Right the Aborigines of this Country (all or any of them) had or have to lands in it."[73] According to Bulkley, this principle

[69] For Mason's petition, see *Collections of the Connecticut Historical Society*, Volume V, 384–390; and the discussion in De Forest, *History*, 319–320.

[70] For biographical information, see Clifford K. Shipton, ed., *Sibley's Harvard Graduates* (IV) 1690–1700 (Cambridge: Harvard University Press, 1933), 450–454. The letter in which Bulkley complains about having to live in the wilderness is quoted on page 451. With the exception of Perry Miller's brief discussion, Bulkley has been neglected by modern scholars. Miller sees Bulkley as representative of a growing rationalism in New England life in the eighteenth century. See Miller, *The New England Mind: From Colony to Province* (Cambridge: Harvard University Press, 1953), 430–432.

[71] Quoted in Shipton, ed., *Sibley's*, 452–453.

[72] On his relationship with Wolcott, see Miller, *New England Mind*, 431. When the Mohegan case was heard again in 1743, Wolcott was one of three men appointed by the colony to appear before the commission on its behalf. See *The Governor and Company*, 11–12.

[73] John Bulkley, *Preface* to *Poetical Meditations, Being the Improvement of Some Vacant Hours* by Roger Wolcott (New London: J. Green, 1725), xv.

has "not wanted many Advocates among us, especially of late years, who have endeavour'd to advance or set it up as our only Valuable Title to whatever Lands are in the Country."[74]

Bulkley's concerns were heightened by the events of the early 1720s. As Richard Bushman has argued, this period was the high point of the conflict over native rights in Connecticut, with the Mohegans' lands being one of the many disputed territories where ownership rested on the validity of Indian deeds. This strife had affected the town of Colchester, which had been founded on the Mohegans' reserved lands and where Bulkley was a landholder and original proprietor.[75] According to Bulkley, the doctrine of native right had led to a "Train of Evils ... not only to Particular Plantations and Persons, but to the Publick in the great Delay and Embarassment of Business in our Assembly's, as well as the Multiplication of Suits in the Law beyond Account."[76] In particular, he felt that those who "Propagate" the idea of "Native Right" did so "to the Prejudice of New Settlements" and were thus responsible for "the Disturbance of Honest Men in their Possessions and Improvements," including the "Ejectment out of them, as well as the Hurt of the Publick."[77]

To combat these dangers, Bulkley attempted to undermine what he saw as the central proposition of the defenders of native rights: the claim that the Mohegans had left the state of nature, entered into some form of civil polity, and could therefore claim collective ownership of large tracts of land. In arguing against this position, Bulkley was not only attacking the Mohegans and their colonial allies, the Masons, but was also engaging with the arguments of the Privy Council and the royal commission of 1705, which, as we have seen, ruled that the Mohegans were a "considerable tribe or people" with treaty rights that had to be respected.[78]

---

[74] Ibid., xvi.

[75] For the disturbances in Colchester, see Bushman, *From Puritan to Yankee*, 97. An order of the General Court from May 13, 1702, granted an "addition to the township of Colchester to John Bulkley and others out of the Moheagan lands." See *The Governor and Company*, vi (Bulkley is also mentioned as a Colchester landholder on page 53).

[76] Bulkley, *Preface*, lv. Bulkley attributed malign motives to those in the colony advocating the Mohegans' rights (and frequently referred to them as "Bigots"). In addition to accusing them of a desire to avoid taxes on the land in question, he also claimed that they were telling people about native right that "'tis the Only Security of Our Interests against the Claim of One beyond the Seas; and that if Native Right will not Invalidate the Duke's Pretensions, we have nothing else that will." The quote is at ibid., lv–lvi. This is most likely a reference to the proprietorial holdings of James II when he was the Duke of York.

[77] Ibid., liv.

[78] In the words of the Dudley commission quoted earlier in the text.

To undermine what he saw as the pernicious effects of this conception of native rights, Bulkley adumbrated a sweeping natural law argument against the Mohegans' claims to both property and political autonomy. In doing so, he went beyond the particular case of the Mohegans and laid out a broad ranging critique of the rights of all of the Native Americans of eastern North America.

In making his argument about native rights, Bulkley drew on several texts, the most important of which was John Locke's *Second Treatise of Government*.[79] Indeed, Bulkley's use of Locke was likely the first extended deployment of his ideas in British America.[80] Bulkley drew on Locke to describe the differences between a state of nature and civil society, to explain the origins of property in labor, and to argue that peoples who lacked money and trade were unlikely to have entered into civil society and determined their property rights collectively.[81] For Bulkley, as for Locke, the fact that the Native Americans had not left the state of nature meant that their lands were legally vacant and could be appropriated without their consent.

Bulkley also drew on scripture to support his argument about Native American rights. According to Bulkley, the "voice of the Law of Nature, viz. that Labour in this State shall be the beginning of Property, seems well to agree [with] the voice of God Himself."[82] In addition, Bulkley cited scripture to support his contention that the state of nature was a historical reality, and thus it was plausible to think that there were places

[79] As an important series of recent studies have shown, Locke's political theory was heavily influenced by his engagement with empire and his concern to justify English settlement in America in the face of the presence of Native Americans. For the major contributions, see the works cited in the introduction.

[80] This claim is based on an extensive reading in the pamphlet and newspaper literature of eighteenth-century British America.

[81] For Bulkley's direct citations of Locke, see *Preface* at xiii, xxii–xxiii, and xxv. Bulkley also drew on the writings of the Spaniard, Joseph Acosta. However, his use of Acosta seems to have been lifted directly from Locke's similar use of him in the *Second Treatise*. Compare the quote on page xxi of Bulkley's *Preface* with the one in Locke's chapter 8, para. 102 (the citation of Acosta's treatise is also similar). On the use of Acosta in the English debates about empire in the early seventeenth century, see Andrew Fitzmaurice, *Humanism and America: An Intellectual History of English Colonization, 1500–1625* (Cambridge: Cambridge University Press, 2003), 141; and "Moral Uncertainty in the Dispossession of Native Americans," in Peter Mancall, ed., *The Atlantic World and Virginia, 1550–1624* (Chapel Hill: University of North Carolina Press, 2007), 405–408. Bulkley also used Ovid's *Metamorphoses* to argue that the classical and the Christian views of Creation were compatible, as well as (though Bulkley does not name the poet) to describe the conditions of a people in a state of nature. See ibid., iii–iv and xxxvii.

[82] Bulkley, *Preface*, xxvi. Bulkley gives the book of Genesis as the source for this argument.

in the world where land was still open to appropriation, the inhabitants
not having fixed their properties in it by positive law.[83] This marrying of
reason and revelation can also be seen in a later sermon where Bulkley
argued that most of the teachings of faith are "no other than what nature
teaches," adding that belief in them would be justified even "had we never
been assisted by Supernatural Revelation."[84]

At the heart of Bulkley's discussion of Native American rights lay a distinction between natural law and positive law, the state of nature and civil
society. Although he did not deny native property rights altogether, arguing
that "it is an undoubted Truth, that the Aborigines of this Country, some
or all of them had rights to Land in it," he held that "it is equally certain
that of what Extent soever it was it arose from one of these Two Things,
viz, Either the Law of Nature or Positive Laws or Constitutions of their
own (Tacit or Express) Regulating or Determining the matter of Property,
one or other of these must give them what they had."[85] For Bulkley, then,
"nothing with any certainty can be Determin'd upon the extent of the
Claims or Properties of any Single Person or Number of them, till first it
be determin'd what their condition was, whether they were a People in
the State of Nature, and so had only what the Law of Nature gave them,
or had quitted that State, [and] entered into Communities."[86]

   To determine whether the Native Americans had adopted "Positive
Laws or Constitutions" before the arrival of the English, Bulkley laid out

---

[83] Citing the example of Abraham, Bulkley argued that "in those Days men did not always
immediately upon Entering into Society, set out the Bounds of their distinct Territories,
and by Laws within themselves respectively Settle the matter of Property." As a result,
Abraham could seek pasture "in a Country where he was a Stranger," and even in places
where there were "Kingdoms or Communities of Men." Ibid., xxxix. This is so close
to Locke's account of Abraham that one wonders if the learned minister was not also
getting his scriptural evidence from the *Second Treatise*. Compare Bulkley with *Second
Treatise*, chapter 5, para. 38.

[84] Quoted in Miller, *From Colony to Province*, 433. This is from an ordination sermon
given in 1730, a year before Bulkley died, entitled "*The Usefulness of Reveal'd Religion,
to Preserve and Improve that which is Natural.* Miller claims that "it is indeed hard to
see how a Calvinist could go so far." Bulkley's combination of natural law and scripture
was also characteristic of Locke's political theory. For Locke's use of biblical examples
(including Abraham, Lot, Cain, and Abel) to demonstrate the origins of property in labor
and the origins of government out of the need to fix the bounds of property as a result of
scarcity, see *Second Treatise*, chapter 5, para. 38.

[85] *Preface*, xvii–xviii. For Locke, once men entered into society, the property rights that
had been generated by labor were now subject to the positive law of the community. See
Second Treatise, chapter 5, para. 45 and para. 50.

[86] *Preface*, xviii.

the salient characteristics of the state of nature. For Bulkley, the state of nature lacked a "Common, Establish'd, Positive Law (Tacit or Express) or Judicature to appeal to, with Authority to decide Controversies between them, and punish Offenders." As a result, "Every man is Judge for himself, and Executioner."[87] By contrast, in civil society there are "Laws for a Measure or Standard of Right and Wrong, and this Right of Judging and Executing is given up by every Individual into the hands of the Community."[88] In such a state, all "Private Judgment in any matter ceases, and the Community is Umpire."[89]

Given these criteria, Bulkley contended that the Native Americans were still in a state of nature. As he put it, "Who that is not a Stranger to them will say the aforementioned Essentials of a state of Civil Policy are to be found among them? that they have any Established, Settled, common Law received and allowed so much as by a Tacit Consent to be the Standard of Right and Wrong and the Common Measure to decide Controversies?" Furthermore, he argued, they lacked "a known, Indifferent Judge with Authority to determine differences according to this Established Received Law?" As he acidly remarked, "Who knows not that an Attempt to find these things among them is like a search for the Living among the Dead?"[90] As a result of the absence of a functioning legal and political system among the Native Americans, Bulkley contended that "every one looks on himself as Vested with the Rights of the Law of Nature, and accordingly is Judge for himself and Executioner!"[91]

Taking the Mohegans – and, indeed, all of the Native Americans of eastern North America – to be in this prepolitical state of natural equality, Bulkley applied Locke's account of the origins of property in labor to the question of their land rights.[92] According to Bulkley, in the state of nature "all have a Right or Claim to the Earth, as well as other things made for the Use and Comfort of Man." However, as individuals in such a state

---

[87] Ibid., xxi.

[88] Ibid., xxiv.

[89] Ibid., xxiii–xxiv. Bulkley's discussion of the state of nature was preceded by three block quotations from the *Second Treatise* (the first of which is from para. 87). Bulkley gave the following page numbers for his quotes: "Treatise of Government, p. 247 and afterward p. 280." The quotes from Locke run from xxii to xxiii.

[90] Ibid., xxx.

[91] Ibid.

[92] See ibid., xxv. Bulkley quotes at length Locke's argument (in chapter 5, para. 30) that the law of reason "makes the Deer the Indians who has Kill'd it." Unlike in the earlier passage of Locke's on the distinction between the state of nature and civil society, Bulkley gives no page number, merely noting that "Worthy to be Inserted here are the Words of that Great Man." The accompanying note says "Mr. Lock."

are "made but commoners in them, and can Claim only as such," Bulkley argued that "there is ... but one way whereby any particular person can begin a Property in any thing, be it Land or anything else, exclusive of the rest of Mankind, and this is by adding to it ... his Labour, which is his alone, and no one else has any Right to."[93] For Bulkley, then, the Native Americans only had title to "what they had Improved, and so held by the Law of Nature."[94] Furthermore, any land they had not cultivated "must remain still in the same Common State it was made in."[95] As a result, "the Mohegs in particular, or any of them, concerning whose Pretended Claims there has been so much Noise and Strife in the Country, which even to this Day is not ended" have no legitimate claim to the "large Territories they have been ignorantly (as well as knavishly enough no doubt) tho't by some to have." Instead, "they had really good Right, but to here and there a few spots of it."[96]

Although he believed that the lack of a functioning legal and political system among the Mohegans made it highly unlikely that they had in fact left the state of nature, for the sake of argument Bulkley devoted the rest of the preface to an extended critique of his opponents' contention that, in his words, the Mohegans had "entered into Communities, and by Compact, and at least Tacit Constitutions of their own, settled the matter of Property, both with their Neighbours respectively, & severally among themselves."[97] According to Bulkley, even if this were the case "it does not from thence necessarily follow that Lands were brought under the Regulation of Compact, or any Positive Constitutions of their own, (tacit or express:) Or that they were held by them any otherwise than as in the State and by the Law of Nature." For, according to Bulkley, "there is no necessary Connexion between those things, the Former does not infer the Latter; A People may put on some Form of Policy without any Determination of the matter of Property in Lands whether by Compact with Neighbouring Polities or any Positive Constitutions of their own."[98]

Suppose, he said, drawing on Locke's *Second Treatise*, that there was an island cut off from the rest of the world, "embodied together in Civil

93 Ibid., xxiv–xxv.
94 Ibid., xli.
95 Ibid., xxvii.
96 Ibid., xxviii–xxix.
97 Ibid., xxxv.
98 Ibid., xxxvi.

Societies, yet Living almost entirely on what Nature prepared to their Hands."[99] And suppose that there were so few inhabitants relative to the bounty of nature that there was a surplus left over after their basic needs had been met. And further assume that there was nothing that was common or perishable enough to serve as money, nor anyone to trade with. "What Inducement," Bulkley asked, "could such Societies have by any Compact either with one another, or among themselves respectively, to fix a Property in Lands, beyond what was done in the way before mentioned by the Law of Nature."[100]

Before the arrival of the English, then, Bulkley contended that the natives were in a similar state as these isolated islanders. As he put it, because of "their poor, mean, barbarous way of Living," and "the great Plenty of all the Provisions of Nature that requir'd," they made "very little use ... of the Earth further than to walk upon it."[101] In particular, land could not be of any value to them as long as "the Spontaneous Provisions of Nature" ensured them "that there is no danger of Want."[102] In addition, they lacked "all means of Communication or Trade with other parts of the World, together with the use of Money, among themselves (which things might impair their stock of Provisions and give a Value to them over and above what their Necessities did)."[103] As a result, "it is next to a Certainty that such Lands only as their Poor way of Living rendered their Tillage of necessary (and how small a part was that compared to the rest of the Country?) they put any Value upon: the rest they looked upon as of no more Price, nor Advantage to be Impropriated than the Air they Breathed in."[104]

Bulkley added to his account of the natives' base material condition a further argument intended to undermine the claim that they had entered civil society and collectively demarcated their property both internally and externally. According to Bulkley, "its not enough" for the advocates of native rights "to assert ... that our Aborigines had quitted the State of Nature and put on some form of Policy." Rather, he held, they also

---

[99] See *Second Treatise*, chapter 5, para. 48, for Locke's island example.
[100] *Preface*, xxxviii.
[101] Ibid., xxxvii.
[102] Ibid., xxxvii–xxxviii.
[103] Ibid., xxxviii.
[104] Ibid., xxxix. On the tensions in Locke's thought between his view of the Native Americans as living in a state of ease and plenty as well as in one of poverty and backwardness, see James Tully, "Rediscovering America: *The Two Treatises* and Aboriginal Rights," in Tully, *An Approach to Political Philosophy: Locke in Contexts* (Cambridge: Cambridge University Press, 1993),161.

needed to produce some kind of evidence "that they had by Compact one with another, & Positive Constitutions (Tacit or Express) Determined and Settled their Bounds and the terms of each Community respectively." In addition to demonstrating "what bounds by Compact with its Neighbours" each tribe had set, Bulkley also stated that the advocates of native rights would have to show "what Settlement its Constitutions made of the Lands within it." Bulkley was certain that neither of these questions could be answered "without the help of Divination."[105]

Bulkley was skeptical that the Native Americans had in fact agreed on the external boundaries of each tribe. As he put it: "Certain it is if they were Communities, or Bodies Politick properly so Called, they had a Federative Power, and, if in the Exercise of it, they made a Partage of the Lands, in this part of the Country among them, their Title Respectively was good, & as good in one Community as another."[106] However, he argued, there was no clear evidence for such an agreement. As Bulkley noted, Connecticut had tried "to enquire in the Claim of the Moheags," but the subsequent report to the General Court (in 1721) was of little "value," because, "at the same time their Neighbours, the Pequots, Quinebaugs, Nahanticks (all of them as worthy of Credit as the Moheags,) give another account, some of them claiming all the Lands within those Limits, saying the Moheags had none, & others of them claiming at least Large Tracts within them."[107] As a result, it was impossible to know "which of them speaks Truth, & consequently where the Right is and of whom to be obtained?" Because of these competing and contradictory claims, Bulkley concluded that it cannot "satisfy any but Fools to be able in this case to say they have Purchased of the Natives."[108]

Bulkley also contended that even if "the common Right of each Community" were "set out by Monuments," and it was known "where or in whom it is, and to whom we must Apply for the fixing a Property in them," the English would still need to know "what Disposition or Settlement the Constitutions (Tacit or Express) of each Society made of the Lands within their Limits respectively."[109] To address this question of the division of property within each tribe, Bulkley posited that all property was originally in the community and remained so until the community decided, via adopting some form of positive law or constitution, how the

[105] Ibid., xlii–xliii.
[106] Ibid., xliv.
[107] Ibid., xliii–xliv.
[108] Ibid., xliv.
[109] Ibid., xlv.

land was to be distributed. According to Bulkley, "all Men by Virtue of the Grant of the Most High before mentioned, are not only Commoners of the Earth, but equally so, none having a Right by that to Claim more or larger Portions of it than others." As such, "when any numbers of them enter into Society and by Compact with Neighbouring Societies Settle their Limits, the Lands within such Limits are the common Right of the Community, and equally so ... till by Constitutions of their own they make another Settlement of them."[110]

Given this original communal ownership, Bulkley asked of those who "assert the Politick State of the Natives" what "Settlement did the Constitutions of any one Community (to Instance in the Moheags Our Neighbours) make of the Lands within their Limits?" In particular, "Where or in whom did they place the Lands?" Did they place them "in any one Single Person ... or in a Certain Number of Men?"[111] According to Bulkley, "nothing can be Determin'd of the Extent ... of the Property of any of them till this be Resolved."[112] Although Bulkley posited that the Native Americans could have made any kind of settlement of property they chose, for the sake of argument he assumed that the community's property rights had been placed with the sachems.[113] He did this for several reasons. As we have seen, Uncas and Oweneco had in fact been the principal grantors of land to the colony (much to the chagrin of the other Mohegans). And, as Bulkley pointed out, the proponents of native rights in Connecticut had contended that the Mohegans' land was vested with the sachems. "I know very well Our Bigots say here, that their Constitutions vested all the Lands in their Kings, or in the Crown (to use our English Phrase)."[114]

---

[110] Ibid., xlv–xlvi.

[111] Ibid., xlvii.

[112] Ibid.

[113] Bulkley had earlier argued that the sachems in fact lacked any real political authority (save by election in time of war) and were not to be considered as possessing the authority of European monarchs. See ibid., xxxi–xxxiv. Locke held a similar view, arguing that "the kings of the Indians in America ... are little more than generals of their armies; and though they command absolutely in war, yet at home and in time of peace they exercise very little dominion, and have but a very moderate sovereignty." *Second Treatise*, chapter 8, para. 109. For a discussion of the political authority – as well as the control over property – of the New England sachems, see William Cronon, *Changes in the Land: Indians, Colonists, and the Ecology of New England* (New York: Hill and Wang, 1983), 58–61, and Yasuhide Kawashima, *Puritan Justice and the Indian: White Man's Law in Massachusetts, 1630–1763* (Middletown: Wesleyan University Press, 1986), who argues that the sachems held the tribe's collective territories in trust.

[114] *Preface*, xlvii.

Bulkley employed this idea that all property originally rested in the community to systematically undermine his opponents' contention about the *dominum* of the sachems, arguing that "Property in lands is not included in the notion of a King, or the want of it in that of a Subject." As such, "the making of one Person a King, and another a Subject simply in it self, will not make a Right of Property, and give it to the One, or Banish it from the Other, without some other Acts or Acts concurrent with it."[115] For Bulkley, then, even if the sachems claimed the right to own (and thus alienate) property, their authority would still need to be derived "from the Concession or Grant of the Community." This in turn meant that Uncas and any of the other sachems that the English "would obtain Lands" from needed to be "King or Monarch according to the Fundamental Law or Constitutions of the Society." If not, "they can't have any pretence to it; nor possibly make out a Good Title to any other."[116] Furthermore, even if it could be shown that the Native Americans had legitimately vested property in their sachems, Bulkley argued that, as in the determination of each tribe's external boundaries, the exact terms of their grant would still have to be known and recorded. Bulkley envisioned three ways in which the community might have transferred land to the sachems: inalienably, with the sachems having no ability to then grant the land away; alienably, allowing the sachems to grant the land away in any manner they chose; and in trust, with the sachems then distributing the land for the benefit of the community.

According to Bulkley, if the Natives had vested their lands inalienably in their sachems, there could have been no transfer of that property to the English settlers. As he put it: "For if the Communities in Vesting the Lands in them gave them no power of Alienation they could have none."[117] In particular, he argued that "it can't be imagined they had a Right or Power to make a Partage or Division of their Dominions among their own Children, to the Exclusion of the rest of the Community."[118] Conversely, Bulkley contended that it was impossible to imagine that the community would ever have granted the land to the sachems with a full power of alienation. As he put it, "I say this is Incredible; For if Lands were of such Value with them that they saw it worth their while to bring them under the Regulation of Positive Constitutions, its unreasonable to

---

[115] Ibid., lii.

[116] Ibid., xlviii. Bulkley also asked whether the sachems were hereditary or elected, though he doesn't develop the implications of this point.

[117] Ibid.

[118] Ibid., xlix

think they should in this sense put them into the Hands of any Person or Persons whatever."[119] Finally, even if their constitutions vested the lands in the kings in trust (as he thought the English and colonial constitutions had done), it still must be shown "whether any Alienations were made by their Kings to their Subjects, and what they were, together with the Tenures in or by which they were holden of the Grantees."[120] Only then, he held, could "the reality and extent of the Right or Property of any particular Member or Members of them" be known.[121]

So, for Bulkley, his opponents' claim that the natives had left the state of nature and adopted positive constitutions did not resolve the question of land rights in the New World. The argument that they had settled their external boundaries was belied by the fact that the claims of the several tribes in New England in fact clashed. And, with respect to the property within the boundaries of each tribe, Bulkley maintained that nothing could be known about whether the English could have acquired it from the sachems until "those Constitutions are declared, and we assured what they Determined upon this matter of property."[122] Given the fact that such written evidence did not exist, the "Hypothesis" that the Native Americans had quitted the state of nature does "no Service to the Interest the Zealous Assertors of it endeavour to Advance by it." On the contrary, "a Supposition of its Truth Inevitably Involves their Rights or Claims in so many Inextricable Difficulties and renders them all so Uncertain, Perplex't and in the Dark than nothing Certain can be Known or Determined upon them."[123] In Bulkley's view, then, "setting aside here and there a Spot this or that Person or Persons Improved and so Impropriated and Held by the Law of Nature, all the rest of the Country Remained in the same Common State wherein it was made, as much the Property of the Kings of the Indies on the Opposite side of the Globe as Theirs."[124]

In place of the arguments of the advocates of native rights, Bulkley advanced an alternate history in which they only became "Sensible" of the value of money and of the profit that could be made from the sale of their land "after the Arrival of the English here, by Conversation and

---

[119] Ibid.

[120] Ibid., l.

[121] Ibid.

[122] Ibid., lii.

[123] Ibid., l. In making this evidentiary demand, Bulkley has dropped his earlier claim that the legal or constitutional evidence for the Mohegans having entered civil society could be either "tacit" or "express."

[124] Ibid., xlii.

Commerce with them." That is, it was only when the English "made
tender" for land "beyond what they Improved, and so held by the Law of
Nature" that the Native Americans began to claim ownership of extensive
territories.[125] And it was because of this that the English, for "Prudential
Considerations," made treaties with the Indians that recognized native
title.[126] For Bulkley, however, such concessions by the English notwithstanding, the bulk of the land in the New World remained "like the Ocean
it self, *Publici vel Communis juris*."[127] As a result, "supposing the English
to be the First (of Civiliz'd Nations) in the Discovery of the Country,
they had (the Royal Allowance and Favour Concurring) an Undoubted
Right to Enter upon and Impropriate all such parts of it as lay Wast or
Unimproved by the Natives and this without any consideration or allowance made to them for it."[128]

By using Locke to posit that the Mohegans were not an independent people but merely individuals in a state of nature, Bulkley was able to argue
for dispossessing the Mohegans, while weakening royal authority in
Connecticut, an authority that rested in part on the Mohegans being able
to claim that they were a separate nation allied to the Crown. In doing
so, Bulkley provided the colony with an entirely natural law defense of its
property rights, one that did not depend on its charter, or on the rights of
Englishmen. Instead, Bulkley contended that the colonists were free – as
individuals – to appropriate land in the New World, irrespective of the
rights of the Native Americans.

After further appeals by the Masons and the Mohegans, the case was heard
again before a royal commission in 1743.[129] William Smith, the eminent
lawyer from New York, represented Connecticut before the commission
and made essentially the same arguments that Henry Ashurst, the colony's agent, had made in his appeal in 1706, contending that the colony
had conquered the land from the Pequots, after which they had allowed
Uncas and the Mohegans to live on the land as a tributary people, subject

---

[125] Ibid., xl–xli.
[126] This is a rare example of Bulkley acknowledging native agency. He usually depicted the
conflict over property in Connecticut as driven by the perfidy of the Masons and others
who held native deeds.
[127] Ibid., liv.
[128] Ibid., liii–liv.
[129] There was also a commission in 1738, but the Crown reversed its decision in favor of
Connecticut on procedural grounds.

to Connecticut's authority and not the Crown's.[130] They had also – out of
a concern for the tribe's welfare – purchased the land several times over
and made a treaty with them, the terms of which they had kept, including the set-aside of the four to five thousand acres as determined by the
1721 commission. Having obtained title by conquest and purchase, the
settlers had then labored on the land, making improvements to it that
only strengthened their rights. Like Ashurst, Smith also invoked prescription or long usage, claiming that by the time the case was litigated the
Mohegans' land had been occupied by the English for many years.[131]

William Bollan, the advocate general of Massachusetts, represented
the Mohegans and the Masons. Like the members of the Dudley commission in 1705, he was hostile to the autonomy enjoyed by the chartered
colonies and believed that better treatment for those Native Americans
loyal to the Crown was necessary for the defense of the empire against
the French.[132] According to Bollan, the Mohegans were "a free and independent people" who were governed by an "ancient established constitution." They were also "the original only owners of a large tract of land
in these parts." When the English arrived, the Mohegans, believing them
to be "a just and honest people, received and entertained them as friends
and entered into a strict alliance with them." This was an alliance, Bollan
insisted, that the Indians had, despite "the severest trials," "at all times
observed and kept." Furthermore, "in order to promote the settlement of
the English," the Mohegans had "from time to time spared them divers
parcels of their lands," save for "the lands in controversy (a small portion
compared to what they owned when the English first settled here)."[133]
Given that the Mohegans had dealt with the colony and the Crown on a
nation-to-nation basis, and given that they had been guaranteed part of
their traditional territory by the colony, Bollan told the commissioners
that they should uphold the verdict of the Dudley commission and return
the disputed land to the tribe.

---

[130] Smith was one of the leading lawyers in the colonies. An opponent of Governor Cosby,
he was involved in the Zenger controversy and also clashed with the governor over
equity jurisdiction in New York. On the latter, see *Mr. Smith's Opinion Humbly Offered
to the General Assembly of the Colony of New-York* (New York, 1734).

[131] For Smith's arguments, see *The Governor and Company*, 76–86.

[132] Little has been written on Bollan, though see the discussion of his role in cracking down
on smuggling in Massachusetts via the use of Admiralty courts, in Conroy, "The Defence
of Indian Land Rights," 405–406. On his growing disaffection from the Crown in the
1760s and 1770s, see Joel D. Meyerson, "The Private Revolution of William Bollan,"
New England Quarterly 41 (1968), 536–550.

[133] *The Governor and Company*, 94, 87.

The tenants who had freeholds on the disputed land also appeared before the commission. They denied the Crown's right to try their titles before a juryless court, arguing that the royal commission was "illegal" as "each of them are *freemen*, natural born subjects of the Crown of Great Britain."[134] As such, the Crown had no right to call their land titles "into question in a court of equity." To do so, they argued, "would be ... contrary to the laws and statutes of that part of Great Britain called England and the laws of this colony," all of which constituted their "undoubted birthright and inheritance."[135]

While the commissioners ruled in favor of Connecticut on the narrow question of whether it had set aside enough land for the Mohegans and thus fulfilled its legal obligations, they did not accept the colony's claims to have acquired the land by conquest or labor. Rather, they held that the land had been transferred to the colony by the royal charter and not by the settlers' efforts. They also denied that either the common law rights of the tenants or the charter were a barrier to the Crown's jurisdiction.[136] The majority of the commissioners were thus in agreement with the rulings of the Board of Trade and the Privy Council in the early 1700s that the Crown had a right to hear an appeal from the Mohegans and to provide them restitution, including, if necessary, the return of the property of individual colonists to the tribe.[137]

Moreover, the decision in favor of the colony was a narrow one. A minority of the commissioners, led by Daniel Horsmanden of New York, sided with the Mohegans. In Horsmanden's view, "The Indians, though living among the king's subjects in these countries, are a separate and distinct people from them." After all, Horsmanden noted, "they have a polity of their own" and "they make peace and war with any nation of Indians when they think fit, *without controul* from the English." Furthermore, according to Horsmanden, the "Crown" in both "Queen Anne's and his present majesty's commission by which we now sit" "looks upon them not as subjects, *but as a distinct people*" who have "the property of the soil of these countries."[138]

---

[134] Ibid., 124.
[135] Ibid.
[136] Ibid., 127.
[137] Ibid., 139.
[138] Ibid., 126–127. Conroy suggests that Horsmanden's arguments "may have been politically motivated" as he was a speculator in Indian land. However, speculators in the eighteenth century usually contended that the Native Americans had property rights that could be transferred to them but not the kind of sovereignty that Horsmanden said the Mohegans had. See Conroy, "Defence of Indian Land Rights," 420, fn. 38.

Although the colony achieved a victory in 1743, the arguments that Bollan and Horsmanden had made in support of indigenous rights were not about to go away. Indeed, as the threat of war with the French grew again in the late 1740s, the Crown was increasingly willing to regulate the relationship between the settlers and the Native American peoples of eastern North America whom it saw as potential allies. In this sense, the Mohegan case was a microcosm of an emerging split in the empire between settlers like Bulkley who wanted to deny indigenous rights, and royal officials who found arguments from chartered conquest, labor, and improvement too conducive to local autonomy and too corrosive of the need for metropolitan control of increasingly dangerous imperial frontiers.

Given his impassioned defense of the Mohegans' rights, it is more than a little ironic that Horsmanden was chiefly responsible for unfairly prosecuting slaves in New York who were accused of a conspiracy to burn the city down. On this, see Jill Lepore, *New York Burning: Liberty, Slavery and Conspiracy in Eighteenth-Century Manhattan* (New York: Alfred A. Knopf, 2005).

5

Daniel Dulany and the Natural Right to English Law

The settlers in Maryland had for the most part received what they wanted in the aftermath of the Glorious Revolution. Unlike the inhabitants of Massachusetts, they were happy to embrace royal government, assuming that the rule of a Protestant prince would be superior to that of the Catholic Lords Baltimore. And the years after the fall of the proprietary government were relatively peaceful, with the lower house of assembly able to build on the gains it had made in the seventeenth century and extend its authority against the often ineffectual checks of a succession of royal governors. However, in 1715, after converting to Anglicanism, the Baltimore family resumed control of the colony. Within a few years, Maryland was plunged into a rancorous constitutional conflict over whether the colony could claim the benefit of English law and rights. The leader of the Maryland lower house, the prominent lawyer, Daniel Dulany, drew on the common law as well as the early modern law of nature to defend the colony's claim against the authority of the proprietor.

The Stuart King, Charles I, created Maryland as a proprietorial colony with his 1632 grant to the Catholic courtier George Calvert (Lord Baltimore). Typical of the early English charters, it delegated a large amount of the king's authority to Baltimore. In fact, it was modeled on a fourteenth-century grant to the Bishop of Durham, and the powers it granted were of a quasi-feudal nature. Under it, Baltimore owned all the land and was the sole source of executive and judicial authority. He was able to establish courts, raise an army, and even exercise martial law in extremis.[1] However, the charter had countervailing elements, for among the vast feudal powers it conferred was a grant to the freemen of the province of the right to be called by the lord proprietor for "advice, assent, and approbation" concerning "the framing of laws."[2] Article VIII of the charter contained a further limit on the proprietor's powers, stating that they had to be

Consonant to reason, and be not repugnant nor contrary, but (so far as may conveniently be done) agreeable to the laws, statutes, or rights of our Kingdom of England: and so that the same ordinances do not, in any sort, extend to oblige, bind, charge, or take away the right or interest of any person or persons in member, life, freehold, goods or chattels.[3]

From the outset, the freemen of the province used the charter's provisions for a representative body to offer their consent to proprietorial decisions. Lord Baltimore, however, had a different conception of their role. He believed that, as he had "full, free, and absolute power ... to ordain, make and enact laws," the freemen should simply ratify his decisions.[4] As a result, Baltimore, through the colony's governor, refused to consent to the laws that the freemen made at the first assembly. The dual legacy of the charter – its grant of both princely powers and the right to representation and English law – was to play itself out over the course of the seventeenth and eighteenth centuries, with both the proprietor and the colonists clashing over their respective rights.

The gradual buildup in the power of the Maryland Assembly, and particularly in its elected lower house, continued through the mid- to late seventeenth century, a time of frequent troubles – religious, political and economic – for the proprietorial camp.[5] The assertiveness of the assembly meant that by the 1670s the proprietor was finding it difficult to govern.[6] However, in the next decade, a reinvigorated proprietor

---

[1] On the charter, see Lois Green Carr and David William Jordan, *Maryland's Revolution of Government, 1689–92* (Ithaca: Cornell University Press, 1974), 5; Newton D. Mereness, *Maryland as a Proprietary Province* (New York: Macmillan, 1901), 8. "The Charter of Maryland" is reprinted in *Maryland as a Proprietary Province*, 507–520.

[2] Mereness, *Maryland as a Proprietary Province*, 510.

[3] Ibid., 512.

[4] Ibid., 510.

[5] On which, see Susan Falb, *Advice and Ascent: The Development of the Maryland Assembly, 1635–1689* (New York: Garland, 1986), 59–78.

[6] David W. Jordan, *Foundations of Representative Government in Maryland, 1632–1715* (Cambridge: Cambridge University Press, 1987), 235. According to Jordan, the Assembly attempted "to emulate the House of Commons to a degree probably unmatched anywhere else in the New World" (235).

making full use of his prerogative powers successfully limited the assembly's powers.[7] In doing so, the proprietorial camp responded to the assembly's claim to control the election of its own members with a powerful denial that the rights of Englishmen extended to Maryland. According to Philip Calvert, the proprietor's uncle and the colony's chancellor, such a privilege was not "Practiced in Virginia, Barbadoes or any other of his Majesties Plantations." Moreover, he contended that "His Majesty hath the Sole Power to Dispose of his Conquests upon terms he Pleases," and thus "he Hath granted his Lordship a Patent with Several Powers and Priviledges amongst which Enacting of Laws is one."[8] The real day of power for the lower house would have to await the fall of the proprietorial regime and its replacement by royal government.

Baltimore lost governing powers

Despite desperate politicking, the Catholic Lord Baltimore fell victim to the political changes that swept through the American colonies in the wake of the Glorious Revolution. Although Baltimore managed to retain his rights to the colony's land, he lost the powers of governance to the Crown, ushering in a "revolution in government."[9] Under royal rule the assembly was able to control its own affairs, and, through the power of the purse, to exercise an increasingly powerful role in the governance of the colony.[10]

The return of the colony to the Calverts in 1715 did not immediately undo the assembly's gains. Charles Calvert, the new heir, was still a minor; and the last royal governor, James Hart, continued to serve in that post under the proprietorship until 1720. But in that year, a distant cousin of the Calverts became governor. Both his attitude and that of the new heir reflected a desire to return to the kind of prerogative powers exercised by the Calverts of old. Such an attitude was unlikely to sit well with an assembly unused to the exercise of a veto and increasingly attached to

[7] See R.C. Simmons, *The American Colonies: From Settlement to Independence* (New York: W.W. Norton, 1976), 81–83. According to Simmons, the assembly was unable to stop the proprietor from narrowing the franchise and restricting the number of representatives allowed from each county, as Baltimore felt that a smaller electorate would render the legislature "more amenable to proprietorial influence." According to Simmons, Baltimore could interfere with the franchise because his "powers legally exceeded those of the King in relation to Parliament."

[8] W.H. Browne, ed., *Archives of Maryland*, Volume 7 (Baltimore: Maryland Historical Society, 1882– ; hereafter cited as *Archives*), 124.

[9] Carr and Jordan, *Maryland's Revolution of Government*, 180.

[10] Aubrey C. Land, *Colonial Maryland: A History* (New York: K.T.O. Press, 1981), 93.

1720

the authority they had accrued since the advent of royal government.[11] But the newly restored proprietorial governor at first affected a moderate tone, claiming that Lord Baltimore had instructed him to act "as a Bountifull Indulgent Father would towards a dutiful Deserving Son"; however, he also expressed a desire to bring "our Prerogative" and "your Privileges into Balance," strongly indicating that the proprietor would attempt to resume the powers he had exercised before 1689.[12]

All remained quiet until the election of 1722, which coincided with a precipitous fall in tobacco prices and which ushered in a new generation of provincial politicians, who arrived with a strong mandate from the electors: reverse the trend of plummeting tobacco prices.[13] In a one-crop economy like Maryland's, such an economic situation was calamitous. Falling prices affected not only planters, large and small, but all who engaged in any but the most rudimentary transactions – for tobacco was not only the main crop but it was also the sole means of exchange.[14] All officers' fees, including those paid to proprietorial officials, were set in tobacco. In addition, the Anglican clergy, part of a state establishment since 1704, received its salary in tobacco.

The new faces in the lower house who attempted to rectify the economic situation were, therefore, embarking on a course of action fraught with potential conflict. One of the new members was Daniel Dulany, a young lawyer from Annapolis, who had come to Maryland twenty years before as an indentured servant from Ireland and had risen to become a prosperous lawyer on the county court circuit. At the time of the election, he held the office of attorney general of the province.[15] He and his new colleague in the assembly, Thomas Bordley, were considered the two best lawyers of their generation in Maryland.[16] They soon put their legal knowledge to

[11] Aubrey C. Land, *The Dulanys of Maryland* (Baltimore: Johns Hopkins University Press, 1958), 45. According to Land, Marylanders knew that following the Glorious Revolution, the "Crown veto over acts of Parliament had ceased to be exercised at all."

[12] *Archives*, Volume 35, 5.

[13] See Land, *Colonial Maryland*, 130, for a discussion of the members of this new generation and their impact on politics in the 1720s.

[14] Charles A. Barker, *The Background of the Revolution in Maryland* (New Haven: Yale University Press, 1940), 71.

[15] See Land, *The Dulanys of Maryland*, 1–43. As well, St. George L. Sioussat, "Economics and Politics in Maryland, 1720–1750," and "The Public Services of Daniel Dulany, the Elder," Johns Hopkins University Studies in Historical and Political Science, XXI, nos. 6–7 (Baltimore: Johns Hopkins University Press, 1903). For Dulany's early life, see Richard Spencer, "Hon. Daniel Dulany, the Elder, 1685–1753," *Maryland Historical Magazine* 13 (1918), 20–28.

[16] See Land, *The Dulanys*, 86–97, for an account of their legal battle in a complicated commercial case, one that ended up being adjudicated in London after several appeals.

use in the Committee of Laws of the lower house, drafting a repealing act
to rid the province of a burdensome tobacco regulation.[17] The members of
the lower house unanimously adopted this act, but the upper house, sensing the danger that this act might pose to the proprietorial prerogative, as
well as to their own fee levels, refused to consent to it.[18]

In 1722, the lower house also initiated a legal challenge to the proprietor by adopting an English statute the provincial courts had previously
held did not extend to Maryland. In addition to adopting this act, it
added language that declared the settlers' right to all English statutes.[19]
In addition, the lower house passed a series of resolutions that included
a clause instructing provincial judges: "To Do equall Law and right to
all the King's subjects rich and poor and not to delay any person of
Common right for the letters of the King, the Lord Proprietary ... or for
any other cause." The intent of the resolutions was to ensure that the
"several Judges and Justices" were able to "Hear, Try and Determine"
their cases "according to the Laws, Statutes and Ordinances and reasonable Customs of *England*, and of this *Province*." The resolutions went
on to claim that "This province hath allwaies hitherto had the Common
Law and such General Statutes of England as are not restrained by words
of Locall Limitation in them."[20]

The resolutions also denied the proprietor's claims about Maryland's
subordinate legal status by stating that "this Province is not under the
Circumstances of a Conquered Country; that if it were the present
Christian Inhabitants thereof would be in the Circumstance, not of the
Conquered, but of the Conquerors."[21] Rather, it was "a Colony of the
English Nation, encouraged by the Crown to transplant themselves
hither for the Sake of improving and enlarging it's Dominions, which,
by the Blessing of God upon their Endeavours, at their own Expence and
Labour has been in great Measure obtained."[22]

[17] See *Archives*, Volume 34, 415. For a contemporary discussion of tobacco regulation, see "A Declaration concerning the Conduct of the London Merchants," in *The Maryland Gazette*, 79, March 18, 1729.
[18] Land, *Colonial Maryland*, 131.
[19] The statute in question was "one of the English Statutes of Limitations." See Sioussat, "The English Statutes in Maryland," Johns Hopkins University Studies in Historical and Political Science, XXI, nos. 11–12 (Baltimore: Johns Hopkins University Press, 1903), 32.
[20] The text of these resolutions can be found in *Archives*, Volume 34, 441–442; they are reprinted in Sioussat, "The English Statutes in Maryland," 73–76.
[21] According to Sioussat, the proprietorial position shifted between 1723 and 1725. In the latter year, Lord Baltimore denied that Marylanders were conquered and affirmed that they were "His Majesty's subjects." See Sioussat, "The English Statutes in Maryland," 45–47.
[22] Quoted in Sioussat, "The English Statutes in Maryland," 74.

To further weaken the claim that the colony had been conquered, the resolutions claimed "That if there be any Pretence of Conquest, it can only be Supposed against the Native Indian infidels." However, this "Supposition cannot be admitted, because the Christian Inhabitants purchased great Parts of the Land they at first took up from the Indians, as well as from the Lord Proprietary." And ever since this purchase, they have "Continued in an amicable Course of Trade with them except some partial Outrages and Skirmishes which never amounted to a General War, much less to a General Conquest, the Indians yet enjoying their Rights and Privileges of Treaty and Trade with the *English*." The resolutions concluded by claiming that "whoever shall advise his Lordship, or his Successors, to Govern by any other Rules of Government, are evil Councillors, ill wishers to his Lordship, and to our present happy Constitution, and intend thereby to infringe our English Liberties, and to frustrate in great Measure, the Intent of the Crown – by the Original Grant of this Province to the Lord Proprietary."[23]

The resolutions were a bid by Dulany and the other leaders of the lower house to limit the proprietorial power by claiming English common law and statute law that the proprietor would find much harder to veto than ordinary acts of the assembly.[24] In doing so, they claimed that they had an equal right to the benefits of English law as the king's subjects within the realm. And what they wanted in particular was the extension of certain statutes (such as the Habeas Corpus Act) that guaranteed basic common-law rights in written form. However, as we saw in Chapter 1, there was no settled case law on the question of whether English laws (and their attendant rights) extended outside the realm.[25]

The assembly's claim for the extension of English statutes to Maryland expressed in the 1722 resolutions met with a firm proprietorial veto. Both sides continued to exchange addresses and messages in the years

---

[23] Ibid., 74–75.

[24] Land, *Colonial Maryland*, 132.

[25] On this question, see Barbara Black, "The Constitution of Empire," 1201. According to Black, "perhaps the most distressing of the many problems presented by [the settlement doctrine] was the inability of the colonists to claim the benefit of certain fundamental protections that had been secured by the English Parliament in post-settlement acts not naming the colonies – for example, in the Habeas Corpus Act." As Black also notes, even when the colonists passed one of these statutes in their own legislatures, there was "nothing to keep a royal governor or proprietor from vetoing it, and nothing to ensure its safe passage through the shoals of disallowance." Black also makes the case that under the "settlement" doctrine, even "the status of pre-settlement acts of Parliament was altogether uncertain," and "acts of Parliament passed after settlement were not in force unless they named the colonies." Ibid., 1201.

between 1722 and 1725. Dulany and the Committee of Laws dug deep
into the provincial archives to prove that Maryland had had the benefit of English statute law in the past.[26] Not surprisingly, it found ample
evidence that there had been such extension. The proprietor countered
by offering to enact any of the statutes Marylanders desired individ-
ually; but he adamantly refused to "Introduce in a Lump ... any of
the English statutes."[27] He was particularly insistent on vetoing all of
the judges' oaths that the lower house attempted to introduce, based on
the 1722 resolutions,[28] because they usually contained a clause instructing the judges to adjudicate cases by reference to English law. The proprietor's conviction was that the people of Maryland would fare better
"If the Statutes of England not expressly Located thither are not in Gross
force among you."[29] In opposing the extension of English statute laws
to Maryland, the proprietor claimed that "the most Common received
opinions of the best lawyers of England have been against it," noting that
"the Habeas Corpus Act has often been Adjudged ... not to extend either
to Ireland or the Plantations."[30]

   This opinion, delivered to both houses of assembly in the fall session of 1725, was answered by Dulany and Bordley in the same session.
Their reply, which one historian has termed "the battle cry of the country
party,"[31] answered all of the proprietor's legal objections as to extension.
In particular, the lower house made a strong argument for the extension
of the Habeas Corpus Act to Maryland, notwithstanding the proprietor's
claim that it did not apply to the colonies. Dulany, writing on behalf of
the lower house, argued that the act was a vital protection for English
rights and had been long used in the province. Dulany also drew on the
settlement doctrine that we discussed in Chapter 1, construing it in a
more liberal fashion than did the Crown lawyers. Because Maryland was
an uninhabited country settled by English subjects, Dulany held that all
English laws extended as of right.[32] Dulany concluded the 1725 address
by arguing "that the Crown has no Right to give us other Conditions

---

[26] See their report in *Archives*, Volume 34, 661–679.
[27] Ibid., 493.
[28] See Dulany's oath bill in *Archives*, Volume 35, 104.
[29] Ibid., 298.
[30] *Archives*, Volume 35, 196–197. The proprietor cited Holt's decision in *Blankard v. Galdy*,
    which held that English laws did not extend to Jamaica (though it could be bound by
    Parliamentary law if "particularly mentioned therein").
[31] Sioussat, "English Statutes in Maryland," 47.
[32] See the discussion of Dulany's address in Sioussat, "The English Statutes in Maryland,"
    47–50.

than in common with our Fellow-Subjects." He also warned the proprietor not to "treat us so much like men that owe their Lives and Liberties only to your Charter."[33]

The exchanges in the fall of 1725 were the last for two years, as the proprietor dissolved the assembly and no new elections were called. These crucial years (1722–1725) had seen the formation of a formidable country party, able and willing to challenge proprietorial power. But the attacks by the lower house on the proprietorial veto led to other political problems. All attempts at tobacco regulation stalled, as the lord proprietor refused to countenance any act that would reduce the fees – paid in tobacco – that his officers received. The lower house, for its part, claimed that officers' fees were already too high and that the upper house "Seem to be Assistants to Prerogative and Dependant on it, Rather than a State in which the people place a Confidence."[34] The lower house, as a result, never offered a bill to raise tobacco prices without including a reduction of officers' fees, often on the order of 25 percent.[35] Proprietorial vetoes left provincial affairs in disarray, depriving officers of any statutory basis for collecting fees, and causing discontent among the Anglican clergy who depended upon receiving their tithes in tobacco. The proprietor's continual vetoes of the judges' oath also left the courts of Maryland in disarray.[36]

Politics remained stalemated from 1725 to 1727. In 1727 a new governor, Leonard Benedict Calvert, the proprietor's younger brother, arrived in Maryland. A scholar and antiquarian, Calvert found the conditions in Maryland something of a shock, referring to it as "this unpolished part of the universe" and complaining that "our Conversation runs on planting Tobacco and such other improvements of trade, as neither the Muses inspire, nor Classic authors treat of."[37] Unfortunately, his attitude toward the settlers did not improve during his governorship. His brother, the proprietor, did not help matters much, delivering more crucial vetoes to provincial legislation in 1728 and 1729. Leonard Calvert, aghast at the situation, wrote to his brother that "This Superiority, as I may term

---

[33] *Archives*, Volume 35, 417.
[34] Ibid., 357.
[35] Land, *Colonial Maryland*, 141.
[36] Charles A. Barker, *The Background of the Revolution in Maryland* (New Haven: Yale University Press, 1940), 129. Newton Mereness notes that "from the time of the restoration of the proprietary government to the year 1729 inclusive, the lord proprietor vetoed ... at least 15 acts." See Mereness, *Maryland as a Proprietary Province*, 226.
[37] Quoted in Land, *Colonial Maryland*, 141.

it, of the people over the Government, seems unaturall, and is I am sure
repugnant to the very End for which Government was Instituted, viz.
An Authoritative Influence for the good order of Society." Calvert added
dolefully that "things can never go well in the plantations, whilst the
Planters are so generally proud, petulant and Ignorant, and have the common necessary Support of Government so much under their thumb."[38]

As the constitutional crisis intensified, Dulany put pen to paper and articulated the provincial position in a pamphlet entitled *The Right of the
Inhabitants of Maryland to the Benefit of English Laws*. It was to be his
final statement in the nearly decade-long constitutional struggle between
the proprietor and the lower house. By December 1728, it was in print
and was advertised for sale in the *Maryland Gazette*.[39]

Dulany began by noting that "there has been a pretty warm Contest"
over the issue of the extension of English law to Maryland. As a result, he
wanted to inquire "into the Right, which the People of Maryland have,
to the Enjoyment of English Liberties; and the Benefit of the English
Laws: which I take to be, and hope to prove are, convertible terms."[40]
According to Dulany, "the Law of England" consisted "of the Common
and Statute Laws." The "Common Law," he held, "takes in the Law of
Nature, the Law of Reason, and the revealed Law of God; which are
equally binding, at All times, in All Places, and to All Persons." It also
included "such usages, and customs, as have been experimentally found,
to suit the Order, and Engagement of Society."[41] According to Dulany,
these "Customs" had "by Consent and Long Use ... obtained the Force
of Laws." Dulany next offered a definition of "Statute Law," which he
claimed "consisted of such Acts of Parliament, as have been made from
Time, to Time, by the whole Legislature." In Dulany's view, these statutes

---

[38] *Archives*, Volume 25, 605.
[39] Daniel Dulany, *The Right of the Inhabitants of Maryland to the Benefit of the English
Laws* (Annapolis, 1728). It is reprinted in St. George L. Sioussat, "The English Statutes
in Maryland," 79–104. All further citations from Dulany's pamphlet will refer to this
reprint. The advertisement appeared in the *Maryland Gazette* of December 17, 1728.
According to Sioussat, this "indicates that it must have had some circulation through
the province." He adds that "only one copy, to the present writer's knowledge, sur-
vives" in "the Calvert papers in the possession of the Maryland Historical Society." "The
English Statutes in Maryland," 51. See also Lawrence C. Wroth, *A History of Printing
in Colonial Maryland, 1686–1776* (Baltimore: Typothetae of Baltimore, 1922), 60–70,
173. For Dulany's library, see Joseph Towne Wheeler, "Reading and Other Recreations of
Marylanders, 1700–1776," *Maryland Historical Magazine* 38 (1943), 52–53.
[40] Ibid., 82.
[41] Ibid.

had often been "declaratory" of English constitutional principles – that is, they had not altered the common law but had "restored the People to the Rights that were theirs, by the Common Law." Dulany claimed that such restorations were often necessary because "ill Men had at Times, invaded, and infringed" these common-law rights; and thus it became essential to make "New Barriers … to prevent future Infringements."[42] Dulany made it clear, then, that he only wanted the extension of those English statutes that had been enacted to secure the subject's fundamental rights, and not, as the proprietorial camp often claimed, the introduction of a plethora of English statutes ill-suited to provincial society.

Dulany based his account of English law on Coke's *Institutes of the Laws of England*. According to Dulany, "the great oracle of the law, the Lord Coke, saith of the Common Law," that it "is the best and most Common Birth-right, that the Subject hath, for the Safeguard and Defence, not only of his Goods, Lands, and Revenues; but of his wife, and Children, his Body, Fame, and Life, also."[43] Echoing Coke, Dulany added that "Tis by virtue of This Law, that a British Subject, may with Courage, and Freedom, tell the most daring and powerful Oppressor, that He must not injure him, with Impunity. This Law uprightly and honestly applied, and administered, will secure Men from all Degrees of Oppression, Violence, and Injustice; it tells the Magistrate what he has to do, and leaves him little Room, to gratify his own Passion, and Resentment, at the Expense of his Fellow-Subject."[44]

According to Dulany, English history was one long cautionary tale about the dangers of unbridled royal power. Drawing on Henry Care's widely read *English Liberties*, Dulany noted the numerous transgressions of the Star Chamber and other prerogative courts against the subject's "antient Rights." These transgressions included allowing "the Great officers of the Crown, and other Great men" (now quoting Care) "to punish, where no Law did warrant, and to make Decrees for Things, having no such Authority; and to inflict heavier Punishment than by any Law was warranted." Dulany (again quoting Care) noted that the Star Chamber "assumed to itself, a Power to intermeddle in civil Causes and Matters only of private Interest, between Party and Party, and had adventured to determine of the Estates and Liberties of the Subject, contrary to the Laws of the Land and the Rights and Priviledges of the Subject." These actions

---

[42] Ibid., 83.
[43] Ibid., 83–84. Dulany is quoting from the first book of Coke's *Institutes*.
[44] Ibid., 84.

constituted "an intolerable Burthen to the Subject"; they were "the Means to introduce an arbitrary Power and Government."[45]

Dulany saw the antidote to such attacks on the "Rights and Priviledges of the subject" in the statutory limits that Englishmen had historically placed on their rulers. According to Dulany, Magna Carta and the Habeas Corpus Act gave English subjects the benefits of due process, protected "the antient and indubitable Right of every Freeman, that he hath full and absolute Property, in his Goods and Estate,"[46] and ensured that no Englishman's property could be taken from him without his consent.[47] These statutes, Dulany argued, constituted "New Barriers" against "ill Men" in authority. They were designed "to prevent future Infringements" on the subject's rights by creating a "bulwark" around his person and property.[48] Rights, then, for Dulany, pertained to the individual subject, securing him from coercion, and protecting him in his person and property. On this rights-centered, jurisprudential understanding of the English polity, the subject's property could not be taken arbitrarily, nor could he be imprisoned or punished without due process of law.[49]

Dulany also denied the proprietorial charge that Marylanders were a conquered people. As Dulany put it, "I have heard it asserted that Maryland is a Conquered Country; which, by the By, is false; and that the Conquered must submit to whatever Terms, the Victor thinks fit to impose on him." However, he argued, if there had been a conquest, "The Indians must be the Vanquish'd, and the English the Victors; and consequently, the Indians would be liable to the Miseries, in which a Conquered People are involved: Otherwise, the Conquerors themselves, must be Loosers [sic] by their Courage, and Success; which would be but a poor Reward of their Valour."[50]

If Maryland was not a conquered province, then what was its legal status? According to Dulany, the settlers in Maryland had voluntarily left the realm and undertaken great hardships in order to expand the King's dominions:

[45] Ibid., 92.
[46] Ibid., 84. Dulany is citing Rushworth's *Historical Collections*.
[47] For Dulany's discussion of Magna Carta, see ibid., 91; for the "writ of Habeas Corpus," see ibid., 84.
[48] Ibid., 83.
[49] For the centrality of consent and the rule of law, see Dulany's use of the important statute of "28 Edw. 3" in ibid., 91.
[50] Ibid., 98.

The First Settlers of Maryland, were a Colony of English Subjects, who left their Native Country, with the Assent and Approbation of their Prince; to enlarge his Empire in a remote Part of the World, destitute of almost all the Necessaries of Life, and inhabited by a People, savage, cruel and inhospitable: To which Place, they (the first Settlers) transported themselves, at a great expence; ran all the Hazards, and underwent all the Fatigues incident to so dangerous and daring an Undertaking; in which Many perished, and Those that survived, suffered All the Extremities of Hunger, Cold and Diseases.[51]

The original settlers in Maryland, then, "were not banished from their Native Country, nor did they adjure it." Rather, they and "their Posterity, and others that followed, met with such Success, as to raise a Subsistence for Themselves, and to become very beneficial to their Mother-Country, by greatly increasing its Trade and Wealth." As a result of their efforts, "They have been as advantageous to England, as any of Her Sons, that never went from their own Homes, or underwent any Hardships."[52] Given the fact that they freely migrated, endured great hardships, and benefited England by their endeavors, Dulany concluded that Marylanders were entitled to equal rights with subjects at home.

Dulany also argued that Marylanders could also claim the "Rights of English, or British Subjects" based on the colony's charter.[53] As Dulany reminded his readers, "Maryland, does not only contain a Grant of the Country, with several Prerogatives to the Lord Proprietary: But also contains a Grant, to the People, of all the Rights, Privileges, Immunities, Liberties, and Franchises, of English Subjects." According to Dulany, "It would be difficult to invent stronger, or more comprehensive Terms than these."[54] However, Dulany added, his argument would be still "good, had the Charter never been made; as were the Rights of English Men, to all the Liberties, confirmed by Magna Charta and other subsequent Statutes, before they were Made."[55] In other words, English subjects had "antient or common-law Rights" before Parliament or any other body – even the king – made the "Grant or Confirmation." Since neither the Crown nor the proprietor had created these rights, the Maryland charter merely provided "Confirmation" of the rights it contained, something that was "advantageous" to the subject's liberty but not constitutive of it. To underscore this conception of fundamental rights, Dulany noted that

M.C.

---

[51] Ibid., 85.
[52] Ibid.
[53] Ibid., 82.
[54] Ibid., 99.
[55] Ibid., 101.

"It is no new thing, even in particular cases, to have a Grant from the King to a private Person, of a Thing in which he really had a right and the King had none."[56]

Dulany next addressed the complex jurisprudence on the rights of Englishmen outside the realm. As he put it, there are "several Book Cases; wherein the Judges have resolved, that the English laws did not extend to Ireland; 'till it was expressly enacted that they should." Moreover, these cases also held "that the English Acquisitions in France, were never governed but by their own Laws." According to Dulany, "the Reason of the adjudged Cases" was based on Coke's opinion in *Calvin's Case*, "where a Distinction is made between the Conquest of a Christian Kingdom, and the Kingdom of an Infidel," the former being allowed to keep its laws until the conqueror "abrogated" them and had "others instituted in their room."[57] In Dulany's view, however, these precedents were not applicable to Maryland, for "the English Acquisitions in France" were "inhabited, by civilized, sociable People, conversant with Arts, Learning and Commerce." As a result, they "had Laws, suited, and adapted to the Order, and Engagements of Society; by which, themselves, and others that went to live among them, might be peaceably, and happily governed."[58] By contrast, he argued, Maryland was inhabited by a people "rude, savage, and ignorant; destitute of Letters, Arts, or Commerce; and almost, of the common Notions, of Right and Wrong."[59] Dulany thought it ridiculous to suppose that their laws should have been left in place, preventing the extension of English law to Maryland. As he added sarcastically: "A People, thus qualified, must make excellent Preceptors for Englishmen."[60]

Dulany's depiction of the Native Americans as uncivilized allowed him to argue that the settlers had a right to English laws in the New World. As he put it: "Maryland, before it was settled by the English, was as to Law, and Government in the same Condition, with an uninhabited Wilderness." And, drawing on the settlement doctrine that had modified Coke's theory in the late seventeenth century, he held that "in Case of an uninhabited Country, newly found out by English Subjects; All Laws in Force in England, are in Force there."[61]

[56] Ibid.
[57] Ibid., 95–96.
[58] Ibid., 95.
[59] Ibid.
[60] Ibid., 95–96.
[61] Ibid. Here Dulany cites Holt's invocation of the settlement doctrine in *Blankard v. Galdy*.

Dulany also based his claim for English rights on the reciprocal relationship between the monarch and his subjects. Once again he quoted Coke: "Between the Sovereign, and the Subject, there is a double and reciprocal Tie; for as the Subject is bound to obey the King, so is the King bound to protect the Subject."[62] For Dulany, "it necessarily followed" from this conception of royal power "that the greatest Advantage, which the Subject can possibly derive, from the Royal Protection, is the Benefit of the Laws." If "He loses It, He loses every Thing." Crucially, Dulany contended that "This Subjection, and this Protection, are not bounded by any Space, less extensive than the British Dominions."[63]

Finally, Dulany drew on the early modern law of nature to make a case for the legal equality of the settlers in the empire. Dulany first adduced the "Opinions of the two great Civilians, and Politicians, Pufendorf, and Grotius, in Relation to Colonies," citing Grotius's treatise *The Rights of War and Peace* to claim that colonists "enjoy the same Rights of Liberty with the Mother City" and "are not sent out, to be Slaves, but to enjoy equal Priviledges, and Freedom." Dulany also cited Pufendorf's *Law of Nature and Nations* to illustrate his claim that "Maryland is undoubtedly part of the British Dominions, and its Inhabitants are Subjects of Great Britain, and so They are called in several Acts of Parliament."[64]

Dulany also adduced the example of St. Paul, who claimed the benefit of Roman law although he was far from the imperial center. Dulany contended that his claim was not based on the fact that "he was born in Rome or Italy; or indeed, in Europe; for he was born in Asia: Nor did he claim the Privilege of a Roman in Rome, Italy or Europe, but in Judea." And most significantly, Dulany noted that "There was no Dispute of his right, because he was born in a remote Province of the Empire; There was no Pretence that the Laws which were securative of the Roman's Rights, were confined within any narrower Limits than those of the Roman Dominions."[65] In Dulany's view, "The Province of Maryland" was "as much a Part of the British Dominions, as Tarsus the City, or Cilicia the Country, of St. Paul's Birth, was Part of the Roman Empire." "Consequently," he argued, "a Man, born in Maryland, hath as good a

---

[62] Ibid., 86. Dulany is citing *Calvin's Case*.

[63] Ibid., 87.

[64] Ibid., 85–86.

[65] Ibid., 87. This use of Roman imperial history to support a claim for colonial equality was unusual. The more common historical example adduced by the colonists was the example of the Greek colonists who had voluntarily left their home cities and established colonies with de jure autonomy.

Right, to demand the Benefit of the Laws of his Mother Country, as the Apostle had, to demand the Privileges of a Roman."[66]

In addition to his use of Grotius and Pufendorf, Dulany also drew on "what the Learned Mr. Locke says of natural Equality."[67] Calling him "that great Man," Dulany cited at length a key passage from the *Second Treatise*, wherein Locke claimed that all men, being naturally equal, had an equal right to be free from the domination of others.[68] And in the pamphlet's concluding pages, Dulany took his use of natural law theory one step further, countering the claim that Marylanders could only have the rights and legal protections that the proprietor would allow them with a powerful Lockean argument about the origins of political authority:

> And I beg leave to add, that Men, from a state of Nature and Equality, formed themselves into Society, for mutual Defence, and Preservation, and agreed to submit to Laws that should be the rule of their Conduct, under certain Regulations. Let us suppose the first Settlers of Maryland, to be a Society of People, united and combined together, for mutual Defence and Preservation; and sensible, not only of the use, but also of the Necessity of Laws, and conscious of their own Incapacity, to make such as might suit their Occasions, and procure their Welfare and Safety: I say, suppose them under these circumstances, without any Regard to their Rights as English or British Subjects, or by Charter: And that they actually agreed to make the Laws of their Mother-Country, (of which it is to be presumed, they had a general, or at least some Notion,) to be the Rule of their conduct ... And that upon long Tryal, and Experience, of those Laws; they became convinced, of the Equality, and Justice of them, and consequently fond of them: Will any one say, that they are obliged to change those Laws? Or, to have them upon other Terms, than they have always had them, without their own Consent...[69]

In this suggestive final passage, Dulany argued that the colonists in Maryland had a natural right to construct political authority on their own, consenting to such law as they saw fit, irrespective of conquest theory or any other metropolitan legal claim.

Dulany's pamphlet was the final word in the controversy over the extension of English laws to Maryland. Within five years sweeping changes

---

[66] Ibid., 87.
[67] Ibid., 87.
[68] Dulany's citation reads "Locke of Civil Government, Chap.2, Sec. 4." The passage from Locke that Dulany cites is as follows: "A State of Equality, wherein all Power and jurisdiction, is reciprocal, no one having more than another; There being nothing more evident than that Creatures of the same species, and Rank, promiscuously born, to all the same Advantages of Nature and the use of the same Faculties, should also be Equal, One, amongst another, without subordination, or Subjection" in ibid., 88.
[69] Ibid., 103.

were to come to Maryland. In 1732, Lord Baltimore arrived in the province in person, determined to break the legislative and administrative impasse. With the aid of a new and more skilful governor, he was able to exercise the full range of his prerogative power. He declared a fee table for proprietorial officers, he passed a modified judges' oath, and he was responsible for issuing paper currency for the first time in the province's history. Following his governor's advice, he offered places to many of the senior provincial leaders, Dulany among them.[70]

Although the dispute ended with this unequivocal assertion of proprietorial authority, there was to be no such decisive solution to the conflicting claims about settler rights in the empire. Indeed, in 1729, at the height of the controversy, a judicial ruling on the extension of the English laws to Maryland written by Sir Philip Yorke, the attorney general, held that "such general statutes as have been made since the settlement of Maryland and are not by express words located either to the plantations in general or to the province in particular, are not of force there." Although Yorke did add the proviso that English statutes could be "introduced and declared to be law by some Acts of Assembly of the province," or by an "uninterrupted usage" of the laws which would imply the "tacit consent of the proprietor and people,"[71] this concession to local legislative autonomy was never accepted by either Crown or Parliament. As a result, the question of what laws the king's subjects could claim on the far shores of the Atlantic remained a source of tension in the empire down to the Revolution.

[70] See Barker, *Background of the Revolution in Maryland*, 135–138.
[71] Quoted in Frederick Madden and David Fieldhouse, eds., *Select Documents on the Constitutional History of the British Empire and Commonwealth: Volume II, The Classic Period of the First British Empire, 1689–1783: The Foundations of a Colonial System of Government* (Westport, CT: Greenwood Press, 1985), 194.

6

Richard Bland and the Prerogative in Pre-Revolutionary Virginia

For nearly thirty years, beginning in the early 1720s, Virginian politics had been calm, free of the clashes with royal authority that had plagued other colonies.[1] However, in the 1750s two disputes, one over the Pistole Fee – a tax on landholdings levied by the royal governor – and the other over the Crown's right to veto colonial laws (the Parson's Cause) engendered a wide-ranging debate about the constitutional status of the oldest royal colony in the empire. In both of these disputes, the leading spokesmen of the lower house of Virginia's assembly (the burgesses) defended their rights with many of the same arguments against royal authority used in other colonies earlier in the century. As well, Richard Bland, a leading member of the burgesses, writing as the Parson's Cause was ending, responded to the repeated assertions of royal prerogative in Virginia by articulating the first explicitly federal vision of the empire. According to Bland, Virginians had (via their elected representatives) a zone of internal legislative autonomy, while still being subject to the external control of the Crown and Parliament in areas that affected the empire as a whole.

The placid politics of early to mid-eighteenth-century Virginia were largely due to the stewardship of the royal governor, William Gooch (1727–1748). In a departure from the stormy tenures of Francis Nicholson and Alexander Spottswood, Gooch chose, for the most part, to work with the

---

[1] On eighteenth-century Virginia, see Richard L. Morton, *Colonial Virginia: Volume II, Westward Expansion and Prelude to Revolution, 1710–1763* (Chapel Hill: University of North Carolina Press, 1960); and Warren Billings, John Selby, and Thad Tate, *Colonial Virginia: A History* (New York: K.T.O. Press, 1986).

assembly, often conceding points of constitutional principle to achieve his ends.[2] In doing so, Gooch was being a good Walpolean, making the empire function by allowing the peripheries to govern themselves with little direct oversight.[3]

Gooch's replacement, Robert Dinwiddie, however, had a very different conception of royal authority. When Dinwiddie arrived in the colony in early 1752, he already had extensive experience in imperial administration, having been a successful merchant in Bermuda, then the island's customs collector, and following that, the surveyor general of the royal customs in the southern colonies (in which post he sat on the Virginia council). Dinwiddie was also the author of several long reports to his superiors in London detailing the commercial and military state of the empire in America.[4] As these reports attest, although a client of Robert Walpole's brother, Dinwiddie's view of the empire was closer to that of George Dunk, the Earl of Halifax, the president of the Board of Trade from 1748, and an ardent advocate of imperial reform. Not surprisingly, Dinwiddie's appointment as lieutenant governor of Virginia in 1751 came as Halifax was in the midst of a wide-ranging attempt to project royal power more effectively across the Atlantic.[5]

---

[2] On Gooch's tenure, David Alan Williams, "Anglo-Virginian Politics, 1690–1735," in Richard Brown and Alison Olson, eds., *Anglo-American Political Relations, 1675–1775* (New Brunswick: Rutgers University Press, 1970), 76–91. Williams argues that the period from 1722 to the early 1750s witnessed a gradual distancing of the colony from the mother country, as peace meant less conflict over taxation and Indian policy, and the Whig hegemony under Walpole reduced the ability of Virginian politicians to lobby effectively in London. On the authority of the burgesses, see Jack P. Greene, "Foundations of Political Power in the Virginia House of Burgesses, 1720–1766," *William and Mary Quarterly* 16 (1959), 485–506.

[3] For example, to raise revenue for a British expedition against New France in 1746, Gooch allowed a committee of the assembly to disburse the funds. On this, see Billings et al., *Colonial Virginia*, 246.

[4] On Dinwiddie, see John R. Alden, *Robert Dinwiddie: Servant of the Crown* (Charlottesville: University Press of Virginia, 1973); and the older works of Louis Koontz, *Robert Dinwiddie: His Career in American Colonial Government and Westward Expansion* (Glendale: Arthur H. Clark, 1941), and *Robert Dinwiddie: Correspondence Illustrative of His Career in American Colonial Government and Western Expansion* (Berkeley: University of California Press, 1951). For Dinwiddie's reports on the military and commercial strength of the British empire in America, see Kenneth Morgan, "Robert Dinwiddie's Reports on the British American Colonies," *William and Mary Quarterly* 65 (2008), 305–346.

[5] On Dinwiddie's vision of imperial reform, one that he shared with many mid-century royal officeholders, see Alden, *Robert Dinwiddie*, 77–89. He was in favor of a colonial union, though he preferred two confederacies (one in the north and one in the south); and he wanted parliamentary taxation of all the colonies to raise revenues for defense.

Given the reformist vision of the new governor, conflict was not long in coming. In April 1752, Dinwiddie obtained permission from the Virginia council to charge a "pistole" (a Spanish coin worth about $4.00) for attaching the official seal to land patents.[6] Once patented, the land would also be subject to the payment of a quit rent to the Crown, further enriching the royal coffers.[7] In asserting his authority to levy the Pistole Fee, Dinwiddie relied on the royal commission as well as the king's instructions. In royal colonies like Virginia, which lacked charters, these two documents formed the basis of the local constitution. The commission, a prerogative instrument issued under the Great Seal, was the source of all legal authority in the colony. Unlike the charters, which usually required court proceedings to be annulled, the power granted by the commission was enjoyed at the king's pleasure. The royal instructions to the governors, which were supposed to remain private, contained detailed guidelines as to how they were to exercise their authority.[8] Although the instructions gave the governors and their councils the right to set officers' fees, in Virginia it had long been the practice to enact them with the consent of the legislature. To ascertain whether he had the authority to levy such a fee on land patents, Dinwiddie asked the Board of Trade in October 1752 for their opinion on the legality of the fee. Early the next year they approved it.[9]

Despite the sanction of the Board of Trade, the Pistole Fee was not popular in Virginia.[10] In addition to levying the fee, Dinwiddie also

6 H.R. McIlwaine and Wilmer Hall, eds., *The Executive Journals of the Council of Colonial Virginia* (Richmond: D. Bottom, superintendent of public printing, 1925–67), Volume V, 385.

7 Koontz, *Robert Dinwiddie*, 212.

8 Leonard Labaree, *Royal Government in America: A Study of the British Colonial System* (1930; New York: Frederick Ungar, 1958), 1–36; and Labaree, ed., *Royal Instructions to British Colonial Governors, 1670–1776*, 2 volumes (New York: D. Appleton-Century, 1935).

9 However, a similar fee levied in the 1680s by the Virginia governor, Francis, Lord Howard of Effingham, had, after a protest from the burgesses, been discontinued on the advice of the Privy Council, as Effingham had not obtained the permission of the council (there was a royal instruction that all officers' fees were to be decided with the council). See W.L. Grant, James Munro, and Sir Almeric Fitzroy, eds., *Acts of the Privy Council of England*, Colonial Series, Volume II (London: His Majesty's Stationery Office, 1910), 142–143 (hereafter, *APCC*). For the legal opinion of the Attorney General, Sir Dudley Ryder, see Colonial Office Papers (hereafter, C.O.) 5/1328, f. 83 (National Archives, United Kingdom) (concurring with the Board of Trade's January 1753 approval).

10 On the conflict over the Pistole Fee, see Glenn Curtis Smith, "The Affair of the Pistole Fee, 1752–55," *Virginia Magazine of History and Biography* 48 (1940), 209–221; Koontz, *Robert Dinwiddie*, 201–235; Morton, *Colonial Virginia*, II, 621–634; and Alden, *Robert Dinwiddie*, 26–37. On land policy in Virginia from Spottswood to Gooch, see Warren R. Hofstra, "'The Extension of His Majesties Dominions': The Virginia Backcountry

required that all surveyed lands be patented, which meant that speculators could no longer hold large tracts without having to pay quitrents
on them.[11] William Stith, Anglican clergyman, chaplain of the burgesses,
and head of the College of William and Mary, rallied opposition to the
fee with the slogan "Liberty, Property and no Pistole."[12] The burgesses,
having received numerous petitions protesting the fee, especially from the
western counties most affected, struck a special committee to investigate
the matter, informing Dinwiddie that they had an "undoubted Right"
to "inquire into the Grievances of the People."[13] This committee then
informed Dinwiddie that "The Rights of the Subject are so secured by
Law, that they cannot be deprived of the least Part of their Property, but
by their own Consent." Furthermore, they contended, the Virginia constitution was founded on this "excellent Principle," and ever since "this
Colony has had the Happiness of being under the immediate Protection
of the Crown." Moreover, the king has always held that no man's life or
property can be taken without "established and known Laws."[14]

According to the burgesses, their right to consent to such fees was also
customary, for under both the Virginia Company and the Crown, all land
patents had been affixed "without Fee or Reward." To alter this manner
of granting land, the committee argued, would be "an Infringement on
the Rights of the People, and a Discouragement from taking up Lands,
and thereby ... the settling the Frontiers of this Country, and the Increase
of his Majesty's Revenue of Quitrents."[15]

On Tuesday, December 4, Dinwiddie addressed the burgesses, arguing
that while he was cognizant of their "just Privileges," his authority to levy
the Pistole Fee "relates solely to Disposal of the King's Land," which was a
"Matter of Favour from the Crown," designed to improve "his Majesty's
Revenue of Quit-Rents." As such, it was founded on "unquestionable

and the Reconfiguration of Imperial Frontiers," *Journal of American History* 84 (1998),
1281–1312. Hofstra characterizes the aim of this policy, which involved the settlement
of foreign Protestants in the backcountry to provide a barrier against the French, as
(especially after 1730) "territorial conquest" (1311).

[11] Alden, *Robert Dinwiddie*, 27.

[12] In a letter to the bishop of London, quoted in Jack P. Greene, ed., "The Case of the Pistole
Fee: The Report of a Hearing on the Pistole Fee Dispute before the Privy Council, June
18th, 1754," in *Virginia Magazine of History and Biography* 66 (1958), 400–401.

[13] H.R. McIlwaine, ed., *Journals of the House of Burgesses of Virginia, 1752–1755, 1756–
1758* (Richmond, VA: The Colonial Press, E. Waddey, 1909), 141 (for a list of counties
that sent in petitions, see pp. 121 and 129).

[14] McIlwaine, ed., *Journals of the House of Burgesses of Virginia*, 143.

[15] Ibid., 143–144.

Authority."[16] The burgesses, however, continued to insist that the fee was "illegal and arbitrary" and "contrary to the Charters of this Colony." And they resolved to send "a loyal Address to the King" in protest.[17] The burgesses also rejected a compromise from the council, whereby the two houses would jointly pass the fee. As a result, on December 15, the council announced in an address to the Crown that it would be supporting the governor. In response, the burgesses prepared to send Peyton Randolph, the king's attorney general, to London to protest the fee before the Privy Council, promising him a handsome salary as well as an annual stipend should he, a royal officer, be dismissed by the governor for disobeying his authority.[18]

Faced with the opposition of the burgesses, Dinwiddie prorogued the assembly on December 19, 1753. While the dispute over the Pistole Fee was coming to a head, tensions were also building with the French in the Ohio Valley. As a result, before sending them home, Dinwiddie chastised the burgesses for their resistance to a small fee when the peace and safety of the colony was imperiled. Instead of showing zeal "for his Majesty's Service," they ignored "the designs of the French," despised "the Friendship of the Indians," and disputed "the Rights of the Crown in the Disposal of their own Lands."[19] Dinwiddie also complained bitterly to his patron Halifax about the burgesses' "republican way of thinking" and their frequent "encroachments on the prerogative of the crown," which, he believed, resulted from "some former governor" who "submitted too much to them."[20]

After Dinwiddie prorogued the assembly, Richard Bland, who was at the center of the opposition to the Pistole Fee, wrote a pamphlet that laid out the burgesses' case in more detail.[21] By the mid-1750s, Bland was emerging as a leading member of the burgesses (he ended up serving for thirty-two

---

[16] Ibid., 154. Dinwiddie also justified the fee by claiming that the council had consented to it. The burgesses, however, denied that the council had the authority to set fees or levy taxes. See ibid., 141.

[17] Ibid., 154. The Privy Council rejected the burgesses' address on June 21, 1754. *APCC*, IV, 232–235.

[18] McIlwaine, ed., *Journals of the House of Burgesses of Virginia*, 168–169.

[19] Ibid., 171; Koontz, *Robert Dinwiddie*, 216.

[20] Quoted in Koontz, *Robert Dinwiddie*, 220.

[21] *A Modest and True State of the Case*. Bland's pamphlet is unfinished and was likely not published. It is reprinted in Paul Leicester Ford, ed., *A Fragment on the Pistole Fee, claimed by the Governor of Virginia* (Brooklyn, NY: Historical Printing Club, 1891), 31–43 (quote on p. 31).

years – 1742 to 1775). He was also a justice of the peace; a colonel of the county militia; a slave-holding plantation owner; an Indian commissioner; and, at the end of his life, a delegate to both the First and the Second Continental Congress as well as to the convention that drafted the Virginia constitution and the new state's declaration of rights in 1776.[22]

Bland based his opposition to the Pistole Fee on an account of the English constitution in which "The Rights of the Subjects are so secured by Law that they cannot be deprived of the least part of their property without their own consent." "Upon this Principle of Law," he argued, "the Liberty and Property of every Person who has the felicity to live under a British Government is founded."[23] For Bland, then, it was not the size of the fee that was the issue but rather the "Lawfulness of it." And, as in the infamous case of Ship Money under Charles I, once the legal restraints on royal authority were breached, the governor – "this Leviathan of Power" – who has the authority to "impose one Pistole" may instead "impose an Hundred."[24] As a result, every infringement on "the legal Forms of government" was, Bland argued, "like a small spark" – if "not extinguished," it will "blaze out into irresistible Flame."[25] Moreover, despite claiming that royal governors in Virginia had not previously levied such fees without consent (i.e., by authority of their instructions alone), Bland did not think that precedent was determinative. After all, he argued, the fact that governors in other colonies collected such fees did not justify them, for in doing so "they Demand that which the Law does not give them & therefore are guilty of taking from the subjects without legal authority."[26]

Following the prorogation of the burgesses in December 1754, Peyton Randolph, the attorney general, and now the colony's agent, sailed for London.[27] Dinwiddie, outraged that a royal officer would act

[22] Despite his central role in the seminal events of the mid-eighteenth century, Bland has not been the subject of a full-length biography. But see Robert Detweiler, *Richard Bland and the Origins of the Revolution in Virginia* (Yorktown: Virginia Bicentennial Commission, 1981); and Clinton Rossiter, *Seedtime of the Republic: The Origin of the American Tradition of Political Liberty* (New York: Harcourt, Brace, 1953), 247–280.

[23] *A Modest and True State of the Case*, 37.

[24] Ibid., 38.

[25] Ibid., 38–39.

[26] Ibid., 40.

[27] As part of his lobbying, Randolph arranged for the publication of Landon Carter's defense of the burgesses: *A Letter from a Gentleman in Virginia to the Merchants of Great Britain, Trading to that Colony* (London, 1754). On Carter's role, see Jack P. Greene, "Landon Carter and the Pistole Fee Dispute, *William and Mary Quarterly* 14

independently of the governor's authority, removed Randolph from office and made George Wythe attorney general. Dinwiddie also retained his friend, James Abercromby, another imperially minded Scot, to represent him in London.

The hearing on the Pistole Fee took place before the Privy Council in June 1754, with an array of legal talent in attendance, including William Murray, later Lord Mansfield, who was the Newcastle administration's attorney general.[28] The Earl of Halifax, president of the Board of Trade was there, as was Lord Granville, president of the Privy Council, who told Peyton Randolph in no uncertain terms that the money the burgesses had promised him was "part of the Revenue of the Crown" and that he "would be liable to an Action from the Governor" should the colony's treasurer pay him.[29]

The hearing opened with William Murray's defense of Dinwiddie. In Murray's view, "the King has an absolute property in all the Lands in this Colony, not already granted out," and may "dispose of them upon what Terms he pleases."[30] Given that the king is the "absolute Proprietor of these Lands," he may in his instructions authorize the governor to "pass grants of Lands in this Colony, upon what Terms he pleases."[31] Moreover, in the absence of royal control of the distribution of land, Murray contended that elites in Virginia had taken up "great quantities of Land," more than they "ever intend to Cultivate." In addition to engrossing huge tracts of land, these speculators had failed to pay quitrents to the Crown.[32] Murray also accused Peyton Randolph of venality, adding that his agency was being paid out of money "to be levied upon the People by the single Authority of one Branch of the Legislature, which is infinitely a greater Burthen than this Patent can be."[33]

Murray's cocounsel was another Scot, Alexander Hume Campbell. Campbell echoed Murray's argument about the absolute right of the king to dispose of lands in Virginia, adding that he could certainly do so "without the leave of *this little Assembly*, who, because they may now

---

(1957), 66–69. Randolph brought the case to the attention of the Privy Council on February 18, 1754. See *APCC*, IV, 232–235.

[28] The briefs before the Privy Council are reprinted in Greene, ed., "The Case of the Pistole Fee, 399–422.

[29] Ibid., 422.

[30] Ibid., 408.

[31] Ibid.

[32] Ibid., 407.

[33] Ibid., 408.

enjoy the Happiness of a mild Government, have presumed to demand that as a matter of Right, which was heretofore indulged them only as a favour." Like Murray, Campbell also attacked the "Land Jobbers" in the burgesses who, he claimed, have an "inordinate and boundless" "Lust" for "acquiring Lands," which, if it were not curbed, would "produce the total destruction of that Colony." He also charged the burgesses with bribing a king's officer – Peyton Randolph – "*to swerve from his duty to the King*" and "oppose the King's Governor acting under the King's Instructions."[34] In doing so, "this puny House of Burgesses have boldly dared to do, what the House of Commons in England never presumed to Attempt."[35]

The lawyers for the burgesses, Robert Henley and Alexander Forrester, argued that under Gooch's long tenure, Virginians were a "free people," who lived "in a remote Country under so mild a Government." In this period, the royal governor had not levied fees without their consent. As a result, the Crown, even though it "is seized of these Lands," cannot "now demand a Fee, which it has long given up."[36] They also pointed out that the lands in question were not very valuable, being far from settlements and any navigable rivers. Furthermore, keeping the cost of settling new lands low would be "an Encouragement to Protestants to settle there." On the other hand, they asked, what settlers would take up these lands "if the Governor proves this Arbitrary."[37] In addition, they argued, if the Pistole Fee was a discouragement to settlement before the onset of hostilities with the French, it was even more so "now when this Colony is attacked by a powerfull Enemy."[38]

Henley and Forrester also contended that allowing royal governors to levy such taxes without consent was an invitation to the abuse of executive authority, for they "always will, endeavour to oppress the Subjects"; and "the distance they are from a superior Power ... enables them to do it with Impunity."[39] Given the danger that Virginia faced from Dinwiddie's "avarice," the burgesses were justified in sending Randolph to represent them in London. Far from Randolph's appointment being an "Instance of disloyalty in the Assembly," it shows "the great Confidence they have in

[34] Ibid., 410.
[35] Ibid., 411.
[36] Ibid., 412.
[37] Ibid., 414.
[38] Ibid., 412.
[39] Ibid., 413.

his Majesty; since they consider his Servant as the Servant of the People."[40]
In opposing the Pistole Fee, then, the burgesses were defending "the
Rights and Privileges, which have been transmitted to them from their
Ancestors."[41] In addition, the burgesses were responding to "the Cries
of the People," and in doing so they had "proceeded in a Parliamentary
way," gathering sufficient evidence before they "Voted this Fee illegal."
Above all, they were "not inflamed against their Sovereign, but animated
with a just resentment against the Usurpation of a Viceroy."[42]

On June 24, the Privy Council decided that Dinwiddie had the authority to
enact the Pistole Fee, thereby holding that the royal instructions trumped
the right of the burgesses to consent to the raising of revenues. However,
the council held that Dinwiddie could levy the fee only on patents of 100
acres or more that lay on the east side of the Allegheny mountains. To the
west, beyond the mountains in the fertile Mississippi Valley, there would
be no fee on land patents in order to encourage settlement.[43]

News of the Privy Council's decision reached the colony in October
1754. The previous month, following George Washington's surrender at Fort Necessity, the burgesses had refused to vote supplies unless
Dinwiddie finally approved the payment of several thousand pounds
to Peyton Randolph for his service in London as its agent. In response,
Dinwiddie prorogued the assembly.[44] But when the session resumed on
October 17, both sides were in a more conciliatory mood as the decision
of the Privy Council had ended the dispute by giving something to each.
And in May of the following year, Dinwiddie, exhausted by the whole
affair, reappointed Peyton Randolph and agreed to the burgesses' request
for the payment of his agent's salary.[45] In return, the burgesses voted a
large sum of money for the prosecution of the war against the French.[46]
Despite this rapprochement, another clash between the governor and the
burgesses was in the offing, one that also involved the authority of the
legislature, the nature of the royal prerogative, and the constitutionality
of the governor's instructions.

[40] Ibid., 415.
[41] Ibid., 419.
[42] Ibid., 416.
[43] Ibid., 422.
[44] Landon Carter defended the burgesses in an essay in the *Maryland Gazette* on Thursday,
October 24, 1754.
[45] See Koontz, *Robert Dinwiddie*, 231.
[46] Morton, *Colonial Virginia*, II, 632.

In 1748, in the last year of governor Gooch's tenure, the House of Burgesses completed a wholesale revision of Virginia's laws, which they then sent to the Board of Trade for review.[47] They arrived at an auspicious moment, for in 1748, Lord Halifax, the newly appointed president of the Board of Trade, initiated another round of reforms to the empire's ramshackle political structure, attempting to centralize authority in London by strengthening the royal prerogative after decades of lax oversight under Walpole's Whigs. As a result, the laws Virginia submitted in 1748 received real scrutiny. In 1751, the Board of Trade (after consulting with the Crown's law officers) recommended to the Privy Council committee for the plantations that ten of the new laws should be disallowed; and the rest, fifty-seven in total, be formally confirmed.[48]

The Privy Council disallowed these laws in part because they violated a royal instruction issued in 1738, which required the inclusion of a clause in any colonial legislation suspending its operation if it altered an earlier law that had been confirmed by the Crown, or if it was enacted for a period of less than two years (a tactic colonial legislatures sometimes used to avoid review altogether).[49] Laws that met either of these criteria (or both) would not go into effect until they had been vetted by the Privy Council in London. Governor Gooch, closely involved in the revision of Virginia's laws, had ignored this instruction when he approved these laws.

[47] On this episode, see Gwenda Morgan, "'The Privilege of Making Laws': The Board of Trade, the Virginia Assembly and Legislative Review, 1748–1754," *Journal of American Studies* 10 (1976), 1–15. Previously, the Privy Council had often let colonial laws "lye bye," neither confirming nor disallowing them. Although this practice was the product in part of a long period of lax royal oversight of the empire, it may also have been intentional, as it avoided the conflict that a disallowance could bring. As well, if it failed to confirm a law, the Privy Council could always disallow it later. Once confirmed, however, colonial laws were much harder to alter or amend. On this point, see Elmer B. Russell, *The Review of American Colonial Legislation by the King in Council* (New York: Columbia University Press, 1915), 56–57.

[48] For the disallowances, see *APCC*, IV, 131–141 (some were put in a probationary category). The normal procedure was for the laws to be vetted by the Board of Trade in consultation with the Crown's law officers (the Attorney General or Solicitor General). They then rendered an opinion on the legality of the legislation (determining whether it violated the royal instructions, or the terms of the charter, or the powers of the prerogative), which the Board then used as the basis for a recommendation to the Privy Council's committee on plantation affairs, who in turn advised the Privy Council to either accept or reject the laws. Gwenda Morgan argues that the laws were disallowed retroactively (or *ab initio*); that is, they were deemed to have never taken effect. In looking at the Privy Council records, I see no evidence that this was done. In the Parson's Cause, the clergy made this argument about the Two Penny Act, but it was not widely accepted. Morgan, "The Privilege of Making Laws," 3–4.

[49] Labaree, ed., *Royal Instructions*, I, 128.

Dinwiddie, who had just arrived in Virginia, had the unhappy task of informing the burgesses in early 1752 that the king had disallowed some of their painstakingly revised laws. These vetoes caused no small amount of consternation, as Virginians, having waited for several years to see if any of the new laws would be disallowed, had already had them promulgated and would now have to revert to the laws that had been in effect prior to 1748. As well, by formally confirming the rest of the law code, the Privy Council had ensured that (again, because of the 1738 royal instruction) they could not now be altered without the insertion of a clause suspending their operation until royal consent had been obtained. Moreover, the assembly knew that if the Privy Council continued the practice of formally confirming laws, then suspending clauses would become a precondition of almost all legislation, severely curtailing their legislative autonomy.[50]

In April 1752, the burgesses and the council appointed a joint committee to petition the king about the disallowance of their laws. The committee acknowledged the king's right to review and disallow their acts as well as to require the insertion of a suspending clause in certain types of laws. However, they insisted, according to "the ancient Constitution and Usage of this Colony," all laws enacted in the colony "have always been taken and held to be in full Force" until news of a royal allowance arrived. This meant that the assembly had the right to alter or amend their own laws "as our Exigencies may require." But now that the king had confirmed fifty-seven of their laws, they could not alter them without royal approval, "even tho' our Necessities for an immediate Revisal or Amendment may ever be so pressing." This new practice of confirmation, they complained, "will Subject us to great Hardships and Inconveniences, since it is not within the Reach of human foresight to form any Laws but what may from Experience be found to want necessary and sometimes speedy Amendments."[51]

Upon receiving the burgesses' petition, the Board of Trade replied that royal limitations on colonial legislative autonomy were necessary "not only to preserve the Just and proper Influence and Authority, which the Crown ought to have in the Direction and Government of its Colonies in America, but also to secure to its Subjects their just Liberties and

---

[50] Morgan, "The Privilege of Making Laws," 9–10.

[51] For the petition of the joint committee, see H.R. McIlwaine, ed., *Legislative Journals of the Council of Colonial Virginia*, Volume II (Richmond, VA: The Colonial Press, Everett Waddey Co., 1918), 1082–1087; and McIlwaine, ed., *Journals of the House of Burgesses of Virginia, 1752–1758*, 78–80.

Privileges."[52] Although it rejected the burgesses' appeal, the Board did not regularly employ confirmation in subsequent years.[53] Instead, it relied on a more vigorous use of the suspending clause; and it insisted on the regular submission of colonial laws to the Crown for review.[54] And because of the looming war with the French, the Board of Trade sought colonial cooperation in the mid-1750s, which reduced its desire to create constitutional tensions in the empire. However, later in the decade, as a British victory against the French seemed increasingly likely, another dispute flared up in Virginia over the royal power of disallowance.

At the center of this new dispute was one of the 1748 laws that had been confirmed by the Crown. Among other things, it fixed the salaries of the clergy in Virginia at 16,000 pounds of tobacco per annum.[55] In 1753 and again in 1755, the assembly temporarily altered the terms of this 1748 act, allowing payment in money for a limited period of time because of tobacco shortages. In 1758, another shortage caused by a severe drought led the burgesses once again to pass such a temporary law, allowing the payment of all tobacco-denominated debts at two pence to the pound (the market price had risen to six pence). Although it altered the 1748 act that had been approved by the Crown, the new governor, Francis Fauquier, did not insist that this Two Penny Act contain a suspending clause, and it was duly enacted. Already upset by the earlier attempts to reduce their salaries, a number of the clergy, who stood to lose a portion of their annual income, organized against the new act. Although it affected all who had contractual guarantees to be paid in tobacco, the dispute came to be known as the Parson's Cause on account of the heavy participation of the clergy in protesting it.[56]

---

[52] February 14, 1752, C.O. 5/1367, fos. 7–10.

[53] Morgan, "Privilege of Making Laws," 13. This was in part because English interest groups often protested colonial laws, and if they had already been confirmed it was very difficult to change them (it required the consent of the colonial legislature or an act of Parliament).

[54] Russell, *Review of American Colonial Legislation*, 95–96.

[55] It also made the vestry in each parish and not the Crown responsible for the livings of the clergy. See Morton, *Colonial Virginia*, II, 795.

[56] On the Parson's cause, see Billings et al., *Colonial Virginia*, 257–259; Morton, *Colonial Virginia*, II, 751–819; Joseph H. Smith, *Appeals to the Privy Council from the American Plantations* (New York: Columbia University Press, 1950), 607–626; Bernhard Knollenberg, *Origin of the American Revolution, 1759–1766* (New York: MacMillan, 1960), 53–64; and Arthur P. Scott, "The Constitutional Aspects of the 'Parsons Cause,'" *Political Science Quarterly* 31 (1916), 558–577. I will focus on the constitutional arguments. I see no evidence that, contrary to the claims of the Virginia clergy and the bishop

The clergy met in convention in late 1758 and elected John Camm to travel to London to appeal the Two Penny act. Born in England, Camm came to Virginia in the mid-1740s. At the time of the Parson's Cause he was a professor of Divinity at William and Mary, and rector of York-Hampton parish.[57] In their representation to the Board of Trade, the clergy complained that by the 1758 Act they were "deprived of that Maintenance which was enacted for them by his Majesty, whose royal Authority the said Assembly cannot by Law controul." As well, the clergy accused the assembly of duplicity because the act was only "made for 10 or 12 Months," precisely "to prevent the Possibility of "royal Consideration" of it before it expired. And despite its temporary nature and the fact that it altered a law that had received royal confirmation, it still did not contain a "suspending Clause, to wait the royal Judgment and Pleasure."[58]

However, given that the Two Penny Act had already expired, the clergy had to do more than demonstrate its illegality. For if they were to collect the salaries they felt were owed to them, they would have to convince the Privy Council to declare it "null and void *ab initio*," as if it had never taken effect (whereas in an ordinary disallowance, the law was in effect until repealed). Only with such a retroactive disallowance could they collect the salaries they would have been paid in 1758 had the Two Penny Act not been passed.

In his appeal, Camm obtained the support of the influential bishop of London, who wrote to the Privy Council on the June 14, 1759, arguing that to suspend the operation of a royal act without obtaining the Crown's assent was "Treason." The bishop also argued that for the burgesses "to

of London, those opposed to Camm wanted disestablishment (as opposed to a continuation of lay dominance in the church). On the religious dimensions of the Parson's Cause (as one part of a general crisis of authority in late colonial Virginia), see Rhys Isaacs, "Religion and Authority: Problems of the Anglican Establishment in Virginia in the Era of the Great Awakening and the Parson's Cause," *William and Mary Quarterly* 30 (1973), 4–36; and Issacs, *The Transformation of Virginia, 1740–1790* (New York: W.W. Norton, 1988), 144–157.

57 On Camm's life, see "Sketch of John Camm," *William and Mary Quarterly* 19 (1910), 28–30. On the convention, see Morton, *Colonial Virginia*, II, 786–767, who contends that Camm did not represent a majority of the clergy. On Camm's travails at William and Mary, see Morton, *Colonial Virginia*, II, 773–776.

58 "The Humble Representation of the Clergy of the Church of England, in his Majesty's Colony and Dominion of Virginia." (Reprinted in Richard Bland, *The Colonel Dismounted: Or the Rector Vindicated. In a Letter Addressed to His Reverence: Containing a Dissertation upon the Constitution of the Colony* (Williamsburg: Joseph Royle, 1764), xxiv–xxvii.

assume a power to bind the King's hands ... is such an act of Supremacy as is inconsistent with the Dignity of the Crown of England, and manifestly tends to draw the people of the plantations from their allegiance to the King."[59]

In August of 1759, Camm obtained a hearing on the Two Penny Act before the Privy Council. On the Board of Trade's recommendation, the Privy Council disallowed the act, as well as the earlier (1753 and 1755) alterations to the original 1748 law.[60] They also reprimanded Virginia's governor, Francis Fauquier, for giving royal assent to the Two Penny Act without insisting that the burgesses insert a suspending clause in it.[61] However, the colony did get a victory of sorts, as the act was repealed, but not voided *ab initio* (i.e., retroactively) as the clergy had hoped.[62]

In the summer of 1760, when Camm finally returned from his lengthy sojourn in England, he paid a visit to governor Fauquier to present him with a copy of the order-in-council disallowing the Two Penny Act.[63] Fauquier, sympathetic to the burgesses and furious at Camm for taking so long to inform the colony of the decision, ordered him out of the

---

[59] William Stevens Perry, ed., *Historical Collections Relating to the American Colonial Church: Volume I, Virginia* (Hartford, CT: Church Press, 1870), 461–463.

[60] For a copy of the Board's recommendation to the Privy Council, see Perry, ed., *Historical Collections*, 458–460. For the disallowance by the Privy Council, see *APCC*, IV, 420–421.

[61] Fauquier's reprimand read as follows: "An instruction prepared by the Board of Trade, on an order from the Committee on 3 Aug. is approved, requiring the Lieutenant Governor strictly to observe and obey the directions of Article 16 of his instructions relating to the passing of laws, upon pain of his Majesty's highest displeasure, and of being immediately recalled from his government." *APCC*, IV, 421.

[62] On the arguments before the Privy Council about whether the Two Penny Act should be disallowed retroactively, see Smith, *Appeals to the Privy Council*, 613–614. In 1753, the Attorney General and Solicitor General (Sir Dudley Ryder and William Murray, respectively) had held that acts of the colonial assembly "are good till repealed, and, consequently, void only from notification of the repealed." George Chalmers, *Opinions of Eminent Lawyers on Various Points of English Jurisprudence Chiefly Concerning the Colonies, Fisheries, and Commerce* (New York; Burt Franklin, 1971), I, 295. In defending the colony before the Board of Trade in July 1759, James Abercromby had contended that the only way the act could be rendered void *ab initio* was if it had contravened the 1696 Navigation Act (which contained a clause stating that any colonial law opposed to its provisions was null and void). See Smith, *Appeals to the Privy Council*, 612.

[63] The burgesses were informed of the disallowance by Governor Fauquier on October 6, 1760. See McIlwaine, ed., *Journals of the House of Burgesses of Virginia, 1758–1761*, 184. For Fauquier's anger at Camm for tarrying in England and not letting him know about the Privy Council's decision until after his return in June 1760, see Morton, *Colonial Virginia*, II, 802.

governor's residence, never to return. Fauquier then proclaimed the disallowance as an ordinary repeal. Not surprisingly, Camm continued to insist that the Privy Council's disallowance had been retroactive, voiding the 1758 law from the outset.[64] Based on this reading of the decision, Camm and four other clergymen sued their parishes in county court, arguing that because the Two Penny Act had never been a valid law, they were now owed the money they would have been paid under the old 1748 law.

In response, the burgesses and the council once more set up a joint committee to petition the king, denying that the Two Penny Act had undermined the royal prerogative. They also denied that there was any precedent for holding that a disallowed law was void from inception, as Camm was claiming.[65] And in early 1759, after first hearing of the clergy's plans to lobby against the Two Penny Act, both houses of the assembly agreed to appoint their own agent in London who would report back to a permanent committee of correspondence made up of representatives of the burgesses and the council.[66]

As the court cases began in Virginia, John Camm circulated the bishop of London's 1759 letter, which had been scathingly critical of the assembly's conduct. This elicited responses from Richard Bland, as well as Landon Carter, another veteran of the Pistole Fee dispute.[67] In his response to the bishop of London, Carter conceded that the 1758 act had violated the terms of the royal instructions (as had the similar acts in 1753 and 1755); but he contended that it was a temporary expedient, meant to provide relief to the inhabitants of Virginia when the tobacco crop was too poor

---

[64] According to William Robinson's August 12, 1765, letter to the bishop of London, Halifax had told Camm that if the Two Penny Act were brought before the Privy Council on appeal, it would most certainly be rendered void *ab initio* on account of its manifest injustice. See Perry, ed., *Historical Collections*, I, 510.

[65] Morton, *Colonial Virginia*, II, 804–807 (this "Humble Representation" was sent to London in the fall of 1760).

[66] Ibid., 788–793. On the committee of correspondence, see E.I. Miller, "The Virginia Committee of Correspondence, 1759–1770," *William and Mary Quarterly* 22 (1913), 1–19.

[67] Landon Carter, *A Letter to the Right Reverend Father in God, The Lord B – – p of L – – N* (Printed in Virginia and London, 1760). In *A Letter to a Gentleman in London* (1759), Carter also defended the colony from English merchants trading to Virginia who had sent a letter to the Board of Trade complaining that the Two Penny Act made paper money legal tender. For an insightful account of Carter's role in the constitutional conflicts of the 1750s, see Rhys Isaac, *Landon Carter's Uneasy Kingdom: Revolution and Rebellion on a Virginia Plantation* (New York: Oxford University Press, 2004), 123–161.

(and the costs of war with the French too high) for them to fulfill their contractual obligations. Surely, Carter asked, the king would not have denied Virginians such a right if he had been consulted. After all, "Is it not the Pleasure of Princes to listen to, and relieve, the Complaints of their Subjects."[68] Carter also pointed out that the Two Penny Act affected all those who were owed payment in tobacco; as such, it was not, as the bishop of London had charged, an attempt "to ruin the Maintenance of the Clergy."[69]

As for the burgesses' authority to pass such an act, Carter argued that "in a British Government" the "Power" to make such decisions rested with "the Parliament; or, as we call it, the General-Assembly?"[70] Carter also argued that the governor, who is "the Representative of his Majesty," had consented to the act, and therefore it was a valid law, as good as the 1748 act it temporarily replaced. As such, he argued, the 1758 act could not be "a mere Nullity." Indeed, if local laws were routinely declared "null, *ab initio*," it would be "very productive of Evil."

Carter also denied that royal instructions were "Laws of publick Authority," or "Rules" of the "Constitution," for they were intended only to guide the conduct of the governor; and even if they were to bind the inhabitants of Virginia, they would still be subject to "particular Exceptions" of the kind that the Two Penny Act represented.[71] As Carter put it, the king would not "pass an Instruction that shall effect the Ruin of the Community over which he presides." Such an act of prerogative would destroy his "own Regality, as all Sovereignty must cease where the Community ends." Indeed, Carter contended that having to wait for the king's assent in all cases would "render all Laws useless, until his Opinion could be known."[72]

In *A Letter to the Clergy*, Richard Bland also vindicated the conduct of the assembly against the aspersions cast upon it by John Camm and his allies among the clergy. Bland echoed many of Carter's arguments about the need for local legislative authority, especially in times of crisis when "The Father of his People is at too great a Distance to extend his beneficent Hand for their Relief in Time."[73] In such cases, he argued,

---

[68] Carter, *A Letter to the Right Reverend Father in God*, 35.
[69] Ibid., 36.
[70] Ibid., 44.
[71] Ibid., 46.
[72] Ibid., 59.
[73] Richard Bland, *A Letter to the Clergy of Virginia in which the Conduct of the General-Assembly is Vindicated against the Reflexions Contained in a Letter to the Lords of*

the "Instruction to a Governour" cannot be construed in such a way as to violate "the first Principles of Justice and Equity," or "to prevent" the governor's "Assent to a Law for relieving a Colony in a Case of such general Distress and Calamity." Moreover, Bland argued that if the clergy's conception of the royal prerogative ever became the constitutional norm in Virginia, "the People would be reduced to a State scarce superior to Galley-Slaves in Turkey, or Israelites under an Egyptian Bondage."[74] Bland did not, however, deny that Virginians were bound by the royal prerogative. Rather, he argued that there were normative limits on its exercise:

> The Royal Prerogative is without Doubt, of great Weight and Power in a dependent and subordinate Government: Like the King of Babylon's Decree, it may, for ought I know, almost force the People of the Plantations to fall down and worship any Image it shall please to set up; but, great and powerful as it is, it can only be exerted while in the Hands of the best and most benign Sovereign, for the Good of the People, and not for their Destruction.[75]

In 1763, John Camm responded to both Carter and Bland, arguing that their invocation of "*salus populi*" only applied in extreme situations like 1688, when the English had to "set aside an arbitrary Popish and abdicating King." By contrast, a relatively mundane occurrence like a poor tobacco crop was not a sufficient reason to transgress royal authority. After all, he reminded his opponents, Virginia is not "a little independent Sovereignty," but is "dependent on the Crown of Great-Britain."[76] According to Camm, this dependence conferred real benefits on its inhabitants, for all who live in the colony have the "Power and Riches of the Mother Country for their Defence against their Enemies." As well, Virginians have "the same Rights in the Mother Country as other British subjects," and "other British Subjects have equal Rights here."[77] However, Camm argued that the empire could not be a polity that respected the rights of all subjects equally if the Virginia assembly could "suspend Laws confirm'd by the King (which seems a Thing of the same Nature with a dispensing Power in the Crown"), or "Arbitrarily dispose of every Man's Property" by violating contracts and thereby

   Trade and Plantations, from the Lord-Bishop of London (Williamsburg: William Hunter, 1760), 16.

[74] Bland, *A Letter to the Clergy*, 16.

[75] Ibid., 18.

[76] John Camm, *A Single and Distinct View of the Act, Vulgarly Entitled the Two Penny Act: Containing an Account of It's Beneficial and Wholesome Effects in York-Hampton Parish* (Annapolis: Jonas Green, 1763), 37–38.

[77] Ibid., 38.

contravening natural justice. If the assembly continued to act in such an arbitrary manner, Camm warned, those who trade in Virginia would be "as unwilling to Trust their Property here, as in any Foreign Kingdom independent of the Crown of Great Britain."[78]

For Camm, then, the royal prerogative was necessary to preserve liberty: "if we could destroy the substance of the King's Power, or the Rights of the Crown, or the Prerogative ... and reduce it to a mere Shadow ... we should only hereby Sap one of the strongest Batteries, erected for the defense of Liberty and Property."[79] And maintaining inviolably "the Dignity of the Crown" was a necessary check to the potentially arbitrary authority of the Virginia assembly. Given this, Bland's charge that the clergy wished to subvert the constitution was false. Nor was it the case that the royal power of disallowance was a form of tyranny. Indeed, Camm mocked Bland for his extravagant fears: "The Colonel if he pleases, may set his Heart at rest, and be assured, that no body desires to see him reduced even to so bad a Condition as that of the Egyptian Bondage of his Slaves."[80]

Richard Bland's final statement on the Parson's Cause came on the eve of the revolutionary crisis in 1764.[81] In it, he built on the arguments that the burgesses had made throughout the 1750s in defense of their constitutional rights, and added to them an imaginative rethinking of the place of Virginia in the empire. In response to Camm's vigorous argument for a transatlantic polity governed by prerogative, Bland offered the first explicitly federal vision of the relationship between Crown and colony in the British empire, one that allowed Virginia a zone of internal autonomy while still maintaining its subjection to the king and Parliament in its external relations with other Britons.

Bland first asked what the legal status of Virginians was. Were, for example, "the present Inhabitants of Virginia" a "People conquered by the British Arms"? Bland noted that many jurists and philosophers – he cites Bacon, Coke, and Holt – had argued that following the conquest of "a Pagan or Infidel" country, its laws were abrogated, and the inhabitants were subject to whatever laws the conquering king saw fit to impose.[82]

[78] Ibid.
[79] Ibid., 24.
[80] Ibid., 36.
[81] Bland, *The Colonel Dismounted*.
[82] Ibid., 20–21. Bland quotes from both Coke and Bacon's opinions in *Calvin's Case*, as well as from Holt's opinion in *Smith v. Brown and Cooper* (1703), which held that

As such, he conceded that if Virginians were to "be considered only as the savage Aborigines of this Part of America," then they could not "pretend to the Rights of British Subjects."[83] But Bland was emphatic that Virginians had not been conquered. Rather, they were the "Descendants of Englishmen, who by their own Consent, and at the Expense of their own Blood and Treasure, undertook to settle this new Region for the Benefit and Aggrandizement of the Parent Kingdom." As such, the "native Privileges our Progenitors enjoyed" descended to the current settlers and "could not be forfeited by their Migration to America."[84] Indeed, Bland argued that the original settlers could not have been induced "by so inadequate a Reward" to expand "the English dominions," if by "making Conquests" they became "Slaves."[85] Furthermore, Bland contended that even the Native Americans – the "original Inhabitants" – were "never fully conquered." Rather, they had "submitted to the English Government upon Terms of Peace and Friendship fixed and settled by Treaties."[86] As such, they still possessed "their native Laws and Customs, savage as they are, in as full an Extent as they did before the English settled upon this Continent."[87]

So, for Bland, Virginians were not a conquered people. On the contrary, they had an inherent right to live "Under" an "English Government," where "all Men are born free" and are "only subject to Laws made with their own Consent." This, for Bland, was "a vital principle of the constitution"; it places all subjects, as long as they obey the laws, "without the reach of the highest Executive Power in the State."[88] Thus the settlers in Virginia, having lost none of their inherent rights by migrating to the New World, must "necessarily have a legal Constitution," with a legislature composed "in Part, of the Representatives of the People."

Virginia was a conquered country and therefore it could be "governed by such Laws as the King pleases." According to Bland, this "great Judge" was "not acquainted with Virginia," for neither "the original or present Inhabitants" were conquered.

[83] Ibid., 21.
[84] Ibid. He added that even if the ancestors of "the present Inhabitants" had been conquerors, they would not have lost "their native Privileges by their Conquests." Rather, they would still have "had as good a Right to the Liberties of Englishmen, after their Conquest, as they had before."
[85] Ibid.
[86] For Bland's role in the assembly negotiating Indian treaties and alliances, see Detweiler, *Richard Bland*, 23. He was also active in the war effort against the French, serving on several important committees. See also Clinton Rossiter, "Richard Bland: The Whig in America," *William and Mary Quarterly* 10 (1953), 44–45.
[87] Bland, *The Colonel Dismounted*, 21.
[88] Ibid.

Without such representation, Bland held, "I am bold enough to say, no Law can be made."[89] Moreover, these English constitutional principles meant that the Virginia assembly had "a Right to enact ANY Law they shall think necessary for their INTERNAL Government." It was not, as Murray and Campbell had argued before the Privy Council, a "puny" assembly but was in fact the equal of Parliament within its own jurisdiction.

Bland also based his defense of the colony's legislative autonomy on the original royal charter as well as the proposed charter of 1676, which Charles II had disallowed. According to Bland, the right to representation granted by both of these charters had been included in the royal commission, which authorized the governor to call a representative assembly in order to pass laws. Moreover, Virginians had enjoyed their "Right to a legal government" by "a constant and uninterrupted Usage and Custom," which, according to Bland, they had "continued to exercise for more than 140 Years." Such a strong claim, Bland assured his readers, could not be countered, even by "the Rector's Principles of passive Obedience."[90]

Bland denied that this internal autonomy would derogate from Virginia's dependence on the mother country, for just as "we cannot lose the Rights of Englishmen by our Removal to this Continent; so neither can we withdraw our Dependence without destroying the Constitution."[91] Nor did it mean that Virginia would be exempt from English laws. The common law was the "Birth-right" of all Englishmen, the product of the "common Consent of the People from Time Immemorial." As such, it inhered in an Englishman "wherever he goes" and thus must be "the General Law by which the Colony is to be governed."[92] As well, Bland held that the statutes in place at the time of the founding of the colony also bound the colonists, given that they were made by the consent of "our Ancestors." If not, then the empire would have two bodies of laws, both made by consent, one binding and the other not, which would be "absurd."[93]

Moreover, according to Bland, Virginians still needed royal assent for their bills to become laws, but he argued that this should be granted by the governor, with the king reserving the power of "abrogating" these laws "notwithstanding his Commissioner's Assent." However, Bland insisted that this royal disallowance only took effect "FROM THE TIME of such

[89] Ibid., 22.
[90] Ibid., 25.
[91] Ibid., 22.
[92] Ibid.
[93] Ibid., 22–23.

Abrogation, and NOT BEFORE."[94] By contrast, Camm's attempt to have the laws of the Virginia assembly disallowed retroactively would "render their Power a mere Cipher."[95] Although the king had the final say in deciding what became law in Virginia, Bland insisted that the royal prerogative was ultimately limited in its scope. With Camm in mind, he argued that only one of "Sir Robert Filmer's Disciples" could "assert that the King by his Prerogative can establish any form of Government he pleases in the Colony."[96] As for the royal instructions, Bland repeated his earlier claim that to treat them as laws binding on the people's representative would "strip us of all the Rights and Privileges of British Subjects."[97]

Under Bland's imperial constitution, then, the prerogative was circumscribed. Its main function was as a superintending power in a federal empire with near-total internal autonomy, including the right to raise and spend monies and to control the distribution of land within its boundaries. In addition to the prerogative, Bland held that Virginia was also subject in its "EXTERNAL Government" to "the Authority of the British Parliament." However, Bland insisted that this subjection had its limits, because even if "Parliament, as the stronger Power," could "force any Laws it shall think fit upon us," it did not have the "constitutional Right" to do so. For Bland insisted, "if the Parliament should impose Laws upon us merely relative to our INTERNAL Government, it deprives us, as far as those Laws extend, of the most valuable Part of our Birthright as Englishmen, of being governed by Laws made by our own Consent." As such, he warned ominously, it "may be opposed." However, Bland dismissed the possibility of resisting Parliament, assuring his readers that "we have nothing of this Sort to fear from those Guardians of the Rights and Liberties of Mankind."[98]

As Bland put down his pen in 1764, the clergy's lawsuits were still wending their way through the courts. In only one of them did a judge or jury accept the clergy's claim that the Two Penny Act had been retroactively disallowed. But even in this case (that of the Reverend James Maury),

[94] Ibid., 25.
[95] Ibid., 29.
[96] Ibid., 23.
[97] Ibid., 26.
[98] Ibid., 22. On the connection between Bland's defense of the internal autonomy of Virginia in the Parson's Cause and the colony's resistance to the Stamp Act in the fall of 1764, see Jack P. Greene, "*Virtus et Libertas*: Political Culture, Social Change, and the Origins of the Revolution in Virginia," in Greene, ed., *Understanding the American Revolution: Issues and Actors* (Charlottesville: University Press of Virginia, 1995), 184–185.

the young Virginian lawyer Patrick Henry managed to get the damages Maury had been awarded reduced to a paltry one penny – a pyrrhic victory indeed – with an eloquent denunciation of the clergy's abuse of the royal prerogative. In his closing argument, Henry told the jury that the royal disallowance of the Two Penny Act amounted to a breach of "the original compact between the King and people, stipulating protection on the one hand, obedience on the other." And as cries of treason echoed around the courtroom, Henry contended that in doing so, the king "degenerated into a tyrant, and forfeits all rights to his subjects' obedience."[99]

The conflicts in Virginia in the 1750s were in part the product of a new reform agenda begun by royal officials in London in the late 1740s and which would ultimately put Bland's question about parliamentary authority at the center of political debate in the empire. To understand these larger developments, which were to convulse the Atlantic world in the 1760s and 1770s, we need to go back to the 1720s, as, in the aftermath of the Board of Trade's failed attempt to revoke the charters, a new centralizing vision was taking shape.

---

[99] As recorded by Reverend Maury. Quoted in Morton, *Colonial Virginia*, II, 811. See also Perry, ed., *Historical Collections*, 497, 514, for William Robinson's recounting of the Maury trial to the bishop of London (August 17, 1764 and August 12, 1765).

PART III

REVOLUTION

7

In Search of a Unitary Empire

By the time the controversies over the prerogative in Virginia had died down in 1764, the empire was on the brink of a more serious dispute, one that involved the very question that Bland had raised only to dismiss: What was the extent of parliamentary authority in the internal affairs of the British American colonies? That this became the point of contention in the mid-1760s indicates that the locus of authority in the empire had shifted from the royal bureaucracy to the ministry. To understand this evolution, we need to go back to the oft-forgotten decades of the early to mid-eighteenth century, when, following the ill-fated attempt on the colonial charters, the empire experienced several decades without any serious constitutional strife. In an era of Whig hegemony at home and peace abroad, the colonies were left largely to their own devices. This laissez-faire policy facilitated the gradual accretion of power by the colonial assemblies at the expense of royal authority. However, a small group of officials in London saw these decades of lax oversight as anything but "a wise and salutary neglect."[1] As a result, they called for a wide-ranging reform of the empire's loose and unwieldy political structure. These reforms, predicated on the claim that Parliament was the ultimate sovereign in the empire, would tear the British Atlantic world apart in the 1770s.

In September 1721, as Jeremiah Dummer was inveighing against its final attempt to revoke the charters, the Board of Trade completed the most

---

[1] Edmund Burke, "Speech on Conciliation," in David Bromwich, ed., *On Empire, Liberty and Reform: Speeches and Letters* (New Haven: Yale University Press, 2000), 79.

comprehensive report on the state of the American colonies to date.[2] Its principal author was Martin Bladen, who, in his long service at the Board (1717–1741), kept alive the vision of a unitary empire that had been held by the bureaucrats of Edward Randolph and William Blathwayt's generation.[3]

Prior to writing the Board's report, Bladen had served on the commission that negotiated the boundaries between Britain and France in North America following the Treaty of Utrecht. This experience made him acutely aware of the French threat. For despite ceding Hudson Bay, Newfoundland, and Acadia (roughly present-day Nova Scotia and eastern New Brunswick), the French still held Cape Breton and therefore controlled the gateway to the St. Lawrence. As well, a disaffected French population remained in Acadia. And, beginning with the founding of Biloxi and Mobile, they began to make good on their long-standing claim to all the land between French Canada and the Gulf of Mexico. This was followed by the chartering of the Mississippi Company and the settlement of New Orleans in 1718.

In writing the Board's report, Bladen spent considerable time detailing the extent of France's territorial ambition, noting that it was building a series of forts from "the entry of the River St. Lawrence" to the mouth of the "Mississippy into the Bay of Mexico," thereby extending "the French Dominions" from "north to south thro' the whole Continent of America."[4] In doing so, the report contended, the French have "robbed" the English settlers of a great part of the trade "they formerly drove with the Indians"; as well, should another war break out, the French "may greatly incommode if not absolutely destroy" the English settlements.[5] The military threat from the French was compounded by their successful attempts "to bring over the Indians to their intrest." As the report pointed out, the French "missionaries have been so successful in this point, they have even seduced some part of the Iroquois commonly called by the

[2] "Council of Trade and Plantations to the King," September 21, 1721, in W. Noel Sainsbury, ed., *Calendar of State Papers, Colonial*, Volume 32 (1720–1721), #656, pp. 408–449 (hereafter CSPC). On the report's genesis, see Charles M. Andrews, *The Colonial Period of American History*, Volume IV (New Haven: Yale University Press, 1938), 389–390; and Ian K. Steele, *Politics of Colonial Policy: The Board of Trade in Colonial Administration* (Oxford: Clarendon Press, 1968), 167–170.
[3] Rory T. Cornish, "Martin Bladen (1680–1746)," *Oxford Dictionary of National Biography* (http://www.oxforddnb.com/view/article/2551; accessed online November 24, 2008).
[4] CSPC, 437.
[5] Ibid., 440.

name of the Five Nations, from their ancient friendship and dependence on your Majesty's colony of New York."[6]

To combat the French, the report urged that the English make "treaties and alliances of friendship with as many Indians as they can."[7] The Board also called for bolstering the "British intrest in those parts" by intermarriage, presents to the Indian chiefs, and evangelization "amongst those poor infidels." But above all, the Board urged that the English begin to outbid the French by "furnishing" the Indians with European commodities at "honest and reasonable prices," something that, the Board noted, had been made difficult by "the unreasonable avarice of our Indian traders." As such, the report proposed that this trade be put under "good regulations," a policy it thought would "greatly contribute to the increase of your Majesty's power and intrest in America." To achieve this end, the Board's report called for the Indian trade to be "equally free in all parts to all your Majesty's subjects in America; and all monopolies thereof discouraged, that no one colony or sett of people whatsoever may engross the same to the prejudice of their neighbours."[8]

The Board also lamented the weakness of royal authority in the colonies. In the private colonies in particular, the "large powers and privileges subsisting by virtue of several Charters" meant that "not only the soil but likewise the dominion or government of several colonies is absolutely alienated from the Crown."[9] The report recited the by now familiar litany of charges against the private colonies: they flouted the laws of trade; they failed to contribute to imperial defense; they sheltered pirates (which further undermined the empire's trade); they refused to send their laws home for review; and, on the rare occasions when they did so, and one of them met with royal disapproval, they simply reenacted it with a proviso that it expire before it had to be sent to London again.[10] All of these transgressions by the private colonies were "detrimental to your Majesty's authority, and tends to ye shaking of that dependency which they owe to your Majesty and to their Mother Kingdom."[11]

---

[6] Ibid., 439.

[7] Ibid., 444.

[8] Ibid., 443–445.

[9] Ibid., 445.

[10] The report gave the example of the proprietary colony of Pennsylvania whose charter gave it five years to send its laws to London and only five months for the Crown to review them (in the meantime they were in force). Ibid., 419.

[11] Ibid., 447.

The Board also decried the lack of revenue generated in the colonies, claiming that "whole provinces have been granted without any, or upon very small reservations to the Crown." As well, the governors had made "exorbitant grants to private persons" without ensuring that quit rents were collected.[12] The Board was also concerned that the royal woods in America were being cut down by private interests, thereby "destroying timber fit for the service of the Royal Navy."[13]

The Board's report argued that the weakness of royal authority in the empire was detrimental to Britain's wealth, and, by extension, to its military and strategic power. To rectify this situation, the report urged the Crown to secure "the intire absolute immediate dependency" of all of the colonies on England.[14] To this end, it once again urged the king to revoke the colonial charters, arguing that all of the private colonies "should be reassumed to the Crown, either by purchase, agreement or otherwise." In this way, they will be "under your Majesty's absolute and immediate government." In addition, by making "all the British Colonies in America hold immediately of one Lord," the "Indians" and the colonies' European rivals will respect English authority as there will no longer be "so many different interests on the Continent of America."[15]

In addition to the removal of the charters, the Board called for all of the colonies to be under the control of "one Lord Lieut. or Captain General" from whom the royal governors would "receive their orders." This captain general would have a "fixed salary ... independent of the pleasure of the inhabitants." He would be attended "by two or more councilors deputed from each plantation," forming a colonial union of a limited kind, and allowing "a general contribution of men or mony" to "be raised, upon the several colonies in proportion to their respective abilities."[16] The report also recommended that jurisdiction over the colonies be concentrated in the Board of Trade.[17] At present, it lamented, the

---

[12] Ibid., 446–447.
[13] On the conflict over timber rights in New England, see Joseph J. Malone, *Pine Trees and Politics: The Naval Stores and Forest Policy in Colonial New England, 1691–1775* (London: Longmans, 1964).
[14] CSPC, 445. The Board did claim that "their religion, liberties and properties should be inviolably preserved to them." (446).
[15] Ibid., 445.
[16] Ibid., 448.
[17] Recall that the Board as constituted in 1696 lacked any executive authority and had to refer all decisions to the secretary of state for the Southern Department, as well as the Privy Council (which, from 1714, had a standing committee for the colonies). In addition, the Treasury, the Customs department, and the Admiralty all had jurisdiction

lines of communication were too diffuse and cumbersome for the proper governance of the empire, with the Board having to share authority with the Privy Council and the secretary of state, which was conducive "to much delay and confusion," as "no one office is thor'ly informed of all matters relating to the Plantations."[18]

The Board's vision of the empire in 1721 was strikingly similar to the one it had articulated earlier in the century. Political centralization would allow for a more effective enforcement of the empire's commercial regulations, rendering the colonies economically beneficial to England as well as providing the wherewithal to match the French in the contest for North America. The demand for political reform in the empire was thus driven by both commercial and geopolitical considerations.

In the decade following the Board of Trade's report, there was some centralization of the empire's loose political structure. The proprietors of the Bahamas surrendered their chartered rights to the Crown, the last of the islands to do so.[19] And in 1723, the Board used the pretext of an ongoing boundary dispute between Connecticut and Rhode Island to suggest that both colonies surrender their charters voluntarily. Not surprisingly, they demurred, citing the protection their charters afforded basic liberties. In its reply to the Board, Rhode Island noted the travails of the first settlers who had founded the colony in "a Wild and Howling Wilderness … Inhabited by Salvage [*sic*] and Barbarous People," and "through their Labour, industry and paines" had "made such improvement in a few Years" that they were able to petition the king for a charter to secure the rights their labors had won. Moreover, the Rhode Islanders insisted they were loyal subjects of the Hanoverian king, who, because of "his Princely goodness," would surely respect the "Liberty and property" of his subjects.[20] And citing Jeremiah Dummer's *Defence*, they reminded "their Lordships" that "wee have a Tincture of the ancient Brittish Blood

---

over the colonies. For the structure of colonial governance in the 1720s, see James Henretta, *Salutary Neglect: Colonial Administration under the Duke of Newcastle* (New Jersey: Princeton University Press, 1972), 3–59.

[18] *CSPC*, 448–449.

[19] For the surrender of the Bahamas' charter, see Louise P. Kellogg, *The American Colonial Charter: A Study of English Administration in Relation Thereto, Chiefly after 1688* (Washington, DC: Government Printing Office, 1904), 250–251. On the Carolina settlers' resistance to the proprietors, which had been one of the chief reasons for the parliamentary resumption bill of 1715, see ibid., 246–250.

[20] Quoted in ibid. 322–323. Rhode Island's reply also noted that they had purchased the land from the natives.

in our veines and that wee esteem our liberty and property granted by our
Royall Charter equall to any Corporation in great Britain."[21]

Connecticut responded to the Board's request in a similar fashion.
They too argued that they had settled in America at their "own Cost," an
undertaking that was "attended with so much difficulty & danger" that
it "may well be look'd on as a dear purchase." Following their efforts in
America, Charles II had acknowledged "the Addition" they had "made
to his Dominions" by granting the settlers in Connecticut a charter.
Moreover, Connecticut informed the Board of Trade, "We are persuaded
We have a King on the Throne, who will esteem It among the Prerogatives
of his Crown, to be the Support & Protector of the Rights of his faithful
subjects."[22]

Although the Board was unable to convince Connecticut and Rhode
Island to give up their charters, it was presented with an opportunity to
weaken (if not revoke) the Massachusetts charter when Governor Shute
became embroiled in a conflict with the assembly over his demand for a
permanent salary in the early 1720s. Stymied by the assembly, he appealed
to London for support. In 1725, the Privy Council issued an explanatory charter strengthening Shute's powers. However, the Massachusetts
assembly, which grudgingly accepted the explanatory charter in a narrow vote, refused to comply with the royal instructions regarding the
governor's salary.[23] The assembly based their opposition to a permanent salary on their rights as Englishmen, arguing that the power of the
purse was the best way to check gubernatorial authority. In the words of
the lower house, "The Taxing of the People ... belongs to the House of
Representatives." The assembly grounded this claim on "their Rights by

---

[21] Quoted in ibid., 325–326. By contrast, in "an arbitrary Reigne" under the rule of "Sir
Edmund Andrases Government" all of the New England charters were "crush't and
Trampled under Foot" "in defiance of Magna charta and the Liberty of a Brittish Subject"
(325).

[22] Quoted in ibid., 332.

[23] On the vote, see Richard Bushman, *King and People in Provincial Massachusetts* (Chapel
Hill: University of North Carolina Press, 1985), 77–78. Bushman notes that the assembly (really the popular party) continued to battle Governor Belcher over control of the
Treasury, refused to grant a permanent salary, and insisted on a land bank that would be
able to issue paper currency. The house, following a Privy Council ruling, backed down
on treasury requisitions; the governor and the royal officials also backed down on the
salary question; and it took an act of Parliament to stop the land bank. According to
Bushman, "Gubernatorial influence may have had its way on lesser issues, but on the big
constitutional and fiscal questions, the governor's power crumpled" (78).

Charter," but added that they also were entitled to it "as *Englishmen* and rational Creatures."[24]

In 1724, in the midst of the conflict with Massachusetts, Thomas Pelham-Holles, the Duke of Newcastle, was appointed as the southern secretary, which was the ministry with responsibility for the American colonies. Newcastle replaced the Earl of Carteret (later Lord Granville), a Carolina proprietor who was so friendly to the chartered colonies that Dummer dedicated the *Defence* to him in 1721.[25] Along with Robert Walpole, the Crown's chief minister, Newcastle supported the Board's attempt to bolster royal authority in Massachusetts, where, since the granting of the new charter in 1691, there had been periodic clashes between the lower house and the governor.[26]

Although the Board of Trade was willing to pay the governor's salary out of English funds, arguing that the expense was worth it in order to strengthen royal authority in the empire, the Treasury disagreed, insisting that the colonists should bear more of the cost of royal government, a view that Robert Walpole shared. As a result, the Privy Council backed Shute's demand for a permanent salary, threatening to get Parliament involved should the assembly continue to be recalcitrant.[27] However, before Shute could be sent back to the colony to confront the assembly, George II replaced him with William Burnet, the governor of New York, in order to grant Burnet's job to a favored courtier.[28] Despite the support of the Duke of Newcastle, Burnet proved no more successful than Shute had been in procuring a permanent salary. In 1729, a frustrated Newcastle threatened to bring the matter before Parliament, with the very real possibility that the charter would be abrogated in its entirety by statute.[29]

---

[24] Quoted in Albert Southwick, "The Molasses Act – Source of Precedents," *William and Mary Quarterly* 8 (1951), 402–403.

[25] Newcastle's appointment thus coincided with the brief reformist period under Walpole in the late 1720s and early 1730s. See Henretta, *Salutary Neglect*, 73–74.

[26] See Henry Russell Spencer, *Constitutional Conflict in Provincial Massachusetts: A Study of the Opposition between the Massachusetts Governor and General Court in the Early Eighteenth Century* (Columbus, OH: Press of Fred J. Herr, 1905), 64–94.

[27] Henretta, *Salutary Neglect*, 70.

[28] Ibid., 71. Henretta argues that this amounted to "the destruction of policy by patronage," as it undermined the Board's plan to send Shute back for a confrontation with the assembly. As such, it did not augur well for the fortunes of metropolitan authority in the years ahead.

[29] Ibid., 81. Indeed, in 1728, worried about the impact of Massachusetts' intransigence on other colonies, Newcastle denied Deputy Governor Gooch of Virginia the right

At this crucial moment, with the ministry contemplating radical action and the Massachusetts House equally intransigent, Burnet died and with him the momentum for reform.[30] Samuel Shute refused to resume his old post; and, to the consternation of the reformers, the ministry – principally Lord Townshend – appointed as governor Jonathan Belcher, who was Massachusetts' agent in London, and thus had been responsible for opposing the very policy that he would now be charged with implementing. Within a few months of his appointment, Belcher asked the Board of Trade if, as a concession to the assembly, he could accept an annual salary. The Board said no, but Belcher's son lobbied Newcastle and the Privy Council who eventually acquiesced. After a nearly decade-long struggle, the Massachusetts assembly had secured its right to control the funding of the royal executive.[31]

The successful resistance of Massachusetts emboldened other colonies. In 1728, the Privy Council disallowed Connecticut's intestacy law.[32] However, Connecticut challenged the validity of the Privy Council's interference with its legislative authority, arguing that "it is the privilege of Englishmen and the natural right of all men who have not forfeited it to be governed by laws made by their own consent."[33] In the early 1730s, the New York assembly clashed with Newcastle's appointee, Governor Cosby, over the removal of Chief Justice Lewis Morris, a conflict that

to accept a monetary gift from the assembly in lieu of a raise in salary as it was contrary to the royal instructions and "would be a very ill precedent for others." Quoted in ibid., 75.

[30] Ibid., 79, argues that this was a moment when a wide-ranging reform of the empire could have been achieved (also see pp. 89–91).

[31] Ibid., 82–88 (although in 1735 the governor's allowance was made permanent).

[32] Passed in 1699, it allowed for partible inheritance (estates could pass to all sons and daughters). The colony felt that this was in accord with scripture, but the Privy Council held that it was contrary to the common law's rule of primogeniture. As in the Mohegan case, this was brought to the attention of the Privy Council by an appeal and not via a review of the colony's laws (the case was called *Winthrop v. Lechmere* and the Winthrop in question – John Winthrop IV – turned it into an indictment of the colony for not sending its laws to England for review; denying the right of appeal to the Crown; and failing to have its officials take oaths of allegiance). Jeremiah Dummer, the colony's agent, prepared a brief for Lechmere, but his lawyers ignored it and the law was disallowed in February 1728. The colony then considered seeking an act of Parliament validating its intestacy law but decided that the price of parliamentary intervention would be too high. In the 1740s, Connecticut was able to get this decision reversed. See Robert J. Taylor, *Colonial Connecticut: A History* (New York: K.T.O. Press, 1979), 195–199. As Taylor points out, the colony could, when it suited it, claim the right to English laws (as in the Mohegan case when it denied the validity of the royal commission).

[33] Quoted in Kellogg, *American Colonial Charter*, 274–275.

eventuated in the Zenger trial.[34] As well, the assembly challenged Cosby's use of equity courts, arguing that they violated the right of Englishmen everywhere in the king's dominions to trial by jury. As William Smith argued (Smith later represented Connecticut against the Mohegans before another kind of juryless prerogative court), "the Subjects inhabiting the remotest Dominion, belonging to England, are to be governed by the same Laws, as the People inhabiting within the Realm." As such, "to affirm this Power in the Crown ... supposes his Majesty to be vested with an Arbitrary Authority over his American Subjects, with Power to impose New Laws, without their Consent." The setting up of an equity court by prerogative would, Smith argued, "alter the Constitution, and deprive us of one of the chief Privileges, which we justly glory in, as the Birth-right of English-men."[35]

The death of Burnet in 1729 had stopped the ministry from using Parliament to revoke the Massachusetts charter. But in the same year, Parliament purchased the proprietor's rights in South Carolina, after their misrule in the wake of an Indian attack in 1715 had led to an insurrection by settlers demanding royal government.[36] The purchase of the

[34] On the dispute between Morris and Cosby as an episode in Anglo-American (or transatlantic) politics, see Stanley N. Katz, *Newcastle's New York: Anglo-American Politics, 1732–1753* (Cambridge, MA: Belknap Press, 1968), 61–132. For a compelling account of the rights-consciousness of mid-Atlantic elites in the eighteenth century, see Alan Tully's comparative study of political culture in Pennsylvania and New York: *Forming American Politics: Ideals, Interests and Institutions in Colonial New York and Pennsylvania* (Baltimore: Johns Hopkins University Press, 1994).

[35] William Smith, *Mr. Smith's Opinion, Relating to Courts of Equity within the Colony of New-York* (New York, 1734), 12. On the neglected topic of equity jurisdiction in the American colonies, see Stanley N. Katz, "The Politics of Law in Colonial America: Controversies over Chancery Courts and Equity Law in the Eighteenth Century," in Katz, ed., *Colonial America: Essays in Politics and Social Development* (Boston: Little, Brown, 1976), 401–423. In the 1720s, Pennsylvania politics was consumed by a battle between David Lloyd, the fiery Welsh Quaker leader of the popular party in the assembly, and James Logan, the Penn family's faithful secretary. The irony was that the popular party invoked the 1701 Charter of Privileges that Penn had granted them in case the Board was successful in its quest to make the Holy Commonwealth a royal colony. For the arguments of the principal antagonists, see David Lloyd, *A Vindication of the Legislative Power* (Philadelphia, 1725); and James Logan, *The Antidote* (Philadelphia, 1725). On the long dispute between proprietor and assembly in Pennsylvania, see Gary Nash, *Quakers and Politics: Pennsylvania, 1681–1726* (Princeton, NJ: Princeton University Press, 1968), 181–305. For the Quaker assembly's invocations of English constitutionalism, see ibid., 266.

[36] An expenditure of funds that was authorized by Walpole. See Henretta, *Salutary Neglect*, 66.

Carolina proprietary reduced the number of chartered colonies in British
America to four. However, as the experience of Virginia in the 1750s
demonstrated, royal government was hardly a recipe for more effective
political control of the empire.[37] As well, Parliament, at the behest of
English commercial interests, passed the Hat Act in 1732. And in 1733,
it passed the Molasses Act to help the West Indian planters who were
being hurt by the colonial smuggling of French sugar. The act made the
purchase of French sugar legal for the first time, but subjected it to a 6
percent duty. Not surprisingly, this had the effect of alienating the northern colonies.[38] As well, in 1732 Parliament established the new colony of
Georgia, supporting it financially with annual grants (as it would do from
1749 in Nova Scotia).[39]

Finally, in 1734, a committee of Parliament, concerned that colonial
autonomy was harming the interests of English merchants and manufac-
turers, attempted to introduce a bill that would have prevented colonial
laws from having "any effect" until they "have received his Majesty's
approbation in Council." It would also have required each colony to send
over a complete copy of all of its laws. If any of them were detrimental
to the prerogative of the Crown or the trade of the realm, they were
to be disallowed, charter rights notwithstanding. Moreover, all subsequent colonial laws had to be sent to England for review within twelve
months.[40] No action was taken on the committee's resolutions, however,
as Parliament was still wary of impinging on chartered rights and was
content to leave imperial governance largely to royal officials.

This brief period of reform (lasting roughly from the mid-1720s to the
early 1730s) had produced parliamentary legislation in favor of British

[37] As Alan Tully notes, even those Pennsylvanians in the mid-eighteenth century who desired
"the termination of the proprietary role in government" wanted to maintain "a dominant
Assembly, a weak chief executive, a reasonably independent judiciary, and widespread
enjoyment of traditional popular rights." Tully, *William Penn's Legacy: Politics and Social
Structure in Provincial Pennsylvania, 1726–1755* (Baltimore: Johns Hopkins University
Press, 1977), 167.

[38] Henretta, *Salutary Neglect*, 322. The Board of Trade's Martin Bladen saw the Molasses
Act (1733) as a way of weakening Massachusetts in the wake of the salary controversy
(he was also a landholder in the West Indies). Ibid., 95–96.

[39] Henretta, *Salutary Neglect*, 94, argues that this legislation amounted to a "new phase"
in the administration of the empire: "For the first time, parliament took an active role
in the management of the empire." However, since Parliament refused to interfere in the
internal affairs of the colonies, it's hard to see how these commercial regulations were
different in principle from the Navigation Acts passed in the seventeenth century.

[40] Leo F. Stock, ed., *Proceedings and Debates of the British Parliament Respecting North
America*, Volume IV (Washington, DC: Carnegie Institute, 1927), 236–237. The Lords

merchants and West Indian planters; but apart from the purchase of the Carolina charter, it did not achieve any significant reform of the colonial governments. There were several reasons for this. As the conflict in Massachusetts indicated, the Crown was unwilling to invest the resources necessary to centralize authority in the empire, leaving the governors at the mercy of increasingly assertive assemblies. As well, the American colonies were less important to officials in London than were the diplomatic maneuverings in Europe they thought so vital to the defense of the realm.[41] And the overriding concern of the Walpole ministry (and later of the Newcastle-Pelham ministry) was with maintaining power at home, which led them to grant important colonial posts to those who could support the ministry in Parliament.[42] This policy had the effect of taking patronage away from the royal governors, thereby weakening their ability to create a court party to bolster executive authority. Venality aside, Walpole's ministry also believed that the empire was best governed with a light hand, a policy encapsulated in the following advice from the Privy Council to Francis Nicholson, the new governor of South Carolina, in 1722: in the "Plantations" the "Government should be as Easy and as mild as possible to invite people to Settle under it."[43]

With imperial authorities unwilling to support the governors, and important colonial posts held by place seekers (or their deputies), the assemblies were able to slowly usurp executive authority.[44] As a result, "by the third decade of the eighteenth century many of the American representative bodies had achieved a degree of strength and confidence which allowed them to deal with royal officials on a basis of near-equality."[45] This encroachment on royal authority was underwritten by

had asked the king to require the Board to compile a report on the state of governance and trade in the colonies (the Board's 1734 report was published in London). A committee was then formed that recommended the reforms proposed in the bill. On the background to this episode, see Andrews, *Colonial Period*, IV, 402–407; and Kellogg, *American Colonial Charter*, 275.

[41] For an argument about the centrality of Europe to British foreign policy in the eighteenth century, see Brendan Simms, *Three Victories and a Defeat: The Rise and Fall of the First British Empire* (New York: Basic Books, 2009), passim.

[42] A policy documented at damning length in Henretta, *Salutary Neglect*, passim. For a more sanguine view, see Philip Haffenden, "Colonial Appointments under the Duke of Newcastle, 1724–1739," *English Historical Review* 78 (1963), 417–435.

[43] Charles Delafaye to Francis Nicholson, in Jack P. Greene, ed., *Settlements to Society: A Documentary History of Colonial America* (New York: W.W. Norton, 1975), 232.

[44] The classic account is Jack P. Greene, *The Quest for Power: The Lower Houses of Assembly in the Southern Royal Colonies, 1689–1776* (Chapel Hill: University of North Carolina Press, 1963).

[45] Henretta, *Salutary Neglect*, 105.

the increasingly assertive rights-consciousness of the settlers.[46] In 1735, the assembly in the new royal colony of South Carolina informed the governor that "His Majesty's subjects in this province are entitled to all the liberties and privileges of Englishmen." The representatives added that "by the laws of England and South Carolina, and ancient usage and custom," they had "all the rights and privileges pertaining to Money bills that are enjoyed by the British House of Commons."[47]

Despite the ongoing disagreement over the rights of the settlers, it would be a mistake to view the empire in these years as beset by endemic political conflict. Indeed, the decades following the peace of Utrecht were ones of increasing social, commercial, political, and cultural integration in the broader Atlantic world.[48] Under the Hanoverians, support for the monarchy grew in British America, as the settlers came to see these Protestant kings as liberty-loving rulers who provided protection in return for allegiance.[49] As well, this era of Walpolean rule was also the period when, as David Armitage has argued, there emerged an ideology of the British empire as "Protestant, commercial, maritime and free."[50] Moreover, the British constitution in these years was the object of veneration by both domestic and foreign observers, many of whom

---

[46] There is no history of British American political ideas for this period, although there are a number of excellent studies of politics in individual colonies. For a suggestive synthesis, combining ideas and institutions, see Bernard Bailyn, *The Origins of American Politics* (New York: Vintage Books, 1967).

[47] Quoted in Max Savelle, *Seeds of Liberty: The Genesis of the American Mind* (New York: Alfred A. Knopf, 1948), 294.

[48] On the Atlantic world in this period, see Ian K. Steele, *The English Atlantic, 1675–1740: An Exploration of Communication and Community* (New York: Oxford University Press, 1986). On the role that colonial lobbies played in binding the empire together, see Alison Olson, *Making the Empire Work: London and American Interest Groups, 1690–1790* (Cambridge, MA: Harvard University Press, 1992). In her earlier work, Olson dated the breakdown of transatlantic political ties to the end of Queen Anne's reign. But in this later study, she argues that transatlantic lobbies functioned to keep the empire together (providing information to ministers on colonial interests and grievances) until about a decade before the revolution. For the earlier work, see Olson, *Anglo-American Politics, 1660–1775: The Relationship between Parties in England and Colonial America* (London: Oxford University Press, 1973). For a series of essays showing the gradual drifting apart of English and American interests in the mid-eighteenth century, see Olson and Richard M. Brown, eds., *Anglo-American Political Relations, 1675–1775* (New Brunswick, NJ: Rutgers University Press, 1970).

[49] On the ideology of monarchy in British America, see Brendan McConville, *The King's Three Faces: The Rise and Fall of Royal America* (Chapel Hill: University of North Carolina Press, 2006).

[50] David Armitage, *The Ideological Origins of the British Empire* (Cambridge: Cambridge University Press, 2000), 182.

asserted that the way it balanced democracy, aristocracy, and monarchy was peculiarly suited to the preservation of liberty.[51] The settlers in America were, for the most part, content with being part of a larger British world that embodied these values. As a result, they did not think systematically about the political structure of the empire, beyond a desire for a degree of local autonomy compatible with what they took to be their rights as Englishmen. However, as with the earlier episodes of conflict in the empire, the exigencies of war and trade led to a renewed round of centralization in the 1740s. And as these geopolitical concerns grew in importance, so the old dream of a unitary empire gained a new purchase among imperial officials in London.

In 1739, on the eve of war with Spain, Martin Bladen, the principal author of the 1721 report, and now the leading figure at the Board of Trade, presented a proposal to Robert Walpole for a colonial union designed to combat the threat from the Spanish and French.[52] Central to Bladen's proposal was the idea, which he had first expressed in 1721, that the American colonies were crucial to both the commercial and military strength of Britain. According to Bladen, the trade of the colonies is "of so great consequence, That the General Voice of the People has called upon the Crown, to enter into a War for the preservation of it."[53]

To hold on to these valuable assets, Bladen once again argued for a colonial union led by a royally appointed captain general who would be responsible for defense against the French. He would also oversee diplomacy with the Native Americans, "whose Friendship," Bladen contended, was "of the highest Consequence to the British Interest in America."[54] Bladen hoped that the captain general would also be able to use his authority to make the colonies "pay more Respect to the orders of the Crown," and "more Regard to the Laws of Trade and Navigation, than they have hitherto done."[55]

Bladen's plan of union also included provision for local consent via a bicameral "Plantation Parliament," with Crown-appointed councilors and a lower house of elected representatives. Bladen argued that his

---

[51] Most famously, in Montesquieu's *The Spirit of the Laws* (Book XI, chapter 6).

[52] Martin Bladen, "Reasons for Appointing a Captain General for the Continent of North America," in Jack P. Greene, ed., "Martin Bladen's Blueprint for a Colonial Union," *William and Mary Quarterly* 17 (1960), 516–530.

[53] "Martin Bladen's Blueprint," 521–522.

[54] Ibid., 528.

[55] Ibid., 530.

proposal for a colonial union would allow for the enacting of "such Laws as shall be agreed on by Common Consent, according to the Custom of British Parliaments." Such a plan, he hoped, would weaken the autonomy of the chartered colonies without the need to revoke their charters.[56]

If the colonies were united in this way, Bladen argued, they could "drive all other European Nations out of the North Continent of America." For in Bladen's view, despite being "under One Uniform Government" and thus able to "direct their Force to the Point, where it may be most needful," the French really had but an "imaginary Empire," potentially much weaker than the English colonies, assuming the latter's strengths could be properly marshaled.[57] Although Bladen wanted the union to be enacted "by virtue of the Prerogative still inherent in the Crown,"[58] he conceded that, given the strength of the colonial assemblies, his plan "may perhaps want the Assistance of the Legislature [that is, the British Parliament] to carry into Execution."[59]

Bladen's ambitious proposal fell on deaf ears, its centralizing goals put aside in order to get colonial cooperation for wars against Spain (beginning in 1739) and then France (from 1744–1748). In the midst of these conflicts, Walpole finally fell from power (in 1742); but the governance of the empire did not substantially change under the ministries of the Earl of Carteret (later Lord Granville) and then the Pelhams (both Newcastle and his brother Henry). Indeed, according to James Henretta, in the 1740s Newcastle continued to treat the colonies in a "completely exploitative" fashion, granting colonial offices to men who would support the ministry in Parliament.[60] As such, even after Walpole had left the scene, the empire continued to be "a great national system of relief for the privileged classes."[61]

As a result of the strains of war and the cumulative effects of years of patronage, there was a breakdown of royal authority in the empire in the 1740s. In 1744, the Board of Trade, concerned about colonial emissions of paper money, introduced a bill in the House of Commons invalidating all acts, orders, votes, or resolutions of the colonial assemblies

---

[56] Ibid., 526. Bladen saw them as "mere Corporations only," with the same legal status as London and other chartered bodies in England. However, he insisted that "within their respective Precincts, their Several Patents would still retain their full effect" (526).

[57] Ibid., 528.

[58] Ibid., 525.

[59] Ibid., 522.

[60] Henretta, *Salutary Neglect*, 259.

[61] Ibid., 238.

that were contrary to the royal instructions.[62] Although Parliament was prorogued before the bill got beyond first reading, it met with strong opposition in the colonies. The New York assembly worried that it would "establish such an absolute power of the crown in all the British plantations as would be inconsistent with the liberties and privileges inherent in an Englishmen whilst he is in a British dominion."[63] For its part, the Connecticut assembly contended that if the bill became law we would "no longer be freemen but slaves."[64]

In Massachusetts, Governor William Shirley was able to use the funding for the war against the French to build up a powerful court party in the assembly.[65] But even under such a powerful and popular governor (he had led the successful expedition against Louisbourg in 1744), there was widespread opposition to naval impressments, imperial control of the colonial militia, and Parliament's attempts to limit paper money emissions. The *Independent Advertiser*, the newspaper founded by a young Samuel Adams, invoked Locke and Cato against Shirley's policies.[66] And in *An Address to the Inhabitants of the Province of Massachusetts Bay*, an anonymous author (most likely Samuel Adams) defended the anti-impressment riots on the grounds that the people were in a "state of nature," and had "a natural right" to band together for "their mutual Defence."[67]

There were also land riots in New Jersey in the late 1740s, which the Board blamed on the weakness of the royal executive. In its response, the Board proposed to make the governor independent of the legislature by granting him a fixed salary out of the British treasury and backing his

---

[62] Stock, ed., *Proceedings and Debates*, Volume V, 183–187. In pushing this legislation, the Board of Trade was looking after the interests of English merchants who feared the inflationary consequences of paper money. According to Leonard Labaree, if this bill had passed it "might have resulted in an enormous extension of the prerogative in America." Leonard Labaree, *Royal Government in America: A Study of the British Colonial System before 1783* (1930; New York: Frederick Ungar, 1958), 34. On the attempts to give parliamentary sanction to royal instructions, see Joseph Smith, *Appeals to the Privy Council from the American Plantations* (New York: Columbia University Press, 1950), 599–603.

[63] Quoted in Labaree, *Royal Government in America*, 440.

[64] Quoted in Smith, *Appeals*, 600, n. 394.

[65] John A. Schutz, *William Shirley: King's Governor of Massachusetts* (Chapel Hill: University of North Carolina Press, 1961).

[66] On these conflicts, see William Pencak, "Warfare and Political Change in Mid-Eighteenth-Century Massachusetts," in Peter Marshall and Glyn Williams, eds., *The British Atlantic Empire before the American Revolution* (London: Frank Cass, 1980), 51–73. On the opposition to impressment in the 1740s, see Pencak, "The Knowles Riot and the Crisis of the 1740s in Massachusetts," *Perspectives in American History* 10 (1976), 163–214.

[67] (Boston: Rogers & Fowle, 1747), 4.

authority by dispatching troops to the colony.[68] Also in the late 1740s, Governor Clinton of New York was locked in a battle with the assembly, which had taken control of the nomination of officers, the mustering and pay of the militia, the repair of forts, and the control of Indian policy (often paying the militia directly without the governor's authorization). As well, the assembly had used the governor's need for money in time of war to extract concessions from him, including the right to control the disbursement of public funds.[69]

Farther south, James Glen, the governor of South Carolina, wrote an anguished letter to the Board of Trade in 1748 complaining of the erosion of his authority at the hands of the assembly. According to Glen, "the whole frame of Government" in the colony was "unhinged," and "the political balance in which consists the strength and beauty of the British Constitution ... entirely overturned." According to Glen, the assembly had arrogated to themselves "much of the executive part of the Government." They appointed the treasurer, the Indian commissioners, and the comptroller of the duties on imports and exports. The assembly also controlled "all Ecclesiastical Preferments," including the appointment of the ministers of the Church of England. "Thus by little and little," Glen warned, "the People have got the whole administration into their Hands, and the Crown is by various Laws despoiled of its principal flowers and brightest Jewells."[70]

Peace came in 1748, though it was widely seen as merely a truce, a short interlude in a long struggle against the French in both Europe and

[68] The Board's report on New Jersey is discussed in Olive Dickerson, *American Colonial Government, 1696–1765: A Study of the British Board of Trade in Its Relation to the American Colonies, Political, Industrial and Administrative* (Cleveland: Arthur H. Clarke, 1912), 190–191. On the land riots, see Brendan McConville, *These Daring Disturbers of the Public Peace: The Struggle for Property and Power in Early New Jersey* (Ithaca, NY: Cornell University Press, 1999). Imperial officials failed to act in part because the Treasury (now headed by Henry Pelham, Newcastle's brother) balked at paying the cost of the civil list in New Jersey (much as it had done in the dispute with Massachusetts in the late 1720s). As well, despite a rare joint meeting of the Privy Council and the Board of Trade in 1749 (and a real worry that the riots were revolutionary), the ministry could not agree about whether to recall Governor Belcher or not (a disagreement that led Halifax to push for the 1752 reforms discussed below). See Henretta, *Salutary Neglect*, 297–304.

[69] On the conflict between royal and local authority in New York in the decades before the Seven Years' War, see Mary Lou Lustig, *Privilege and Prerogative: New York's Provincial Elite* (Madison, NJ: Fairleigh Dickinson University Press, 1995), 53–77.

[70] Glen's letter is reprinted in Jack P. Greene, ed., *Great Britain and the American Colonies, 1606–1763* (Columbia: University of South Carolina Press), 261–267.

America. As a consequence, the fears that Bladen had expressed of encirclement by the French dominated strategic discussions in imperial circles in the late 1740s and early 1750s. This concern about French power was compounded by the palpable erosion of royal authority in many of the colonies, as well as by a growing sense among metropolitan officials that if Britain lost political and economic control over its American empire it would eventually lose its own wealth, military power, and, ultimately, its liberty.[71]

One consequence of this new concern about the empire was the emergence of a reinvigorated Board of Trade in 1748, led by George Dunk, the Earl of Halifax. Halifax was appointed by the Duke of Bedford, who had replaced Newcastle as the southern secretary. In a report prepared soon after Halifax assumed the presidency, the Board lamented the growing political independence of the colonies, as well as their refusal to obey the laws of trade, or provide for their own defense, all of which, it argued, called for the regulation of "the several Constitutions of the plantations in America" so that they "may be usefull to, and not rival in Power and Trade their Mother Kingdom."[72] In addition to repeating its earlier call for the revocation of the charters, the Board wanted to ensure that "no Law whatsoever should be in Force in the Plantations" until it "had obtained the Assent of the Crown." As well, it called for all the colonies to send their laws to London for review so that "the King should have the power of making any proper Alteration in them," as he does, the Board noted, with laws "sent from Ireland."[73]

---

[71] The best account of the origins of this new imperial policy is Jack P. Greene, "'A Posture of Hostility': A Reconsideration of Some Aspects of the Origins of the American Revolution," in Jack P. Greene and William G. McLoughlin, eds., *Preachers and Politicians: Two Essays on the Origins of the American Revolution* (Worcester: American Antiquarian Society, 1977), 5–46. Daniel Baugh also sees the late 1740s as a turning point, as imperial officials abandoned the "blue water" policy that had left the colonies on their own (apart from commercial regulations) and adopted in its place a policy of more aggressive centralization, on the grounds that America was vital to national security. However, Baugh argues that the Duke of Newcastle – unlike the Whig opposition under Pitt – continued to see Europe and not America as the primary focus of British foreign policy. See Baugh, "Maritime Strength and Atlantic Commerce: The Uses of 'a Grand Marine Empire'," in Lawrence Stone, ed., *An Imperial State at War: Britain from 1689 to 1715* (New York: Routledge, 1994), 210–212. On the post-1748 Board, see Arthur H. Basye, *The Lords Commissioners of Trade and Plantations, 1748–1782* (New Haven: Yale University Press, 1925).

[72] "Some Considerations relating to the Present Conditions of the plantations; with Proposals for a better Regulation of them," in Jack P. Greene, ed., *Great Britain and the American Colonies*, 267–271 (quote at 267–268).

[73] Greene, ed., *Great Britain and the American Colonies*, 271.

The Board also insisted on colonial obedience to royal instructions, a policy that, as we have seen, was the cause of much discontent in Virginia in the 1750s. In 1749, the Board brought a bill before the Commons which would have made all colonial acts contrary to royal instructions null and void.[74] By insisting on the authority of the royal instructions, the Board intended to limit the legislative power of the lower houses of assembly. The Board also instructed the governors to ensure that suspending clauses were inserted into certain kinds of colonial bills, preventing them from going into effect until they received royal approval. And in 1752, after much lobbying, Halifax procured an order in council which gave the Board the power to nominate to the Privy Council all colonial officials. As well, the Board became the sole channel for all civil correspondence with governors and other officials.[75]

The instructions issued to Danvers Osborne, the governor of New York, in 1753, typify the Board's new policy of asserting royal authority in the empire. Written by Charles Townshend, a new member of the Board, they directed Osborne to insist on a salary that "shall be indefinite and without limitation."[76] Osborne was also to be in sole charge of the disbursement of military funds. According to Horace Walpole, Osborne's instructions were "better calculated" for "the latitude of Mexico and for a Spanish tribunal, than for a free, rich British settlement."[77] William Bollan, the Massachusetts agent in London, portrayed the Board's reforms in an ominous light, comparing them to the way that Ireland was governed, "with a body of standing forces, a military chest," and "the abridgement of their legislative powers."[78]

The Board's post-1748 drive to restructure the empire inspired a spate of proposals from those who had held royal office in the colonies, and had experienced the ill effects of colonial autonomy. Like Governor Dinwiddie

[74] On the 1749 bill, see Stock, ed., *Proceedings and Debates*, Volume V, 298, 304–307, 313–321, 367; and Greene, "'Posture of Hostility'," 25.
[75] On the Board's enhanced powers, see Dickerson, *American Colonial Government*, 48–50; and Basye, *Lords Commissioners of Trade and Plantations*, 69–82. Labaree, however, claims that the changes to the royal instructions were not that drastic (*Royal Government*, 64–66). According to Basye, in 1761 much of the power that the Board received in 1752 was rescinded (174). For the circular letter to the governors, see Leonard Labaree, ed., *Royal Instructions to British Governors, 1670–1776*, Volume II (New York: D. Appleton, 1935), 748–749.
[76] Labaree, ed., *Royal Instructions to British Colonial Governors*, I, 190–193 (quote at 192).
[77] Quoted in Greene, "'Posture of Hostility'," 34.
[78] Quoted in Henretta, *Salutary Neglect*, 343.

in Virginia, many of these reformers were Scots. Inspired by the benefits of the Union of 1707 and suspicious of local authority, they desired a unitary empire, with the colonies subordinate to the king-in-Parliament.[79]

Henry McCulloh was typical of the breed. An associate of the North Carolina governor in the 1740s, he was a sometime land speculator, whose patron was Martin Bladen. In 1751, McCulloh submitted a large manuscript to Halifax calling for significant reforms of the empire. Although disavowing any designs on colonial liberties, McCulloh praised the government of New France, where royal power was respected and the Crown's territories were not fragmented into multiple jurisdictions. In contrast, English settlers ignored royal instructions, clung to their charters, and thereby thwarted the Crown's ability to govern the empire. To rectify the situation, McCulloch called for Parliament to enact a stamp tax, the revenue from which would go to the royal governors, freeing them from their reliance on the assemblies. McCulloh also advocated an intercolonial assembly, along with a renewed alliance with the northern Indians to ward off the threat of a French invasion.[80]

Like McCulloch, James Abercromby was a Scot who had served in the colonies and experienced the intransigence of the assemblies at firsthand. In 1752, drawing on his long colonial experience, he wrote a lengthy treatise (circulated in manuscript to ministerial officials) on the governance

---

[79] On this mid-century attempt to rethink the empire – including the ways that some of these reformers envisioned the status of Native Americans – see Brendan McConville, *The King's Three Faces*, 220–245. J.M. Bumsted argues that these reformers had concluded (after witnessing the excessive autonomy of the assemblies firsthand) that imperial officials had a choice: reform the empire to strengthen the prerogative, or "risk American separation." See Bumsted, "'Things in the Womb of Time': Ideas of American Independence, 1633 to 1763," *William and Mary Quarterly* 31 (1974), 545. On the Scots in British America, see Ned Landsman, "The Provinces and the Empire: Scotland, the American Colonies and the Development of British Provincial Identity," in Stone, ed., *An Imperial State at War*, 258–287; and "The Legacy of British Union for the North American Colonies: Provincial Elites and the Problem of Imperial Union," in John Robertson, ed., *A Union for Empire: Political Thought and the British Union of 1707* (Cambridge: Cambridge University Press, 1995), 297–317. Landsman argues that these Scots were not authoritarians; rather, they believed in "an expansive commercial union," one based on Scottish political economy and the ideas of the provincial enlightenment, in which Britons everywhere would have equal rights. However, he concedes that many of these reformers were "firm administration men" (304) – that is, they held royal office (or aspired to) and therefore wanted to increase the authority of the Crown in America.

[80] Henry McCulloh, *Proposals for Uniting the English Colonies on the Continent of America, So as to Enable them to Act with Force and Vigour Against their Enemies* (London, 1757). This (and several other pamphlets) were originally part of a large manuscript submitted to Halifax in 1751.

of the empire, the centerpiece of which was a comprehensive plan to use parliamentary authority to reform "the Interior Government" of the colonies.[81] Abercromby's bill was a Magna Carta in reverse; instead of a grant of liberties, it proposed revoking the colonial charters, and requiring that all colonial laws be sent to Britain before they could take effect (much like Poynings's Law in Ireland). As well, all colonial laws repugnant to those of England were to be void from the moment of passage. And finally, Abercromby's new Magna Carta gave parliamentary sanction to royal instructions that forbade the assemblies from adjourning themselves without the Crown's approval, and took away their exclusive right to frame money bills.

Archibald Kennedy and Cadwallader Colden, two Scots long resident in New York, who had experienced the weakness of royal authority in that colony at firsthand, also proposed reforms to the empire in the early 1750s.[82] They argued that the growing power of the New York assembly had led to unbalanced government, with an executive too weak to check the depredations of colonial elites in this strategically vital part of the empire.[83] In particular, both Kennedy and Colden were concerned that local autonomy was undermining the vital diplomatic and military ties to the Iroquois Confederacy. In his 1751 tract titled *The Importance of Gaining and Preserving the Friendship of the Indians*, Kennedy described the mutual assistance in war and trade between the English and the "Five Nations" as an "original Contract and Treaty of Commerce." However,

---

[81] James Abercromby, *An Examination of the Acts of Parliament Relative to the Trade and Governance of our American Colonies* (1752), in Jack P. Greene, Charles F. Mullett, and Edward Papenfuse, eds., *Magna Carta for America* (Philadelphia: American Philosophical Society, 1986), 45–169 (quote at 149). On Abercromby's career, see Andrews, *Colonial Period*, IV, 409–411.

[82] On their role as "imperial agents," defending metropolitan authority against New York's provincial elites, see Daniel Hulsebosch, *Constituting Empire: New York and the Transformation of Constitutionalism in the Atlantic World, 1664–1830* (Chapel Hill: University of North Carolina Press, 2005), 71–104; and Paul Tonks, "Empire and Authority in Colonial New York: The Political Thought of Archibald Kennedy and Cadwallader Colden," *New York History* 91 (2010), 25–44.

[83] For the encroachment of the New York assembly on the governor's power in the late 1740s and early 1750s, see Lustig, *Privilege and Prerogative*, 53–77. On the much-neglected figure of Colden, see John Dixon, *Cadwallader Colden and the Rise of Public Dissension: Politics and Science in Pre-Revolutionary New York* (doctoral dissertation, UCLA, 2007). For Colden's account of these turbulent years, see "The Rise and Progress of the Publick Dissensions in the Province of New-York" (October 18, 1748. New York Historical Society, Colden Papers, Scientific and Political Papers and Notes). I am indebted to John Dixon for providing me with a transcript of this document.

the commissioners in charge of the treaty were a group of Anglo-Dutch traders who "have so abused, defrauded and deceived those poor, innocent, well-meaning People" that "we have very few *Indians* left that are sincerely in our Interest." Kennedy warned that if this situation wasn't remedied, it will lead to "fatal Consequences," especially given that the French are "our natural Enemies and Competitors in every Corner of the World," who continually try and "seduce" the Indians in order to weaken British power.[84]

In his *Essay on Government* written the following year, Kennedy charged the assemblies with being "the Authors of this Neglect." As he pointed out, neither the governor nor the council can "command one shilling of the publick Money, if that Shilling would save the Province, while the Speaker has it in his Power, by order of the House, to dispose of it as he pleasest, without being accountable to any but themselves."[85] By abusing the power of the purse, the assemblies were able to erode royal authority, forcing the governors to give up "every Instruction ... one after another" in order to obtain a salary and money for the civil list.[86]

According to Kennedy, the assemblies' attack on the Crown's authority was unjustified, for their very existence was based on either royal charters or commissions, both of which were merely revocable grants from the king. As such, Kennedy argued, the settlers were "but Tenants at Will," who enjoyed their rights only "during Pleasure and good Behaviour."[87] Given their subordinate status, Kennedy advised the assemblies to "drop those parliamentary Airs and Stile, about Liberty and Property, and keep within their Sphere, and make the best Use they can of his Majesty's Instructions and Commission, because it would be High-Treason to sit and act without it." And if they did not, Kennedy warned them that the stakes were high: "it is not impossible, (considering how indefatigable the French are in this Matter) but that *Fresh-Water* may become our Frontier."[88] Given the dire consequence of leaving the governance of the empire to "the Caprice of the Assemblies,"[89] Kennedy called for the reform of the empire to be "enacted, by a British Parliament."[90]

---

[84] Archibald Kennedy, *The Importance of Gaining and Preserving the Friendship of the Indians to the British Interest, Considered* (New York, 1751), 6.
[85] Kennedy, *An Essay on the Government of the Colonies* (New York, 1752), 37.
[86] Ibid., 34.
[87] Ibid., 15.
[88] Ibid., 37.
[89] Ibid., 39.
[90] Ibid., 37.

These plans for reforming the empire were all driven by a growing fear that war with the French and their native allies was inevitable.[91] And then in the summer of 1753 what Kennedy had warned about came to pass, as news reached the Board of Trade that the Mohawk leader Hendrick, angry at his treatment by the Albany commissioners, had told the New York governor that the Covenant Chain, the venerable diplomatic alliance between the English and Iroquois, was no more.[92] Soon after receiving this news, the ministry heard reports of French encroachments in the Ohio Valley. In response, it sent a letter to the royal governors (in August 1753) to "repel by Force" any incursions within the "undoubted limits of His Majesty's Dominions."[93] The Board of Trade also sent word to the governor of New York to convene all of the colonies for a conference designed to restore the alliance with the Six Nations. This led to a meeting at Albany in June 1754. Although originally charged only with repairing the Covenant Chain, the delegates exceeded the mandate given them by the Board of Trade and agreed to create a colonial union, largely at the urging of Benjamin Franklin and William Shirley, the governor of Massachusetts.[94]

Franklin had been thinking about such a union since the early 1750s. Indeed, he had corresponded about it with, among others, Colden and Kennedy.[95] In early 1751, his plan for a union was printed as an appendix

---

[91] On the fear (from at least 1748 or 1749) in the ministry that the French wanted to encircle if not conquer the British colonies, see T.R. Clayton, "The Duke of Newcastle, the Earl of Halifax, and the American Origins of the Seven Years' War," *Historical Journal* 24 (1981), 571–603.

[92] See Eric Hinderaker, *The Two Hendricks: Unraveling a Mohawk Mystery* (Cambridge, MA: Harvard University Press, 2010), 216–228.

[93] Quoted in Clayton, "The American Origins of the Seven Years' War," 584.

[94] In what follows I am indebted to Timothy Shannon's superb account: *Indians and Colonists at the Crossroads of Empire: The Albany Congress of 1754* (Ithaca: Cornell University Press, 2000). On the long history of such attempts, see Harry M. Ward, "*Unite or Die*": *Intercolonial Relations, 1690–1763* (Port Washington, NY: Kennikat Press, 1971).

[95] See Shannon, *Indians and Colonists*, 89–93, for Franklin's connections to Kennedy, Colden, James Alexander, and William Douglass (among other mid-century elites with an expansive vision of the empire). Shannon contrasts this group with other reformers like William Shirley, James Abercromby, and Thomas Pownall who were only "sojourners in America" (104), and who had a much more limited vision of the empire's territorial reach; as well, in contrast to Franklin's vision of a white empire of settlement that would unite all Britons, this latter group saw the empire as a multiracial *imperium*, with a strong distinction between colonists and those in the metropole. On Franklin's vision of empire, see Gerald Stourzh, *Benjamin Franklin and American Foreign Policy* (Chicago: University of Chicago Press, 1954), 33–82; and Gordon Wood, *The Americanization of Benjamin Franklin* (New York: Penguin Press, 2004), 61–104.

to Kennedy's *Importance of Gaining ... the Friendship of the Indians*. And in 1754, on the eve of the Albany Congress, he drafted a similar but more detailed plan, which provided the blueprint for the discussion at Albany.[96] Franklin saw union as the precondition for an expansive empire to the west. Once the Indians had faded away, he hoped that "the greatest Number of Englishmen will be on this side of the Water." Franklin exulted in such a prospect: "What an Accession of Power to the British Empire by Sea as well as Land! What Increase of Trade and Navigation! What Numbers of Ships and Seamen!"[97]

The delegates at Albany agreed to create a colonial union with a "President General" appointed by the Crown, and a "Grand Council" to be chosen by the assemblies. The council had the power to choose its own speaker, and it could not be dissolved or prorogued without its own consent, or by the "Special Command of the Crown."[98] All acts passed by the council required the assent of the president general who would then execute them. This new government would also have control over all Indian affairs, including the making of peace and war, the regulation of trade, the signing of treaties, and the purchasing of all land not within the current boundaries of any one colony. It would also decide on the settlement of western territories (purchased from the Indians), granting land and reserving to the Crown a quit rent. And it would be responsible for making laws for these "new settlements" until the Crown formed them into governments. It was also to be in charge of colonial defense, with the authority to raise and pay for troops, and the power to "Levy such General Duties, Imposts, or Taxes, as to them shall appear most equal and Just." Its laws would conform to those of England and be transmitted

[96] "Short hints towards a Scheme for uniting the Northern Colonies," in Leonard Labaree, ed., *The Papers of Benjamin Franklin*, Volume V (New Haven: Yale University Press, 1962), 337–338. This differed from the 1751 plan (appended to Kennedy's pamphlet) in that Franklin now called for the union to be enacted by Parliament (as he had seen the unwillingness of the Pennsylvania assembly to help the Virginians in the Ohio Valley in the winter and spring of 1754).

[97] Franklin, *Observations Concerning the Increase of Mankind, Peopling of Countries*, 12–13. He compared the Native Americans to the Britons who were conquered by the Saxons and driven from their lands, after which "the Saxons increas'd on their abandoned Lands" (6–7). *Observations* was written in the early 1750s but only published in 1755 (at the behest of William Shirley) as an appendix to William Clark's *Observations on the Late and Present Conduct of the French, with Regard to their Encroachments upon the British Colonies in America* (Boston, 1755). See Shannon, *Indians and Colonists*, 99, on Franklin's vision of empire in the *Observations*. On Franklin's role in the Albany Conference, see Gordon Wood, *The Americanization of Benjamin Franklin*, 72–78.

[98] Labaree, ed., *The Papers of Benjamin Franklin*, V, 389.

to the king in council for approbation, who would have three years to disallow them. However, each colony was, with the exception of ceding authority in the above areas, to "retain its present Constitution."[99]

Despite the backing of prominent colonial elites, the Albany Plan was uniformly rejected by the assemblies who were worried that it would undermine their autonomy by creating a new level of government with taxing powers, the ability to raise troops, control over coveted western lands, and a monopoly on relations with Native Americans.[100] The Massachusetts General Court, despite being one of the few assemblies that had been supportive of a colonial union, opposed the Albany Plan as it would "be subversive of the most valuable rights & Liberties of the several Colonies included in it, as a new Civil Government is thereby proposed to be establish'd over them with great & extraordinary powers to be exercis'd in time of Peace, as well as War."[101]

Two of the backers of the Albany plan – the royal officeholder William Shirley and the imperially minded provincial, Benjamin Franklin – had very different responses to its demise. After failing to get the Albany Plan through the Massachusetts assembly, Shirley wrote to London that the Albany Plan did not sufficiently "strengthen the dependency of the colonies on the Crown."[102] In its stead, he proposed a colonial union with a commander in chief for all of British North America, but without a potentially troublesome pan-colonial assembly. The governors and councilors in each colony would estimate the costs of conducting Indian diplomacy and raising troops, after which the commander in chief would obtain the necessary funds from the British treasury. Parliament would then levy a tax on the colonists sufficient to cover these expenditures.[103]

Franklin was in Boston in the fall of 1754 and Shirley showed him his plan.[104] While Franklin shared Shirley's desire for a more unified empire,

---

[99] For a copy of the Plan of Union, see Labaree, ed., *The Papers of Benjamin Franklin*, V, 387–92.

[100] On the colonial response to the Albany Plan, see Shannon, *Indians and Colonists*, 212–220; and Alan Rogers, *Empire and Liberty: American Resistance to British Authority, 1755–1763* (Berkeley: University of California Press, 1974), 10–21.

[101] Quoted in Savelle, *Seeds of Liberty*, 331.

[102] Quoted in Alison Olson, "The British Government and Colonial Union, 1754," *William and Mary Quarterly* 17 (1960), 31.

[103] Shirley left no copy of this plan. Shannon, *Indians and Colonists*, 227–228, reconstructs it from the comments of Franklin (who said in the December 3 letter that he was returning "the loose sheets of the plan"), and Thomas Hutchinson. See also Labaree, ed., *The Papers of Benjamin Franklin*, V, 442.

[104] John A. Schutz, *William Shirley: King's Governor of Massachusetts* (Chapel Hill: University of North Carolina Press, 1961), 184–185.

he objected to the lack of colonial representation in Shirley's plan. And in three letters to Shirley in December 1754, Franklin made an impassioned plea for an empire based on equality and consent. In the first letter on December 3, he argued that "excluding the People of the Colonies from all share in the voice of the Grand Council, will give extreme dissatisfaction," as would "taxing them by Act of Parliament, where they have no Representative." In the next letter (December 4), Franklin complained that taxing colonists in Parliament without their consent was the equivalent of treating them "as conquer'd People, and not as true British Subjects." He also decried the power of Shirley's military governor, who would have the power to march colonial militiamen "from one End of the British and French Colonies to the other" without the "Consent of their Representatives," a power he compared to the treatment of the French Canadians "that now groan under such Opposition from their Governor." Above all, Franklin was concerned that in Shirley's centralized union the colonial assemblies would be "dismiss'd as a useless Part of their Constitution."[105] For the settlers to be governed in such a fashion would be unjust, he argued, for how can it be that "by hazarding their Lives and Fortunes in subduing and settling new Countries, extending the Dominion and encreasing the Commerce of their Mother Nation, they have forfeited the native Rights of Britons."[106]

In his final letter to Shirley on December 22, Franklin reiterated this point with a thought experiment. Suppose, he said, that land was dredged off the coast of England and peopled by British subjects. Would it be right, he asked, "to deprive such Inhabitants of the common privileges enjoyed by other Englishmen"? If not, Franklin reasoned, then there was even less reason for treating valuable colonies in such a fashion. After hearing Franklin's reservations about his plan, Shirley suggested that the colonies be granted parliamentary representation. Franklin agreed that this would be "vastly more agreeable to the people, than the method lately attempted to be introduced by Royal Instructions." The settlers would, Franklin thought, submit more easily to laws in which they had a say, and which were therefore "agreeable to the nature of an English constitution" and in conformity "to English Liberty." A parliamentary

---

[105] Franklin to William Shirley, December 4, 1754, in Labaree, ed., *Papers of Benjamin Franklin*, Volume V, 445. Wood, *Americanization of Franklin*, 77–78, says that the only copies we have of the letters of December 3 and 22 are the ones reprinted in a London newspaper in 1766 (we have a later copy of the letter from December 4) and so Franklin's boldness might have been a post facto addition.
[106] Labaree, ed., *Papers of Benjamin Franklin*, V, 447.

union would also, he hoped, make the empire "one Community with one Interest." However, Franklin insisted that the colonies be allowed a sufficient number of MPs, and that "all the old Acts of Parliament restraining the trade or cramping the manufactures of the Colonies, be at the same time repealed and the British Subjects on this side of the water put, in those respects, on the same footing with those in Great Britain"[107]

In these divergent reactions to the collapse of the Albany Plan, we can see the contours of the debate about the constitutional structure of the empire that would take place in the 1760s and 1770s.[108] While Franklin's fellow Pennsylvanian Joseph Galloway (along with William Smith, Jr.) would propose a variety of plans for a colonial union in the 1760s and 1770s (including ones that allowed for representation in Parliament), they did not gain any real traction. Instead, Shirley's post-Albany plan to subordinate the colonies to the control of a royal executive funded by parliamentary taxes would become the dominant one among imperial officials in London.[109] By contrast, Franklin's vision of an expansive empire in the west predicated on colonial equality and government by consent was much closer to the view of most of the settler elites who had so soundly rejected the Albany Plan (even though they disagreed with Franklin about the benefits of colonial union). And indeed, in the 1760s, having come to the conclusion that a parliamentary union was impossible, Franklin was in the forefront of those proposing a federal division of authority in the empire, with the colonies having a constitutional connection solely to the Crown.[110]

As the Albany Plan was being debated in the colonies, the Board of Trade, concerned about the deteriorating military situation in the colonies, put forward its own plan of union. The Board's aim was to take the defense of the empire out of the control of the assemblies and place it with a royally appointed military and civilian governor for all of mainland English

---

[107] Ibid., 449–451. See also Richard Koebner, *Empire* (Cambridge: Cambridge University Press, 1961), 88–89.

[108] Shannon, *Indians and Colonists*, 227–228, argues that "their exchange foreshadowed the constitutional dispute over the Anglo-American connection that would split the empire apart after 1763."

[109] According to Shannon, Shirley wanted the union to "strengthen the hierarchies of authority and dependence that held the *imperium* together." Ibid., 231. On eighteenth-century understandings of *imperium*, see Koebner, *Empire*, 1–17, 85–104.

[110] On this, see Wood, *The Americanization of Benjamin Franklin*, 120–124; and Shannon, *Indians and Colonists*, 231.

America.[111] The Board's plan did, however, allow for "the mutual consent and agreement of the Colonies themselves" (via a meeting of commissioners whom they would nominate). But if the colonists refused to voluntarily contribute to the defense of the empire, the Board threatened to make "an application for an interposition of the Authority of Parliament."[112]

This threat of parliamentary intervention was supported by members of a younger generation of MPs and royal officials, who, having experienced the rise of Parliament under Walpole, had no qualms about asserting its authority outside the realm. One of these men was Charles Townshend, the author of the Board's instructions to Danvers Osborne in 1753. When consulted by Newcastle about the Board's plan of union, he argued that the colonies would never agree to unite against the French without the threat of parliamentary sanction (in this he was joined by William Murray, later Lord Mansfield).[113] And in a subsequent memo to Newcastle, Townshend proposed a parliamentary duty on imports and exports, with the revenue going to support royal government, thereby making the colonial executives independent of the assemblies. According to James Henretta, Townshend's proposal "differed radically" from previous proposals for union in its "constitutional reliance on parliamentary legislation rather than the royal prerogative."[114] As chancellor of the Exchequer in the 1760s, Townshend would get a chance to put his ideas into action.

The onset of war against the French in 1755 meant that the Board of Trade's plan was dropped. In its place, Halifax opted for a limited form

[111] On this plan, see Olson, "The British Government and Colonial Union, 1754," 22–34; and Shannon, *Indians and Colonists* 209–210.

[112] Greene, ed., *Great Britain and the American Colonies*, 285–288.

[113] As Townshend rightly pointed out, none of the colonies had come to the aid of Virginia in the summer of 1754 following Washington's defeat. See Olson, "The British Government and Colonial Union," 29–30.

[114] On the ideas about parliamentary authority held by this new generation, see Henretta, *Salutary Neglect*, 340–341; and Paul Langford, "Old Whigs, Old Tories, and the American Revolution," in P.J. Marshall and Glyn Williams, eds., *The British Atlantic Empire before the American Revolution* (London: Frank Cass, 1980), 106–130. Alison Olson argues that after 1750 a "new legalism" came into vogue among metropolitan jurists, replacing an older Whig flexibility about the application of parliamentary law to the colonies with a desire for a more rigid enforcement of its acts in America. See Olson, "Parliament, Empire & Parliamentary Law, 1776," in J.G.A. Pocock, ed., *Three British Revolutions, 1641, 1688, 1776* (Princeton: Princeton University Press, 1980), 289–322. (Olson also notes that the colonies had obeyed the Toleration Acts and the Naturalization Acts, the implication of which is that they didn't resist all legislation that affected their internal affairs).

of centralization: the appointment of a military commander for all of the colonies, and the establishment of two Indian superintendents, the latter a recognition of the strategic importance of alliances with the Native Americans and a reflection of the concern in imperial circles that the depredations of colonial traders and land speculators would drive them into the hands of the French.

But even this limited form of centralization engendered resistance, as many colonies refused to contribute adequate funds to the war effort, comply with the Navigation Acts, or cede authority over Indian affairs to the new commissioners. And in Virginia, at the epicenter of the struggle against the French in the Ohio Valley, the assembly made funding contingent on Dinwiddie paying Peyton Randolph's salary. In Pennsylvania, whose borders were even more endangered, the assembly would not grant the governor, Robert Hunter Morris, funds for colonial defense unless they were backed by a tax on the proprietary lands. Since this was contrary to his instructions, Morris refused to assent to the bill. In reply, the assembly informed him that they "cannot admit of Amendments to a Money Bill" according to "the arbitrary Pleasure of a Governor, without betraying the Trust reposed by us in our Constituents, and giving up their just Rights as Freeborn Subjects of England." After all, the assembly argued, "the Freeborn Subjects of England" should "not lose their essential Rights by removing into the King's Plantations," for in doing so they had increased the "British Dominions at the Hazard of their Lives and Fortunes." Indeed, the assembly contended that the settlers had "particular Privileges" "added to their native Rights, for their Encouragement in so useful and meritorious an undertaking."[115]

The Pennsylvania assembly also resisted ceding control over Indian affairs to the new superintendent. In the spring of 1756, the governor declared war against the Delawares and the Indians allied to them who had attacked the colony. However, the new Indian commissioner, William Johnson, as well as William Shirley, then the commander in chief of British forces, overrode this declaration because the Delawares were allied to the Six Nations.[116] William Smith, the Anglican provost of the College of Philadelphia, appalled at the assembly's intransigence in such

---

[115] "Message of the Pennsylvania Assembly to Governor Morris" (November 25, 1755), in Gertrude MacKinney, ed., *Pennsylvania Archives* (1931), Eighth Series, Volume V, 4176–4177.

[116] See Rogers, *Empire and Liberty*, 30–31. There was another incident the same year when Loudon, Shirley's replacement, forbade the colony from negotiating with the Six Nations or their allies. Both the council (which supported the proprietor) and the assembly (largely Quaker) agreed that this was a violation of their charter rights.

perilous times, accused the representatives of acting as if they were "a pure republic," warning them that if they did not change their behavior the colony would fall "into the Hands of the French."[117]

Partly as a result of the unwillingness of most of the colonies to contribute to the war effort, the first years of the conflict went badly for the English. But in 1757, William Pitt took control of the ministry and changed strategy, putting in place a funding system whereby the Crown offered subsidies to encourage the colonial assemblies to make voluntary contributions to the cost of the war.[118] This policy proved successful, but it meant the ministry incurring debt that would become a source of tension in the empire in the 1760s. As a result of Pitt's new strategy, the tide of war turned in 1758 and 1759, with stunning victories at Louisbourg and then Quebec.

Despite an upsurge of British patriotism on both sides of the Atlantic following the defeat of the French, the aftermath of war revealed a fault line in the empire.[119] On the colonial side, the experience of impressments, the conflicts over the quartering of British soldiers, the treatment of the colonial militias by British redcoats, and the restrictions on wartime trade all led to discontent with British rule. These concerns were compounded when the settlers learned that the British army would be staying in the colonies, and that there would be limitations on westward expansion. Given that they had fought alongside the British, many settlers had assumed that they would share equally in the fruits of victory. Their disappointment would prove explosive in the years ahead.[120]

[117] William Smith, *A Brief State of the Province of Pennsylvania* (London, 1756), 8–9, 43.
[118] On Pitt's strategic changes, see Fred Anderson, *Crucible of War: The Seven Years' War and the Fate of Empire in British North America, 1754–1766* (New York: Vintage Books, 2000), 202–239 (Anderson notes that to win the war, Pitt turned his back on the post-1748 centralization plans of Halifax and the Board); and Simms, *Three Victories and a Defeat*, 422–462.
[119] On this, see Jack P. Greene, "The Seven Years' War and the American Revolution: The Causal Relationship Reconsidered," *Journal of Imperial and Commonwealth History* VII (1980), 85–105. John Murrin is skeptical of the claim that the Seven Years' War was a precondition for the Revolution by removing the French threat, arguing instead that postwar conditions did not necessitate reform and then revolution; rather, it was the propensity of British policy makers to insist on implementing old, failed, and unnecessary policies – taxation instead of voluntary requisitions; quartering of troops; tight regulation of imperial trade; and, finally, revoking colonial charters. Murrin, "The French and Indian War, the American Revolution, and the Counterfactual Hypothesis: Reflections on Lawrence Henry Gipson and John Shy," *Reviews in American History* 1 (1973), 307–318.
[120] On the American fear of British tyranny, see Rogers, *Empire and Liberty*; and the older study by Eugene McCormac, *Colonial Opposition to Imperial Authority during the*

From London's perspective, colonial behavior during the war only intensified the need to resume the prewar reforms. In particular, there was a widespread perception that colonial legislators had abused their privileges, failing to adequately contribute to the war effort with money or men, refusing to quarter troops, and continuing to disobey the acts of trade. There was also a concern that the rapacity and duplicity of colonial traders and land speculators were alienating the Indians from the "British Interest."[121]

The war also removed the military threat posed by the French, while leaving a large number of royal troops in the colonies.[122] British officials thus had "a freer hand" to act in defense of metropolitan interests in the years after 1763.[123] To effect the necessary reforms, these officials called on Parliament to alter the constitutional structure of the empire.[124]

In 1748, the same year that Halifax was appointed to the Board of Trade, a dispute over taxation in Maryland revealed a very different conception of legislative sovereignty in America from the one that was becoming dominant in mid-century Britain, and which, in the hands of Townshend and others, was to transform political debate in the empire in the 1760s and 1770s.

The dispute began when the Maryland assembly asserted its statutory power to authorize the county courts to levy a tobacco tax. However, instead of using the funds for maintenance of the existing courthouse, Prince George's county put the money toward the construction of a new one. A series of essays ran in the *Maryland Gazette* debating the legitimacy of the county's decision.[125] While disagreeing over whether the

French and Indian War (Berkeley: University of California Publications in History, 1914). On the tensions between the colonial militia and British regulars, see Fred Anderson, *A People's Army: Massachusetts Soldiers and Society in the Seven Years' War* (Chapel Hill: University of North Carolina Press, 1984).

[121] Greene, "The Seven Years' War," 88.
[122] On the idea to use the army to enforce British edicts, see Greene, "The Seven Years' War," 93.
[123] Ibid., 94.
[124] Ibid., 92.
[125] *Maryland Gazette* (Annapolis, MD: J. Green, 1745–1813). There is as yet no definitive list of all of the essays. The ones that I have identified so far are January 20 (a Freeholder); February 10 (a Freeholder); March 16 (a Freeholder); March 23 (Native of Maryland); April 20 (a Freeholder); April 27 (Philanthropos); May 4 (Native of Maryland); May 11 (Native of Maryland); May 18 (Philanthropos); June 4 (Americano-Britannus). All of the essays appeared with pseudonyms. Given the paucity of secondary sources, I have been unable to identify the participants or much about the debate save the information in the

Maryland assembly was right to delegate its taxing power in this manner, all of the participants agreed that a representative legislature could not violate fundamental rights.

The exchange began with an essay by a "Freeholder" who asked "Whether a Parliament (or in *America*, an Assembly, for I presume none will pretend to make any material distinction) has a Power, i.e., a Right to enact anything contrary to a fundamental part of the *British* Constitution." He answered in the negative: The right to consent to taxation was "a fundamental part of the Constitution." And if the people's representatives gave up this right to a county court, which could in principle tax as much as it wanted, then the "original Compact" "would be broken," and the "People loos'd from all Types of Obedience." If unchecked, he warned, this power – "instead of *rebuilding* Court Houses" – might "in Time build *Fortifications? Standing Armies*, levy *Ship Money*, or, in short, raise any [levy] upon the People for whatever they thought proper to give the title of publick Charges to."

"Americano-Britannus" supported the "Freeholder," drawing on "Mr. Lock" to make the argument that the constitution derived from an *"an original Contract betwixt the People and their Rulers."* "It was this alone," he argued, "which did, or could give Beginning to any lawful Government in the World." As such, for the Maryland assembly to delegate its power to tax to a county court violated "that Agreement of the Society (to be govern'd after such a particular Manner) which constituted them." "Such a Power," he argued, "would be to all Intents and Purposes, giving away *an absolute Power over the Estates of the People*, which Mr. Lock calls *a Breach of Trust in the Legislative;* or in other Words, a Breach of the *Constitution.*"

Two essayists defended the assembly's delegation of its taxing power. "Philanthropos" challenged a "Freeholder" to explain "how a Law can be supposed to strike at the Liberties of the People; which is made by the Consent of the People? Or, which is the same Thing, by their Representatives?" In other words, the delegated power enjoyed by the county courts had been granted by the people's representatives and was therefore legitimate. A "Native of Maryland" also argued that there was no danger in having local magistrates exercise such discretionary

essays themselves. The essay of May 4 is unsigned, but internal evidence indicates that the author is a Native of Maryland. On local government in Maryland, see Lois Green Carr, "The Foundations of Social Order: Local Government in Colonial Maryland," in Bruce C. Daniels, ed., *Town and County: Essays on the Structure of Local Government in the American Colonies* (Middletown: Connecticut University Press, 1978), 72–110.

214

Revolution

power, for if they violated the "fundamental Laws of the Kingdom," the people could "return to their original, State of Nature, and chuse a new Government, or resume the old One."

Despite their disagreements, then, all of the participants held that colonial legislatures (which they equated with Parliament) were trustees of the people's rights, limited by the power delegated to them and by the norms of the constitution. Moreover, if they exceeded the bounds of their delegated authority, the people could resist them. This view was in marked contrast to the increasingly widespread belief at the seat of the empire that the British Parliament was an absolute sovereign, which could, if it wanted, pass laws abrogating the subjects' rights. For most of the eighteenth century, however, Parliament had resisted the attempts of royal officials to use its authority to alter the colonial constitutions. That was to change in the 1760s.

8

The Final Imperial Crisis

In 1774, Lord Chief Justice Mansfield handed down an important ruling about the rights of settlers in the new territories conquered from the French in the Seven Years' War.[1] Campbell, the plaintiff, was a planter on the conquered French island of Grenada who objected to paying a new duty on all sugar exports on the grounds that the 1763 Royal Proclamation had promised the settlers on the island a representative government. Having extended such a right to a conquered territory, Campbell contended, the king could not then raise money by prerogative without local consent. Mansfield agreed, holding that "the King had precluded himself from the Exercise of a Legislative Authority over the Island of Grenada" by pledging to grant the settlers an assembly of their own.[2]

At first glance, Mansfield's decision was a striking victory for the rights of settlers in the newly expanded empire. In holding that rights once granted were irrevocable, it removed the ambiguity about royal power outside the realm that had existed since Coke's equivocal ruling in Calvin's Case.[3] But on closer inspection, the verdict provided cold

---

[1] I have used the published version of Mansfield's judgment, *Lord Mansfield's Speech in Giving the Judgment of the Court of King's-Bench … in the Cause of Campbell against Hall …* (London, 1775). On this decision, see A.B. Keith, *The Constitutional History of the First British Empire* (Oxford: Oxford University Press, 1930), 15–16. This duty was intended to make the levy in the newly conquered sugar islands the same as the one in the previously settled islands.

[2] *Lord Mansfield's Speech*, 20.

[3] Mansfield also repudiated "Coke's absurd Exception, as to Pagans," holding that Coke's denial that the laws of non-Christians survived a conquest only "shews the Universality and Antiquity of the Maxim" that "the Laws of a Conquered Country continue until they are altered by the Conqueror." Ibid., 11.

comfort to Englishmen in the Crown's dominions. For despite limiting the power of the prerogative over them, Mansfield placed no such limits on Parliament. Indeed, Mansfield simply transferred the authority that the Crown had enjoyed by conquest to the king-in-Parliament. As he put it: "A Country, conquered by the British Arms, becomes a Dominion of the King in Right of his Crown, and therefore, necessarily subject to the Legislature, the Parliament of Great Britain."[4] In other words, while royal authority could be limited by an explicit grant of rights, the territories that received such a grant would be subject to the British Parliament, now seen as the supreme sovereign in the empire.

Mansfield's view of parliamentary authority in the empire was shared by William Blackstone, the most influential legal writer in the late eighteenth-century British world. In his *Commentaries on the Laws of England*, first published at the time of the Stamp Act, he held that the American colonies were conquests, and, as such, "the whole of their Constitution" was "liable to be new-modeled and reformed by the general superintending power of the legislature in the mother country."[5] Blackstone also defended Parliament's authority in both the realm and the royal dominions by arguing that in every state "there is and must be a supreme, irresistible, absolute, uncontrolled authority, in which the *jura summi imperii*, or the rights of sovereignty, reside."[6] The corollary of this argument was the belief that no state could long survive where sovereignty was divided, where there was an *imperio in imperium*, a sovereignty within a sovereignty.[7]

---

[4] Ibid., 10. Mansfield added that "if the King has a Power, (and when I say the King, I always mean the King without the Concurrence of Parliament) to alter the old, and introduce new Laws in a conquered Country, this Legislation being subordinate, that is, subordinate to his own Authority in Parliament, he cannot make any change contrary to fundamental Principles: – He cannot exempt an Inhabitant from that particular Dominion; as, for Instance, from the Laws of Trade, or, from the Power of Parliament, or give them Privileges exclusive from other Subjects; and so in many other Instances which might be put" (11–12).

[5] William Blackstone, *Commentaries on the Laws of England*, Volume I, ed. Stanley N. Katz (1765; Chicago: University of Chicago Press, 1979), 107. See also H.T. Dickinson, "The Eighteenth-Century Debate on the Sovereignty of Parliament," *Royal Historical Society Transactions* 26 (1976), 189–210.

[6] Blackstone, *Commentaries*, I, 49.

[7] Bernard Bailyn dates the origin of the idea that every state must have one source of sovereignty to the English Civil Wars of the mid-seventeenth century. See Bailyn, *The Ideological Origins of the American Revolution* (Cambridge: Harvard University Press, 1967), 198–229. Bailyn errs, however, when he claims that it was, therefore, a venerable, and widely accepted doctrine by the late eighteenth century. As H.T. Dickinson argues, this conception of "the sovereign legislature of king-in-parliament as the ultimate,

For Blackstone, it followed from this conception of sovereignty that the scope of parliamentary authority was necessarily unlimited, for it "hath sovereign and uncontrollable authority in making, confirming, enlarging, restraining, abrogating, repealing, reviving, and expounding of laws, concerning matters of all possible denominations, ecclesiastical or temporal, civil, military, maritime, or criminal." It could, he contended, "do every thing that is not naturally impossible; and therefore some have scrupled to call it's power, by a figure rather too bold, the omnipotence of Parliament. True it is, that what they do, no authority on earth can undo."[8]

Although Blackstone glorified the British constitution as the apotheosis of liberty, he was adamant that there could be no challenge to Parliament's authority from the people. While Locke and "other theoretical writers," he conceded, had made a "just" argument "in theory" that the people had a right to resist the legislature when it violated the trust reposed in it, Blackstone argued that such a "devolution of power, to the people at large, includes in it a dissolution of the whole form of government established by that people; reduces all the members to their original state of equality; and, by annihilating the sovereign power, repeals all positive laws whatsoever enacted." As such, Blackstone held that the English constitution could make no "provision for so desperate an event," which "at once must destroy all law" and "compel men to build afresh upon a new foundation."[9]

---

absolute and irresistible authority in the state" was a "more recent constitutional doctrine" than that of the American colonists who held "that parliament was constrained by customary and immemorial rights of the people." H.T. Dickinson, "Britain's Imperial Sovereignty: The Ideological Case against the American Colonies," in Dickinson, ed., *Britain and the American Revolution* (London: Wesley Longman, 1988), 81. The work of John Elliott and H.G. Koenigsberg on multiple monarchies in early modern Europe also suggests that Parliament's claim to be the sole sovereign in the empire was aberrant compared to prevailing practice in composite or multiple monarchies, where the several dominions of the King were usually governed by their own laws and legislature, subject to royal approval (a system that entails some sort of division of governing authority). See J.H. Elliott, "A Europe of Composite Monarchies," *Past and Present* 137 (1992), 48–71; and H.G. Koenigsberger, "Composite States, Representative Institutions and the American Revolution," *Bulletin of the Institute of Historical Research* 62 (1989), 135–153.

[8] Blackstone, *Commentaries*, I, 143, 156–157.

[9] Ibid., 157. Gerald Stourzh argues that Blackstone did countenance a right of revolution in extremis, and that he and not Locke was invoked by the more conservative of the American revolutionaries (for example, the South Carolinian, William Henry Drayton). See Stourzh, "William Blackstone: Teacher of Revolution," in Stourzh, ed., *From Vienna to Chicago and Back: Essays on Intellectual History and Political Thought* (Chicago: University of Chicago Press, 2007), 60–79. David Lieberman, however, argues

Why did legal and political elites in eighteenth-century England believe so strongly in Parliament's absolute sovereignty over all Britons? First, there was a widespread conviction that Parliament's triumph over the Crown in the Glorious Revolution had ushered in an era of unprecedented liberty and prosperity for all Britons. To challenge Parliament's sovereignty, then, was to jeopardize the entire revolutionary settlement, and in particular the limits it had placed on the powers of the Crown. Parliament was also – as J.G.A. Pocock has recently argued – seen as the only thing standing between England and a return to civil war. Thus, for Pocock, "it was not English hegemonic solidarity, but underlying English instability, which accounts for the uncompromising insistence on the undivided sovereignty of the crown-in-parliament." As such, its sovereignty "could not be compromised without threatening – especially in times of dynastic instability – a resumption of the processes which had led to civil war and dissolution in the remembered past."[10] Given these interrelated concerns about sovereignty, liberty, and stability, any challenge to Parliament from subjects in the empire was likely to meet with a decidedly hostile response.

In the aftermath of the Seven Years' War, exultant in the worldwide victory of British arms, the settlers in America did not foresee that Parliament, which they also venerated as the guarantor of English liberty, would challenge their autonomy. Indeed, apart from the Board of Trade's attempts to revoke the New England charters via statute earlier in the century, they had not had to confront any parliamentary legislation that seriously affected their internal governance. However, that was to change in 1763, when the ratification of the Treaty of Paris gave Britain control of all of

that Blackstone "blunted the radical implications of his own appeal to natural rights and natural equality." David Lieberman, "The Mixed Constitution and the Common Law," in Mark Goldie and Robert Wokler, eds., *The Cambridge History of Eighteenth-Century Political Thought* (Cambridge: Cambridge University Press, 2006), 317–349 (quote at 323). See also David Lieberman, *The Province of Legislation Determined: Legal Theory in Eighteenth-Century Britain* (New York: Cambridge University Press, 1989), 52–55. Lee Ward attributes Blackstone's wariness about invoking a right of resistance as well as his insistence on Parliament's sovereignty to the influence of Samuel Pufendorf (an insight that deserves more scholarly attention). See Ward, *The Politics of Liberty in England and Revolutionary America* (Cambridge: Cambridge University Press, 2004), 320–323.

[10] J.G.A. Pocock, "Political Thought in the English-speaking Atlantic, 1760–1790, Part 1: The Imperial Crisis," in J.G.A. Pocock, Gordon J. Schochet, and Lois G. Schwoerer, eds., *The Varieties of British Political Thought* (Cambridge: Cambridge University Press, 1993), 257–258.

North America east of the Mississippi, including New France, the Spanish territories in Florida, and the vast lands of the Ohio Valley where the war had begun.[11]

The need to govern and defend these new territories led a succession of parliamentary ministries to propose reforms whose unpopularity in the colonies was to tear the empire apart a little over a decade after its greatest military triumph. In late 1762, the king's favorite, Lord Bute, decided to keep 10,000 troops in America after the war's end, both to defend the empire against the French and to control the valuable lands beyond the Appalachians in the Ohio Valley, which were inhabited by Native Americans and coveted by the settlers.[12]

After Bute fell in early 1763, a new ministry under George Grenville came to power. His cabinet consisted of men with extensive experience in colonial governance, chief among them Lord Halifax, the new secretary of state for the Southern Department, who in his time as president of the Board of Trade had been an ardent advocate of imperial reform. In the summer of 1763, Halifax, along with the Earl of Hillsborough, his successor at the Board, were hard at work on a plan to govern the newly acquired territories. Their work was given a sense of urgency by news of an Indian uprising in the west. Dubbed Pontiac's War after the Ottawa chief at the heart of the rebellion, it had been triggered by Sir Jeffrey Amherst, the British commander in chief, who had decided to withhold customary gifts of shot and gunpowder from the Native Americans, and it soon reached the frontiers of the colonies with deadly results. The rebellion was also driven by the natives' concern that following the defeat of the French, the British, desirous of the rich lands of the Ohio Valley,

[11] On 1763 as a pivotal year, see Colin Calloway, *The Scratch of a Pen: 1763 and the Transformation of North America* (New York: Oxford University Press, 2006).

[12] On the problems of the postwar empire, see Fred Anderson's masterful account in *The Crucible of War: The Seven Years' War and the Fate of Empire in British North America, 1754–1766* (New York: Vintage Books, 2000), 557–637. For the impact of the army in America, see John Shy, *Towards Lexington: The Role of the British Army in the Coming of the American Revolution* (Princeton: Princeton University Press, 1965). George III was also in favor of keeping troops in the colonies at the settlers' expense in order to defend Florida and Quebec. See Jeremy Black, *George III: America's Last King* (New Haven: Yale University Press, 2006), 210. On the connection between war and imperial reform, see Jeremy Adelman, "An Age of Imperial Revolutions," *American Historical Review* 113 (2008), 319–340. On the growing sense among Britons that they were now in possession of a worldwide empire, see H.V. Bowen, "British Conceptions of Global Empire," *Journal of Imperial and Commonwealth History* 26 (1998), 1–27.

would not live up to their agreement (in the Treaty of Easton in 1758) to withdraw from the west after the war.[13]

The Grenville ministry's response was the Royal Proclamation of 1763, which proposed the establishment of new colonies in Quebec and East and West Florida, each with a royal governor and an elected assembly.[14] But to restore peace to the empire's frontiers, the rest of the newly acquired territory – from the Great Lakes to Florida, and from the Mississippi to the Appalachians – was to be reserved for the Native Americans. By the terms of the Proclamation, no colonial governments could grant these lands to settlers, and no Briton could settle on them. As well, all of the Indian trade would now be under the control of the two superintendents, William Johnson and John Stuart (for the north and south, respectively), and could take place only at locations approved by them.[15]

In addition to organizing territory, Grenville sought to raise sufficient revenue to meet the costs of stationing the army in America as well as to cover the large debt incurred fighting the French. Many in the ministry felt that the colonies had benefited from the defeat of the French without paying their fair share to prosecute the war. As a result, in the fall of 1763, Grenville began to tighten up the collection of customs duties, sending the Royal Navy to police the coast, and requiring that all customs officials reside in the colonies to combat the endemic smuggling and bribery that had so reduced the Crown's revenues in America.

In March 1764, with strong parliamentary majorities, Grenville passed the Sugar Act, which cut the duty on foreign molasses from sixpence to three, enough, Grenville thought, to make smuggling less attractive while still raising a substantial revenue.[16] The Sugar Act also strengthened the

---

[13] Gregory Dowd, *War Under Heaven: Pontiac, the Indian Nations, and the British Empire* (Baltimore: Johns Hopkins University Press, 2003).

[14] This arguably contravened the guarantee in the Treaty of Paris that the French in the conquered province of Quebec would be able to keep their own laws and religion. See Anderson, *Crucible of War*, 568.

[15] On British plans for the west, see J.M. Sosin, *Whitehall in the Wilderness: The Middle West in British Colonial Policy, 1760–1775* (Lincoln: University of Nebraska Press, 1961). At the same time, the Board of Trade was working on a comprehensive plan for Indian affairs; however, it was never implemented due to the cost of stationing troops in the trans-Appalachian west. See Daniel Richter, "Native Americans, the Plan of 1764, and a British Empire that Never Was," in Robert Olwell and Alan Tully, eds., *Cultures and Identities in Colonial British America* (Baltimore: Johns Hopkins University Press, 2006), 269–293.

[16] According to the Massachusetts' agent, Israel Maudit, "there did not seem to be a single man in Parliament, who thought that the conquered provinces ought to be left without Troops, or that England, after having run so deeply in Debt for the conquering of

customs service in the colonies by allowing officials to sue violators of the Navigation laws in a new vice-admiralty court in Halifax rather than in the local courts where convictions were much harder to come by. It also placed the burden of proof upon the accused in all cases and limited the damages that customs officers could face if they were successfully sued by a merchant wrongly accused of smuggling. Merchants and ship captains also had to post bonds to ensure their compliance with the act, and, as in previous reforms, the governors were required to take oaths to uphold the law.[17]

Most explosively, in the spring of 1765, with strong majorities in both the Lords and the Commons, the Grenville ministry passed the Stamp Act, which required the settlers to purchase special stamped paper before they could enter into a contract, print a newspaper, make a will, fill out a customs form, or even purchase a pack of playing cards. Also in 1765, the ministry passed a Quartering Act compelling the colonial assemblies to provide accommodations and supplies for the army in America.[18]

The reforms that the Grenville ministry passed in the aftermath of the Seven Years' War were an attempt to realize the long-standing metropolitan vision – stretching back to Martin Bladen and before him Edward Randolph and William Blathwayt – of a more centralized empire. The ministry (along with the Board of Trade) strengthened the Navigation Acts, stationed an army in the colonies, attempted to direct the pattern of settlement from London, set aside land for the Native Americans, and levied taxes that would be used to bolster royal authority in the empire. But unlike previous attempts at reform, Grenville's emanated from the ministry, not the royal bureaucracy, and thus had the full legal force of Parliament behind them.

As news of Grenville's reforms crossed the Atlantic in the spring and summer of 1764, a wide-ranging debate began over Parliament's right to tax the colonies; and more broadly, over what the exact relationship was

these provinces, by which Stability & Security is given to all the American Governments, should now tax itself for the maintenance of them." Quoted in Anderson, *Crucible of War*, 574.

[17] See Carl Ubbelohde, *The Vice-Admiralty Courts and the American Revolution* (Chapel Hill: University of North Carolina Press, 1960).

[18] The definitive account is still Edmund S. Morgan and Helen M. Morgan, *The Stamp Act Crisis: Prologue to Revolution* (Chapel Hill: University of North Carolina Press, 1953). For the British perspective, see P.D.G. Thomas, *British Politics and the Stamp Act Crisis: The First Phase of the American Revolution, 1763–1767* (Oxford: Clarendon Press, 1975).

between the center and periphery of this constitutionally indeterminate transatlantic empire. In responding to these reforms, settler elites, both in the official pronouncements of the assemblies and in an increasingly rich pamphlet literature, drew on the long tradition of thinking about their rights in the empire that had originated in the late seventeenth-century resistance to the Stuarts. Although cautious at first, their response eventually transcended the narrow question of taxation to address the broader issues of self-government and sovereignty. And faced with an increasingly intransigent assertion of Parliament's sovereignty, they began to articulate a federal vision of the empire, in which authority was based entirely on the natural rights of settlers who had voluntarily migrated to the New World conceived of as a state of nature.[19] In this account of the empire's constitution, their relationship to Parliament was based solely on a delegated authority to regulate the trade of the empire. In all other respects, the colonies were free states bound solely to the person of the king, who provided them protection in return for allegiance.[20] Moreover, this defense of their sovereignty was predicated on the replacement of the Native Americans by industrious settlers whose success in turning a wilderness into flourishing civil societies gave them a superior title to America.[21]

Beginning in the fall of 1764, the colonial assemblies produced numerous petitions and resolves protesting both the Sugar Act and the proposed Stamp Act. In almost all cases, they denied that Parliament had the right to levy taxes on them without their consent.[22] Indeed, so important was this principle that, in the words of the New York assembly's petition to the House of Commons in 1764, "an Exemption from the Burthen of

---

[19] On this point, see the important article by Michael Kammen, "The Meaning of Colonization in American Revolutionary Thought," *Journal of the History of Ideas* 31 (1970), 337–358.

[20] On this aspect of revolutionary thought, see Pocock, "Political Thought in the English-speaking Atlantic," 262–263.

[21] In this final chapter, I can only discuss a small sample of the vast outpouring of political writing in the final imperial crisis. For a comprehensive bibliography, see T.R. Adams, *American Independence: The Growth of an Idea: A Bibliographical Study of the American Political Pamphlets Printed between 1764 and 1776 Dealing with the Dispute between Great Britain and Her Colonies* (Providence: Brown University Press, 1965).

[22] For an argument that the colonies always maintained an exclusive right to tax themselves and thus were not, contrary to the claims of the progressive historians, inconsistent or opportunistic in their opposition to British policy, first objecting only to internal taxes, and then external, see Edmund Morgan, "Colonial Ideas of Parliamentary Power, 1764–1766," *William and Mary Quarterly*, 5 (1948), 311–341.

ungranted, involuntary Taxes, must be the grand Principle of every free State." Without such a right "vested in themselves, exclusive of all others," the assembly argued, "there can be no Happiness, no Liberty," and "no Security," "for who can call that his own, which may be taken away at the Pleasure of another." The principle of consensual taxation was, the assembly insisted, "the natural Right of Mankind."[23]

The New York assembly's petition contained other arguments that had long been employed by the settlers in defense of their rights in the empire. As the assembly informed the Commons, in settling America they had "submitted to Poverty, Barbarian Wars, Loss of Blood ... and ten Thousand unutterable Hardships, to enlarge the Trade, Wealth, and Dominion of the Nation." As such, they claimed an "Exemption" from Parliamentary taxation not as a "Privilege" but "as their Right."[24] In other words, because they had created an empire for the Crown by their own efforts, defending themselves against a "barbarian Enemy," they had a right to "a civil Constitution" that was "permanent" and could be "transmitted to their latest Posterity."[25] Although the assembly conceded that Parliament had the right to levy duties for the sole purpose of regulating the empire's trade, it resisted any further extension of Parliament's authority. Indeed, it argued that "History" cannot "furnish an Instance of a Constitution" that permits "one Part of a Dominion to be taxed by another, and that too in Effect, but by a Branch of the other Part." Having reduced Parliament to merely a "Branch" of the government of one part of the empire, the New York assembly added that it had a financial interest in making Britons "on one Side of the Atlantic" "submit to the most unsupportable Oppression and Tyranny."[26] And it warned that the imposition of such a tyranny would "turn a vast fertile, prosperous Region, into a dreary Wilderness; impoverish Great-Britain, and shake the Power and Independency of the most opulent and flourishing Empire in the World."[27]

In December 1764, the Virginia House of Burgesses sent a petition to the king with a similar message. They too insisted that it was

---

[23] The New York Petition to the House of Commons, October 18, 1764, in Edmund S. Morgan, ed., *Prologue to Revolution: Sources and Documents on the Stamp Act Crisis* (Chapel Hill: University of North Carolina Press, 1959), 9–10.

[24] Ibid., 10.

[25] Ibid., 11, 9.

[26] Ibid., 10. The New York assembly even claimed to prefer absolute monarchy to rule by Parliament on the grounds that it tended to treat its subjects more equally.

[27] Ibid., 13–14.

"a fundamental Principle of the British Constitution" that "the People are not subject to any Taxes but such as are laid on them by their own Consent."[28] Moreover, like the New York assembly, the burgesses contended that they had not "forfeited" their rights by "their Removal hither." Rather, they had been "licensed and encouraged by their Prince," and "animated with a laudable Desire of enlarging the British Dominion and extending its Commerce." In return for their efforts, the king had granted them a royal charter that confirmed their "ancient ... Right of being governed by such Laws respecting their Polity and Taxation as are derived from their own Consent." The burgesses also insisted that they had this "Right" of self-government not only as "Descendents of Britons" but also as "Men." Moreover, the burgesses claimed that they could ill afford any new taxes as they were still laboring under debts contracted in the war against the French, and continued to face the "Expense" of "providing for the Security of the People against the Incursions of our savage Neighbours."[29]

In the spring of 1765, when news reached America that the Stamp Act had passed Parliament with strong majorities, more petitions and resolves issued from the colonial assemblies. In addition to the rejection of all taxation without consent as a violation of their rights as British subjects, some of the assemblies based their claim to equal rights with those at home on the universal grounds of the law of nature. Moreover, they rested their case against parliamentary authority on the efforts they had undertaken to expand the king's dominions as well as on the fact that they had long possessed a right to control their internal affairs. In addition, they reminded British officials that they had always been willing to grant the Crown funds via voluntary requisitions. Finally, they all complained that the Sugar Act's extension of the powers of the vice-admiralty courts violated their right to trial by jury.[30]

As the protests against the Stamp Act became increasingly violent in the summer and fall of 1765, nine of the colonies gathered in a pan-colonial Stamp Act Congress in New York in October.[31] Not surprisingly, the

[28] Ibid., 15.
[29] Ibid.
[30] The claims in this paragraph are based on a close reading of the protests against the Stamp Act from the assemblies of Rhode Island, Pennsylvania, Maryland, Connecticut, Massachusetts, South Carolina, New Jersey, and New York, in Morgan, ed., *Prologue to Revolution*, 50–62. On the opposition to vice-admiralty courts, see David S. Lovejoy, "Rights Imply Equality: The Case against Admiralty Jurisdiction, 1764–1776," *William and Mary Quarterly* 16 (1959), 459–484.
[31] Virginia, North Carolina, and Georgia were unable to send delegates as their governors had prevented their assemblies from meeting.

Declaration of the Stamp Act Congress mirrored the resolves of the colonial assemblies, arguing that the settlers were "entitled to all the inherent Rights and Liberties of" the "Natural born Subjects, within the Kingdom of Great-Britain." In particular, the declaration proclaimed that it was "inseparably essential to the Freedom of a People, and the undoubted Right of Englishmen, that no Taxes be imposed on them but with their own consent."[32] In addition to complaining about parliamentary taxation, Congress also objected to the violation of trial by jury entailed in Grenville's extension of the "Jurisdiction of the Courts of Admiralty beyond its ancient Limits," which, it claimed, had "a manifest tendency to subvert the Rights and Liberties of the Colonists."[33]

In making its case for settler rights, Congress also emphasized the colonial contribution to the empire's development. After all, they informed the king, they had turned "the inhospitable Desarts of America" into "Flourishing Countries," where "Science, Humanity and the Knowledge of Divine Truths" were "diffused through Remote Regions of Ignorance, Infidelity, Barbarism," all of which, the Congress argued, had increased the "Wealth and Power of Great-Britain."[34]

In all of its official pronouncements, the Stamp Act Congress was careful to acknowledge its allegiance to the Crown and to profess "all due Subordination to that August Body the Parliament of Great Britain." But it was adamant that the colonies "cannot be, Represented in the House of Commons" due to their "remote Situation."[35] Moreover, it contended that Parliament had "never hitherto Tax'd any, but those who were actually therein Represented." For example, it had never, the Congress claimed, taxed Ireland or "any other of the Subjects without the realm."[36] As for what the limits should be on Parliament's authority in the empire, the Congress could only ask "Whether there be not a material Distinction ... between the necessary Exercise of Parliamentary Jurisdiction in general Acts, for the Amendment of the Common Law, and the Regulation of Trade and Commerce though the whole Empire, and the Exercise of that Jurisdiction, by imposing Taxes on the Colonies."[37] The search for an answer to this question would shape political debate on both sides of the Atlantic in the tumultuous decade to come.

---

[32] Morgan, ed., *Prologue to Revolution*, 62–63.
[33] Ibid., 63.
[34] Ibid., 64.
[35] Ibid., 62, 67.
[36] Ibid., 67.
[37] Ibid., 68.

The Grenville ministry commissioned Thomas Whatley, an undersecretary of the Treasury and one of the drafters of the Stamp Tax, to answer the settlers' objections.[38] Whatley argued that "the zealous Exertion of the civil, the military, and the naval Powers in the Colonies"[39] was necessary for the security of the empire; and that this required revenue, hence the need "to charge certain Stamp Duties in the Plantations."[40] Moreover, the settlers could not claim any exemption from "general Burthens." Rather, "being a part of the British dominions," they were obligated "to share all necessary Services with the rest." This obligation was heightened by the fact that Britain had to pay off "the national debt," the "heaviest Part" of which "has been incurred by a War undertaken for the Protection of the Colonies."[41]

Whatley did, however, agree that the colonists had "the Privilege, which is common to all British Subjects, of being taxed only with their own Consent, given by their Representatives."[42] Indeed, he extended the principle of consent beyond taxation, holding that "No new Law whatever can bind us that is made without the Concurrence of our Representatives." According to Whatley, even the Navigation Acts required colonial consent, since they "are still Levies of Money upon the People," and the "Constitution" "knows no Distinction between Impost Duties and internal Taxation."[43] However, Whaley argued, there was no lack of consent in the empire, for "the Colonies" were "virtually represented in Parliament." This was because "every Member of Parliament sits in the House, not as Representatives of his own Constituents, but as one of that august Assembly by which all the Commons of Great Britain are represented." As such, each MP has a "Duty" not to sacrifice the interests of the whole nation to those of the place he represents.[44] The fact that the colonies had their own assemblies did not, according to Whatley, affect Parliament's right to levy taxes on them. After all, he argued, the "Citizens of London" were also represented "in their Common Council," and yet they were still

---

[38] Thomas Whatley, *The Regulations Lately Made Concerning the Colonies, and the Taxes Imposed upon them, Considered* (J. Wilkie, 1775; originally published: London, 1765). On Whatley, see Ian R. Christie, "A Vision of Empire: Thomas Whatley and the Regulations Lately Made Concerning the Colonies," *English Historical Review* 113 (1998), 300–320.

[39] Whatley, *The Regulations Lately Made*, 100.

[40] Ibid., 101.

[41] Ibid., 102–103.

[42] Ibid., 104.

[43] Ibid., 105.

[44] Ibid., 108–109.

subject to the "general Superintendance" of Parliament.[45] As well, the "great Corporation" of the East India Company, which exercised "Rights" over their possessions that "fall little short of Sovereignty," was not represented in Parliament yet was subject to its taxing power. The American colonies, Whatley contended, were in "exactly the same Situation."[46]

Whatley's idea of virtual representation met with a forceful response from Daniel Dulany, the son of the leader of the Maryland House in the 1720s. Dulany had studied at both Cambridge and the Inns of Court in London, and, like his father had been, was one of the leading lawyers in the colonies. Dulany denied the identity of interests between members of Parliament and residents of the colonies on which Whatley's idea of virtual representation rested. As he pointed out, neither parliamentarians nor their electors would be affected by a tax levied on Americans. As a result, the colonists "may be oppressed in a thousand shapes without any sympathy or exciting any alarm" among Englishmen at home.[47] And in any case, Dulany contended, there was no need for the settlers to be represented in Parliament for "the colonies have a complete and adequate legislative authority" in their own assemblies.[48]

Although Dulany granted that "the supreme authority vested in the king, Lords, Commons may justly be exercised to secure or preserve their dependence," he maintained that parliamentary authority in the empire had limits. For example, Parliament did not have the right to "seize the property" of an "inferior" when it pleased, nor could it "command" the colonies "in everything." According to Dulany, "there may very well exist a *dependence* and *inferiority* without absolute *vassalage* or *slavery*." In fact, the relationship between the mother country and the colonies was defined by the colonial charters, which were an "express compact" by which "the powers vested in the inferior" "limited" those of the "superior."[49] Dulany's account of the empire's constitution, then, depended on the idea that the powers of government could in fact be divided, and that the colonies, though subordinate to the authority of the British Parliament, were not so absolutely.[50]

[45] Ibid., 110.
[46] Ibid., 108–109.
[47] Daniel Dulany, *Considerations on the Propriety of Imposing Taxes in the British Colonies for the Purpose of Raising a Revenue by Act of Parliament* (1765), reprinted in Bernard Bailyn, ed., *The Pamphlets of the American Revolution, 1750–1776*. Volume I: 1750–1765 (Cambridge: Belknap Press, 1965), 607–658 (quote at 615).
[48] Dulany, *Considerations*, 618.
[49] Ibid., 618–619.
[50] Ibid., 620.

Dulany's pamphlet, though it successfully rebutted Whatley's argument for virtual representation, was unable to answer the arguments of other defenders of the ministry, who, following Blackstone and Mansfield, insisted that Parliament's sovereignty was unlimited and indivisible. One of these was William Knox, who had worked at the Board of Trade under Halifax, and then served on the governor's council in Georgia, where he formed the view that the autonomy the colonists had enjoyed prior to 1763 made them republics in all but name.[51]

In his 1765 pamphlet, *The Claim of the Colonies*, Knox perfectly expressed the prevailing metropolitan consensus that "the parliament of Great Britain has a full and compleat jurisdiction over the property and person of every inhabitant of a British colony." Moreover, he argued, "the prosperity and security of the colonies has arisen from, and is connected with that jurisdiction."[52] And the fact that the colonists had charters that granted them the rights of Englishmen did not, Knox insisted, exempt them from Parliament's reach, but only from that of the Crown.[53] Indeed, Knox held that the colonial claim to be exempt from taxes based on their royal charters threatened to revive the prerogative, endangering the rights of Britons everywhere. After all, if an appeal to royal authority could "dispense with acts of parliament," then it could also "deprive the same subject of the benefit of common law." "Thank God," Knox exclaimed, that "the constitution of Great Britain admits of no such power in the crown."[54]

Knox also maintained that Parliament had always had the authority of "altering, and in some cases entirely annulling" royal charters. The

[51] On Knox's authorship of a memo to Grenville in 1763 about reforming the empire, see Thomas Barrow, "A Project for Imperial Reform: 'Hints Respecting the Settlement for Our American Provinces,'" *William and Mary Quarterly* 24 (1967), 108–126. On his career in imperial administration, see Franklin B. Wickwire, *British Subministers and Colonial America, 1763–1783* (Princeton: Princeton University Press, 1966), 42–44. For Knox's view that the colonies were republics in all but name, see Jack P. Greene, "William Knox's Explanation for the American Revolution," *William and Mary Quarterly* 30 (1973), 293–306.
[52] Knox, *The Claim of the Colonies to an Exemption from Internal Taxes Imposed by Authority of Parliament Examined: In a Letter from a Gentleman in London, to his Friend in America* (London: W. Johnston, 1765), 2.
[53] Ibid., 4–5.
[54] Ibid., 8–9. He added that the post-Glorious Revolution constitution "acknowledges no authority superior to the legislature, consisting of king, lords, and commons. The crown, considered as the executive power, cannot controul the legislature, nor dispense with its acts. On the contrary, the legislature can controul the crown in the exercise of its prerogative, and has frequently done so, particularly in the circumstances of grants or charters made by the crown."

fishmongers of London, to take but one example, had their charter "destroyed" by Parliament along with the "peculiar privileges the crown had granted them." And as Knox reminded his colonial readers, "the charter of that company stood upon as good authority, as does the charter of any colony in America."[55] In Knox's view, then, Parliament had "supreme and uncontrouled jurisdiction, internally and externally, over the properties and persons of the subjects in the colonies."[56]

The confrontation with this metropolitan conception of parliamentary sovereignty shaped settler thought in decisive ways in the crucial decade following the Sugar and Stamp Acts. While the mercurial James Otis drove himself nearly mad trying to square a commitment to settler rights with a belief in the absolute sovereignty of Parliament,[57] others pursued the more promising path that Dulany had opened up and tried to draw some line between parliamentary authority and the rights of the settlers. The most sophisticated attempt to do so was that of Richard Bland, who, in his 1766 *Inquiry into the Rights of the British Colonies*, built on the distinction he had made the year before (in *The Colonel Dismounted*) between internal and external spheres of authority.[58]

In developing his earlier insight, Bland made a radical move and suggested that it was a mistake to think of the British constitution as applicable to the complex structure of a transatlantic polity. In Bland's view, it was "in vain to search into the civil Constitution of *England* for Directions in fixing the proper Connexion between the Colonies and the Mother Kingdom."[59] Nor, he argued, were classical models of empire of much help, for the colonies in "*North America*, were planted in a Manner, and under a Dependence, of which there is not an Instance in all the Colonies of the Ancients." Like the Spanish colonies to the south, the Roman colonies had been established in the middle of "vanquished

[55] Ibid., 9.

[56] Ibid., 13.

[57] In *The Rights of the British Colonies Asserted and Proved* (Boston: Edes and Gill, 1764), Otis conceded that Parliament's authority was "supreme, sacred and uncontroullable not only in the realm but through the dominions" (65), but called for (citing Coke's decision in Bonham's Case) the courts to "void" any Parliamentary acts that violated fundamental rights.

[58] Richard Bland, *An Inquiry into the Rights of the British Colonies, Intended as an Answer to The Regulations lately made concerning the Colonies, and the Taxes imposed upon them considered. In a Letter Addressed to the Author of that Pamphlet* (Williamsburg: Alexander Purdie, 1766).

[59] Ibid., 13.

nations" as conquests, whereas "the colonies in North America" were "founded by Englishmen" in "this uncultivated and almost uninhabited country," and "without any expence to the nation."[60] Because we "can receive no Light from the Laws of the Kingdom, or from ancient History, to direct us in our Inquiry," Bland argued, "we must have recourse to the Law of Nature, and those Rights of Mankind which flow from it."[61] According to Bland[62]:

Men in a State of Nature are absolutely free and independent of one another as to sovereign jurisdiction, but when they enter into a Society, and by their own Consent become Members of it, they must submit to the Laws of the Society according to which they agree to be governed; for it is evident, by the very Act of Association, that each Member subjects himself to the Authority of that Body in whom, by common Consent, the legislative Power of the State is placed: But though they must submit to the Laws, so long as they remain Members of the Society, yet they retain so much of their natural Freedom as to have a Right to retire from the Society, to renounce the Benefits of it, to enter into another Society, and to settle in another Country; for their Engagements to the Society, and their Submission to the publick authority of the State, do not oblige them to continue in it longer than they find it will conduce to their Happiness, which they have a natural Right to promote. This natural Right remains with every Man, and he cannot justly be deprived of it by any civil Authority.[63]

For Bland, it followed from this natural right of migration that

when Subjects are deprived of their civil Rights, or are dissatisfied with the place they hold in the Community, they have a natural Right to quit the Society of which they are Members, and to retire into another Country. Now when Men exercise this Right, and withdraw themselves from their Country, they recover their natural Freedom and Independence: The Jurisdiction and Sovereignty of the State they quitted ceases; and if they unite, and by common Consent take Possession of a new Country, and form themselves into a political Society, they become a sovereign State, independent of the State from which they separated.[64]

[60] Ibid., 13–14.
[61] Ibid., 14.
[62] Bland cited "Vattel's Law of Nature. Locke on Civil Govern. Wollaston's Rel. of Nat." in support of the idea that men in a state of nature are free and independent of one another. For Bland, the corollary of this natural right of exit was that anyone who elected to remain under a government in which he was not represented had tacitly consented to be bound by the laws of that state. It was this, and not the metropolitan idea of "virtual" representation, that justified Parliament's right to bind the vast majority of the populace of Britain who were not represented in it. Ibid., 9–10.
[63] Ibid.
[64] Ibid., 14.

As such, Bland argued, all of the "Subjects of *England*" had "a natural Right to relinquish their Country, and by retiring from it, and associating together, to form a new political Society and independent State."[65] Moreover, when, in the early seventeenth century the first settlers had ventured across the Atlantic, "*America* was no Part of the Kingdom of *England*." Instead, Bland argued, "it was possessed by a savage People, scattered through the Country, who were not subject to the *English* Dominion, nor owed Obedience to its Laws."[66] Given that America was unoccupied save for the "savage" and therefore stateless Native Americans, the original settlers faced no barriers to the exercise of their natural right to choose the form of government they wanted to live under. And what choice did they make? In Bland's account, they made a compact with the English king, who granted them a royal charter with all "the rights and privileges of Englishmen," in return for which they had expanded the royal dominions. "In such a Case," Bland argued, "the Terms of the Compact must be obligatory and binding upon the Parties; they must be the Magna Charta, the fundamental Principles of Government, to this new Society; and every Infringement of them must be wrong, and may be opposed."[67] According to Bland, under the terms of the charter (and here he adduced the history of Virginia to make his case), they "were respected as a distinct State, independent, as to their *internal* Government, of the original Kingdom, but united with her, as to their *external* Polity, in the closest League and Amity, under the same Allegiance, and enjoying the Benefits of a reciprocal Intercourse."[68]

For Bland, then, the settlers had, by the law of nature and by the terms of their compact with the king, a right to control "their *internal* Government." But did this mean that they were entirely free of Parliamentary jurisdiction? Bland did not "dispute" that the "Colonies are subordinate to the Authority of Parliament," which was "without doubt, supreme within the body of the kingdom," and "cannot be abridged by any other power." However, he insisted that the king also had "prerogatives" that he had used to "license" "his subjects to remove into a *new* country." After all, without a royal power independent of Parliament, the king could never have secured to the settlers the rights contained in their charters. Bland did not think, however, that the settlers' rights rested on royal prerogative. On the contrary, he insisted that even if there had been

[65] Ibid.
[66] Ibid., 20.
[67] Ibid., 14–15.
[68] Ibid., 20.

no exemption from parliamentary taxation granted in the royal charter, the settlers would have been entitled to it from "that great principle in the British constitution, by which freemen in the nation are not subject to any laws, but such as are made by representatives elected by themselves to parliament." In "either case," Bland contended, the settlers had a right of "directing their internal government by laws made with their own consent."[69]

Bland conceded that Parliament could levy "Taxes or Impositions" upon the colonies' "Import and Export Trade," as "after the Restoration the Colonies lost that Liberty of Commerce with foreign Nations they had enjoyed before that Time." In Bland's view, this loss "deprived the Colonies, so far as these Restrictions extended, of the Privileges of *English* Subjects, and constituted an unnatural Difference between Men under the same Allegiance, born equally free, and entitled to the same civil Rights."[70] Although he was prepared to allow Parliament the right to regulate trade, he was insistent that its power over the settlers was circumscribed. For example, "if by a Vote of the *British* Senate the Colonists were to be delivered up to the Rule of a *French or Turkish* Tyranny," Bland contended that "they may refuse Obedience to such a Vote, and may oppose the Execution of it by Force." So for Bland, "Great" as "the Power of Parliament ... is," "it cannot constitutionally, deprive the People of their *natural* Rights; nor, in Virtue of the same Principle, can it deprive them of their *civil* Rights, which are founded in Compact, without their own Consent."[71]

But could the settlers resist an unconstitutional infringement of their rights by Parliament? Bland at first appeared to sanction such resistance, claiming that "*Power* abstracted from *Right* cannot give a just Title to Dominion. If a Man invades my Property, he becomes an Aggressor, and puts himself into a State of War with me: I have a Right to oppose this Invader." But Bland quickly drew back from the implications of this full-throated defense of a right of resistance, counseling moderation instead. If, for example, subjects "are deprived of their civil Rights, if great and manifest Oppressions are imposed upon them by the State on which they are dependent, their Remedy is to lay their Complaints at the Foot of the Throne, and to suffer patiently rather than disturb the publick Peace, which nothing but a Denial of Justice can excuse them in breaking."[72]

[69] Ibid., 21, 22, 26.
[70] Ibid., 16, 23.
[71] Ibid., 26.
[72] Ibid., 25, 26–27.

Faced with such a moderate stance, Bland hoped that the ministry would withdraw the offending legislation, allowing the colonies to "enjoy the Freedom, and other Benefits of the *British Constitution*, to the latest Page in History!"[73]

Widespread protests in the colonies led to the repeal of the Stamp Act by the new Rockingham ministry in the spring of 1766. But in the Parliamentary debates, even those members who were sympathetic to the colonies' claim to be exempt from parliamentary taxation agreed that it had the right to bind them by legislation. Indeed, William Pitt (now Lord Chatham), venerated in the colonies for his role in the great victory over the French and for his opposition to the Stamp Act, maintained that "Parliament has a right to bind, to restrain America. Our legislative power over the colonies, is sovereign and supreme."[74] On the question of where the ultimate locus of authority lay, Pitt's account of the imperial constitution was in essence the same as that of hard-liners like Lord Mansfield, who argued that "the British legislature, as to the power of making laws, represents the whole British empire" and "has the authority to bind every part and every subject without the least distinction, whether such subjects have a right to vote or not, or whether the law binds places within the realm or without."[75]

To secure a majority to repeal the Stamp Act, the Rockingham ministry passed the Declaratory Act, which proclaimed "That the said colonies and plantations in *America* have been, are, and of right ought to be, subordinate unto, and dependent upon the imperial crown and parliament of *Great Britain*; and that the King's majesty, by and with the advice and consent of the lords spiritual and temporal, and commons of *Great Britain*, in parliament assembled, had, hath, and of right ought to have, full power and authority to make laws and statutes of sufficient force and

---

[73] Ibid., 30.

[74] Chatham's speech (January 14, 1766), in R.C. Simmons and P.D.G. Thomas, eds., *Proceedings and Debates of the British Parliaments Respecting North America, 1754–1783*, Volume II, 1765–1768 (Millwood, NY: Kraus International Publishers, 1983), 89. Pitt added, however, that this authority should not be used to contradict "fundamental principles," such as the subject's right to grant taxes to the sovereign voluntarily. He also contended that Durham, Chester, and Wales had never been taxed until they were incorporated (and thereby represented); and that virtual representation was nonsense. Moreover, he claimed that the right of taxation was not part of the governing or legislative power, as legislation requires the consent of all three estates, whereas taxation is the purview of the Commons alone (86).

[75] Mansfield's speech (February 3, 1766), in Simmons and Thomas, eds., *Proceedings and Debates*, II, 130.

validity to bind the colonies and people of *America*, subjects of the crown of *Great Britain*, in all cases whatsoever."[76]

The year after repeal of the Stamp Act the Rockingham Whigs fell from power and were replaced by a new ministry under the control of Pitt. However, due to Pitt's ill health, Charles Townshend, who had been at the Board of Trade under Halifax in the 1750s, held the reins of power. Townshend had been an advocate of parliamentary taxation of the colonies since his time at the Board. In May 1767, he secured the passage of a Revenue Act that levied duties on certain commodities imported into the colonies, among them tea, glass, lead, and paper.[77] Townshend planned to put the monies raised from these duties toward the support of royal government in the colonies.[78] Moreover, the duties would be collected in America by a reorganized customs service, which included a new American Board of Customs Commissioners headquartered in Boston whose salaries would also be paid out of the duties they collected.[79] The following year, four new vice-admiralty courts were established in the major colonial ports.[80] Townshend also decided to move the troops who had been guarding the Proclamation line in the west into the cities to

---

[76] The Declaratory Act (March 18, 1766), in Jack P. Greene, ed., *Colonies to Nation: A Documentary History of the American Revolution, 1763–1789* (New York: McGraw-Hill, 1967), 85. On the colonial response to the Declaratory Act, see Morgan and Morgan, *The Stamp Act Crisis*, 298.

[77] Townshend claimed that these taxes were "external" as opposed to the hated tax on stamps, which was "internal." It's likely that he thought the colonies wouldn't object to such "external" taxes on the basis of Benjamin Franklin's misleading testimony before Parliament in early 1766, in which he suggested that the colonies only objected to "internal" taxes such as the Stamp Tax. Of course, Townshend, like most in Parliament, thought any such distinction was nonsensical as Britain possessed an absolute right to levy any kind of tax it wanted on the colonies. On Franklin's misleading testimony, see Edmund S. Morgan, *Benjamin Franklin* (New Haven: Yale University Press, 2002), 156–159. By 1766, Franklin had given up his early dream of a pan-colonial legislature (as well as colonial representation in Parliament) and was beginning to conceive of a federal empire with the colonies connected solely to the Crown and not Parliament. See Gordon Wood, *The Americanization of Benjamin Franklin* (New York: Penguin Press, 2004), 120–124.

[78] On which, see Lawrence H. Gipson, *The Coming of the Revolution, 1763–1775* (New York: Harper Brothers, 1954), 174–175.

[79] See Olive M. Dickerson, *The Navigation Acts and the American Revolution* (Philadelphia: University of Pennsylvania Press, 1951); and Thomas C. Barrow, *Trade and Empire: The British Customs Service in Colonial America, 1660–1775* (Cambridge: Harvard University Press, 1967).

[80] James Munro and Sir Almeric Fizroy, eds., *Acts of the Privy Council Colonial Series*. Volume V (1766–1783) (London: His Majesty's Stationery Office, 1912), 151–153.

better assert Parliament's authority.[81] And in the summer of 1767, the Townshend ministry passed an act suspending the New York assembly, which, in contravention of the Quartering Act, had refused to provide the troops in the colony with sufficient supplies.[82]

Taken together, these measures revived colonial fears that Parliament intended "to destroy constitutional rights in America."[83] Although no pan-colonial congress met to protest Townshend's Revenue Act, there was a widespread campaign to boycott British goods, which culminated in non-importation and nonconsumption agreements enforced by local commit-tees throughout America.[84] The epicenter of the resistance to these measures was Massachusetts, where, in early 1768, the assembly, at the instigation of Samuel Adams, sent a circular letter to the other colonies protesting the new duties on the grounds that "it is an essential, unalterable right in nature, engrafted into the British constitution, as a fundamental law ... that what a man had honestly acquired is absolutely his own" and "cannot be taken from him without his consent." The circular letter went on to claim that colonial representation in Parliament "will forever be impracticable," and it expressed concern that Townshend's plan to pay the salaries of the governors, judges, and "other civil officers" would "endanger the happi-ness and security of the subject."[85] When the assembly refused to rescind

---

[81] In April 1768, following the Treaty of Stanwix, a new boundary line running to the west of the Appalachians was drawn, opening more land for settlement in the Ohio Valley than the Proclamation line decreed in 1763. This in turn facilitated the movement of troops into the colonial cities as the protests over the new Revenue Act gathered pace. See John Alden, *A History of the American Revolution* (New York: Alfred A. Knopf, 1969), 93–94.

[82] On these measures, see Robert Middlekauff, *The Glorious Cause: The American Revolution, 1763–1789* (1982; expanded edition, New York: Oxford University Press, 2005), 149–158. On the suspension of the New York legislature, see Nicholas Varga, "The New York Restraining Act: Its Passage and Some Effects," 1766–1768, *New York History* 37 (1956), 233–258.

[83] Middlekauff, *The Glorious Cause*, 157. Ian Christie argues that Townshend's reforms were a more serious attack on colonial self-government than the Stamp Tax, for they threatened to remove the financial leverage that the settlers had long had over the royal governors. See Christie, *Crisis of Empire: Great Britain and the American Colonies, 1754–1783* (New York: W.W. Norton, 1966), 71.

[84] For the nonimportation agreements adopted in Boston (in August 1768, after earlier attempts had fallen though), and in Charleston (July, 1769), see Merrill Jensen, ed., *American Colonial Documents to 1776*, Volume IX of David Douglas, ed., *English Historical Documents* (London: Eyre and Spottiswoode, 1955), 724–726.

[85] Jensen, ed., *American Colonial Documents*, 714–716. The circular letter went on to state that "American subjects" had these rights "exclusive of any consideration of charter rights"; rather, they had "natural and constitutional" rights as "free men and subjects." And it insisted that the constitution of all "free states" was "fixed."

the letter, Governor Bernard, under orders from Lord Hillsborough, the new secretary of state for America,[86] dissolved it.[87] Hillsborough also sent a letter to the rest of the colonial governors advising them to prorogue or dissolve their assemblies if they took any notice of this "seditious paper" that denied "the authority of Parliament" and subverted "the true principles of the constitution."[88] The dissolution of the Massachusetts assembly did not dampen the resistance to British measures in Boston. After they seized John Hancock's sloop *Liberty* on charges of smuggling, the officers of the new Board of Customs Commissioners were forced to retreat to an island in Boston harbor so fierce was the opposition to their presence. By September 1768, two regiments of troops were on their way to Boston with two more to follow.[89]

The most widely read response to the Townshend Acts came from the pen of John Dickinson, a Pennsylvanian lawyer, who had been a leading member of the Stamp Act Congress. In a series of *Letters from a Farmer in Pennsylvania*, which were published in colonial newspapers as well as in England, Dickinson argued that Parliament's attempt to tax the colonies was unconstitutional. Drawing on Locke, Dickinson argued that "Those who are taxed without their own consent, expressed by themselves or their representatives, are slaves."[90] Dickinson made it clear the amount of the tax was not the issue, for, he contended, if "they have a right to levy a tax of one penny on us, they have a right to levy a million upon us." Moreover, he noted, the new duties were levied for the sole purpose of raising a revenue. What was worse, they would be

---

[86] This was a new cabinet post that took over responsibility for the American colonies from the secretary of state for the Southern Department. It was abolished in 1782.

[87] The vote to rescind the letter was taken in June 1768 and was defeated 92 to 17. Those who voted against were afterward celebrated as the "ninety-two."

[88] For Hillsborough's letter (of April 21, 1768), see Jensen, ed., *American Colonial Documents*, 716–717. The nonimportation agreements started with Boston in August 1768 and spread to all of the colonies except New Hampshire by the end of 1769.

[89] The troops were withdrawn from the west in 1768. This marked the end of the Board's postwar attempt to implement a new Indian policy. See Jensen, ed., *American Colonial Documents*, 704–707, for Hillsborough's April 1768 letter to Gage informing him of the change in policy. See also Peter Marshall, "Colonial Protests and Imperial Retrenchment: Indian Policy, 1764–1768," *Journal of American Studies* 5 (1971), 1–17. In response, Boston called a convention of the towns to protest the presence of troops, which, its meeting claimed, was against their natural, constitutional, and charter rights (this was in September 1768).

[90] Dickinson, *Letter VII*, in Forrest McDonald, ed., *Empire and Nation* (1962; Indianapolis: Liberty Fund, 1999), 44.

used to pay the salaries of royal governors in the colonies, further weakening settler rights. Dickinson also worried that judges in the colonies, who already held their commissions "at pleasure," would now have their salaries paid by the Crown and thus be more likely to comply when customs officers requested writs of search and seizure. "Is it possible," Dickinson lamented, "to form an idea of a slavery more complete, more miserable, more disgraceful, than that of a people, where justice is administered, government exercised, and a standing army maintained, at the expense of the people, and yet without the least dependence on them."[91]

Despite his denial of Parliament's right to tax the colonies for revenue, Dickinson conceded to Parliament an overarching yet ill-defined legislative authority, which included a right to levy duties for the sole purpose of regulating trade.[92] But another Philadelphian, William Hicks, issued a more radical challenge to Parliament, contending that it had no legitimate jurisdiction over the colonies at all.[93] Hicks built his case against Parliament on the basis of "that equality which we have received from nature, and which we find so firmly supported by the laws of our mother country."[94] Moreover, Hicks argued, when the settlers "crossed the Atlantic to settle the deserts of America, they bro't with them the spirit of the English government."[95] Once in America and unable to be represented in Parliament, they had applied to "their Prince for such protection and assistance as might raise them to an equality with their brethren of England."[96] As a consequence, the settlers were only subject to laws made "by regular agreement with the deputy of the Crown." And it followed from this that "the Lords and Commons of England" cannot "covenant with the Crown for the limiting and restraining our natural liberty."[97]

What this meant was that the colonists were not only exempt from parliamentary taxation but also from its legislation. For, as Hicks put it,

---

[91] Dickinson, *Letter IX*, 57.

[92] As he put it, the "colonies are dependent on Great Britain," which has a "legal power to make laws preserving that dependence." Dickinson, *Letter V*, 27–29.

[93] William Hicks, *The Nature and Extent of Parliamentary Power Considered* (John Holt: New York, 1768). Hicks originally wrote it in the wake of the repeal of the Stamp Act. Before it was published in 1768, he added a consideration of the measures passed by Townshend.

[94] Ibid., 25.

[95] Ibid., 22.

[96] Ibid., 23.

[97] Ibid., 20.

we may be as "effectually" ruined by one as by the other.[98] Indeed, Hicks
went so far as to say that no one in America could be free "when all that he
holds valuable in life must lie at the mercy of that unlimited power, which
is so repeatedly said to be sovereign and supreme."[99] Hicks singled out
the Declaratory Act as particularly egregious, for it allowed Parliament
to exercise its "unbounded legislative power for the horrid purpose of
reducing three millions of people to a state of abject slavery."[100] Such an
assertion of parliamentary power reduced the king's subjects in America
"to a state of subordination inconsistent with their natural rights and not
to be reconciled to the spirit of our own constitution."[101] If Parliament,
Hicks concluded, was supreme in "every respect whatsoever" then the
"liberty of America is no more than a flattering dream, and her privileges
delusive shadows."[102]

   Not surprisingly, Hicks thought the Navigation Acts were illegitimate.
No "inhabitant of Birmingham or Manchester" had a "natural right," he
contended, to "prevent an industrious settler of the colonies from engaging in those manufactures which may interfere with the business of his
own profession."[103] But without Parliament's supervening authority how
would the empire hold together? Hicks did acknowledge "the necessity
of lodging in some part of the community a restraining power, for the
regulating and limiting the trade and manufactures of each particular
county or colony, in such a manner as most effectually promote the good
of the whole," but he called for the monarch to play this role.[104] It was
no "paradox," he claimed, to assert that the "freemen settled in America
may preserve themselves absolutely independent of their fellow subjects
who more immediately surround the throne, and yet discharge, with the
strictest fidelity, all their duties to their sovereign."[105] In other words, the
settlers in America could be "loyal and valuable subjects to their Prince"
as well as "neighbours" to Britain. This was an explicitly federal vision
of the empire – the colonies were, for Hicks, "so many different counties
of the same kingdom," who, because they were unable to be represented
in the "general council," were governed by their own assemblies with

[98] Ibid., 28.
[99] Ibid., 26.
[100] Ibid., 27.
[101] Ibid., 11.
[102] Ibid., 39.
[103] Ibid., 30.
[104] Ibid., 12.
[105] Ibid., 24.

the concurrence of the king. In such an arrangement, "the restraining power lodged in the Crown" will "insure" that this "policy" was conducive to the general good. After all, Hicks claimed, "we cannot suppose that a wise and just Prince would ever consent to sacrifice the interest and happiness of any one part to the selfish views of another."[106]

Due to widespread opposition in the colonies, the new ministry under Lord North repealed all of the Townshend duties in the spring of 1770, save the one on tea, which was kept on the books to uphold Parliament's right of taxation.[107] Lord Hillsborough, the American secretary, told the colonies that the ministry would be no longer tax them for revenue. Hillsborough also allowed Governor Bernard to recall the Massachusetts assembly, despite the fact that they had not rescinded the circular letter. Three years of commercial prosperity and relative calm ensued, though in the spring of 1770 there was a clash between British troops and Bostonians that left several locals dead. During this time, the settlers imported tea and paid the duty that Townshend had levied in 1767. But the Board of Customs Commissioners remained, the Royal Navy patrolled the coasts looking for smugglers, and British troops were still in Boston.

As with the repeal of the Stamp Act, a crisis had been averted but not resolved. The idea of parliamentary sovereignty still resonated in official circles in London; and even those who were sympathetic to America like Thomas Pownall, ex-governor of Massachusetts and author of *The Administration of the Colonies*, maintained that Parliament was the supreme legislature of the empire.[108] In a speech in Parliament calling for the repeal of all the Townshend duties, he made it clear that "Parliament hath ... from the nature and essence of the constitution ... a sovereign supreme power and jurisdiction over every part of the dominions of the

---

[106] Ibid., 25.

[107] Alden, *A History of the American Revolution*, 104, notes that the cabinet almost voted to get rid of all the duties, but the king was opposed.

[108] First published in 1765, Pownall's treatise went through several editions in response to the changing constitutional situation in the empire in the 1760s and 1770s. See G.H. Guttridge, "Thomas Pownall's *The Administration of the Colonies*: The Six Editions," *William and Mary Quarterly* 26 (1969), 31–46. John Shy argues that the revolution was inevitable, given that both Pownall, who was friendly to the colonies, and Governor Ellis of Georgia, who most certainly was not, both agreed that Parliament must be the ultimate sovereign in the empire. See Shy, "Thomas Pownall, Henry Ellis, and the Spectrum of Imperial Possibilities," in Alison Olson and Richard M. Brown, eds., *Anglo-American Political Relations, 1675–1775* (New Brunswick, NJ: Rutgers University Press, 1970), 155–186.

state, to make laws in all cases whatsoever."[109] Indeed, many defenders of parliamentary authority were now claiming that there could be no middle ground between colonial subordination to Parliament and total independence.[110] In 1769, William Knox, now one the undersecretaries of state in the new American department, argued that "There is no alternative: either the colonies are a part of the community of Great Britain, or they are in a state of nature with respect to her, and in no case can be subject to the jurisdiction of the legislative power which represents her community, which is the British Parliament."[111]

The new governor of Massachusetts, Thomas Hutchinson, made the same argument in early 1773 in a debate with the Massachusetts General Court. In 1772, the ministry had decided to pay Hutchinson's salary, as well as that of Andrew Oliver, the lieutenant governor, and all of the superior court justices, from the duty on tea.[112] In response, Samuel Adams, who was at the center of the opposition to British authority in Massachusetts, created a committee of correspondence as part of the Boston Town Meeting in the fall of 1772. Concerned that powerful royal officials would now be beyond the reach of popular control, the committee issued "A State of the Rights of the Colonists," stating that "Among the natural Rights of the Colonists are these: First, a Right to Life; Secondly, to Liberty; thirdly to Property." And, the committee argued, "All Men have a Right to remain in a State of Nature as long as they please," so when they enter into civil society they do so "by voluntary consent," forming an "original compact," the terms of which "should conform as far as possible to the Law of natural reason and equity." In the committee's view, the policies of the British ministry – rendering the executive independent of the legislature via nonconsensual taxation, stationing an army among them in peacetime, and abrogating the right to a trial by a jury of one's peers – violated the settlers' natural rights.[113]

[109] April 19, 1769, in Simmons, eds., *Proceedings and Debates*, III, 154.
[110] And plans for a union in the late 1760s came to nothing. See Richard Koebner, *Empire* (Cambridge: Cambridge University Press, 1961), 173–193.
[111] Knox, *The Controversy between Great Britain and Her Colonies Reviewed* (London, 1769), 22.
[112] See Oliver M. Dickerson, "Use Made of the Revenue from the Tax on Tea," *New England Quarterly* 31 (1958), 232–243.
[113] It was published as a pamphlet entitled *Votes and Proceedings of the Freeholders and other Inhabitants of the Town of Boston* (Boston: Edes and Gill, 1772). It was sent to the selectmen of the Massachusetts towns and was also printed in London and Dublin. See Richard D. Brown, *Revolutionary Politics in Massachusetts: The Boston Committee of Correspondence and the Towns, 1772–1774* (Cambridge: Harvard University Press, 1970).

In January 1773, Hutchinson called a meeting of the General Court to denounce the stance of the Boston committee of correspondence. According to Hutchinson, there was "no line that can be drawn between the supreme Authority of Parliament and the total Independence of the Colonies." This was because it is "impossible that there be two independent Legislatures in one and the same State, for though there be but one Head, the King, yet two Legislative Bodies will make two Governments as distinct as the Kingdoms of England and Scotland before the Union."[114] Moreover, the fact that most of the colonies had been settled under charters from the Crown did not mean that they were free of Parliament's jurisdiction. According to Hutchinson, when the settlers first arrived in America they did so "under a Grant and Charter from the Crown of England," which meant that "they were to remain subject to the supreme Authority of Parliament."[115]

Empire for Hutchinson necessarily involved a diminution of the rights of settlers. As he told the General Court, those "who claim Exemption from Acts of Parliament by Virtue of their Rights as Englishmen, should consider that it is impossible the Rights of English subjects should be the same, in every respect in all Parts of the Dominions."[116] And, he insisted, it was an error to suppose, as so many of the settlers had, that "the Government, by their Removal from one Part of the Dominions to another, loses it's Authority over that Part to which they remove, and that they are freed from the Subjection they were under before."[117]

In May 1773, as Hutchinson was locked in rhetorical battle with the Massachusetts assembly, Lord North passed the Tea Act, which retained the import duty levied by Townshend in 1767 but eliminated all export duties paid on tea when it left England. The act also gave the financially troubled East India Company a monopoly on the sale of tea in the colonies. By doing so, North intended to undercut the much cheaper tea smuggled into the colonies by the Dutch, thereby increasing the Crown's revenues as well as the profitability of the East India Company.[118] Convinced that

---

[114] "The Address of the Governor," in John Phillip Reid, ed., *The Briefs of the American Revolution* (New York: New York University Press, 1981), 20.

[115] Ibid., 15.

[116] Ibid., 19.

[117] Ibid.

[118] According to Ian Christie, by the early 1770s, the ministry was dominated by hard-liners opposed to conciliation. As well, the king "had become increasingly apprehensive about the attitude of the colonists and was prepared to support a firm policy." Christie, *Crisis of Empire*, 82.

this was yet another attempt at parliamentary taxation, committees of correspondence across the colonies organized protests; and in late 1773, as the first shipments arrived, mobs pressured the consignees and the ship captains to turn around without landing the tea.[119] However, in Boston, Governor Hutchinson insisted that the ships remain in the harbor until they had unloaded the tea. On the night of December 16, 1773, a mob ensured that this would not happen by dumping 90,000 pounds of tea into Boston harbor.[120]

The ministry's response to yet another act of resistance in Boston was swift and all-encompassing. In the spring of 1774, Parliament passed legislation known collectively as the Coercive Acts. The first closed the port of Boston to all commerce until the East India Company was compensated for the loss of tea. The second altered the Massachusetts charter for the first time since 1691, giving the king the power to appoint the previously elected council (the upper house of the General Court). It also allowed the governor to appoint all provincial judges and sheriffs, and limited the number of town meetings to one a year without the permission of the governor. A third act provided for the removal out of the colony of any magistrate, soldier, or customs official indicted for a capital offense and unlikely to receive an impartial trial in a colonial court. A fourth act provided for the quartering of troops in private dwellings anywhere it was thought necessary. Finally, General Gage, who was the commander in chief of British forces, also became the civil governor of the colony.[121] Having failed to maintain order in his native province, Thomas Hutchinson headed into a long exile in England.[122]

In the summer of 1774, Parliament also passed the Quebec Act, which finally established civil government in that conquered province. However, unlike the proposals in the 1763 Royal Proclamation, there would be no representative assembly allowed, the Catholic church was to retain all of its rights, and French civil law would remain in force.[123] As well, the boundaries of Quebec were to be extended into the Mississippi Valley as

[119] In Charleston, Christopher Gadsen, "the Sam Adams of South Carolina," mobilized men to send the tea back. The captain refused and a compromise was reached on December 22. The tea was landed and put in a locked warehouse. It was later sold by the revolutionary government. See Alden, *A History of the American Revolution*, 139–140.

[120] Benjamin Labaree, *The Boston Tea Party* (New York: Oxford University Press, 1964), 141.

[121] For the Coercive Acts, see Jensen, ed., *American Colonial Documents*, 779–785.

[122] Bernard Bailyn, *The Ordeal of Thomas Hutchinson* (Cambridge: Belknap Press, 1974), 274–330.

[123] Philip Lawson, *The Imperial Challenge: Quebec and Britain in the Age of the American Revolution* (Montreal: McGill-Queens University Press, 1989), 126–145.

far south as the Ohio River. To the settlers, this was an ominous development as there would now be a new colony, lacking English constitutional government and the Protestant religion, which excluded them from the valuable lands to the west of the Appalachians.[124]

Upon his arrival in Massachusetts in May 1774, General Gage found that his writ ran no farther than Boston, such was the opposition to the Coercive Acts in the province. He was unable to obtain compensation for the East India Company or to punish the tea rioters. And when he tried to call a new General Court into session in Salem, the elections produced a legislature dominated by those opposed to the Coercive Acts. In August, his attempt to convene another General Court, this time with the appointed councilors promised in the Coercive Acts, caused an outburst of popular fury such that the new councilors had to flee to Boston for their lives. By the end of the summer, royal government had been replaced by county conventions and town meetings everywhere but in Boston. In September, the resolves of the convention of Suffolk county denounced the Coercive Acts as unconstitutional, called for a commercial boycott of Great Britain, and urged that the colony begin to prepare for armed resistance.[125]

As Massachusetts was being singled out in the summer of 1774, James Wilson, a Scottish émigré lawyer from Pennsylvania, published a forceful pamphlet in response to the Coercive Acts. In it, Wilson, who was a legal protégé of John Dickinson, adopted a more radical stance than his teacher, and, like William Hicks, claimed that Parliament had no right to bind the colonies legislatively.[126]

For Wilson, it was a fundamental maxim that "All men are, by nature, equal and free." In particular, he insisted that all men have "rights" to which they are "entitled by the supreme and controulable

[124] Sosin, *Whitehall in the Wilderness*, 239–255.

[125] On the upheavals in Massachusetts in the summer and fall of 1774, see Christie, *Crisis of Empire*, 89–90.

[126] James Wilson, *Considerations on the Nature and Extent of the Legislative Authority of the British Parliament* (Philadelphia, 1774). Wilson had originally written it in 1768, at the same time as Hicks's similar pamphlet, but had left it unpublished. On Wilson's political ideas, see John V. Jerzierski, "Parliament or People: James Wilson and Blackstone on the Nature and Location of Sovereignty," *Journal of the History of Ideas* 32 (1971), 95–106. For a wider range of Wilson's political and legal writings, see Robert Green McCloskey, ed., *The Works of James Wilson*, 2 volumes (Cambridge: Belknap Press, 1967).

laws of nature" as well as "the fundamental principles of the British constitution."[127] Chief among these was the right to consent to all laws that bound them. As Wilson put it, "No one has a right to any authority over another without his consent: All lawful government is founded on the consent of those, who are subject to it." In Wilson's view, "Such consent was given with a view to ensure and to encrease the happiness of the governed above what they could enjoy in an independent and unconnected state of nature." And because "This rule is founded on the law of nature," Wilson argued, "It must control every political maxim: it must regulate the Legislature itself. The people have a right to insist that this rule be served; and are entitled to demand a moral security that the Legislature will observe it."[128] Given this, Wilson denied that Parliament had a "supreme irresistible uncontrolled authority over" the colonies.[129] Indeed, since all just authority derived from the people's natural rights, Parliament could have no authority over Britons who had not consented to its laws. To argue otherwise, Wilson insisted, implied that one group of subjects could bind another without their consent, even though both had equal natural rights.

Wilson contended that the legal history of the relations between realm and dominion supported his denial of parliamentary authority in the empire. Citing a medieval case concerning Ireland, he argued that the decision of "all of the Judges of England, met in the exchequer-chamber" was that the Irish were not bound by acts of the English Parliament because they did not "send KNIGHTS TO PARLIAMENT."[130] For Wilson, the decision of "those reverend sages of the law" was based on exactly the same principle on which "the Americans have founded their opposition to the late statutes made concerning them." Moreover, Wilson insisted, their decision applied to "*every* Statute" and not just those concerning taxation. After all, he asked, "Have those a right to imprison or gibbet us, who have not a right to tax us?"[131] And if the Irish were not subject to Parliament, Wilson reasoned, then the Americans certainly were not, as Ireland was directly subject to English courts (a writ of error ran from their courts to the King's Bench), whereas colonial courts were only subject to "an appeal to the King in Council."[132] For Wilson, it followed from

[127] Ibid., 2–3.
[128] Ibid., 3.
[129] Ibid., 3–4.
[130] Ibid., 19–20. This was a case from the reign of Richard II, but I have not been able to identify which one from Wilson's footnote (4. Modern Reports, 225).
[131] Ibid., 21.
[132] Ibid., 22.

this "that parliamentary authority is derived SOLELY from representation – that those, who are bound by Acts of Parliament, are bound for this ONLY reason, because they are represented in it." After all, Wilson added, "the law never ceases, but when the reason of it ceases also."[133]

Wilson also adduced two more cases in support of his position, one concerning late seventeenth-century Jamaica, and the other early eighteenth-century Virginia. In the first case, Wilson held that the judges "expressly determined – *That the Acts of Parliament or Statutes of England were not in force in Jamaica*," adding that "This decision is explicit in favour of America; for whatever was resolved concerning Jamaica is equally applicable to every American colony."[134] In the second case, according to Wilson, "Lord Chief Justice Holt held, that the laws of England did not extend to Virginia."[135] However, Wilson acknowledged that these decisions rested on Coke's opinion in Calvin's Case, where the great jurist determined that Ireland, being conquered, could be bound by statutes of the English Parliament if it were "especially named." "Nor will I conceal," Wilson added, "that the same exception is taken notice of, and seems to be allowed by, the Judges in the other cases relating to America."[136] Confronted with the equivocal nature of this jurisprudence on the rights of subjects outside the realm, Wilson chose to reject the legitimacy of the conquest doctrine on which both Coke and Blackstone had based the authority of Parliament over the dominions.[137] As Wilson put it: "Does naming them give those, who do them that honor, a right to rule over them? Is this the source of the supreme, the absolute, the uncontrouled

---

[133] Ibid., 19, 21.

[134] Ibid., 22–23.

[135] The two cases were *Blankard v. Galdy* (1694) and *Smith v. Brown and Cooper* (1703). However, as I discussed in Chapter 1, they typify the uncertainties of the jurisprudence on English rights in the empire. Drawing heavily on Coke's opinion in *Calvin's Case*, they both based nonextension on the fact that the two colonies were conquered and thus subject to their own laws until the king decided whether to accord them English law. Although the fact that they were conquered allowed Holt to decide that English laws did not extend, it also allowed the king to alter their laws by prerogative alone; and as Coke's *obiter* in *Calvin's Case* suggested, the English Parliament could bind conquered dominions if it "named" them in an act. Curiously, Wilson did not seize on Holt's doctrine of settlement, first laid out in *Blankard*, which, as we saw in Chapter 1, held that in "uninhabited countries" the settlers were entitled to English law and rights, though, according to Blackstone, this meant that the settlers were then bound by Parliament.

[136] Wilson, *Considerations*, 23–24.

[137] In his footnotes, Wilson attributes the naming doctrine to Coke's decision in *Calvin's Case*, while noting that Coke later had some qualms about Parliament's authority in Ireland. Wilson cited the passage about the American colonies as conquests in Blackstone's *Commentaries*. He also noted that "Lord Chief Justice Holt, in a case above-cited, calls Virginia a conquered country." Ibid., 24–25.

authority of Parliament? These positions are too absurd to be alledged; and a thousand judicial determinations in their favour would never induce one man of sense to subscribe his assent to them."[138]

Wilson also denied that the American colonies had ever been conquered territories. "How come the Colonists to be a conquered people?" he asked. "By whom was the conquest over them obtained? By the House of Commons? By the constituents of that house?"[139] Far from being conquered, Wilson argued, the settlers had been the conquerors, for they had undertaken "at their own expence, expeditions to this distant country, took possession of it, planted it, and cultivated it." Given the extent of their labor, Wilson insisted that they never would have "suspected that their descendants would be considered and treated as a conquered people."[140] After all, he asked,

Do those, who embark, freemen, in Great-Britain, disembark slaves, in America? Are those, who fled from the oppression of regal and ministerial tyranny, now reduced to a state of vassalage to those, who, then, equally felt the same oppression. Whence proceeds this fatal change? Is this the return made us for leaving our friends and our country – for braving the danger of the deep – for planting a wilderness, inhabited only by savage men and savage beasts – for extending the dominion of the British Crown ...?[141]

The American settlers, then, had undertaken a risky migration to a territory inhabited by "savages" who had no sovereignty or property rights the settlers had to respect. But if the empire had been founded in such a decentralized fashion, then what was "the connexion between Great-Britain and her Colonies?" Drawing on another aspect of Coke's protean decision in Calvin's Case, Wilson argued that the settlers owed an allegiance solely to the person of the king. "Every subject," Wilson contended, "so soon as he is born, is under royal protection, and is entitled to all the advantages arising from it. He therefore, owes obedience to that royal power, from which the protection, which he enjoys, is derived."[142]

---

[138] Ibid., 24–25. Wilson claimed that Coke later doubted the validity of the naming doctrine, resolving in "12 Report, 111" that the "Acts of Parliament, made in England, since the Act of the 10th H.7, (he makes no exceptions) do not bind them in Ireland; but all Acts made in England before 10 H. 7, BY THE SAID ACT MADE IN IRELAND, An. 10, H. 7, c.2, do bind them in Ireland."

[139] Wilson held that "it would be somewhat difficult to deduce it satisfactorily" in the case of Ireland, adding that "it is foreign to my purpose to enquire into the reasonableness of founding the authority of the British Parliament over Ireland upon the title of conquest." Ibid., 25.

[140] Ibid., 26.

[141] Ibid., 16.

[142] Ibid., 31. Wilson cited "7 Report. 52. Calvin's Case."

And this allegiance was, as Coke had argued, nonterritorial; that is, it followed English subjects wherever they went.[143]

For Wilson, the allegiance that subjects owed to the Crown differed from subordination to a legislative body like Parliament, for the "former is founded on protection: The latter, on representation." "An inattention to this difference," Wilson argued, "has produced, I apprehend, much uncertainty and confusion in our ideas concerning the connexion which ought to subsist between Great-Britain and the American Colonies."[144] According to Wilson, the colonists recognized the Crown's authority because "they have hitherto enjoyed, and still continue to enjoy his protection."[145] After all, Wilson argued, they "took possession" of America "in the *King's* name: They treated, or made war with the Indians by *his* authority: They held land under *his* grants, and paid *him* the rents reserved upon them: They established governments under the sanction of *his* prerogative, or by virtue of his charters." And, as Wilson reminded his readers, "No application for those purposes was made to the Parliament," and "No ratification of the charters or letters patent was solicited from that Assembly, as is usual in England with regard to grants and franchises of much less importance."[146]

So for Wilson, the empire was bound together by the fact that subjects on both sides of the Atlantic owed allegiance to "the same Prince." But what exactly was the role of the Crown in the governance of the empire? According to Wilson,

the King is entrusted the direction and management of the great machine of government ... He makes war: He concludes peace: He forms alliances: He regulates domestic trade by his prerogative; and directs foreign commerce by his treaties, with those nations, with whom it is carried on. He names the officers of government; so that he can check every jarring movement in the administration. He has a negative in the different legislatures throughout his dominions, so that he can prevent any repugnancy in their different laws.[147]

In Wilson's view, the empire was far better served "by the operation of the legal prerogatives of the Crown, than by the exertion of an unlimited authority in Parliament."[148]

[143] Ibid., 32.
[144] Ibid., 21–22.
[145] Ibid., 31.
[146] Ibid., 29–30.
[147] Ibid., 33.
[148] Ibid., 34.

The result of Wilson's closely reasoned pamphlet was a vision of "the different Members of the British Empire" as "DISTINCT STATES, INDEPENDENT OF EACH OTHER, BUT CONNECTED TOGETHER UNDER THE SAME SOVEREIGN IN RIGHT OF THE SAME CROWN."[149] Wilson did not, however, intend simply to replace the absolute authority of Parliament over the colonies with that of the Crown. Rather, he held that "The Constitution of Great-Britain is that of a limited monarchy," and thus the colonists' "dependence" on the Crown was "not a dependence like that contended for on Parliament, slavish and unaccountable." Rather, Wilson insisted, "It is a dependence founded upon the principles of reason, of liberty, and of law."[150]

Farther to the south, as resistance mounted to the Coercive Acts in the summer of 1774, Thomas Jefferson, a then relatively unknown member of the Virginia House of Burgesses, penned *A Summary View of the Rights of British America*.[151] Intended as a guide for the Virginia delegation to the Continental Congress, it was his first publication and was partly responsible for establishing him as a leading spokesman for colonial rights, as well as a suitable candidate for drafting the Declaration of Independence. Along with Wilson's recently published *Considerations*, Jefferson's *Summary View* was read on both sides of the Atlantic and influenced the delegates at the first Continental Congress in September, 1774.[152]

Like Bland, Hicks, and Wilson, Jefferson defended settler rights by arguing that "our ancestors, before their emigration to America, were the free inhabitants of the British dominions in Europe, and possessed a right which nature has given to all men, of departing from the country in which chance, not choice, has placed them, of going in quest of new habitations, and of there establishing new societies, under such laws as to them shall seem most likely to promote public happiness."[153] "America was conquered," Jefferson claimed, "and her settlements made, and

---

[149] Ibid., 34.

[150] Ibid., 11, 31.

[151] Thomas Jefferson, *A Summary View of the Rights of British America. Set Forth in Some Resolutions Intended for the Inspection of the Present Delegates of the People of Virginia* (Williamsburg, 1774). On Jefferson's life during these crucial years, see Noble E. Cunningham, Jr., *In Pursuit of Reason: The Life of Thomas Jefferson* (New York: Ballantine Books, 1988), 23–35.

[152] Cunningham, *In Pursuit of Reason*, 31. Both Wilson and Jefferson had sat in local revolutionary committees in 1774, as well as in similar colony-wide bodies.

[153] Jefferson, *A Summary View*, 6.

firmly established, at the expence of individuals, and not of the British public."[154] It was "for themselves they fought, for themselves they conquered, and for themselves alone they have a right to hold." Britain, Jefferson argued, did not expend a "shilling" to assist the American colonies until after they were firmly established, and had become commercially valuable.[155] After these "settlements" had been made "in the wilds of America," Jefferson contended that the "emigrants" chose "to adopt that system of laws under which they had hitherto lived in the mother country, and to continue their union with her by submitting themselves to the same common sovereign, who was thereby made the central link connecting the several parts of the empire thus newly multiplied."[156] In place of parliamentary sovereignty, then, Jefferson envisioned a federal empire, wherein the only tie to Britain was through the monarch.

Given this view of the empire, Jefferson argued that Parliament's attempts to legislate for the colonies were a violation of "those rights which God and the laws have given equally and independently to all." This oppression had a long history, beginning with Cromwell's attempts to restrict the trade of Virginia in the 1650s, a policy that Charles II continued after the Restoration. Jefferson objected to the Navigation Acts because they violated the "natural right" that the colonists "possessed" to "exercise of a free trade with all parts of the world."[157] But the ill effects of these trade regulations paled in comparison to Parliament's repeated attempts, beginning with the Sugar and Stamp Acts, to tax and legislate for the colonies without their consent. Jefferson evoked the tenor of the tumultuous decade just past in characteristically eloquent terms: "Scarcely have our minds been able to emerge from the astonishment into which one stroke of parliamentary thunder has involved us, before another more heavy, and more alarming, is fallen on us. Single acts of tyranny may be ascribed to the accidental opinion of a day; but a series of oppressions, begun at a distinguished period, and pursued

---

[154] Jefferson compared the migration to America with that of the Saxons to Britain. For a full account of the role that this historical understanding played in Jefferson's political thought, see H. Trevor Colbourn, *The Lamp of Experience: Whig History and the Intellectual Origins of the American Revolution* (Chapel Hill: University of North Carolina Press, 1965), 158–184; and, more broadly, Colin Kidd, *British Identities before Nationalism: Ethnicity and Nationhood in the Atlantic World, 1600–1800* (New York: Cambridge University Press, 1999).

[155] Jefferson, *Summary View*, 6.

[156] Ibid., 7.

[157] Ibid., 8.

unalterably through every change of ministers, too plainly prove a delib-
erate and systematical plan of reducing us to slavery."[158]

Jefferson singled out Parliament's suspension of the New York
legislature for failing to comply with the Quartering Act as a particularly
egregious example of parliamentary tyranny: "One free and independent
legislature hereby takes upon itself to suspend the powers of another,
free and independent as itself." Jefferson condemned the Coercive Acts
on the same grounds. They were, he argued, "acts of power, assumed by
a body of men, foreign to our constitution, and unacknowledged by our
laws." "Not only the principles of common sense," he proclaimed, "but
the common feelings of human nature, must be surrendered up before his
majesty's subjects here can be persuaded to believe that they hold their
political existence at the will of a British parliament." For Jefferson, no
"reason" could be given "why 160,000 electors in the island of Great
Britain should give law to four millions in the states of America, every
individual of whom is equal to every individual of them, in virtue, in
understanding, and in bodily strength."[159]

Given that he viewed the empire as an association of equal states
under one common sovereign, Jefferson called for the king, as "the only
mediatory power between the several states of the British empire, to rec-
ommend to his parliament of Great Britain the total revocation of these
acts."[160] According to Jefferson, the Crown, because it held "the executive
powers of the laws of these states," should refuse "to pass into a law
any bill which has already passed the other two branches of legislature."
Although the Crown had, "for several ages past," "modestly declined the
exercise of this power in that part of his empire called Great Britain,"
Jefferson argued that "the addition of new states to the British empire has
produced ... new, and sometimes opposite interests." As such, he called
for the king "to resume the exercise of his negative power, and to prevent
the passage of laws by any one legislature of the empire, which might
bear injuriously on the rights and interests of another."[161]

Jefferson was not, however, calling for Parliament's authority to be
replaced by an equally unbounded subordination to the Crown. Indeed,
he decried the role that prerogative power had played in the empire. He
charged the Stuart monarchs with taking land that "had been acquired

[158] Ibid., 11.
[159] Ibid., 12–13.
[160] Ibid., 16.
[161] Ibid., 16.

by the lives, labours, and the fortunes of individual adventurers," and distributing it among their "favourites," who then "erected" it "into distinct and independent governments."[162] Eventually, however, the Stuarts' "treasonable crimes against their people" had led to "the exertion of those sacred and sovereign rights of punishment reserved in the hands of the people for cases of extreme necessity, and judged by the constitution unsafe to be delegated to any other judicature."[163] But, as Jefferson lamented, even after the overthrow of the Stuarts, royal governors in America had continued to prorogue and dissolve the colonial assemblies, after which they often "refused to call another, so that, for a great length of time, the legislature provided by the laws has been out of existence." For Jefferson, this was a violation of the people's rights, because "from the nature of things, every society must at all time possess within itself the sovereign powers of legislation." And if the king interferes with this right, then, Jefferson argued, "the power reverts to the people, who may exercise it to unlimited extent, either assembling together in person, sending deputies, or in any other way they may think proper."[164]

Jefferson also accused the king of allowing colonial "laws" to "lie neglected in England for years, neither confirming them by his assent, nor annulling them by his negative." The king had "rendered this grievance still more oppressive" by instructing his governors to pass "no law of any moment unless it have such suspending clause; so that, however immediate may be the call for legislative interposition, the law cannot be executed till it has twice crossed the Atlantic."[165] And, finally, the Crown had rendered the settlers' property rights insecure by imposing on British North America the kind of feudal tenures that had been introduced by the Normans into England. However, Jefferson contended that "America was not conquered by William the Norman, nor its lands surrendered to him, or any of his successors," and thus "Possessions" in the colonies were "undoubtedly of the allodial nature." For Jefferson, the existence of such allodial (i.e., unencumbered) property rights meant that "each individual of the society may appropriate to himself such lands as he finds vacant, and occupancy will give him title."[166] This clear implication of this stance was that any attempt by the Crown to preserve Native American rights

---

[162] Jefferson was referring to the creation by the English Crown of quasi-feudal proprietorships in America in the seventeenth century.
[163] Ibid., 7.
[164] Ibid., 19.
[165] Ibid., 17.
[166] Ibid., 21.

by limiting western settlement was an illegitimate exercise of the prerogative. In Jefferson's view, individual settlers (or the governments to which they delegated their authority) had the sole right to appropriate and distribute land in America.[167]

In response to these outrages, Jefferson insisted that British Americans had a right to petition the king for redress. After all, "he is no more than the chief officer of the people, appointed by the laws, and circumscribed with definite powers, to assist in working the great machine of government, erected for their use, and consequently subject to their superintendence."[168] For Jefferson, only the wise rule of such a monarch, who was willing to "deal out to all equal and impartial right," could hold "the balance of a great, if a well poised empire." And only such an empire, Jefferson thought, was suitable for "a free people claiming their rights, as derived from the laws of nature, and not as the gift of their chief magistrate."[169]

In its response to the Tea Party, Parliament had intended to isolate Massachusetts, but the Coercive Acts had the opposite effect, largely due to the committees of correspondence and the intercolonial cooperation that had been built up in the decade of escalating controversy since the Stamp Act. In September 1774, as Massachusetts descended into open rebellion, delegates from all but one of the mainland colonies met in a Continental Congress in Philadelphia.[170] For such a pan-colonial body to meet was illegal, even treasonous, especially since its delegates had, in many cases, been sent by provincial conventions that were in effect revolutionary governments, the royal governors having dissolved the old colonial assemblies.[171]

The delegates began their deliberations by approving the Suffolk Resolves, which declared that no allegiance was due to the Coercive Acts. After some debate, they also rejected the Pennsylvanian Joseph Galloway's plan of union, which, like the Albany Plan in 1754, would have created a pan-colonial legislature with representation from all of

---

[167] On the tensions between this Jeffersonian view and that of the Crown, see Robert A. Williams, *The American Indian in Western Legal Thought: The Discourses of Conquest* (New York: Oxford University Press, 1990), 233–286.

[168] Jefferson, *Summary View*, 5–6.

[169] Ibid., 22–23.

[170] In what follows, I have drawn largely on Jack Rakove's judicious account, *The Beginnings of National Politics: An Interpretive History of the Continental Congress* (New York: Alfred A. Knopf, 1979), 42–62.

[171] Middlekauff, *The Glorious Cause*, 240.

the colonies, overseen by a president appointed by the Crown.[172] The delegates also agreed on an association to forbid all imports of goods from Britain, India, and the Ireland after December 1, 1774.[173]

The Congress then constituted a committee to draft a statement of rights. Some of its members, like Richard Henry Lee of Virginia, argued that Congress should make its claim "upon the broadest bottom, the ground of nature" for, according to Lee, when "our ancestors" arrived in America they "found ... no government." Lee was also adamant that rights to "Life and liberty" cannot "be given up when we enter society." However, Lee did not see these natural rights as inconsistent with those based on the common law, and he argued that the Congress should rest its claims on a "fourfold foundation: on nature, on the British constitution, on charters, and on immemorial usage." John Jay of New York agreed that it was "necessary to recur to the law of nature" as well as "the British constitution to ascertain our rights," adding that the settlers originally had "a right to emigrate" and "erect what government they please." As for whether the settlers could sever their connection to the Crown, Jay contended ominously that "there is no allegiance without protection."[174]

However, several prominent members of the committee wanted Congress to make its case solely on the basis of the British constitution. John Rutledge of South Carolina held that subjects could not "alienate" their "allegiance," and that the original emigrants to America did not have the right to establish "what constitution they please." For Rutledge, colonial claims were "well founded on the British constitution, and not on the law of nature." James Duane of New York concurred, holding that "the law of nature" was but "a feeble support" and that the Congress should rest its case on "the laws and constitutions of the country from whence we sprung." The future Loyalist, Joseph Galloway, insisted that he could not find "the rights of Americans" in the "state of nature," but only in "political society" – that is, in "the constitution of the English government."[175]

---

[172] For a copy of the plan, see Julian P. Boyd, ed., *Anglo-American Union: Joseph Galloway's Plans to Preserve the British Empire, 1774–1778* (Philadelphia: University of Pennsylvania Press, 1941), 112–114; and for a discussion of why it failed to win approval, see Jon E. Ferling, *The Loyalist Mind: Joseph Galloway and the American Revolution* (University Park: The Pennsylvania State University Press, 1977), 26–31.

[173] Jensen, ed., *American Colonial Documents*, 813–816.

[174] Ibid., 803–805.

[175] Ibid.

The Declaration of Rights that emerged from this committee combined all of the modes of argument that had characterized settler discourse in the empire for more than a century. It held that "the inhabitants of the English colonies in North America, by the immutable laws of nature, the principles of the English constitution, and the several charters or compacts" had rights to "life, liberty and property," which they "have never ceded to any sovereign power." Moreover, their ancestors, "who first settled these colonies, were at the time of their emigration from the mother country, entitled to all the rights, liberties, and immunities of free and natural-born subjects within the realm of England." Since the "foundation of English liberty, and of all free government, is a right in the people to participate in their legislative council," and since they "cannot properly be represented in British Parliament," Congress claimed that the settlers "are entitled to a free and exclusive power of legislation in their several provincial legislatures," subject only to the "negative" of the "sovereign, in such manner as has been heretofore used and accustomed."[176]

The Congressional Declaration called for the repeal of all of the post-1763 parliamentary legislation, including the Coercive Acts and the Quebec Act, which, they claimed, erected a "tyranny" in a country the settlers had helped to conquer. As well, the declaration denounced the presence of a standing army in the colonies, and reiterated the colonists' right to jury trials, and to the benefit of such parliamentary statutes as they found "by experience" to be suitable to local circumstances. The Congress did concede that Parliament had the authority to regulate colonial trade but made it clear that this was only with the settlers' "consent," and only when its acts were truly for the "commercial advantage" of the "whole empire."[177]

At the end of October 1774, their work done, the delegates headed home, having agreed to convene again the following spring. Despite the hopes of many in the colonies, the ministry showed no sign that it would repeal the Coercive Acts and wind the constitutional clock back to 1763. In October, after Gage had refused to call the General Court into session, the Massachusetts towns defied him and sent representatives to a provincial congress, giving the colony "something approaching a revolutionary government."[178] All across America in the winter of 1774–1775,

[176] Ibid., 805–808.
[177] Ibid.
[178] Middlekauff, *The Glorious Cause*, 259.

authority at the provincial and local level was falling into the hands of extra-legal bodies. In December, the associations authorized by Congress began to enforce the boycott on British imports, adding another layer to the proliferation of extra-constitutional committees and conventions. In response to the breakdown of royal authority, Joseph Galloway, disillusioned by the rejection of his plan of union, launched a bitter attack on what he saw as "clear, palpable treason and rebellion." Galloway worried that continued resistance would place the colonists in "the deplorable condition of a conquered people, subject to the oppression and tyranny of a military government ... with British forces in all your capital cities, commanding your allegiance to the British state."[179]

Galloway was not the only subject in America who felt this way in the tense winter and spring of 1775. Daniel Leonard, a lawyer and scion of an old Bay Colony family, wrote a series of essays defending Parliament's policies under the pseudonym *Massachusettensis*.[180] Leonard had been appointed by General Gage to the ill-fated royal council and then been forced to seek safe haven in Boston after an angry mob attacked his house. In response to the claims of the radicals in Massachusetts, Leonard argued that the colonies were part of the empire and thus subject to the authority of the king-in-Parliament, "the most perfect system that the wisdom of the ages has produced." And, he insisted, it had always been the case that Parliament could bind the royal dominions without their consent, adding that even if a subject of the king left the realm "he and his posterity are and ever will be subject to the authority of the British Parliament."[181] As well, like all of the defenders of Parliament in the imperial crisis, Leonard maintained that "two supreme or independent authorities cannot exist in the same state," for it "would be what is called *imperium in imperio*, the height of political absurdity."[182]

---

[179] Joseph Galloway, *A Candid Examination of the Mutual Claims of Great-Britain and the Colonies: With a Plan of Accommodation on Constitutional Principles* (New York: James Rivington, 1775), 31, 62. Galloway contended that "all the treatises on the common law" held that resistance to the Crown was treason (31).

[180] The bulk of the essays are reprinted in Bernard Mason, ed., *The American Colonial Crisis: The Daniel Leonard-John Adams Letters to the Press* (New York: Harper Torchbooks, 1972), 3–97. Leonard's essays ran from December 1774 to April 1775. Leonard and Joseph Galloway and Thomas Hutchinson all became Loyalists. On the emergence of Loyalism, see Mary Beth Norton, *The British-Americans: The Loyalist Exiles in England, 1774–1789* (Boston 1972), 10–41; and Robert M. Calhoon, *The Loyalists in Revolutionary America* (New York: Harcourt Brace Jovanovich, 1973).

[181] Letter VI, in Mason, ed., *The American Colonial Crisis*, 43.

[182] Letter V, in Mason, ed., *The American Colonial Crisis*, 33.

John Adams, recently returned from the Continental Congress, responded to Leonard under the pseudonym, *Novanglus* (or the New Englishman). Adams's letters were the most comprehensive articulation of the colonial case against parliamentary authority in the entire revolutionary crisis.[183] As a lawyer, Adams was particularly concerned with countering Leonard's constitutional argument that all of the dominions of the Crown were legally subject to Parliament's authority. In doing so, he had to confront the complex jurisprudence about the rights of subjects outside the realm that stretched from Coke in the early seventeenth century to Blackstone and Mansfield in the late eighteenth century. After what he called a "fatiguing ramble" through a thicket of complicated precedents, Adams ended up rejecting this jurisprudence, and in particular its claim that conquest allowed the king or Parliament to bind the dominions legislatively without their consent.[184]

Adams began with Wales, which he claimed had been "conquered" by the English king, and was therefore "always held of the crown of England," but was not "parcel of the realm or the kingdom, nor bound by the laws of England."[185] As conqueror, the English king was an "absolute monarch," who could "govern this country with or without the advice of his English lords and commons." However, according to Adams, following the conquest, the Welsh became "fond of the English laws, and desirous of being incorporated into the realm, to be represented in parliament, and to enjoy all the rights of Englishmen." As a result, despite the desire of the English king to retain "the power in his own hands of giving it what system of law he pleased," a "union and incorporation were made by the consent and upon the supplication of the people of Wales ... so that there was an express contract between the two bodies of people,"

---

[183] *Novanglus; Or, A History of the Dispute with America*, reprinted in C. Bradley Thompson, ed., *The Revolutionary Writings of John Adams* (Indianapolis: Liberty Fund, 2000), 148–284. Adams's essays were written between January and April, 1775. The citations to *Novanglus* that follow refer to Thompson's edition. On Adams's political ideas, see C. Bradley Thompson, *John Adams and the Spirit of Liberty* (Lawrence: University Press of Kansas, 1998). See also James Muldoon, "Discovery, Grant, Charter, Conquest, or Purchase: John Adams on the Legal Basis for English Possession of North America," in Christopher L. Tomlins, ed., *The Many Legalities of Early America* (Chapel Hill: University of North Carolina Press, 2001), 25–46.

[184] *Letter XII*, in Thompson ed., *The Revolutionary Writings of John Adams*, 278. A point made in Michael Zuckert's superb essay, "Natural Rights and Imperial Constitutionalism: The American Revolution and the Development of the American Amalgam," *Social Philosophy and Policy* 22 (2005), 27–55.

[185] *Letter VIII*, in Thompson ed., *The Revolutionary Writings of John Adams*, 246.

a contract that included the extension of English laws, as well as Welsh representation in the English Parliament.[186]

Adams next turned to Ireland. He held that it, like Wales, was "a conquered country" and thus not "annexed to, or parcel of the realm." As a consequence, for several hundred years (following its conquest by Henry II), "the king's powers" were "absolute there," such that "he might govern it without his English parliament, whose advice concerning it he was under no obligation to ask or pursue." However, as Adams was aware, since the conquest Ireland had become subject to the authority of the English Parliament despite having a representative body of its own. In order to weaken the force of this unfortunate precedent, Adams contended that Ireland had, in the reign of Henry VII, consented to be bound by the English Parliament. This occurred under the aegis of Henry's proconsul, Sir Edward Poynings, who arrived in 1495 to put down a Yorkist rebellion. Sensing that the Irish were disaffected, and following Henry's advice that "he should gain more by clemency and indulgence than by rigor and severity," Poynings "called a parliament" in which "all former laws of England were made to be in force in Ireland, and no bill can be introduced into the Irish parliament unless it previously received the sanction of the English privy council." As a result, Adams argued, the power of the English Parliament to bind Ireland by "acts of parliament, if specially named," was "grounded entirely on the voluntary act, the free consent of the Irish nation."[187]

But Adams was too careful a lawyer to leave the story there. As he acknowledged, Coke's claim that countries conquered by the English king could be bound by his Parliament if it "named" them in an act was still widely accepted in the eighteenth century, having been incorporated into Blackstone's recently published *Commentaries*. While conceding that what he called Coke's "parenthesis" was a valid precedent, Adams contended that Parliament's power to legislate for unrepresented dominions was "arbitrary and groundless," based solely on the dubious legal force of conquest, which was part of the law of nations but not the law of nature.[188] Moreover, as Adams noted, "the Irish nation" has "never been convinced" of the "justice" of their situation, which was one reason there was "a standing army of twelve thousand men"

[186] *Letter VIII*, Ibid., 248, 251–252.
[187] *Letter X*, Ibid., 266–267.
[188] *Letter XI*, Ibid., 272.

stationed there, despite the fact that the English Parliament has "never once attempted ... to tax them."[189]

Having probed the limits of the English jurists' account of the empire, Adams offered the radical suggestion that no coherent account of the relationship between realm and dominions had ever been given. For Adams, the great "defect" in the imperial constitution was that "*colonization*" was "*casus omissus* at common law." That is, "no provision" had been "made in this law for governing colonies beyond the Atlantic, or beyond the four seas, by authority of parliament; no, nor for the king to grant charters to subjects to settle in foreign countries."[190] As a result, instead of invoking principles of "law, or justice, or reason," Britain was asserting its sovereignty on the basis of "mere power," and was preparing to "resort to war and conquest" in a vain attempt to subdue the colonies.[191] In doing so, it was betraying the true nature of its constitution as "a limited monarchy," which, in its respect for the rule of law, was "much more like a republic than an empire."[192]

"How, then," Adams asked, "do we New Englandmen derive our laws? I say, not from Parliament, not from common law, but from the law of nature, and the compact made with the king in our charters." Furthermore, Adams argued, the king had no legitimate authority in America that was not derived from that of the settlers. This was because America was "not a conquered, but a discovered country." That is, it "came not to the king by descent, but was explored by the settlers. It came not by marriage to the king, but was purchased by the settlers of the savages. It was not granted of the king by his grace, but was dearly, very dearly earned by the planters, in the labor, blood, and treasure which they expended to subdue it by cultivation." As a result, the rights of the settlers stood "upon no grounds, then, of law or policy, but what are found in the law of nature, and their express contracts in their charters, and their implied contracts in the commissions to governors and terms of settlement."[193]

For Adams, this meant that the legal foundation of the empire was based on the fact that "English liberties" were "but certain rights of nature, reserved to the citizen by the English constitution," which "cleaved to our ancestors when they crossed the Atlantic." And, Adams argued,

---

[189] *Letter XI*, Ibid., 268.
[190] *Letter VII*, Ibid., 221; *Letter VIII*, Ibid., 237.
[191] *Letter VII*, Ibid., 227.
[192] *Letter VII*, Ibid., 226–227.
[193] *Letter XII*, Ibid., 238, 278.

these rights would "have inhered in them if, instead of coming to New England, they had gone to Otaheite or Patagonia, even although they had taken no patent or charter from the king at all." Indeed, Adams went so far as to argue that the original settlers "had a clear right to have erected in this wilderness a British constitution, or a perfect democracy, or any other form of government they saw fit."[194] Upon their arrival in America, however, Adams claimed that they had made a contract with the English king in which he granted them protection in return for allegiance.[195] As such, each of the American colonies had a separate tie to the Crown, just like Wales and Ireland and the Channel Islands did. As Adams put it, "Massachusetts is a realm, New York is a realm, Pennsylvania another realm, to all intents and purposes, as much as Ireland is, or England or Scotland ever were. The King of Great Britain is the sovereign in all of these realms."[196]

When Adams put down his pen in the spring of 1775, the war of words was coming to an end and the real one was about to begin. The second Continental Congress met in May, not long after the first shots had been fired at Lexington and Concord. Soon after convening, it began to prepare for war, putting George Washington in charge of a Continental army, and issuing a declaration, written by both Jefferson and John Dickinson, justifying the taking up of arms.[197] At the same time, the congressional moderates, with Dickinson again in the lead, insisted on sending one last petition to the king seeking reconciliation. However in August, two days after he received this Olive Branch petition, George III issued a royal proclamation declaring the colonies in open rebellion.[198] This was followed by a forceful speech before Parliament in October in which he vowed to defeat the rebellion. And in December, the king assented to the Prohibitory Act, which ended all trade with the colonies and sanctioned the seizure of their ships on the high seas as if they were "open enemies."[199]

---

[194] *Letter VIII*, Ibid., 238.
[195] According to Brad Thompson, "Adams trimmed the colonists' allegiance to the king from one grounded on Coke's quasi-medieval teaching in *Calvin's Case* to one squarely within the radical social contract tradition of Locke's *Second Treatise*." See Thompson, *The Spirit of Liberty*, 79.
[196] *Letter VIII*, in Thompson ed., *The Revolutionary Writings of John Adams*, 239.
[197] Jensen, ed., *American Colonial Documents*, 842–847.
[198] Both the Olive Branch Petition and the King's proclamation are in Jensen, ed., *American Colonial Documents*, 847–851.
[199] Ibid., 853.

In taking these actions, George III made it impossible for the settlers'
vision of an empire of independent states under a common monarchy to
be realized. By putting them out of his protection, he was unilaterally
sundering the reciprocal bonds of protection and allegiance.[200] In such
circumstances, the radicals in Congress contended that they could withdraw their allegiance and invoke their natural right to resist constituted
authority. In May, 1776, Congress passed a resolution that accused the
king and Parliament of excluding "the inhabitants of these united colonies from the protection of his Crown." It then instructed the colonies
to suppress all royal authority and to "adopt such government as shall,
in the opinion of the representatives of the people, best conduce to the
happiness and safety of their constituents."[201] And on June 7, responding
to instructions from the Virginia House of Burgesses, its senior delegate,
Richard Henry Lee, moved "that these United Colonies are, and of right
ought to be, free and independent States."[202]

The resulting Declaration of Independence, written largely by
Jefferson, traced the arc of constitutional conflict in the empire since the
Restoration, its powerful indictment of the king capturing the essence
of the settlers' concern for their constitutional rights in an uncertain
imperial polity, from the repeated dissolution of their legislative bodies,
to the suspension of their laws, to the interference with judicial tenure,
to the denial of the right to trial by jury, to the presence of standing
armies in their midst, and, finally, to the annulling of their charters. The
Declaration's opening paragraphs, however, show the extent to which
this long transatlantic constitutional conflict had brought the idea of
natural rights to the forefront of the settlers' political theory. Although
the common law and English constitutional rights remained central to
early American political culture long past independence, they would

[200] For the argument that in the final years of the imperial crisis George III was "actively
committed to a policy of coercion in America," see Andrew Jackson O'Shaughnessy,
"'If Others Will Not Be Active I Must Drive': George III and the American Revolution,"
Early American Studies I (2004), 9, and passim. On the "abrupt transformations in
popular attitudes" to the King between 1774 and 1776, see William D. Liddle,
"'A Patriot King or None': Lord Bolingbroke and the American Renunciation of George
III," *Journal of American History* 65 (1979), 968, and passim. On the attachment to
monarchy in British America, see Brendan McConville, *The King's Three Faces: The
Rise and Fall of Royal America, 1688–1776* (Chapel Hill: University of North Carolina
Press, 2006).
[201] Jensen, ed., *American Colonial Documents*, 854.
[202] Ibid., 867–868.

now – as Bland, Hicks, Wilson, Adams, and Jefferson himself had all argued in the years leading up to independence – be grounded in the law of nature, the violation of which had, according to the Declaration, triggered a right of revolution, a total dissolution of the tie to the monarch, an act that was not conceivable within the confines of the customary ancient constitution.[203]

Natural law was also the basis of the Declaration's assertion that the "United Colonies are, and of Right ought to be, FREE AND INDEPENDENT STATES." In the parlance of the eighteenth century, the phrase "free state" had "come to mean specifically a nonmonarchical regime" – that is, a republic.[204] The culmination of the long debate about rights in the British Atlantic was thus the creation of thirteen new republican governments, whose "separate and equal station" among "the Powers of the earth" was based on the "Laws of Nature and of Nature's God," as well as on the claim that their rights were superior to those of the indigenous peoples in their midst, whom the Declaration, echoing over a century of settler discourse about native rights, referred to as "merciless Indian savages."[205] In the uncertain years after 1776, these new republican states would have to decide on terms of union as they tried to survive in a dangerous world, surrounded by European empires and powerful native confederacies.[206] In doing so, they would build on the federal division of

---

[203] According to Mark Goldie, "a right of resistance was ultimately an appeal beyond history to natural or divine right, exercised by the community beyond the framework of the constitution." Goldie, "The Roots of True Whiggism," *History of Political Thought* 1 (1980), 209–210. For the centrality of natural rights to post revolutionary American jurisprudence, see Douglas Bradburn, *The Citizenship Revolution: Politics and the Creation of the American Union, 1774–1804* (Charlottesville: University of Virginia Press, 2009).

[204] David Armitage, *The Declaration of Independence: A Global History* (Cambridge: Harvard University Press, 2007), 38. Armitage attributes the revolutionaries' use of the phrase "free state" to the influence of Vattel, who explicitly connected the natural rights of individuals to the sovereign powers of the independent states they formed: "Nations being composed of men naturally free and independent, and who, before the establishment of civil societies, lived together in the state of nature, nations, or sovereign states, are to be considered as so many free persons living together in the state of nature." Emer de Vattel, *The Law of Nations; or, Principles of the Law of Nature applied to the Conduct and Affairs of Nations and Sovereigns* (London, 1793), lii.

[205] For the text of the Declaration, see Cynthia A. Kierner, ed., *Revolutionary America, 1750–1815: Sources and Interpretation* (New Jersey: Prentice Hall, 2003), 137–139.

[206] For the descent of the trans-Appalachian territories into a lawless state of nature after the collapse of British authority, see Patrick Griffin, *American Leviathan: Empire, Nation and Revolutionary Frontier* (New York: Hill and Wang, 2007).

authority they had so cherished in the years before 1776, combining it
with revolutionary ideals of rights and equality to create a new republican
empire on the far side of the Atlantic, which was, in the words of Alexander
Hamilton, "in many respects the most interesting in the world."[207]

[207] Alexander Hamilton, Federalist One, in Jack Pole, ed., *The Federalist* (Indianapolis: Hackett, 2005), 1. On the problems of union in the 1780s, see David Hendrickson, *Peace Pact: The Lost World of the American Founding* (Lawrence: University Press of Kansas, 2003). For a nuanced account of the connections between pre- and postrevolutionary American federalism, see Peter Onuf, *Jefferson's Empire: The Language of American Nationhood* (Charlottesville: University of Virginia Press, 2000), 53–79; as well as Jack P. Greene, *Peripheries and Center: Constitutional Development in the Extended Polities of the British Empire and the United States, 1607–1788* (Athens: University of Georgia Press, 1986), passim. On the new American "empire of liberty" in the west, see Eric Hinderaker, *Elusive Empires: Constructing Colonialism in the Ohio Valley, 1673–1800* (New York: Cambridge University Press, 1997), 187–225.

Conclusion

Settlers, Liberty, and Empire has traced the emergence of a distinctive settler strand of Anglo-American political thought in the crucial decades between the Glorious Revolution in America and the American Revolution against Britain. Confronted by a succession of centralizing initiatives emanating from London, settler elites drew on the common law and the early modern law of nature to defend their rights in a legally contested transatlantic empire. They supported this claim to equal rights by pointing to the risks they had taken to establish flourishing polities in a New World they persisted in seeing as a wilderness, inhabited by indigenous peoples whose sovereignty and property they had supplanted by purchase, conquest, and labor. This account of the rights of the English settlers in the empire was both coherent, based as it was on the fundamental right that each subject had to liberty and property throughout the king's dominions, and widely shared, being employed at moments of constitutional tension irrespective of whether the colonies using it to defend their autonomy were corporate, proprietary, or royal.

The result of this century-long debate about rights in the empire was the emergence of a revolutionary conception of political authority on the far side of the Atlantic in the decade leading up to 1776. Laid out in its fullest form in a series of late colonial pamphlets, it held that the settlers had a natural right to migrate from England, establish self-governing polities in America, and then delegate political authority to the Crown in return for the benefits of royal protection. Their tie to the center, then, was conditional on its respect for their autonomy in a loosely confederated empire, one they had helped to create, and which was dependent on their freedom for its flourishing. And when faced with Parliament's assertion in the 1760s and 1770s that the empire was in fact a unitary state in which it was the ultimate sovereign, settler elites invoked a natural right to resist constituted authority and establish new republican governments based on popular consent.

The settler political theory described in this book was not the inevitable outcome of a process of Americanization. Rather, it was the long-term result of a confluence of factors, from the presence of indigenous peoples in eastern North America, whom the settlers could construe as living in a Lockean state of nature; to the centralizing policies of metropolitan officials concerned about geopolitical and commercial threats in a world of competing empires; to the Atlantic world itself, which, as we have seen, privileged a universal discourse of law and rights over municipal legal systems like the English common law, whose conceptual resources had, as John Adams and other settlers came to realize, proved inadequate to deal with the legal complexity of a transoceanic empire. Settler political thought was thus fundamentally reactive, a product of the pressure they felt from the center as well as the peculiar features of the world they encountered on the far shores of the Atlantic.

This settler adoption of natural rights was a radical departure from traditional English legal norms in that it supplied a justification for a right of resistance and thus a renunciation of all royal and parliamentary authority, a stance that, as J.G.A. Pocock reminds us, the ancient constitution was unable to justify.[1] But the move to natural rights was not a sudden "leap out of history" on the eve of the Revolution, a last-minute shift from an older world of traditional English liberties and privileges.[2] Rather, it was the result of a long debate about settler rights in the empire, out of which emerged a peculiarly American amalgam of natural law and common law, with natural law supplying the ultimate foundation of political authority, and common law much of the substantive content of the civil rights that Americans claimed during the founding era. As we have seen,

---

[1] According to J.G.A. Pocock, "the ancient constitution has no origin and contains no provision for its own dissolution." Pocock, *The Ancient Constitution and the Feudal Law: A Study of English Historical Thought in the Seventeenth Century* (1957; revised edition, Cambridge: Cambridge University Press, 1987), 354.

[2] A claim made by T.H. Breen in his Harmsworth lecture, *The Lockean Moment: The Language of Rights on the Eve of the American Revolution* (Oxford: Oxford University Press, 2001), 12, as well as in his "Ideology and Nationalism on the Eve of the American Revolution: Revisions *Once* More in Need of Revising," *Journal of American History* 84 (1997), 13–39, and echoed in much of the literature on the revolution. See, for example, Edward Countryman, "Indians, the Colonial Order, and the Social Significance of the American Revolution," *William and Mary Quarterly* 53 (1996), 342–362; and Richard Johnson "'Parliamentary Egotisms': The Clash of Legislatures in the Making of the American Revolution," *Journal of American History* 74 (1987), 338–362.

the Declaration of Independence contained an eloquent defense of both individual and collective rights based on natural law, alongside a list of complaints about the king's violation of English legal norms. Many of the new republican state constitutions formed in the crucial years between 1776 and 1780 followed a similar pattern: their preambles contained stirring declarations of fundamental natural rights, while the body was largely composed of claims to English legal rights.[3] That British North Americans should combine these two intellectual traditions is not surprising for, despite their differences, they both understood rights as grounded in something more fundamental than mere positive law (whether it be "nature," or "custom," or "history"). The widespread claim that English rights were the subject's "birthright" was compatible with the law of nature as both saw rights as inhering in the individual rather than being the grant of a sovereign authority.[4] As well, both natural law and common law placed a premium on consent as the foundation of all legitimate political authority; and they were as one in rejecting the idea that law was the mere will or command of the sovereign. Metropolitan legal and political culture, by contrast, eschewed what was seen as a politically radical invocation of natural rights, especially after the upheaval of Civil War and regicide in the mid-seventeenth century, and the subsequent rise

[3] On the attempt by postrevolutionary American jurists to incorporate republican ideals of natural rights, equality, and choice into the common law, see Ellen Holmes Pearson, "Revising Custom, Embracing Choice: Early American Legal Scholars and the Republicanization of the Common Law," in Eliga H. Gould and Peter Onuf, eds., *Empire and Nation: The American Revolution in the Atlantic World* (Baltimore: Johns Hopkins University Press, 2005), 93–111. On the understudied topic of the state constitutions, see Willi Paul Adams, *The First American Constitutions: Republican Ideology and the Making of the State Constitutions in the Revolutionary Era* (1980; expanded edition, Lanham: Rowman and Littlefield, 2001).

[4] In arguing that early modern natural law theory was primarily concerned with rights and not duties, I am drawing on the work of Richard Tuck, as well as the broader literature on natural rights and empire discussed in the introduction and Chapter 1. See Richard Tuck, "The Modern Theory of Natural Law," in Anthony Pagden, ed., *The Languages of Political Theory in Early Modern Europe* (Cambridge: Cambridge University Press, 1987), 99–119. For a contrary view, see Knud Haakonssen, "From Natural Law to the Rights of Man: A European Perspective on American Debates," in his *Natural Law and Moral Philosophy: From Grotius to the Scottish Enlightenment* (Cambridge: Cambridge University Press, 1996), 310–342, as well as Barry Shain, "Rights Natural and Civil in the Declaration of Independence," in Shain, ed., *The Nature of Rights at the American Founding and Beyond* (Charlottesville: University of Virginia Press, 2007), 116–162. Unlike Shain, I don't see a sharp divide in British American discourse between natural rights and the rights individuals enjoy in civil society, nor between the Declaration's conception of individual rights and its defense of the rights of states. Indeed, as I argued at the end of the last chapter, the latter were derived from the former. For a discussion of this question, see the contributions to the "Critical Forum: David Armitage, *The Declaration of Independence: A Global History*," *William and Mary Quarterly* 65 (2008), 347–369.

of the idea of the unitary sovereignty of the king-in-Parliament in the eighteenth century.[5]

The nexus of ideas that I have called settler political theory, with its amalgam of English rights and natural rights, also appealed across denominational and regional lines, helping to create a common understanding of the place of British North Americans in the empire. This process of integration was fostered by the growing Anglicization of the colonies in the eighteenth century, which bolstered the prestige of the common law, as well as by the shared experience of living outside the realm, in legally tenuous polities, and among indigenous peoples whose claims to land and authority often clashed with those of the settlers.[6]

This settler use of natural law was also fundamentally eclectic. Although Locke was clearly important to settlers much earlier than usually thought, they also invoked other thinkers in the broader natural law tradition, among them Grotius, Pufendorf, Burlamaqui, and Vattel. However, they did so in a way that elided the differences among them. For example, in the 1720s, Dulany saw no incongruity in citing Grotius, Pufendorf, and Locke to bolster his claim that Marylanders were entitled to English law and rights. And in the 1760s, Bland defended a natural right of migration by citing (though not quoting) both Locke and Vattel.[7] As such, *Settlers*,

---

[5] This is the main conclusion of the revisionist school of Stuart historiography. Mark Goldie's exhaustive analysis of the English pamphlet literature during the Glorious Revolution shows that radical arguments positing a natural right of resistance as a justification for the change in government formed only a small percentage of the arguments surrounding the taking of the oath. According to Goldie, "only 10% articulated a natural law theory of resistance and only 16% were prepared explicitly to defend a right of deposition." See Mark Goldie, "The Revolution of 1689 and the Structure of Political Argument: An Essay and an Annotated Bibliography of Pamphlets on the Allegiance Controversy," *Bulletin of Research in the Humanities* 83 (1980), 489.

[6] The fact that figures as religiously diverse as William Penn, Jeremiah Dummer, Daniel Dulany, John Bulkley, John Adams, and Thomas Jefferson (to name just a few) had a similar view of the status of the settlers in the empire suggests that religious differences did not significantly shape colonial legal and constitutional thought. Carla Pestana has recently argued for the integrative force of Protestantism in the early modern British world. Pestana, *Protestant Empire: Religion and the Making of the British Atlantic World* (Philadelphia: University of Pennsylvania Press, 2009). For an argument that the British Atlantic was divided by intra-Protestant religious differences which culminated in revolution, see J.C.D. Clark, *The Language of Liberty, 1660–1832: Political Discourse and Social Dynamics in the Anglo-American World* (New York: Cambridge University Press, 1994). On Anglicization, see John Murrin, "The Legal Transformation: The Bench and the Bar of Eighteenth-Century Massachusetts," in Stanley Katz and John Murrin, eds., *Colonial America: Essays in Politics and Social Development* (New York: Alfred A. Knopf, 1983), 540–572.

[7] In defending the idea that political power inheres inalienably in individuals as well as the idea that there is an individual right of armed resistance, Locke was departing in some respects from earlier theorists of natural rights, including not only Hobbes but also Grotius

Liberty and Empire has focused on the ways that the settlers used these English and European ideas in particular contexts, rather than engaging in a debate about which thinker had the dominant influence (a besetting sin of the old debate between liberalism and classical republicanism in which Locke's influence was either exaggerated or denied altogether).

The law of nature (and the related doctrine of the *ius gentium*, or the law of nations) was also important in the 1760s and 1770s as the settlers argued that they had an individual natural right to leave the realm and govern themselves in "free states" loosely confederated in a treaty relationship to the Crown, much like any number of contemporary European leagues or alliances.[8] The early modern law of nations also shaped the settlers' conception of the confederation they entered into in the crucial years after 1776, based as it was on the autonomy each of the former colonies enjoyed once they had become, to borrow Peter Onuf's apt characterization, independent "state-republics."[9]

While not denying the importance of the much-studied years after 1763, *Settlers, Liberty, and Empire* shifts scholarly attention away from the late eighteenth century and instead recaptures the experience of settler elites as they faced an early modern world of constitutional uncertainty, imperial centralization, and geopolitical rivalry. In doing so, it stresses the continuity between the politics of the colonial and revolutionary eras, in contrast to much recent scholarship that studies the social and cultural history of the colonies in the Atlantic world, while largely ignoring the political origins of

and Pufendorf. The question of the relationship between Locke and the other early modern natural law theorists is too big a topic to be covered in this study. However, it is interesting to note that when the natural law treatises of both Barbeyrac and Pufendorf reached English audiences in the eighteenth century, they were translated from the editions produced by the French Hugenot, Jean Barbeyrac. Barbeyrac appended copious notes to his edition of Pufendorf, correcting what he saw as errors in Pufendorf's arguments with insights drawn from Locke's *Second Treatise*. Barbeyrac was particularly concerned in drawing the reader's attention to the superiority of Locke's theory of resistance as well as his theory of property over those of Pufendorf. The impact that Barbeyrac's editorial interventions had on the reception of natural law theory in the Anglo-American world in the eighteenth century remains to be studied. For a selection of these notes, see Mark Goldie, ed., *The Reception of Locke's Politics*. Volume II (Brookfield, VT: Pickering and Chatto, 1999), 263–282. For the influence of Burlamaqui on Jefferson, see Morton White, *The Philosophy of the American Revolution* (New York: Oxford University Press, 1978).

[8] On the continental tradition of divided authority, see Alison LaCroix, *The Ideological Origins of American Federalism* (Cambridge: Harvard University Press, 2010), 18–20. For Vattel and the idea of a free state, see David Armitage, *The Declaration of Independence: A Global History* (Cambridge: Harvard University Press, 2007), 37–40.

[9] See Peter Onuf, *Jefferson's Empire: The Language of American Nationhood* (Charlottesville: University of Virginia Press, 2000), 11; and David Hendrickson, *Peace Pact: The Lost World of the American Founding* (Lawrence: University Press of Kansas, 2003).

the revolutionary upheaval that created the new nation.[10] *Settlers, Liberty, and Empire* also takes seriously the impact of the indigenous peoples of the New World on the formation of settler political theory, as well as the complicated relationship between law, institutions, and political theory in the eighteenth-century British world. As such, it sees the settlers' long-term engagement with empire as a necessary (if not a sufficient) cause of the Revolution that sundered the British world.

The story that *Settlers, Liberty, and Empire* tells also has implications for the years after 1776 when the new nation, surrounded by hostile European empires and powerful native confederacies, embarked on a fraught experiment with republican government. At the heart of this book's account of the eighteenth-century Anglo-American world lies a vision of empire in which rights-bearing settlers carved out a sphere of autonomy from the center by virtue of the labor and risk they had undertaken to create flourishing polities on the far periphery of the Atlantic world. This vision of the empire held that the rights of the settlers would be best protected in a loose federal system in which the colonies had a large degree of local control and in which the rights to sovereignty and property of the native peoples they encountered were necessarily diminished.

In the aftermath of independence, this decentralized settler vision was no longer constrained by the authority of Crown or Parliament. Taking their place was a much weaker central government that, even after the constitution was ratified in 1788, remained a federal polity with the states continuing to enjoy a large degree of autonomy. As a consequence, the citizens of the new United States were free to migrate west and south into the coveted lands of the trans-Appalachian west, where, as Eliga Gould argues, they reenacted "in each territory the home rule proclaimed in 1776," while "asserting rights of conquest and self-government that went well beyond those of their own predecessors, let alone of those American subjects still subject to the British Crown."[11] As in the old empire, then, territorial jurisdiction followed the establishment of property rights by migrating settlers, but after independence their claims were animated by a powerful conception of popular sovereignty born of revolution.[12]

[10] On the "disjunction" between scholarship on the colonies and the revolution, see Pauline Maier, "Disjunctions in Early American History," in Donald Yerxa, ed., *Recent Themes in Early American History: Historians in Conversation* (Columbia: University of South Carolina Press, 2008), 9–17.

[11] See Eliga Gould, "The Question of Home Rule," *William and Mary Quarterly* 64 (2007), 258, as well as Jack P. Greene, "Colonial History and National History: Reflections on a Continuing Problem," *William and Mary Quarterly* 64 (2007), 235–250.

[12] On which, see Countryman, "Indians, the Colonial Order, and the Social Significance of the American Revolution," 342–362.

Despite the brief interval of respect for native autonomy and property under Washington's secretary of war, Henry Knox, in the 1790s,
this process accelerated following Jefferson's election in 1800 and the
proclamation of an expansive "empire of liberty"; for, as Jefferson asked
rhetorically in his Second Inaugural, "who can limit the extent to which
the federative principle may operate effectively?"[13] With the withdrawal
of both Spain and Great Britain following the War of 1812, the native
nations who remained in the southeast and the northwest were no longer
able to count on European allies as a counterweight to this expansive
empire of liberty.[14] As John Quincy Adams told the British delegation
at the treaty negotiations in 1814 (who had wanted native autonomy
to be respected), "to condemn vast regions of territory to perpetual bar-
renness and solitude that a few hundred savages might find beasts to
hunt upon it" would never be tolerated by the "people of the United
States," who, Adams insisted, did not want to be precluded from "settling
and cultivating these territories."[15] Adams's sentiments were echoed by
Andrew Jackson in his second State of the Union message in 1830. Using
language steeped in the long history of settler justifications for empire,
Jackson asked his fellow citizens, "What good man would prefer a country covered with forests and ranged by a few thousand savages to our
extensive Republic, studded with cities, towns, and prosperous farms,
embellished with all the improvements which art can devise or industry
execute, occupied by more than 12,000,000 happy people, and filled with
all the blessings of liberty, civilization, and religion?"[16]

Jackson's words were a prelude to removal, as the long argument
about the rights of the settlers, dating back to the seventeenth century,

[13] "Second Inaugural Address," March 4, 1805, in Merrill D. Peterson, ed., *The Portable Thomas Jefferson* (New York: Penguin Books, 1988), 318. On Knox's Indian policy, see Joseph J. Ellis, *American Creation: Triumphs and Tragedies of the American Founding* (New York: Alfred A. Knopf, 2007), 127–164. On the new empire of liberty that Americans were building in the west, see Eric Hinderaker, *Elusive Empires: Constructing Colonialism in the Ohio Valley, 1673–1800* (Cambridge: Cambridge University Press, 1997), 268–270.
[14] On the momentous consequences of this transition, see Jeremy Adelman and Stephen Aron, "From Borderlands to Borders: Empires, Nation-States, and the Peoples in Between in North American History," *American Historical Review* 104 (1999), 814–841.
[15] Quoted in Leonard Sadosky, *Revolutionary Negotiations: Indians, Empires, and Diplomats in the Founding of America* (Charlottesville: University of Virginia Press, 2009), 203. According to Sadosky, the entrance of the United States into the Westphalian system of states marked the end of any attempt by the new republic to negotiate with the native peoples of North America as sovereign nations.
[16] "State of the Union Address," December 6, 1830, in Theda Purdue and Michael D. Green, eds., *The Cherokee Removal: A Brief History with Documents* (New York: Bedford/St. Martins, 2005), 127.

was reenacted on a continental scale in nineteenth-century America. Viewed in this way, the political and legal theory of the American founding is ripe for comparison with that of other settler colonies around the world, from Canada to the Antipodes, many of which were also federal states where indigenous peoples stood in the way of the settlers' continental ambitions, and whose expansion has been a central feature of the global history of the modern world.[17]

Out of the crucible of an Atlantic empire, then, emerged powerful ideas of rights and equality, ideas that led, ultimately, to revolution and republicanism. By any standard, this was a momentous achievement, with revolutionary ideals animating an increasingly democratic political culture, while written constitutions ratified by popular consent secured the rights of the new republic's Euro-American citizens far better than the old empire had done. But in explaining the intellectual origins of this new expansive, rights-conscious republican empire, it is important to remember that these ideas had less happy consequences for its non-European inhabitants. The settler political theory that developed in the interstices of the British empire was intimately connected to the dispossession of the indigenous peoples of North America. Indeed, it was the settlers rather than the Crown who argued that the Native Americans were, in effect, stateless, and could, therefore, be pushed aside in the scramble for land that followed the defeat of the French in 1763 and the British in 1783. Moreover, the autonomy that the new republican states enjoyed after 1776 blunted the antislavery thrust of the revolutionary idea of natural rights and equality, ensuring that what remained of the British empire would emancipate its slaves long before the states that had seceded from it.[18] This intellectual legacy meant that after the settlers left one empire, they created another on a continental scale, whose emancipatory and exploitative impulses had deep roots in their past, and continued to shape their history well into the next century.

---

[17] On which, see James Belich, *Replenishing the Earth: The Settler Revolution and the Rise of the Angloworld, 1783–1939* (New York: Oxford University Press, 2009); and Carole Pateman, "The Settler Contract," in Carole Pateman and Charles Mills, eds., *Contract and Domination* (Cambridge: Polity Press, 2007), 35–78.

[18] On which, see Christopher Brown, "Empire without Slaves: British Concepts of Emancipation in the Age of the American Revolution," *William and Mary Quarterly* 61 (1999), 273–306.

Index